DONAT PHARAND

The Law of the Sea
of the Arctic

with Special Reference to Canada

UNIVERSITY OF OTTAWA PRESS
OTTAWA, CANADA
1973

To Yolaine

FOREWORD

The "international law community" of lawyers, Government officials, scholars, and others interested in the development of customary international law, treaties and international institutions, will welcome this book by Professor Donat Pharand of the University of Ottawa. Its field of the international law of the Arctic, and of the sea generally, is particularly timely.

In the long range perspective of the centuries, world-wide interest is focussed more and more on the northern parts of the Earth. Several decades ago Stefansson and others pointed to the gradual shift of the centers of world power, and of economic and intellectual activity, from the warm lands of the Mediterranean and low latitudes to northern Europe, northern America, and northern Asia. The Arctic Ocean and its surrounding seas, bordered by territories of Canada, the United States (Alaska), the U.S.S.R., Norway, Iceland, and Denmark (Greenland), lie in the center of these regions of ever-increasing world importance. The airplane and the submarine, as well as the ice-breaker, have made the Arctic a present and potential route of transport. Large deposits of oil, gas and other minerals have been found beneath its shores and its seabeds, while a wealth of marine life thrives in its cold waters. The world is becoming more and more concerned with the North, and with the international law problems of which nations may properly assert control and jurisdiction over persons and activities in the Arctic.

At the same time, since World War II we have seen rapid new developments in the international law of the sea. The once-traditional "three-mile-limit" no longer marks the internationally permissible outer limit of the littoral state's jurisdiction over the sea (if, indeed, it ever did !). Recent years have seen coastal nations asserting broader limits of territorial waters, new methods of measurement which broaden the *marginal sea belt, claims to waters of archipelagoes, exclusive rights over the resources of their continental shelves, claims to regulate and to exclude others from fisheries further and further out from shore, and attempts to prevent and to deal with pollution of the seas. There may be some hope that agreement can be reached on at least some of these problems of the international law of the sea at the forthcoming United Nations Conference on the Law of the Sea; but at least for the present, and probably for years to come, these will remain unsettled questions of international law.*

Professor Pharand's book concerns both the contemporary law of the Arctic, and the international law of the sea. It is thus most timely, and it affords a real contribution based on careful study and thought. It was prepared as his dissertation for the S.J.D. degree at the University of Michigan Law School, which has been happy to award him its doctorate. I have enjoyed the opportunity to be associated with his work on this volume as the chairman of his doctoral committee. This collection of studies forms a valuable addition to the scholarly literature dealing with the law of the sea and with Arctic problems. It will undoubtedly be of greatest interest in the nations most directly concerned with the Arctic, and especially Canada, but I am sure that it will also be read with interest and profit by those who are thinking about the general development of law in the world community.

William W. Bishop Jr.,
Edwin DeWitt Dickinson University Professor
of International Law,
University of Michigan.

ACKNOWLEDGMENTS

This book is an enlarged and revised version of a dissertation accepted by the Michigan Law School in satisfaction of the partial requirements for the S.J.D. degree. My most sincere appreciation and gratitude go to Professor W. W. Bishop Jr., of the University of Michigan Law School, who acted as Faculty Advisor throughout the years covering the preparation of the dissertation. In spite of his heavy teaching load and his many other onerous duties, in particular those of editor-in-chief of the *American Journal of International Law* until last year, Professor Bishop always managed to find time to give much-needed advice and guidance. The writer is grateful to Professors Eric Stein of the Michigan Law School and Inis L. Claude Jr., formerly of the Michigan Political Science Department and now Director of the Center for Advanced Studies of the University of Virginia, who were members of the Faculty Committee in 1968 when a preliminary part of this work was completed. A special word of appreciation goes to Mary B. Gomes, Professor Bishop's competent assistant, who was good enough to read a substantial part of the original manuscript and make helpful suggestions to improve the form. I am also grateful to the Michigan Law School teaching, administrative and library staffs, for the consideration shown me during my various stays at the Law School.

My gratitude extends to my friends and colleagues, both at universities and in government, who encouraged me to complete this study. It extends in particular to Professor Maxwell Cohen of the McGill Law Faculty, to Dean Ronald St. John Macdonald of the Dalhousie Law School and to Leonard Legault, until recently head of the Law of the Sea section in the Department of External Affairs, all of whom took the time to read parts of the draft and made very useful suggestions. J. E. Cooper, of the Marine Sciences Branch, of the Department of the Environment, saw to the preparation of all the maps, except the one on North Polar Regions (which is my own modest effort), and I am greatly indebted to him.

Dr. Tore Gjelsvik, Director of Norway's Polar Institute, and Dr. Finn Sollie, of the Fridtjof Nansen Foundation, were especially helpful in reading and commenting on the draft of the last part of this book dealing with the Arctic continental shelf and sea-bed. A special debt to the Arctic Institute of North America and to its research coordinator, Dr. John E. Sater, is gratefully acknowledged; indeed, part of this work was sponsored by the Arctic Institute with the approval and financial support of the Office of Naval Research under contract N00014-70-A-0219-0001 (subcontract ONR-435).

I am greatly indebted to my dean, Gérald A. Beaudoin, who has always given me strong encouragement in my research, as well as to the authorities of the University of Ottawa who have made this publication possible. I wish to pay tribute also to Léopold Lanctôt, the tireless director of the University of Ottawa Press, who has shown me the utmost consideration and has seen to the editing and printing in record time and efficiency. I am pleased to include in my acknowledgments two University of Ottawa professors: Paul Dussault, of the Political Science Department, and Anne-Marie Jacomy-Millette, of the Faculty of Law; they helped me greatly in the collection of materials while acting as research assistants for a brief period of time during the preliminary stages of my research. I also gladly acknowledge the competent assistance of Mrs. Jeanne d'Arc Vaillant-Lefebvre, who assisted me with the final verification of the bibliography.

Most of the proof reading assistance came from my son Michel, a student in English at the University of Ottawa; his cooperation went beyond filial obligations. I owe a particularly heavy debt of gratitude to my sister, Mrs. Florence Lalonde, who provided me with desperately needed financial assistance during an early period of study and research in Europe which proved to be a valuable beginning for the present work.

Finally, I will be forever grateful to my wife Yolaine who not only provided me with vital moral support and understanding, but acted as private secretary for most of the time this book was in preparation.

I also wish to express my appreciation to those who have graciously given me permission to draw upon some of my previous publications, namely:

"Innocent Passage in the Arctic", 6 *Canadian Yearbook of International Law* 3 (1968);

"The Legal Status of Ice Shelves and Ice Islands in the Arctic", 10 *Les Cahiers de droit* 461 (1969);

"The Continental Shelf Redefinition, with Special Reference to the Arctic", 18 *McGill Law Journal* 536 (1972);

"Oil Pollution Control in the Canadian Arctic", 7 *Texas International Law Journal* 45 (1971);

"Freedom of the Seas in the Arctic Ocean", 19 *University of Toronto Law Journal* 210 (1969);

"Historic Waters in International Law, with Special Reference to the Arctic", 21 *University of Toronto Law Journal* 1 (1971).

University of Ottawa,
September 1973.

D. P.

CONTENTS

Part VII

THE ARCTIC CONTINENTAL SHELF AND SEABED

LIST OF FIGURES

Introduction

Recent years have witnessed the discovery of vast oil reserves in the Arctic, particularly on the North slope of Alaska and in the Canadian Arctic islands. Those reserves within the Arctic circle are conservatively estimated by geologists to be in excess of 500 billion barrels of oil. This is as much as the total known reserves of the rest of the world. The problem now is to discover economic methods of transporting the oil which is about to be extracted.

Of the various methods available — water, rail, highway, air, pipeline — water is bound to be chosen, either by itself or in conjunction with others, as an important means of transportation. In spite of the presence of ice, technology is developing to the point where navigation is now possible in the Arctic seas and will become possible in the Arctic Ocean itself. Scientific expeditions of the Soviet Union and the United States have been installed on ice islands for some twenty years, drifting in the Arctic Ocean while pursuing their research and increasing their knowledge of the ocean floor, the ice movement and the whole marine environment. Large icebreakers and ice-strengthened ships have been tested in the high Arctic waters and super submarine tankers have been designed to cross the Arctic Ocean while remaining completely submerged under the pack ice. Considering these developments, Canada decided to establish a pollution prevention zone of 100 miles from its Arctic coast, in order to protect the delicate ecology of the region. It also extended its territorial waters from 3 to 12 miles so as to gain greater control over the waters of its Arctic archipelago.

The above developments have raised a number of legal questions which touch upon nearly all aspects of the law of the sea. The major questions which will be examined in the course of this study are the following: 1. Is the right of innocent passage applicable to the Northwest and Northeast Passages ? 2. What is the legal status of the waters of the Canadian Arctic Archipelago ? 3. Could the Arctic states claim a historic title to some of the Arctic waters ? 4. Does the principle of "the freedom of the seas" apply to the Arctic Ocean ? 5. What is the legal status of ice shelves and ice islands ? 6. What is the international legal validity of the Canadian legislation on the prevention of pollution in the Arctic ? 7. What should be the polar and lateral boundaries of the Arctic continental shelf and sea-bed ?

The study will endeavour to shed light on those seven major questions, as well as on a number of related issues. A separate part will be devoted to each major question.

PART I

Innocent Passage in the Arctic

The question of innocent passage through straits will undoubtedly be one of the major issues at the Third Law of the Sea Conference scheduled to begin its first substantive session at Santiago de Chile, in April 1974. The whole concept of innocent passage will have to be revised and the Conference will have to bear in mind some of the straits of the Arctic regions. Consequently, this investigation will bear mainly on the legal status of the Arctic waters constituting what are commonly known as the Northwest Passage, on the North American side of the Pole, and the Northeast Passage or Northern Sea Route on the Soviet side. The basic question is whether or not the right of innocent passage in favour of foreign ships applies to those waters.

The inquiry will be divided into three sections: the first will review the international law principles applicable to innocent passage in general; the second will inquire into the right of innocent passage through the Northeast Passage, and the third will do the same for the Northwest Passage.

I. — THE LAW OF INNOCENT PASSAGE

The object of this first section is to review briefly the legal principles necessary for an intelligent discussion of the main question under investigation: the applicability of the concept of innocent passage to the Arctic sea routes on either side of the Pole.

The law relating to innocent passage, like the law of the sea in general, is quite ancient in origin and finds its legal basis primarily in custom. It was not until 1958 that general conventions were adopted, thus codifying and specifying a good deal of the principles of relevant customary law. On the whole, there was little innovation in the Law of the Sea Conventions and, indeed, their primary purpose was not to make new law but to clarify the old. However, in this case it is not sufficient to refer to these conventions, since two states whose coasts are involved do not consider themselves fully bound by them. Canada has ratified one convention only, the Continental Shelf Convention, and it is uncertain to what extent that country considers itself bound by the principles contained in the others. The Soviet Union has ratified three of the conventions, but it has attached an important reservation relating to the passage of warships to its ratification of the Territorial Sea Convention. In the circumstances, it is therefore necessary to refer to both customary and conventional law; the emphasis will vary in accordance with the nature of the questions being examined. The questions are: 1. Is innocent passage really a right ? 2. What does innocent passage mean ? 3. Is innocent passage applicable to warships ? 4. How is innocent passage applicable to oil tankers ? 5. To what bodies of water does innocent passage apply ?

1. Is Innocent Passage Really a Right ?

Innocent passage is as old as the law of the sea itself and is a normal consequence of freedom of navigation; it was practised by maritime powers throughout the centuries with such consistency that Jessup was able to affirm in 1927: "As a general principle, the right of innocent passage requires no supporting argument or citation of authority; it is firmly established in international law." [1]

A similar opinion was expressed by Gidel when he pointed out that certain treaty provisions recognizing this right after World War I merely confirmed an existing customary rule: " . . . ce droit de passage existait dès auparavant comme une règle coutumière certaine." [2] And the same author emphasized that innocent passage consists of not merely a privilege but a real right: "Cette limitation consiste dans l'existence, au profit des navires étrangers, non seulement d'une

---

[1] JESSUP, *The Law of Territorial Waters and Maritime Jurisdiction*, at 120 (1927).
[2] III GIDEL, *Le Droit International Public de la Mer*, at 195 (1934).

faculté de passage, mais d'un véritable droit de passage dans la mer territoriale, sous la réserve que ce passage soit 'inoffensif'. . ." [3] Innocent passage being a right in the strict sense, the sovereignty of the coastal state is qualified by a correlative duty not to prevent foreign vessels from the normal exercise of that right. This was recognized explicitly in an arbitral award between Panama and the United States in 1933; presiding Commissioners Van Heeckereen and Root stated in their majority decision:

> There is a clear preponderance of authority to the effect that this sovereignty is qualified by what is known as the right of innocent passage, and that this qualification forbids the sovereign actually to prohibit the innocent passage of alien merchant vessels through its territorial waters . . . [4]

Indeed, the preponderance of authority is such that innocent passage, as a right, has become a well-established principle of customary law. Lauterpacht accurately sums up the legal position:

> It is occasionally maintained that all nations have the right of inoffensive passage for their merchantmen by usage only, and not by the customary Law of Nations, and that, consequently, in strict law a littoral State may prevent such passage. This view cannot be accepted. An attempt on the part of a littoral State to prevent free navigation through the maritime belt in time of peace would not be legally warranted. [5]

This right and duty relationship relating to innocent passage was given express recognition by the 1958 Convention on the Territorial Sea. On the one hand, it is stipulated that "ships of all States, whether coastal or not, shall enjoy the right of innocent passage through the territorial sea" (Art. 14); on the other hand, coastal states have a double duty not to hamper innocent passage and to "give appropriate publicity

---

[3]   GIDEL, *ibid.*, at 197.
[4]   *Campania De Navegacion Nacional (Panama)* v. *United States* (1933), in BISHOP, *International Law Cases and Materials*, at 512-513 (2nd ed., 1962).
[5]   OPPENHEIM, *International Law*, at 494 (Lauterpacht's 8th ed., 1955).

to any dangers to navigation, of which it has knowledge, within its territorial sea" (Art. 15). This provision, which had been recommended by the International Law Commission, confirmed the principles upheld by the International Court of Justice in its judgment of 1949 in the *Corfu Channel Case*. A further consequence of the characterization of innocent passage as a right is that "no charge may be levied upon foreign ships by reason only of their passage through the territorial sea" (Art. 18, para. 1). This does not, however, bar the coastal state from levying tolls as payment for specific services rendered to a foreign ship, such as pilotage, towage, etc. (Art. 18, para. 2).

2. WHAT DOES "INNOCENT PASSAGE" MEAN ?

As for the term "passage" it is fully defined in the 1958 Territorial Sea Convention and, since the definition is essentially a reiteration of customary law as confirmed by the 1930 Codification Conference, [6] it would be superfluous to trace the origin of the custom. Article 14 makes it clear that passage means navigation through territorial waters (para. 2); as a rule, it does not include stopping or anchoring; these are permitted only if incidental to ordinary navigation or made necessary by *force majeure* or distress (para. 3). The meaning of "innocent" is considerably more difficult to appreciate and neither case law nor conventions are very helpful to find a clear answer to the new problem posed by oil tankers. The International Court had to examine the meaning of innocence of passage in relation to warships, in the *Corfu Channel Case*. It held that it was not the character of the ship which was the determining factor, but rather the character of the passage itself. In the words of the Court, the question to consider is "whether the manner in which the passage was carried out was consistent with the principle of innocent passage". [7] It had to apply this rule to two passages effected by British warships. With respect to the passage of four warships on October

---

[6]   See "Commentary" to Article 15, in (1956) *I.L.C. Yearbook* II, at 272.

[7]   (1949) *I.C.J. Rep.*, at 30.

22nd 1946, the Court was satisfied that the passage was innocent. The evidence showed "that the ships were not proceeding in combat formation, but in line, one after the other, and
that they were not manoeuvring until after the first explo-
sion". [8] With respect to the second passage on November 12th
and 13th, the United Kingdom government itself recognized
that it was not mere innocent passage. The mine clearing
operation was carried out against Albania's express objection
and "under the protection of an important covering force composed of an aircraft carrier, cruisers and other war vessels". [9]

The 1958 Convention expressed the principle underlying
the *Corfu Channel* decision, namely that "[p]assage is innocent
so long as it is not prejudicial to the peace, good order or
security of the coastal State" (Art. 14, para. 4). In each case,
it must be decided whether a particular passage may be considered to be prejudicial to the protected rights of the coastal
state. From the positive way in which Article 14 is worded,
it would seem that passage is to be presumed innocent until
shown otherwise. This is the view of Leo Gross who maintains that "the text as adopted clearly puts the burden on the
coastal state to show that the passage itself rather than the
passage of a particular ship, its purpose or cargo, was prejudicial to the stated values of the coastal state". [10] If this is
so, the coastal state must be in a position to secure the necessary evidence to discharge its heavy burden as to the non-
innocent nature of the passage. Consequently, the state may
regulate the passage of foreign ships to guard against the
possibility of a passage being dangerous to its security; and,
if the passage is effected in a manner contrary to the protective
regulations, the coastal state may point to the prohibited act

---

[8]   *Ibid.*, at 30-31.

[9]   *Ibid.*, at 33.

[10]   L. GROSS, "The Geneva Conference on the Law of the Sea and
the Right of Innocent Passage through the Gulf of Aqaba", 53 *A.J.I.L.*
564, at 582 (1959). Prof. McDougal would seem to give a different interpretation when he states: "The ships of other states are said to have a
right of innocent passage, but within the geographic zone the burden is
put upon such ships of proving their innocence". See ALEXANDER (ed.),
The Law of the Sea, 3-23, at 17 (1967).

or omission as evidence of the violation. This would constitute proof of offensive passage. The International Court recognized this right of protection of the coastal state in its *Corfu Channel* judgment. If stated clearly that Albania "would have been justified in issuing regulations in respect of the passage of warships through the Strait . . ." [11] *A fortiori,* the right of protection exists in ordinary territorial waters. The Court did, however, go on to say that regulating did not mean prohibiting. Thus Albania would not have been justified "in prohibiting such passage or in subjecting it to the requirement of special authorization". [12]

The 1958 Convention contains an express guarantee of this right of protection of coastal states and gives them the general power "to take necessary steps [13] in its territorial sea to prevent passage which is not innocent" (Art. 16, para. 1); the coastal state may even go so far as to "suspend temporarily in specified areas of its territorial sea the innocent passage of foreign ships if such suspension is essential for the protection of its security" (Art. 16, para. 3). But the power of temporary suspension does not extend to straits used for international navigation between two parts of the high seas (Art. 16, para. 4). In the case of warships, the coastal state has a special power of expulsion if the warship refuses to comply with the local regulations (Art. 23).

3.   Is INNOCENT PASSAGE APPLICABLE TO WARSHIPS ?

Although the right of innocent passage for merchant ships has been recognized for a long time, the same does not hold true for warships. Indeed, Hall affirmed categorically that "[t]his right of innocent passage does not extend to vessels of war". [14] And Elihu Root argued on behalf of the government of the United States in the North Atlantic Fisheries arbitration

---

[11]   (1949) *I.C.J. Rep.*, at 29.
[12]   *Ibid.*
[13]   For specific examples of what those steps might entail, see "Peacetime Passage by Warships through Territorial Straits", 50 *Colum. L. Rev.*, at 224-225 (1950); and the "Commentary" to Article 17, in (1956) *I.L.C. Yearbook* II, at 274.
[14]   HALL, *International Law,* at 163 (7th ed., 1917).

in 1910 that "[w]arships may not pass without consent into this zone, because they threaten". [15] This often-quoted statement represented the traditional United States' position and probably also the majority opinion on the question. Jessup regarded this as a "sound rule", and maintained that warships "should not enjoy an absolute legal right to pass through a state's territorial waters any more than an army may cross the land territory". [16] This restriction on warships seemed to apply even when passing through straits. After a thorough study of states' practice up to World War I, regarding both merchant ships and warships, Bruël arrived at the following conclusion: " . . . the legal position of straits as regards the right of passage in time of peace, seems to be briefly this at the outbreak of war: the right of innocent passage for both merchant-vessels and ships of war, the right of the latter, however, not yet being fully established." [17]

The situation remained uncertain until the decision of the International Court in the *Corfu Channel Case*. There, Albania argued that no legal regime was applicable to straits in general; it contended that, in devising a legal regime for a particular strait, the two elements to consider were "l'importance du détroit pour la navigation internationale, et son intérêt stratégique pour les Puissances riveraines". [18] In the exchange of diplomatic correspondence with the United Kingdom, Albania had also asserted that "foreign warships and merchant-vessels had no right to pass through Albanian territorial waters without prior notification to, and the permission of, the Albanian authorities". [19] The International Court rejected all of those contentions, and stated the law in the following terms:

> It is, in the opinion of the Court, generally recognized and in accordance with international custom that States in time of peace have a right to send their warships through

---

[15]　See I HACKWORTH, *Digest of International Law,* at 646 (1940).
[16]　JESSUP, *supra* note 1, at 120.
[17]　I BRUËL, *International Straits,* at 108 (1945).
[18]　Duplique de l'Albanie, I *Corfu Channel Case, I.C.J. Pleadings,* at 354 (1949). The pleadings of Albania were in French only.
[19]　(1949) *I.C.J. Rep.,* at 27.

straits used for international navigation between two parts of the high seas without the previous authorization of a coastal State, provided that the passage is innocent. Unless otherwise prescribed in an international convention, there is no right for a coastal State to prohibit such passage through straits in time of peace. [20]

It is worth noting that only two of the sixteen judges expressed a clear dissent on this specific question of the right of warships to innocent passage through straits. The two judges were Azevedo and Krylov. Even Dr. Ecer, the judge *ad hoc* for Albania, did not go beyond the expression of a "doubt" as to the correctness of the above statement of the law. Having just referred to the opinion of the majority, he simply stated: "I doubt whether this argument is well founded." [21] At the end of his "dissenting" opinion, he explains his doubt as to the legal situation and concludes that the first passage of the British warships on October 22nd 1946 was not offensive. The relevant conclusions of Dr. Ecer are the following:

(a) In 1946, there was no clear rule of customary international law concerning the right of passage for a warship through straits. The juridical situation was doubtful; each of the two Parties could put forward good arguments in support of his claim.

(b) I do not think it has been judicially established that the passage of the four British vessels on October 22nd, 1946, was offensive, from the subjective standpoint (intention). [22]

On the other hand, Judge Krylov was categorical that warships possessed no right of innocent passage in territorial waters, because "warships constitute a menace — 'they threaten', [23] that is not the case with merchant ships". [24] The fact that the territorial waters in question lay within an international strait made no difference. "Contrary to the opinion of the majority of the judges", he wrote, "I consider that there is no such thing

---

[20] *Ibid.*, at 28.
[21] *Ibid.*, at 128.
[22] *Ibid.*, at 130.
[23] The expression is borrowed from Elihu Root, to whom he had just referred with approval in his dissenting opinion.
[24] (1949) *I.C.J. Rep.*, at 74.

as a *common regulation* of the legal régime of straits. Every strait is regulated individually." [25] However, the decision of the Court made it quite clear that a warship does possess the right of innocent passage *in peacetime* through a strait, although made up of territorial waters, connecting two parts of the high seas.

The right of innocent passage of warships was fully debated in the International Law Commission and at the 1958 Conference on the Law of the Sea. The International Law Commission began by granting passage to warships without prior authorization or notification. However, due to the strong opposition of certain members [26] of the Commission and to comments from certain governments, it later completely reversed its position. The Commission did, however, add that normally innocent passage should be granted. [27] At the 1958 Conference, Tunkin and Nikolaev of the USSR led the debate for the retention of the provision of the I.L.C. requiring prior authorization from the coastal state. [28] Sir Gerald Fitzmaurice of the United Kingdom argued for its deletion, and stated that "his government had no record of any prior authorization having been required from its warships in time of peace, by any country, for the purpose of passage through the territorial sea". [29] This is the position which the Conference finally adopted. It deleted completely the specific article giving the right of innocent passage to warships, and made other provisions (Arts. 14 to 17) applicable to all ships. It retained, however, the article providing for the expulsion of warships from the territorial sea in case of refusal to comply with the regulations of the coastal state (Art. 23). As properly pointed out by Jessup, "[t]he implication is that warships do have the right

---

[25] *Ibid.*

[26] See the positions taken by ZOUREK, in (1954) *I.L.C. Yearbook* I, at 158-159, and by KRYLOV, in (1955) *I.L.C. Yearbook* I, at 145.

[27] See "Commentary" to Article 24, in (1956) *I.L.C. Yearbook* II, at 276-277.

[28] See U.N. Conference on the Law of the Sea, Official Records, U.N. Doc. A/CONF. 13/39, Vol. III, at 78, 94 and 130 (1958).

[29] *Ibid.*, at 133.

of innocent passage". [30] Tunkin's interpretation is different, nevertheless; even after the Conference, he still maintained that coastal states remain free to pass regulations requiring warships to obtain prior permission for innocent passage through territorial waters. His analysis of the Convention on this point is worth noting:

> They [the Western Powers] succeeded in securing the deletion from the draft convention of the clause giving coastal states the right to grant or deny foreign warships the right of passage through their territorial waters. However, the clause requiring that foreign warships observe the rules governing passage through territorial waters laid down by the coastal state remained. Such rules can, of course, include a requirement that prior permission be obtained or prior notification of passage given. [31]

Regardless of one's personal view on the right of innocent passage of warships, an objective interpretation of the Convention does not lend support to Tunkin's conclusion. It is contrary to the provisions contained in Articles 14 to 17, headed *Rules applicable to all ships*, and specifically granting the right of innocent passage to *all ships*. On this point, the well known legal historian Professor Verzijl made a review of the deliberations of the 1958 Conference, both in Committee and in Plenary, and came to the following conclusion:

> Many voices will, of course, be raised in future against the unhampered passage for warships, but there would seem to be little chance, in view of the text of the Convention as it now runs, that an unbiassed Judge will question that right. After the rejection of the exceptional provision for passing warships, their freedom of passage is clearly covered by the general rules in sub-section A "applicable to all ships". No falling back upon a pretended contrary rule of

30   JESSUP, "The U.N. Conference on the Law of the Sea", 59 *Colum. L. Rev.* 234, at 248 (1959). For a similar interpretation, see the following: Arthur H. DEAN, "Freedom of the Seas", 37 *Foreign Affairs* 83, at 92 (1958-59); J. H. W. VERZIJL, "The United Nations Conference on the Law of the Sea, Geneva, 1958", VI *Netherlands Int'l L. Rev.* 1, at 34 (1959); R. A. BAXTER, *The Law of International Waterways*, at 167-168 (1964); and Wm. E. BUTLER, "The Legal Regime of Russian Territorial Waters", 62 *A.J.I.L.* 51, at 69 (1968).
31   TUNKIN, "The Geneva Conference on the Law of the Sea", 1 *Int'l Aff.* 47, at 49 (1958).

customary law, said to allow a coastal State to prevent the
passage of warships without its authorization, — a rule,
for the rest, resolutely opposed by others —, would seem to
be of any judicial avail against the explicit provisions and
the logical context of section III of Part I of the first
Convention. [32]

It follows from the analysis just made that warships do enjoy
the right of innocent passage under the 1958 Territorial Sea
Convention. The question remains: what is the situation for
oil tankers ?

4. How is Innocent Passage Applicable to Oil Tankers ?

Under existing international law, both customary and
conventional, no special provision is made for the pollution
threat posed by oil tankers. They fall in the category of commercial vessels and benefit from the right of innocent passage.
The unanswered question remains: when does the passage of
an oil tanker become non-innocent and what may the coastal
state do to prevent such passage ? As seen earlier, a passage
is deemed innocent so long as it does not prejudice the peace,
good order or security of the coastal state. It is obvious from
the language used in the Territorial Sea Convention that it was
primarily intended to cover the case of warships effecting a
passage in a manner which poses a threat to the security of
the coastal state. Is it possible for an oil tanker to pose such
a threat ? The question was studied by the Institute of International Law at the time of the *Torrey Canyon* disaster and
it came to the conclusion that a ship, which does not conform
with certain anti-pollution standards, does pose a threat to
the coastal state. Consequently, it provided in the articles
relating to accidental pollution of the seas, adopted at its
Edinburg Session of 1969, that coastal states could act as
follows:

> States have the right to prohibit any ship that does not
> conform to the standards set up in accordance with the
> preceding articles for the design and equipment of the

---

[32] J. W. H. VERZIJL, *International Law in Historical Perspectives*,
Vol. IV, at 188 (1971).

> ships, for the navigation instruments and for the qualifi-
> cations of the officers and members of the crews, from
> crossing their territorial seas and contiguous zones and from
> reaching their ports. [33]

In the measures set up in the preceding articles are included
"traffic regulations in areas where such regulations are necessary and in particular provisions concerning the routes to be
followed, the maximum speeds and the compulsory pilotage
procedures". [34] The Institute of International Law further
provided that nothing could prevent a state from enacting
such measures until they are established internationally or in
the event that they are inadequate to prevent pollution. [35]
Under existing international law, such measures could be
taken under the general customary law right of self-protection
or under the "sanitary regulations" recognized in the Territorial
Sea Convention (Article 24). It also presumes that Article 14
of the Convention, defining innocent passage, is given a restrictive interpretation. More specifically it means restricting the
meaning of "innocent" so as to exclude a tanker not conforming with certain anti-pollution standards. It also means that
a prejudice to the marine and territorial environment of the
coastal state is tantamount to a prejudice "to the peace, good
order or security" of that state. In other words, a tanker which
so menaces the coastal state constitutes a threat to its living
in peace and security. The present writer subscribes to this
view, although he would prefer to have the anti-pollution
standards and their method of control by the coastal state
agreed upon internationally.

5. To What Bodies of Water Does Innocent Passage Apply ?

The examination of the previous questions has already
made it clear that the right of innocent passage applies primarily to the territorial sea. Indeed, it is the right of innocent

---

[33]   Article VI of "Measures concerning accidental pollutions of
the seas", Institute of International Law, Geneva (1969).
[34]   *Ibid.*, at Article II.
[35]   *Ibid.*, at Article IV.

passage that distinguishes the legal status of territorial waters from that of internal waters. Gidel is succinct and accurate when he says: "Le droit de passage . . . caractérise la condition juridique particulière de la mer territoriale par opposition aux eaux intérieures. Les eaux intérieures de l'État riverain peuvent être interdites par lui aux navires étrangers." [36] The rule is that innocent passage of foreign ships may be prohibited in internal waters but not in territorial waters. It is only by way of special exception to that rule that the 1958 Convention grants a right of innocent passage in some newly-acquired internal waters. The exceptional case may arise where states such as Norway have a deeply indented coastal line or a fringe of coastal islands; such states may draw straight baselines from which to measure their territorial waters, providing they also meet certain other requirements set out in Article 4 of the Convention. If the effect of establishing such baselines is to enclose "as internal waters areas which previously had been considered as part of the territorial sea or of the high seas, a right of innocent passage as provided in articles 14 to 23, shall exist in those areas" (Art. 5). Although this is a provision of exception, it does indicate the extent to which the right of innocent passage has become a fundamental principle of the law of the sea. The International Law Commission would have preserved this right only "where the waters have normally been used for international traffic", [37] but the 1958 Conference decided to drop the qualification. As was pointed out by Sir Hersch Lauterpacht, if Article 5 had not been adopted the coastal state could have interfered at its discretion with freedom of navigation in those waters. [38]

The right of innocent passage is not only applicable to territorial waters and to newly-enclosed internal waters; it also applies to straits connecting two parts of the high seas, whether or not they are formed entirely of territorial waters. And since the right of innocent passage in territorial waters finds its legal justification in the wider principle of freedom

---

[36] GIDEL, *supra* note 2, at 197.
[37] Article 5, para. 3, (1956) *I.L.C. Yearbook* II, at 267.
[38] See (1954) *I.L.C. Yearbook* I, at 67.

of navigation on the high seas, it follows logically that the same right should be recognized — perhaps even more so — when those waters form the connecting link between two parts of the high seas. On this question, Bruël comes to the following conclusion:

> ... the right of "passage inoffensif" through territorial waters in time of peace established for merchant vessels already ab. [sic] the middle of the 19' [sic] century was sufficient, in the main, to guarantee them a right of passage also in the part of the territorial waters which lies in straits. [39]

The determining consideration is the fact that a strait connects two parts of the high seas. In his oral argument before the International Court in the *Corfu Channel Case*, Sir Eric Beckett of the United Kingdom put it in these terms: "It is simply the geographical fact that the strait connects two parts of the open sea where ships may lawfully wish to pass, which distinguishes it as a strait subject to a special régime in international law." [40] True, the question at issue was the right of passage of warships, but the same right exists even more for all other ships. In its judgment, the International Court rejected the volume of international traffic as the test and accepted the geographical situation as being the decisive criterion for the application of the right of innocent passage. On this point, the French text of the judgment, which is the only authoritative one, reads as follows: "Le critère décisif paraît plutôt devoir être tiré de la situation géographique du Détroit, en tant que ce dernier met en communication deux parties de haute mer, ainsi que du fait que le Détroit est utilisé aux fins de la navigation internationale." [41]

Thus it appears that the real test of the applicability of the right of innocent passage in a strait is the geographical connection of two parts of the high seas, although the fact that a strait is used for international navigation is an important consideration. The interpretation given to this passage

---

[39] I BRUËL, *supra* note 17, at 101-102.
[40] I *Corfu Channel Case, I.C.J. Pleadings,* at 278 (1949).
[41] (1949) *I.C.J. Rep.,* at 28.

by Professor Rousseau centres even more on the geographical situation and warrants a full quotation of his interpretative statement:

> ...la Cour internationale de justice a retenu comme *critère* décisif des détroits internationaux non le volume du trafic ou l'importance plus ou moins grande du détroit pour la navigation internationale, mais la *situation géographique* du détroit, c'est-à-dire le fait qu'il met en communication deux parties de la haute mer. [42]

The English translation of the relevant passage of the Court's judgment is not entirely accurate; it gives the impression that the right of innocent passage does not exist unless two criteria are met, both of which are equally important. The translated judgment reads: "But in the opinion of the Court the decisive criterion is rather its geographical situation as connecting two parts of the high seas and the fact of its being used for international navigation." [43]

Interpreting the English text only, Mr. Mervyn Jones appears to be fully justified in saying that "[t]he limitation which the Court makes is that the fact must be shown that it is being used for international navigation". [44] In other words, proof of use for international navigation would be an indispensable element for the right of innocent passage to exist in a territorial strait. McDougal and Burke seem to give a similar interpretation, although they do emphasize the importance of the geographical element; they concede that "... the Court considered the essential criterion to be geographical". [45] However, in the next sentence they add: "As long as the strait connects two parts of the open sea and is used for international navigation, the coastal state does not possess the competence to prohibit the innocent passage of warships." [46] It must be admitted that both of those elements were present in the *Corfu Channel Case*. It is therefore pos-

---

[42] ROUSSEAU, *Traité de Droit International Public,* at 446 (1953).
[43] (1949) *I.C.J. Rep.,* at 28.
[44] M. JONES, "The *Corfu Channel Case*: Merits", 26 *Brit. Y. B. Int'l L.* 447, at 453 (1949).
[45] McDOUGAL and BURKE, *The Public Order of the Oceans,* at 207 (1962).
[46] *Ibid.*

sible to argue that, on a strict interpretation of the *ratio decidendi*, the judgment does not cover more than the specific issue it had to decide, regardless how widely phrased was the statement of the law.

The effect of the 1958 Convention, however, is to give fuller recognition to the existence of the right of innocent passage in straits made up of territorial waters. If such straits only connect two parts of the high seas but are not used for international navigation, they are governed by the general provision guaranteeing the right of innocent passage through the territorial sea (Art. 14); they have the same status as ordinary territorial waters and are subject to the same limitations. This means that the coastal state may temporarily suspend innocent passage for security reasons (Art. 16, para. 3). If such straits connect two parts of the high seas and are also used for international navigation, a special provision applies; not only is the coastal state precluded from prohibiting the innocent passage of foreign ships in such straits, but it may not even suspend such passage (Art. 16, para. 4). It should also be noted that the "use" envisaged does not have to be extensive for the non-suspension clause to apply; the International Law Commission would only have prevented the coastal state from suspending innocent passage through straits "normally used for international navigation between two parts of the high seas". [47] The 1958 Conference decided to delete the word "normally" and to extend the non-suspension provision to straits between "one part of the high seas and another part of the high seas or the territorial sea of a foreign State" (Art. 16, para. 4).

It is in regard to the second type of strait — the one used for international navigation — that the United States has proposed to replace the rule of innocent passage by that of *free transit*. The draft article which it introduced in the United Nations Seabed Committee on this question reads:

> In straits used for international navigation between one
> part of the high seas and another part of the high seas or

---

[47]   Article 17 (1956) *I.L.C. Yearbook* II, at 258.

the territorial sea of a foreign state, all ships and aircraft in transit shall enjoy *the same freedom of navigation and overflight,* for the purpose of transit through and over such straits, *as they have on the high seas.* [48]

In other words, the concept of international strait contained in the Territorial Sea Convention is preserved, but the right of innocent passage is replaced by a right of "free transit". This would give foreign ships and aircraft the same freedom of navigation and overflight as they have on the high seas. To put it shortly, the claim is for some kind of "high seas corridors". True, however, coastal states could designate corridors suitable for transit by all ships and aircraft through and over such straits and, in straits where there are channels that are customarily used by ships in transit, the corridors should include such channels. As explained by the American Legal Adviser, the coastal state, while retaining its right to enforce "reasonable safety traffic regulations", could not use them "as a way of impairing the right of free transit". [49] This right would prevail apparently over the right of the coastal state to take pollution prevention measures. This would seem to be the inference contained in the following passage in the same speech:

> We recognize the concern of many states bordering straits regarding the need to prevent pollution. Pollution control problems, however, are not unique in straits. For example, the same problems pertain in heavily traveled shipping routes. The doctrine of innocent passage is not adequate to protect both coastal and maritime interests in international straits. It applies only in territorial seas, and as I have mentioned, it is subject to varying interpretations by different coastal states. Specific international agreements are required to insure appropriate protection from the hazards of pollution. [50]

At least two comments should be made about this passage. The first comment is that innocent passage does not apply

---

[48]   See Article II, "Texts & Draft Articles", U.N. Doc. A/AC. 138/SC. II/L. 4, reproduced in 65 *Dep't State Bull.,* at 266 (1971);
[49]   See statement by John R. Stevenson, reproduced in 65 *Dep't State Bull.,* at 263 (1971).
[50]   *Ibid.*

presently to territorial sea only. As already seen, a suspendable right of innocent passage applies to straits not used for international navigation and a non-suspendable right of innocent passage applies to straits that are used for international navigation. The second comment is that, regardless of the adoption of international anti-pollution norms, the coastal state is normally the only one in a position to verify the implementation of those norms when a foreign ship reaches its territorial waters. This verification, of course, should be subject to an adequate dispute settlement procedure, in order to prevent possible abuses by the coastal state.

It seems from the above analysis of the American proposal that "free transit" through territorial sea straits used for international navigation means complete freedom of passage for all ships and aircraft as if they were actually on the high seas. No notice to the coastal state would be required and, since it would apply to "all ships and aircraft", it would include passage of military ships and overflight of military aircraft. It would even allow submarines to cross such straits under water, since the requirement to navigate on the surface and to show the flag is linked to the concept of innocent passage which would no longer apply.

Needless to say that the American proposal has met with opposition, particularly from certain archipelagic states such as the Philippines and Indonesia. For instance, at the New York meeting of the Seabed Committee in March 1972, the representative of Indonesia stated: "It seems to us that the so-called concept of 'free transit' has been evoked to guarantee the unhampered and secret movement of the warships and submarines . . ." [51] Such opposition is understandable since the right of free transit might impinge on a more fundamental right, namely that of the national security of the coastal state. Even Canada has seen fit to envisage special protective measures against the possibility of unknown submarines in its

---

[51]   See "Statement of Dr. Hasjim Djalal . . . before Sub-committee II . . . on 29 March 1972", at 3-4 (text distributed at time of delivery).

Arctic waters. The Canadian White Paper on Defence, published in 1971, contains the following passage:

> Although Canada has a good capability to detect submarines in its waters in the temperate zone, it has only very limited capability to detect submarine activity in the Arctic. It might be desirable in the future to raise the level of capability so as to have subsurface perimeter surveillance, particularly to cover the channels connecting the Arctic Ocean to Baffin Bay and Baffin Bay to the Atlantic. The Government is therefore undertaking research to determine the costs and feasibility of a limited subsurface system to give warning of any unusual maritime activity. The Defence Research Board is playing an important role in these studies. If found to be desirable, the system could be operated as part of the overall surveillance of North America against unknown submarines. [52]

Thinking in terms of North American defence, one can doubt that the right of free transit would be in the best interest of the United States.

SUMMARY OF THE LAW OF INNOCENT PASSAGE

The principles of law discussed may be summarized in four brief statements:

1. Innocent passage is a right, and not merely a privilege to be granted or refused at the discretion of the coastal state.

2. The innocence of the passage is generally determined by reference to the nature of the passage itself but, in the case of ships carrying polluting materials, it may be determined by its conformity with certain anti-pollution standards.

3. The right of innocent passage applies to both merchant ships and warships, although its application to the latter is disputed by some. The passage of merchant ships may be suspended temporarily for security reasons, and warships may be expelled for refusal to comply with regulations of the

---

[52] *Information Canada, Defence in the 70s* (White Paper on Defence), at 18 (1971).

coastal state. Submarines must navigate on the surface and show their flag.

4. The right of innocent passage exists in the following areas.

a) internal waters newly-enclosed by straight baselines;

b) territorial waters, either along the coast or in a strait;

c) straits connecting two parts of the high seas or one part of the high seas and one part of territorial waters. If such straits are used for international navigation, there can be no suspension of the right of innocent passage.

II. — INNOCENT PASSAGE IN THE NORTHEAST PASSAGE

The right of innocent passage in what is now more commonly known as the Northern Sea Route does not appear to be recognized by the Soviet Union. In September 1965, the U.S. Coast Guard Icebreaker *Northwind* came under constant surveillance by Soviet aircraft and warships as soon as it entered the Kara Sea; [53] such surveillance increased in intensity as the *Northwind* proceeded toward Vilkitsky Straits, a key passage of the Northern Sea Route. The situation was such that the captain decided to go no further than thirty miles from the entrance of the straits; the Soviet Union had apparently made a strong protest when it learned of the intended passage. A spokesman from the State Department is reported to have stated that the Soviets made it clear "that they consider the waters of Vil'kitskogo Strait territorial waters, and that anyone intruding in those waters would be intruding on the territory of the Soviet Union. They made it very clear they would go all the way to take appropriate measures." [54] In the circumstances, no real attempt was made to use the straits. [55]

---

[53] For a full account of this voyage in the Barents and Kara Seas, see Richard PETROW, *Across the Top of Russia* (1967). The author was aboard the *Northwind* to cover the historic cruise for the *New York Times*.

[54] *Ibid.*, at 352-353.

[55] The *Northwind* then proceeded north around the northern tip of Severnaya Zemlya and the captain asked his superiors' permission

In August 1967 two U.S. icebreakers, the *Eastwind* and the *Edisto*, attempted to by-pass the Vilkitsky Straits by going around the northern tip of Severnaya Zemlya, but they were blocked by heavy ice at about 82° North latitude. When the Soviet Ministry of Foreign Affairs was informed by the American embassy in Moscow that the ships would have to pass through Vilkitsky Straits, it replied that "the straits constituted Soviet territorial waters". [56] In spite of this answer, the captain of the *Edisto* sent a message to the Soviet Ministry of the Maritime Fleet on August 28, indicating his intention to pass through the straits. There was a negative reaction from the Foreign Affairs Ministry. According to the U.S. State Department, ". . . the Soviet Ministry of Foreign Affairs reaffirmed its declaration of August 24 and made it clear that the Soviet Government would claim that passage of the ships through the Vilkitsky Straits would be a violation of Soviet frontiers". [57] The United States government, through its embassy in Moscow, sent "a note strongly protesting the Soviet position" [58] but it was nevertheless considered advisable to cancel the proposed 8,000 mile circumnavigation of the Arctic Ocean.

The principle of law applicable to the incident was formulated by State Department officials in the following terms:

> There is a right of innocent passage for all ships through straits used for international navigation between two parts of the high seas, whether or not, as in the case of the Vilkitsky Straits, they are described by the Soviet

to continue east. The reply was immediate and negative: "Comply previous orders. Return Seattle by way of Atlantic." — PETROW, *supra* note 53, at 340.

[56]   57 *Dep't State Bull.* No. 1473, at 362 (1967).

[57]   *Ibid.* A reported account of the incident by Captain Benkert of the *Eastwind* states that the negative reply of the Maritime Fleet Ministry specified that a 30-day notice was necessary. "The Russians replied", he said, "that they felt, since the strait was their territorial waters and since we were warships, a 30-day notice to pass through these waters was requested". See *The Polar Times*, at 13 (December 1967). At the Geneva meeting of the Seabed Committee in July 1972, China referred to this incident and pointed out that the USSR, which was now supporting the concept of "free transit" proposed by the U.S.A., seemed to be in favour of "free transit" in straits close to other countries but not to their own. See A/AC.138/SC1136, at 4 (24 July 1972).

[58]   *Ibid.*

> Union as being overlapped by territorial waters, and there
> is an unlimited right of navigation on the high seas of
> straits comprising both high seas and territorial waters. [59]

As a proposition of law, the above statement is difficult, if
not impossible, to challenge. It remains to be seen, however,
to what extent it really governs the incident just briefly described. It must not be forgotten that the American ships
were trying, in effect, to borrow part of a sea route which the
Soviet Union has developed and which it considers strictly
national; the whole legal status of the Northern Sea Route
was, therefore, being put to the test. In order to express an
opinion on the question, one must be reasonably familiar
with the development of the route, the physiography of the
bodies of water involved, and the legal status of those waters.
To gain this knowledge, the following questions will be examined: 1. How was the Northern Sea Route developed?
2. What bodies of water are used by the route? and 3. What
is the legal status of the waters traversed by the route?

1. How Was the Northern Sea Route Developed?

The dream of the British "Company of Merchant Adven-
turers", founded in 1551 with the object of finding a maritime
route to "the mighty Empire of Cathay", has now become a
reality. After unsuccessful attempts by many seafarers, a
Swede, Capt. A. E. Nordenskiöld, succeeded in sailing the
whole length of the Northeast Passage from the Atlantic to
the Pacific in 1878-79. Navigation is made difficult by the
presence of ice for most of the year and, partly for that
reason, it has never become the international route once
envisaged. But it has become an important national route,
that of the USSR. The Soviet Union has long recognized
the importance of developing the route, and has spared no
effort in that direction. A special Committee for the Northern
Sea Route was created as early as 1920; in 1932, it was given
the status of Main Administration [60] and put under the juris-

---

59   *Ibid.*
60   For a summary of the historical background of the Main
Administration (Glavsevmorput) of the Northern Sea Route, see Vladas

diction of the Council of Peoples' Commissars. The Decree of 17 December 1932 gave the Main Administration the task of "final development of the Northern Sea Route from the White Sea to the Bering Strait, full equipment of this route, maintenance of it in proper condition, and procurement of means for the safety of navigation over the same". [61] Subsequent decrees were issued, defining and enlarging the powers of the Main Administration so that it could attain the stated objective; as an indication of the importance of the route, jurisdiction over the Main Administration was transferred to the Council of Ministers in 1946, and to the Ministry of the Navy in 1953. [62]

Ice being the main obstacle to the development of the Northern Sea Route, the Main Administration took two measures of capital importance: it built a fleet of icebreakers, and established a network of fixed and mobile Arctic stations. The present fleet of icebreakers was built gradually over the years; the USSR already had a certain number for use in its northern ports, it acquired some from the British Government during the First War, and it has expanded the fleet continuously to the present. It seems that most of the icebreakers were built by the USSR, but it has bought some from abroad, particularly from Finland and the Netherlands; it was also reported in 1967 that the USSR planned to obtain some from Japan. [63] To-day the Soviet Union owns some 20 conventional icebreakers, the more recent being the 22,000 h.p. *Moskva* and *Leningrad*, both built in Finland. It also has a powerful nuclear-powered icebreaker, the *Lenin*, and more of the same will probably follow. [64] The *Lenin* is a 44,000 h.p. icebreaker equipped with turbo-electric power, automatic piloting and radiation control units; [65] such icebreakers are used to escort

STANKA, *Institutions of the USSR active in Arctic Research and Development*, at 3 (2nd ed. 1963).

[61]   TARACOUZIO, *Soviets in the Arctic*, Appendix III, at 383 (1938).
[62]   See Vladas STANKA, *supra* note 60, at 3.
[63]   See *The Polar Times*, at 30 (June 1967).
[64]   See T. ARMSTRONG, "Northern Sea Route", 39 *Geographical Magazine*, at 24 (May 1966).
[65]   See NEJANOV & GUESIN, "The atomic icebreaker *Lenin* in the Arctic", noted in 12 *Arctic Bibliography*, at 641, No. 74248 (1965).

vessels and barges carrying millions of tons of coal, oil, tin, gold and other natural resources extracted from the northern regions and brought to ports along the sea route; icebreakers like the *Lenin* can cut through ice six feet thick. [66]

However, it is still easier to avoid ice than cut through it, so the Main Administration developed means of doing just that to an appreciable degree; it now uses helicopters to accompany ships for ice scouting, and has developed a series of weather and ice forecast stations on the land and islands along the route. Seven stations were established in 1917, but over one hundred are in operation to-day; [67] with the help of these weather stations and five observatories (Barentsburg, Tikhaya Bay, Dickson Island, Tiksi Bay and Pevek), forecast charts are prepared for the Arctic basin and the sea route. This work is done under the supervision of specialists in the Arctic Research Institute. [68] The forecast charts show such data as air pressure distribution, air stream direction, temperature anomalies and prevailing wind directions, all of which are important in the prognosis of ice movement. [69] The operations of this network of land stations are supplemented by two types of drifting stations; one type operates in the five seas traversed by the route, and the other is installed in the Arctic Ocean itself. Those operating in the five seas are called "ice-drift recorders"; [70] first used in 1953, they consist of radio beacons placed on the ice and used by shore stations to plot their movement. Since 1957, the equipment has been perfected into automatic weather stations (DARMS), having a signal range of about 800 nautical miles. These stations indicate the speed and direction of the current and the ice, thus permitting ice forecasting to help navigation in the sea route; from 1953 to 1965, some 274 radio beacons and auto-

---

[66]   See ARMSTRONG, *supra* note 64.
[67]   Stanka states the figure to be 115 for 1961; see *supra* note 60.
[68]   Since 1958, this Institute is called the "Arctic and Antarctic Research Institute", and has a staff of about 500.
[69]   See G. VANGENGEIM (ed.), Note on "Manual of Weather Prediction", in 12 *Arctic Bibliography*, at 527, No. 73408 (1965).
[70]   They are described in a paper by A. I. YUROKIN and Yu. N. SINYURIN, in *Meteorologiya i Gidrologiya* (1966), No. 9, at 40-43, and summarized in *The Polar Record*, Vol. 13, No. 87, at 793 (Sept. 1967).

matic weather stations have been installed throughout the five seas traversed by the route. [71]

But all the work of forecasting just described could not be done effectively if it were not for the information gained from the second type of drifting stations in the Arctic Ocean itself; these drifting ice stations have been in operation for some thirty years, and constitute probably the most spectacular accomplishment of the Soviet Arctic Institute. The first drifting station "North Pole-1", directed by Papanine, was launched by the USSR in 1937, and the Soviet scientists have operated more than 20 such stations up to now.

In 1962, the Deputy-Director of the Institute, P. A. Gordienko, summarized the scientific accomplishments of the Soviet drifting stations. [72] Up to April 1st 1962, the first ten stations covered by the report had drifted a total of 6224 days, and had covered a total distance of 39,600 kilometers; the scientific parties on those ice stations averaged 13 people and included oceanographers, glaciologists, meteorologists, aerologists, geophysicists and medical doctors; their observations and measurements are recorded, analysed and then used to improve navigation in the Northern Sea Route. Gordienko summed up the result of the drifting stations in these terms: "The processing, analysis and comparison of these data have considerably enlarged our knowledge of the Central Arctic and surrounding seas, with direct practical applications to the requirements of the Northern Sea Route and the domestic economy of the Arctic coastal region." [73] Special emphasis is laid on understanding the two main types of water circulation in the Arctic basin, since only this makes it possible to "evaluate the relationship between formation of ice conditions in the Arctic seas during the navigation season and changes of ice circulation in the Arctic Basin". [74]

---

[71] *Ibid.*
[72] P. A. GORDIENKO, "Scientific Observations from, and the Nature of Drift of the North Pole Stations", in N. A. OSTENSO (ed.) *Problems of the Arctic and Antarctic No. 11*, Leningrad (1962), English translation (1966).
[73] See GORDIENKO, *ibid.*, at b-16.
[74] A. L. SOKOLOV, "Drift of Ice in the Arctic Basin and Changes

It appears from the foregoing that the Main Administration, with all its equipment and thousands of employees, has succeeded in its task of conclusively developing the Northern Sea Route; navigation has been made reasonably safe, and the season is being gradually lengthened. Whereas the navigation season used to last little more than a month, it now extends to nearly four months. [75] Dr. Armstrong, of the Scott Polar Institute, who has been studying and following the progress of the Northern Sea Route for some twenty-years, believes that "there might be a real possibility of year-round navigation in some regions". [76]

Some 300 vessels of the Soviet Union presently carry over 1,000,000 tons of cargo along the sea route; an appreciable part of this cargo comes from the ports of Murmansk and Archangel, thus cutting roughly in half the distance that such cargo would have to travel via the Suez or Panama canals. In the same way, the maritime distance between Europe and Asia could be reduced considerably if the sea route could be used for international traffic. However, there is not much through-traffic, crossing the whole of the Northern Sea Route, and there does not appear to be much interest at the moment for using it as an international waterway because of the likelihood of delays. [77] Better ice-strengthened ships would probably have to be devised in order to develop a greater degree of through-traffic.

---

in Ice Conditions over the Northern Sea Route", in *Problems of the Arctic* . . . , *supra* note 72, at j-15.

[75] Figures on the length of the navigation season vary somewhat, but these appear conservative enough. See the following sources: *The Polar Record*, Vol. 13, No. 87, at 790 (September 1967); Michael MARSDEN, "Resources and Communications in the Arctic", in R. St. J. MACDONALD (ed.), *The Arctic Frontier*, at 42 (1966); and J. E. SATER (coord. by), *The Arctic Basin*, at 257-258 (1969).

[76] ARMSTRONG, *supra* note 64, at 25.

[77] "The idea has been put forward in the Soviet Union that Scandinavian and West European shipping might be interested in using this route and indeed the USSR has lately been quite actively promoting its international use. But the gain in distance from, say, London to Far Eastern ports is not very great, and is effectively offset by the likelihood of delays". See J. E. SATER (coord. by), *The Arctic Basin*, at 258 (1969).

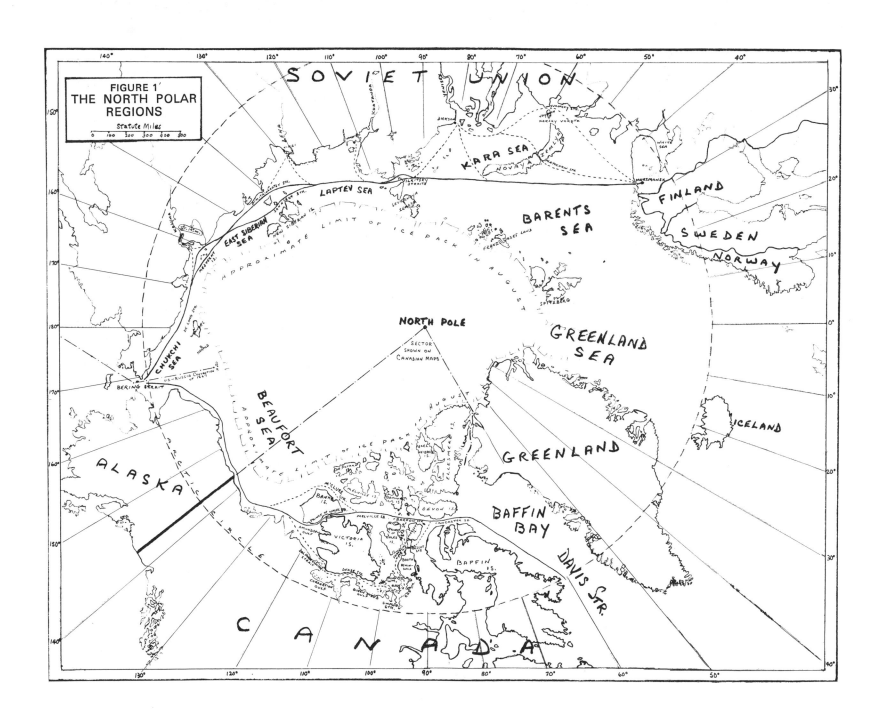

FIGURE 1
THE NORTH POLAR REGIONS

Statute Miles
0 100 200 300 400 500

2. What Bodies of Water Are Used
by the Northern Sea Route ?

Course of the route. — The Northern Sea Route, with its shipping lanes leading to and from ports along the coast, must traverse five seas: Barents, Kara, Laptev, East Siberian and Chukchi (Figure 1). [78] It must also traverse or circumnavigate three groups of islands: Severnaya Zemlya, the New Siberian Islands and the small Medvezhy Islands. Starting from Murmansk, the main lane runs through the Barents Sea, passing north of Novaya Zemlya, and proceeds across the Kara Sea into the Vilkitsky Straits of Severnaya Zemlya; having crossed the straits, the route traverses the Laptev Sea and doubles into a southern lane through the Dimitri Laptev Strait, and into a northern one through the Sannikov Strait, both of which lead into the East Siberian Sea. There, the route divides again to pass on either side of the small Medvezhy Islands; it then resumes as a single lane along the coast south of Wrangel Island, into the Chukchi Sea and through Bering Strait. In August 1965, the U.S. icebreakers thought at first of opening up a new northeast passage by avoiding the three groups of islands altogether; "[t]heir itinerary called for them to travel north of the Soviet islands of Novaya Zemlya, Severnaya Zemlya, and the New Siberian Islands". [79] But ice conditions forced them to attempt to borrow the normal lanes of the sea route.

Nature of the route. — A brief description of some of the physiographic aspects of those seas and straits is a necessary condition for a realistic and meaningful discussion of the legal aspects which will follow. At least three such aspects are important for our present purpose: the depth of the water, the presence of ice, and the width of straits. Four of the five seas are described as continental shelf seas, because their average depth is 200 meters or less; [80] nevertheless, all are

---

[78] The shipping lanes are indicated by small broken lines, and the main lanes are shown by a heavier and solid line.

[79] *Supra* note 56.

[80] See *Encyclopedia of Oceanography*, Vol. I, at 192, 243, 430 and 442 (1966).

suitable for surface navigation and present no major problem on that score. [81] But the presence of ice varies from sea to sea; the Barents Sea is partially isolated from polar ice by the Franz Josef Land archipelago, and benefits from the warm waters of the Gulf Stream, so that it is most favourable for navigation. The Kara Sea is also partly protected from the north by Severnaya Zemlya and is not fully reached by the permanent pack ice. Professor Fairbridge, of the Geology Department at Columbia, states that "[i]n the center of the sea, even in midwinter, the ice is not solid or continuous". [82] The ice pack, however, does reach Severnaya Zemlya, and normally makes it compulsory for ships to go through the Vilkitsky Straits. [83] A group of five small islands, the Geyberga Islands, divides the western entrance of the otherwise single strait, averaging about 40 miles wide, into two straits. As indicated on the map (Figure 2), [84] the strait north of the Geyberga Islands is about 22½ miles wide, whereas the southern one measures approximately 11 miles. [85] The Vilkitsky Straits constitute the most difficult passage of the Northern Sea Route; this is due to the cross currents meeting in the northern portion of the straits and the resulting concentration of ice coming in from the Kara Sea at the western entrance and from the Laptev Sea at the eastern entrance. The use of icebreaker assistance is generally considered necessary to cross these straits. As for the ice in the Laptev Sea, A. S. Ionin, of the Soviet Institute of Oceanography, states

---

[81]   Some shallow areas are nevertheless encountered, the principal one being at the eastern approach of the Dimitri Laptev Strait. There is an extensive area of shoal water which limits the passage through that strait to ships drawing a maximum of 22 feet. See *Sailing Directions for Northern USSR*, Vol. III, at 254 (amended up to 1967).

[82]   The *Encyclopedia of Oceanography, supra* note 80, at 431.

[83]   In September 1965, the U.S. icebreaker *Northwind* navigated completely around the tip of Severnaya Zemlya before hitting any ice whatever, but it seems that such favourable conditions are unusual.

[84]   See also Map 6618, published by the U.S. Naval Oceanographic Office, under the authority of the Secretary of the Navy. It is dated July 17, 1967 and makes use of available data up to 1966.

[85]   The measurements were made by the writer, and so was the positioning of the route; he is indebted to Dr. Melvin G. Marcus, professor of geography at the University of Michigan, who kindly verified the measurements of the Vilkitsky Straits. The exact measurement of the northern strait by Dr. Marcus was 22.51 miles.

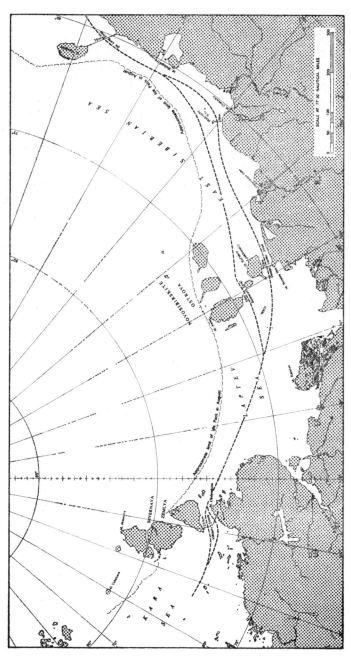

FIGURE 2   THE NORTHEAST PASSAGE

that "[m]ost of the year the sea is covered with ice which sometimes remains in the northern part over the whole summer"; [86] the ice in the Dimitri Laptev and Sannikov straits does not present special difficulty, since these straits are substantially protected from the pack ice by the New Siberian Islands. Both straits are about 29 miles wide [87] but, because of extensive shoal water at its eastern entrance, the Dimitri Laptev Strait is restricted to vessels drawing up to 22 feet. The East Siberian Sea is reached by the pack ice almost as far as the small Medvezhy Islands, of which the closest to the coast is about 19 miles; [88] Ionin states that "[i]n the eastern part of the sea, floating ice often remains off the coast even in summer". [89] Because of the ice, therefore, it is normally advantageous to pass south of the small island and closer to the coast. Both the Laptev and the East Siberian seas are easier to navigate close to the coast, because the waters discharged from the numerous coastal rivers running north contribute to keep the passage free from ice. In so far as the Chukchi Sea is concerned, the pack ice does not usually reach south of Wrangel Island, which is located about 75 miles from the coast and forms Long Strait; conditions of navigation in this sea are comparatively good.

3. WHAT IS THE LEGAL STATUS OF THE WATERS OF THE NORTHERN SEA ROUTE ?

Although the practice of the USSR indicates that it considers the Northern Sea Route a national route, it has not adopted any law to that effect; it has, however, adopted a number of laws and decrees relating to its jurisdiction over certain lands and boundary waters which have relevance to that sea route. These will be examined in the light of international law principles, to determine if they can be invoked

---

[86]   The *Encyclopedia of Oceanography, supra* note 80, at 444.
[87]   Sources consulted for the measurements and positioning of the route include the following: *The U.S. Oceanographic Atlas of the Polar Seas, Part II, Arctic* (1958) and *Sailing Directions for Northern USSR*, Vol. III, with amendments up to 1967 inclusive.
[88]   *Ibid.*, for sources consulted.
[89]   The *Encyclopedia of Oceanography, supra* note 80, at 244.

by the Soviet Union in support of its state practice. The laws in question relate to territorial waters and what are called "internal sea waters".

(1) *Soviet laws relating mainly to territorial waters*

On December 10, 1909, the *Law on Extension of the Maritime Customs Zone* was adopted, claiming jurisdiction over a breadth of 12 miles off Russian coasts for the purpose of customs control; this law is cited by the USSR as having established the breadth of its territorial waters at 12 miles. [90] On May 24, 1921, the USSR adopted a *Decree concerning the Protection of Fisheries and Game Reserves in the Arctic Ocean and the White Sea.* [91] This decree establishes a 12-mile fishing zone in the White Sea, and in the Barents Sea, referred to as the "Arctic Ocean". Both of these laws are permissible in customary international law, but neither one can serve as a basis to bar the innocent passage of foreign ships in the Northern Sea Route.

On April 16, 1926, the Presidium of the Central Committee of the USSR adopted a decree *On the Proclamation of Lands and Islands located in the Northern Arctic Ocean as Territory of the USSR.* [92] This decree is examined here because of the wide meaning often attached to the term "territory" in the legislation of the USSR and the interpretation which the decree has received from some of the Soviet jurists. The relevant part of the decree stated:

> All lands and islands ... located in the Northern Arctic Ocean, north of the shores of the Union of Soviet Socialist Republics up to the North Pole between the meridian 32°04′35″E. long ... and the meridian 168°49′30″W. long ... are proclaimed to be territory of the USSR. [93]

---

[90] U.N. Synoptical table, prepared by the U.N. Secretariat, based upon information received from States; Annex Doc. A/CONF.19/4, in *Second U.N. Conference on the Law of the Sea,* A/CONF.19/8, 157-163 (1960).

[91] U.N. Legislative Series, *Laws and Regulations on the Régime of the High Seas,* Vol. I, at 116 (1951).

[92] *Soviet Statutes and Decisions,* Vol. III, No. 4, at 9 (Summer 1967).

[93] *Ibid.*

This decree, which is in effect the adoption of the sector theory by the USSR in the Arctic, has been interpreted by the Soviet jurists in such a way as to include all maritime areas within the sector described by the decree. [94] The Soviet government, however, has never given such an interpretation; and there is nothing in the decree or in the diplomatic note communicating the decree to foreign governments to indicate any such intention. [95] The decree has been preceded by two diplomatic notes addressed to the American Secretary of State in 1916 and 1924, both of which confined themselves to claiming sovereignty over the lands and islands north of the mainland. [96] Furthermore, as we shall see in a later statute, the term "territory" is used alone, whereas it is the legislative practice of the Soviet legislators to use the expression "water territory" when intending to include water.

It is also worth noting that the textbook in International Law for use in law schools, authored by seven Soviet jurists under the official sponsorship of the Academy of Sciences of the USSR Institute of State and Law, limits its interpretation of the sector decree to lands and islands. Under the heading "Status of the Arctic", it states: "It is in theory and practice recognized that all lands and islands discovered, as well as those which will be discovered in the future within the polar sector adjacent to the coast of a given State constitute part of that State's territory." [97] The text then continues and simply paraphrases the 1926 decree. The conclusion is, therefore, that this decree cannot be and is not being considered by the USSR as a legal basis for its claim of jurisdiction over the Arctic seas under review.

---

94   See in particular the following: KOROVIN, "S.S.S.R. i Poliarnye Zemli, Sovetskoye Pravo", No. 3, at 45-46 (1926), and SIGRIST, "Rabochii Sud", at 984 (1928), cited by TARACOUZIO in *Soviets in the Arctic*, at 348 (1938); LAKHTINE, "Rights over the Arctic", 24 *A.J.I.L.* 703, at 712 (1930); VYSHNYEPOLSKY, "The Problem of a System of Law for the Arctic Region", translated in *Soviet Press Translations*, Vol. 7, No. 18, 371-376 (15 oct. 1952).
95   See text of the Decree and the Note (in French) in Lakhtine, *Rights in the Arctic* (in Russian), Appendix, at 44-45 (1928).
96   See text of the Notes (in French) in LAKHTINE, *ibid.*, at 43-44.
97   F. I. KOZHEVNIKOV (ed.) *International Law*, at 191 (1960).

On June 15, 1927, the *Regulations (Statute) for the Defence of the State Frontiers of the USSR* were enacted. In this legislative enactement, the USSR establishes "along coastal frontiers: a maritime zone extending seaward from the line of the lowest ebb-tide on the mainland and on islands to a distance of twelve miles . . ." (Art. 9, para. c). [98] The statute goes on to provide measures for the protection of the 12-mile maritime zone against violation by foreign vessels. This legislation presents no unusual feature on the point under investigation, since the jurisdiction claim is limited to 12 miles.

On August 5, 1960, preceding its ratification of the 1958 Convention on the Territorial Sea, the USSR adopted a new law entitled *Statute on the Protection of the State Border of the USSR.* [99] This law replaces that of 1927 and is of considerable relevance to the present investigation; it defines the "state border" as being "the line which determines the land and water territory of the USSR" (Art. 1). It is most important to keep in mind this special concept of territory and border when trying to interpret Soviet legal literature. The territorial sea of the USSR is referred to as 'coastal sea waters', and these are defined as follows:

> Coastal sea waters, 12 nautical miles in breadth, computed from the line of lowest ebb-tide both on the mainland and also around islands, or from the line of the farthest extremity of internal sea waters of the USSR, shall constitute the territorial waters of the USSR. In individual instances provided for by agreements of the USSR with other states, the breadth of territorial waters may be otherwise. The line of the farthest extremity of territorial waters shall constitute the state border of the USSR at sea (Art. 3). [100]

These provisions leave no doubt that, in the absence of a convention to the contrary, the breadth of "territorial waters" is only 12 miles and that the outer limit constitutes the "state

[98] U.N. Legislative Series, *Laws and Regulations on the Régime of the Territorial Sea,* at 255-256 (1957).
[99] See *supra* note 92, at 10-24.
[100] *Ibid.,* at 10.

border" of the USSR. The Statute then provides for the establishment of a "border zone" of two kilometers wide within the "state border" for the latter's protection (Art. 8).

The innocent passage of merchant vessels is specifically protected within territorial waters, but it is expressly limited to those vessels.

The relevant article is reproduced hereunder:

> Article 15. — Foreign non military vessels shall enjoy the right of innocent passage through territorial waters of the USSR. By innocent passage is meant navigation through territorial waters for the purpose of crossing them without entry into internal sea waters or for the purpose of passage into internal sea waters or exit from internal sea waters for the high seas. Passage shall be considered innocent if the vessels follow a customary navigational course or a course recommended by competent agencies, observing the established regime, and in places where there are no districts closed for navigation which have been announced in Izveshcheniia moreplavateliam (Notice to Mariners). [101]

The meaning of "innocent passage" just given is quite in accord with the 1958 Convention on the Territorial Sea, [102] except that the right is specifically limited to merchant or non-military vessels.

The innocent passage of warships is subjected to the previous authorization of the government of the USSR. The relevant provision reads:

> Article 16. — Foreign warships shall pass through territorial and enter internal sea waters of the USSR in accordance with the previous authorization of the Government of the USSR ... Foreign submarines whose arrival in territorial and internal sea waters of the USSR has been authorized must only navigate on the surface. [103]

This provision is, of course, contrary to the 1958 Convention, which guarantees the right of innocent passage to both mer-

---

[101]   Ibid., at 13-14.
[102]   For a discussion of Articles 14 and 16 of that Convention see "What does innocent passage mean ?" in Section I of this Part entitled *The Law of Innocent Passage.*
[103]   *Supra*, note 92, at 14.

chant and warships. However, the USSR has never recognized that warships enjoyed this right and its delegates argued against it at the 1958 Conference. Speaking against the Netherland's proposal to give warships the right of innocent passage without previous authorization or notification save in exceptional circumstances, Nikolaev expressed his government's view in the following terms:

> The Netherlands representative had also contended that the requirement of previous authorization could prove prejudicial because of possible delay. The USSR delegation could not accept that view, since the paramount interests of a State should not be subordinated to a desire for haste in some other quarter. [104]

It is not surprising, therefore, that the USSR attached the following Reservation to its instrument of ratification of the Convention on the Territorial Sea: "To Article 23 (Subsection D. The rule as applied to warships): The Government of the USSR considers that a coastal state has the right to establish an authorization procedure for the passage of foreign warships through its territorial waters." [105]

This "authorization procedure" has been set out in the *Rules for Visits by Foreign Warships to Territorial Waters and Ports of the USSR*, adopted on 25 June 1960. [106] These rules replace the 1931 Provisional Rules, [107] and consist of some twenty articles outlining the procedure and conditions for obtaining the necessary consent. A comparison of these Rules with former ones reveal that they are more stringent in a number of important respects. It is now provided that "[c]onsent for the entry of foreign warships shall be sought through the Ministry of Foreign Affairs of the USSR not later than 30 full days prior to the proposed visit..." (Art. 2), whereas the former Rules merely required that "[a]uthoriza-

---

[104] *U.N. Conference on the Law of the Sea,* Official Records, U.N. Doc. A/CONF.13/39, Vol. III, at 130 (1958).
[105] Reproduced in *Soviet Statutes and Decisions, supra,* note 92, at 45.
[106] *Ibid.,* at 24-29.
[107] Reproduced in U.N. Legislative Series, *Laws and Regulations on the Régime of the Territorial Sea,* 412-416 (1957).

tion for the entry of foreign warships shall be requested in good time through the diplomatic channel..." (Art. 3). [108] Exceptions to the consent requirements are provided for, but have been reduced from three to two. These two exceptions are "warships carrying heads of states or heads of governments and warships escorting them" and warships whose entry is due to natural disaster and heavy damage to the ship (Art. 3). The former third exception in favour of warships carrying heads of diplomatic missions accredited to the USSR Government has been deleted. The Rules further specify the preliminary information about the proposed visit which must accompany the request for consent to the Ministry of Foreign Affairs (Art. 2), as well as a list of detailed information to be given to the Soviet communications officer upon approaching port (Art. 10). These rules also contain a list of prohibited acts (Art. 16) and permissible acts (Art. 17). If a foreign warship violates the rules and disregards a warning, "it may be requested to leave the territorial waters of the USSR by order of the proper authorities" (Art. 18).

The rest of the Rules do not present any special feature, except that they apparently apply only to passage through territorial waters *with entry* into internal waters and ports. In this regard, they are in conformity with the enabling provision of the Statute which envisages previous authorization for foreign warships to "pass through territorial and enter internal sea waters of the USSR" (Art. 16). In other words, it is questionable whether a foreign warship could obtain permission to simply pass through territorial waters without wanting to pay a visit to a port. If this is the proper interpretation, both Article 16 of the Statute and the Rules go beyond the Reservation which the Soviet Union attached to Article 23 of the 1958 Convention, and they are tantamount to a complete prohibition. That Reservation enables the USSR "to establish an authorization procedure for the passage of foreign warships through its territorial waters". Any further mental reservation which would add "and enter internal sea

---

[108]   *Ibid.*, at 412.

waters for an approved visit to a port" would be beyond the scope of the reserving possibilities of the Reservation. If the real intention of the USSR had been to prohibit completely the passage of warships through its territorial waters, then it ought to have attached a reservation to Article 15. This article provides that "[t]he coastal State must not hamper innocent passage through the territorial sea" (para. 1); the latter provision forms part of the group appearing under the heading *Subsection A. Rules Applicable to All Ships*. This was well understood by its delegation at the Conference, which submitted a joint proposal with Bulgaria attempting to amend Article 15 (Article 16 of the I.L.C. draft). The amendment would have deprived warships of the right of innocent passage and forced ships to use specified navigational channels. [109] As explained by delegate Nikolaev at the Conference, the reason for the amendment — calling for the deletion of what has become paragraph 1 of Article 15 already cited — was that it "appeared in Subsection A, which contained general rules, and it would apply not only to commercial and other non-military vessels but also to warships". [110] Nikolaev was quite right in his interpretation; Article 15, imposing an obligation on the coastal state not to hamper innocent passage, does apply to warships. Not having made any reservation to this article, it is difficult to understand how the USSR could have intended a prohibition of the innocent passage of warships. Nevertheless, the laws and regulations just examined lead to that conclusion; they limit the right of innocent passage to merchant ships. Leaving aside for the moment the questionable validity of such limitation, the reason for refusing to allow the passage of foreign ships such as the U.S. icebreakers is still not evident. Presuming that the Northern Sea Route does go through part of its territorial waters, what legal basis can the USSR invoke to bar foreign ships crossing from the Kara Sea to the Laptev Sea through the Vilkitsky Straits ? There is no mention of straits in its laws and regu-

---

[109]   See annex Doc. A/CONF.13/c.1/L, at 46 in *U.N. Conference on the Law of the Sea*, A/CONF.13/39, Vol. III (1958).
[110]   *Ibid.*, at 78.

lations relating to territorial waters. But, even if straits are less than 24 miles wide, the right of innocent passage still exists in those territorial waters. What then could be the basis for refusing passage to a foreign ship ? Could it be that the seas traversed by the Northern Sea Route are considered as internal waters and that no access is possible without permission ? Since this is conceivable, the legislation and practice of the Soviet Union ought to be examined in this respect.

(2) *Soviet laws relating to internal sea waters*

The legislation of the USSR contains only one provision relating to internal waters: Article 4 of the 1960 statute. The relevant portion is reproduced below:

> *Article 4.* — Internal sea waters of the USSR shall include:
>
> a) waters of ports of the USSR ...
>
> b) waters of bays, inlets, coves, and estuaries, whose entire shores belong to the USSR, up to a straight line drawn from shore to shore in a place where, from the side of the sea, one or several passages are first formed, if the breadth of each of these does not exceed 24 nautical miles;
>
> c) waters of bays, inlets, coves, and estuaries, seas and straits, historically belonging to the USSR. [111]

This provision must be interpreted in the light of the preceding article, already examined, which stipulates that the breadth of territorial waters is computed "from the line of the farthest extremity of internal sea waters" (Art. 3). Thus any body of water coming within the present definition of "internal sea waters" serves as a baseline for the breadth of territorial waters beyond; the definition appears to be — certainly at first reading — quite in conformity with the Territorial Sea Convention. It respects the 24-mile closing line for bays stipulated by the Convention as a maximum, and includes historic bays which are specifically excepted from the 24-mile rule. It must be observed, however, that the enumeration of bodies of water considered as *"historically belonging to the USSR"* include not only bays, inlets and the like, but also *"seas and straits"*. One

---

[111]   *Supra*, note 92, at 10-11.

is left to wonder what seas and straits are thereby envisaged; [112] there is absolutely nothing else in the enactment which could offer guidance as to the intention of the legislator. Consequently, barring any proof of the contrary by way of historic title, [113] the waters traversed by the Northern Sea Route cannot be considered as internal waters.

(3) Appraisal of the legal situation

If we are correct in the conclusion that the waters traversed by the sea route are not considered by the USSR as internal waters, they must be only territorial waters, with the consequent right of innocent passage. But what then could be the possible basis for refusing to let the U.S. icebreakers through the Vilkitsky Straits ? Under the laws, regulations and practice which we have analysed, there remains only one answer apparently: that the U.S. icebreakers are classified by the USSR as warships; and there is some evidence to support this rationalization. According to a report in the *New York Times* on December 17th 1967, Capt. Benkert of the *Eastwind* stated that the Soviets insisted on a 30-day notice because the icebreakers were warships. The report reads:

> In our only direct communication with the Russians, Capt. William K. Earle, Edisto's skipper and group commander, indicated our desire to pass through the strait. The Russians replied that they felt, since the strait was their territorial waters and since we were warships, a 30-day notice to pass through these waters was requested. [114]

This kind of reply was fully justified under the Soviet authorization procedure for warships. It would also appear that there is some justification for classifying the U.S. Coast Guard ships as warships, since they perform certain police duties, are manned by enlisted personnel, and carry armaments. Appa-

---

[112]   When Krylov raised the question of internal seas in the International Law Commission, he referred only to the Sea of Azov. The report states: "When asking the Rapporteur to insert a passage on internal seas, he had had in mind such cases as the Sea of Azov which, together with its strait, lay entirely within Soviet territory." — (1956) *I.L.C. Yearbook I,* at 261.

[113]   This possibility will be considered in Part III of this work.

[114]   See W. BAMBERGER, *The Polar Times,* at 13 (December 1967).

rently the two icebreakers in question "were armed with twin five-inch .38 calibre guns at the bows, standard Coast Guard equipment" [115] and carried "a crew of 220, composed of 20 officers, 195 enlisted men and five civilians in control of the oceanographic work". [116] The Coast Guard is "a military service and a branch of the armed forces of the United States". [117] It is "a service in the Treasury Department, except when operating as a service of the Navy". [118] This transfer of service occurs either upon "declaration of war or when the President directs". [119] It is not known if, on that occasion, the ships were operating as a service of the Navy and subject to regular naval discipline. However, the appearances seemed to indicate that the essential elements of the definition of a warship contained in the High Seas Convention were present, [120] and the Soviet authorities were probably quite justified in treating the U.S. icebreakers as warships. [121] In the circumstances, the soundness of the position taken by the USSR would depend ultimately on the validity of its authorization procedure in International Law. The net result of this authorization procedure is to turn the right of innocent passage for warships into a mere privilege which the Soviet Union may grant or refuse at will. Such a procedure is of doubtful validity under traditional customary law, and is in violation of the Convention on the Territorial Sea. The latter provides, in its Article 15, that "[t]he coastal State must not hamper innocent passage through the territorial sea" (para. 1). This provision is one of the rules applicable to all ships, and it was so recognized by the delegates of the USSR at the 1958 Conference. The concept of innocent passage as a right in favour of *all*

---

[115]   Peter GROSE, "U.S. Halts Arctic Expedition as Soviet Bars Ships", *New York Times,* August 31, 1967, reproduced in *The Polar Times,* at 14 (Dec. 1967).

[116]   *Ibid.,* at 15.

[117]   14 *U.S. Code,* sec. 1.

[118]   *Ibid.*

[119]   *Ibid.*

[120]   Article 8(2).

[121]   This is also the view of Professor Butler expressed in "The Legal Regime of Russian Territorial Waters", 62 *A.J.I.L.* 51, at 64, note 71 (1968) and in *The Soviet Union and the Law of the Sea,* at 70 (1971).

ships is so basic as to come within the very scope of the object and purpose of the Convention. Consequently, the Reservation relating to warships attached by the USSR to its ratification is hardly compatible with the Convention, and goes to the very integrity of the instrument. And, as stated by the International Court, " . . . it is the compatibility of a reservation with the object and purpose of the Convention that must furnish the criterion for the attitude of a State in making the reservation . . ." [122] It follows that the Reservation of the USSR, at least as interpreted by its government, does not meet the criterion and is, therefore, of doubtful validity. Being a prohibited reservation, any failure to raise a formal objection on the part of the United States cannot be interpreted as an acceptance of the Reservation. Such an interpretation could be possible only if the Reservation had been a permissible one in the first place. In other words, the reservation of one state, which is prohibited because of incompatibility with the object and purpose of the convention or otherwise, can never be validated by the mere silence of another state.

The foregoing analysis does not mean that the USSR may not exercise some control over the passage of a warship; the Territorial Sea Convention gives the right to "require the warship to leave its territorial sea", if it refuses to comply with its regulations (Art. 23). Consequently, the USSR would have been justified in expelling the U.S. Coast Guard ships from the Vilkitsky Straits' area in August 1967, had they refused to comply with its regulations. But regulation of passage does not mean prohibition; this distinction, made by the International Court in the *Corfu Channel Case* and maintained in the Territorial Sea Convention, permits the coastal state to make "laws and regulations relating to transport and navigation" (Art. 17). And, since the passage remains innocent only "so long as it is not prejudicial to the peace, good order or security of the coastal State" (Art. 14, para. 4), the USSR would have been entitled to verify the innocence of

---

[122] *Advisory Opinion on Reservations to the Convention on Genocide* (1951), *I.C.J. Rep.* 15, at 24. The Court's view was incorporated in Article 19 of the Convention on the Law of Treaties in 1969.

the passage if it had reasonable grounds to do so. The Convention does not stipulate how far such protective regulations may go but, in certain circumstances, the coastal state might be justified in insisting on a verification of the innocent character of the passage before letting a foreign warship through.

In so far as merchant ships are concerned, the Territorial Sea Convention permits the USSR to impose a temporary suspension of their passage for security reasons (Art. 14, para. 3). This power of suspension applies to straits also, unless they are used for international navigation (Art. 14, para. 4). On this point, it appears that only three foreign ships have ever traversed the Northern Sea Route; the Swedish ship *Vega,* under the command of Nordenskiöld, became the first to sail the whole length of the Northeast Passage *in* 1878-79; the second was the Norwegian ship *Maud,* led by Amundsen in 1918-19; the third was the *Komet,* of the Third Reich, which traversed the entire passage from August 19 to September 5, 1940. The first two ships made voyages of scientific exploration, before the development of the Northeast Passage by the Soviets; the third voyage was made with the approval of the Soviet Union and with the assistance of its icebreakers. Subject to the few exceptions just mentioned, it is doubtful if any foreign ship has ever crossed the Vilkitsky Straits without being escorted by a Soviet icebreaker or receiving special permission from the Soviet Union. Thus the legal regime of ordinary territorial waters would apply to those straits of the Northern Sea Route which are too narrow to leave a strip of high seas in the middle. Allowing for a breadth of 12 nautical miles from the coast and around the islands, there are two such passages: the Vilkitsky Straits and the strait formed by the Medvezhy Islands and the coast. In those areas the right of innocent passage legally exists at least as much as in any territorial sea. This conclusion would still hold, even if the USSR could justify consideration of the groups of islands traversed by the sea route as separate outlying archipelagoes, with one belt of territorial sea around each group. It would remain doubtful that the water areas within the straight baselines joining the islands could be considered as internal waters. Even so, the Territorial Sea Convention preserves the right of innocent passage in such newly-enclosed water areas (Art. 5, para. 2). It should be mentioned, in addition, that the applicability of the right of innocent passage to the Northern Sea Route does not prevent the U.S.S.R. from adopting regulations to insure the safety of navigation and the protection of its marine environment. The U.S.S.R. did adopt such regulations in September 1971 and they appear perfectly valid. [123]

The foregoing appraisal of the legal situation relating to the Northeast Passage may be summarized as follows:

1.   The right of innocent passage, as guaranteed by both custom and convention, exists in favour of all ships throughout the Northeast Passage.

2.   Although the Vilkitsky Straits and the strait south of the Medvezhy Islands may be properly considered as constituting Soviet territorial waters, the right of innocent passage exists as much as in ordinary territorial waters. Temporary suspension could be imposed by the Soviet Union, since those straits are not used for international navigation.

3.   Presuming that U.S. Coast Guard icebreakers may be classified as warships, they retain the right of innocent passage under the Territorial Sea Convention, but are subject to expulsion for refusal to comply with coastal laws regulating (not prohibiting) innocent passage.

4.   The national legislation of the Soviet Union, subjecting the passage of warships to its complete discretion and control, appears contrary to the Territorial Sea Convention. The Reservation attached by the Soviet Union to its ratification of that Convention, as interpreted by the Soviet authorities, appears incompatible with the object and purpose of the Convention and is of doubtful validity in international law.

---

[123]   See "Statute on the Administration of the Northern Sea Route Attached to the Ministry of the Maritime Fleet" (confirmed by the Council of Ministers of the USSR, 16 September 1971), reproduced in 9 *Int'l Legal Materials,* at 645-646 (1972).

III. — INNOCENT PASSAGE IN THE
NORTHWEST PASSAGE

If the American ships have been prevented by the Soviets from navigating the Northeast Passage, they have been greatly assisted by the Canadians in making experimental crossings of the Northwest Passage. The close cooperation has even been extended to permit the crossing of U.S. nuclear submarines. Does this indicate that Canada considers the Northwest Passage as a sea route open to foreign ships ? Could a foreign ship pass through the Northwest Passage as of right accorded by law, or only as a matter of privilege accorded by Canada ? These are the kind of questions on which the present study may hopefully shed some light. Such a study cannot be really enlightening, however, without some familiarity with the history of the passage, the physiography of the route and the legal character of the bodies of water involved. To acquire this knowledge, the following questions will be investigated: 1. How was the Northwest Passage developed ? 2. What bodies of water are used by the Passage ? and 3. What is the legal status of the Northwest Passage ?

1. How was the Northwest Passage Developed ? [124]

The search for the Northwest Passage goes back to 1576, when Martin Frobisher convinced Queen Elizabeth of the advantages of finding a route to Cathay. After Frobisher, British expeditions continued for over three centuries under such leaders as Davis, Baffin, Hudson, Parry, Ross, Franklin and M'Clure. It was M'Clure who, in 1852, completed the last link of one of the routes of the Northwest Passage, by leading a sled party across the strait now named after him. Having been forced to abandon his ship at Mercy Bay, on the north side of Banks Island, while trying to navigate the strait from west to east, he completed the crossing on foot and reached the northern side of Viscount Melville Sound.

---

[124] For a summary of the explorations of the Canadian Arctic and those relating to the Northwest Passage, see I *Pilot of Arctic Canada* 37-80 (2nd ed., 1970).

The feat of completely sailing the passage, however, was not accomplished until 1906, some 330 years after Frobisher's first voyage. The honour for this spectacular accomplishment goes to Roald Amundsen, [125] a Norwegian, who made it from the Atlantic to the Pacific in his 47-ton herring boat, the *Gjoa;* his route was via Lancaster Sound and Barrow Strait (Figure 1), down Peel Sound and through Franklin, James Ross and Rae Straits. After spending 19 months on the Southeast coast of King William Island, at a bay now known as Gjoa Haven, he crossed Simpson Strait and made his way through the islands at the entrance of Victoria Strait, then through Dease Strait, Coronation Gulf, Dolphin and Union Strait, Amundsen Gulf and along the mainland coast.

In 1910, Captain Bernier was commissioned by the Canadian government to proceed north in command of the *Arctic* to "patrol Davis strait, Baffin bay, Lancaster Sound, Barrow strait, Melville Sound, M'Clure strait, and Beaufort sea to Herschel island, thence through Behring strait to Vancouver or Victoria, B.C." [126] The Commission specified however: "The advisability of attempting to make the North-West Passage is however left to your judgment, after ascertaining the ice conditions on the spot." [127] Unfortunately the ice conditions in M'Clure Strait prevented him from completing the crossing. He turned back at a point 30 miles south of Cape Providence but, in his words, "we had reached the farthest point in this direction of any vessel". [128] Indeed, the Parry Channel route which Captain Bernier came so close to complete has yet to be travelled in its entirety by any surface vessel. A complete crossing of the Northwest Passage by a Canadian ship, although not via M'Clure Strait, was not made until 1940.

Under the command of Sergeant Larsen, the RCMP Schooner *St. Roch* made the Passage from the Atlantic to the

---

[125]   Amundsen was also among the first to navigate the Northeast Passage, in 1918-1919.
[126]   Quoted in J. E. BERNIER, *Master Mariner and Arctic Explorer,* at 347 (1939).
[127]   *Ibid.*
[128]   *Ibid.,* at 355.

Pacific in 1940-1942. The *St. Roch* was a small ship, built in 1928 specially for the RCMP, with extra thick Douglas Fir and equipped with a small 150-horsepower diesel motor. The crossing was made part of a regular tour of duty by the RCMP in the Canadian North. Sergeant Larsen took the same route as Amundsen, except that he went through Bellot Strait and Prince Regent Inlet instead of Peel Sound. This voyage from Vancouver to Halifax, with visits en route to Eskimo groups and RCMP detachments, took some 28 months.

The return trip of the *St. Roch* in 1944 was made through Parry Channel (Lancaster Sound, Barrow Strait and Viscount Melville Sound) as far as Banks Island, down Prince of Wales Strait, along the mainland coast and through Bering Strait. The *St. Roch* covered some 7500 miles from Halifax to Vancouver in 86 days (26 July to 16 October 1944), and accomplished her various duties on the way. In the words of Sgt. Larsen, "[t]hus, for the first time in history, we became the only vessel to complete the Northern Routes both ways, and the only vessel that had completed the Lancaster Sound Route, which is the better of the two. This route will no doubt be used in the future." [129] Larsen predicted that before long powerful icebreakers would ply the Arctic waters regularly and carry supplies to the northern inhabitants.

In 1950, Canada launched a special Arctic service vessel, the *C. D. Howe,* which had a cruising radius of 10,000 miles and a flight deck for use by a helicopter: [130] it made annual patrols to the central and northern Arctic islands, using the eastern part of the Northwest Passage. In 1954, the Canadian Coast Guard *Labrador,* a heavy icebreaker, became the first deep-draft ship to navigate the Passage completely, by following Larsen's route west. [131] In the same year the U.S. Coast Guard *Northwind* became the first ship to cross the entire length of M'Clure Strait, which is fully exposed to the

---

[129]   H. LARSEN, *The Northwest Passage,* at 8 (1948).
[130]   See CANADA (Dept. of Resources and Development), *Transportation and Communications in the Northwest Territories,* at 11-12 (1953).
[131]   See I *Pilot of Arctic Canada,* at 66 (2nd ed., 1970).

ice coming from Beaufort Sea and the Arctic Ocean itself. [132] Three years later, a squadron of three U.S. Coast Guard ships, two hydrographic survey ships and one icebreaker (the *Spar*, *Bramble* and *Storis*) crossed the Northwest Passage from the Pacific to the Atlantic following Larsen's route east. [133] This was a joint hydrographic endeavour between Canada and the United States, and the U.S. squadron was led through the narrow Bellot Strait by the C.C.G.S. *Labrador*. [134]

The crossings accomplished thus far had demonstrated the possibility — albeit with considerable difficulty — of surface navigation accross the whole length of the Northwest Passage. However, some parts of the Passage, in Barrow Strait, are rather shallow and the question remained whether it could be used for undersea navigation. The answer came in 1960 when the U.S.S. *Seadragon*, with the acquiescence of the Canadian government, crossed the Northwest Passage from east to west. The 2360-ton nuclear submarine followed the Parry Channel route (Lancaster Sound, Barrow Strait, Viscount Melville Sound) and M'Clure Strait, remaining under water throughout except for one surfacing at Resolute Bay. It then surfaced in the Beaufort Sea, before making for the North Pole and back through Bering Strait. [135] Equipped with special sonar and electronic aids, the *Seadragon* picked its way through icebergs along the west coast of Greenland and navigated the Northwest Passage without any difficulty. The following description shows the effectiveness of this equipment: "Sonar gave continuous information on: overhead ice thickness, sub-to-ice distance, sub-to-bottom distance, location of holes in the ice (called polynyas), details of polynya outline ridges to allow surfacing, and also provided continuous spotting of iceberg." [136] The manner and facility of the passage is confirmed by the commander of the *Seadragon* who

---

[132]   *Ibid.*, at 131.
[133]   *Ibid.*, at 66.
[134]   See *Polar Times*, at 9 (Dec. 1959).
[135]   For a brief account of the event, see *The Polar Record*, Vol. 10, at 390 (1960-1961).
[136]   Leon DULBERGER, "Sonar Guides Submarines under Polar Ice", *Electronics*, Vol. 34, No. 12, at 18 (1961).

states: "Islands and shoals were carefully and accurately plotted on the chart. There was channel there deep enough for any future nuclear submarine to follow, winter or summer, favorable ice or not." [137] The United States had proved conclusively the feasibility of under-sea navigation in the Northwest Passage.

With the discovery of large oil reserves at Prudhoe Bay in 1968, oil companies began to consider the possibility of using the Northwest Passage to transport the precious commodity. In 1969, the Humble Oil Company had the S.S. *Manhattan*, a 43,000 horsepower tanker, converted into an icebreaking vessel and sent it through the Northwest Passage, in September of that year, in order to determine its feasibility for year-round navigation. In spite of the assistance of the Canadian icebreaker *John A. Macdonald* which rescued her from ice-jams on numerous occasions, the *Manhattan* could not negotiate the polar ice of M'Clure Strait. She was forced to turn back before reaching Mercy Bay and then borrowed Prince of Wales Strait to complete the crossing. The *Manhattan* nevertheless became the first commercial vessel to make its way through the Northwest Passage. [138]

The last vessel to cross the Northwest Passage, at the time of writing, was the Canadian Scientific Ship *Hudson*. [139]

---

[137] J. T. STRONG, "The Opening of the Arctic Ocean", *U.S. Naval Institute Proceedings*, Vol. 87, No. 10, at 62 (1961). For a description of the Seadragon's passage through the island of Barrow Strait, see G. P. STEELE, *Seadragon under the Ice*, 165-173 (1962).

[138] Of the numerous accounts of the *Manhattan* voyage, see B. KEATING, "North for Oil", 137 *National Geographic*, 374-391 (1970).

[139] There was however a report that the first loaded tanker to attempt a crossing of the Northwest Passage left Rotterdam on August 7, 1972, bound for Rae Point on Melville Island. The 16,254-ton Finnish tanker *Palva* was said to be carrying 15,000 tons of aircraft fuel and was to be assisted by a Canadian icebreaker. See *Globe & Mail*, 8 Aug. 1972, at 8. To complete the picture on crossings of the Northwest Passage, mention should be made of two crossings still in progress: one by Tony Dauksza of Grand Rapids, Michigan, who has already made his way across more than four-fifths of the Northwest Passage with his 16-foot canoe *Arctic Ice Breaker* (See *Detroit Free press*, 29 Aug. 1971, at 28 & 29); the other, by Colin Irwin of Bournemouth, England, who has covered about three quarters of the way so far with his 18-foot sail boat *Endeavour* (See the *Globe & Mail*, 22 Sept. 1972, at 37). Both of

It made an easterly crossing in the fall of 1970, thus completing a one-year oceanographic expedition which had taken her on a 41,000 nautical mile voyage from Halifax, south to Cape Horn, north to Bering Strait, east through the Northwest Passage and back to Halifax. [140]

Canada has been increasing its activities in the Arctic for a considerable number of years [141] and maritime navigation has remained the main mode of transportation. In 1964, the Canadian Coast Guard fleet already consisted of over 200 vessels: 50 watchkeeping ships, 10 heavy icebreakers, 8 light icebreakers and 150 landing crafts and tugs. [142] Over 100,000 tons of cargo are being delivered annually to some seventy-five different places in the Arctic; [143] these cover widely-separated parts and include the DEW line stations, numerous Eskimo settlements and weather stations. In 1964, the *Labrador* set a Canadian record by reaching 81°45′ north into Robeson Channel, between Ellesmere Island and Greenland.

This extensive use of the Northwest Passage and of other bodies of water throughout the Arctic islands is constantly increasing as more scientific data are obtained and better navigational aids are developed. To this end, Canada operates an appreciable number of Arctic weather stations, a few of which are manned jointly with the United States.

---

these soloists are following roughly the same route as that of the *St. Roch* for its easterly crossing in 1940-42.

[140] For a brief account of this voyage, see "Circumnavigation of the Americas", 32 *External Affairs Bull.*, No. 2, at 64-66 (Feb. 1971).

[141] In the early 1950's, a special "Advisory Committee on Northern Development" was created, with instructions "to advise the government on questions of policy relating to civilian and military undertakings in northern Canada and to provide for the effective coordination of all government activities in that area" — See *Government Activities in the North,* Doc. ND 441, at 2 (1956). This committee reports periodically to the Cabinet on all phases of development and its reports cover the work of the branches and divisions of all federal departments and agencies carrying on activities in the Canadian North.

[142] See Gordon W. STEAD, "Current Canadian Coast Guard Operations in Ice", *The Polar Record*, Vol. 12, No. 77, 147-155 (1964). The author, an Assistant Deputy Minister of the Department of Transport, gives an excellent account of the work accomplished by the Canadian icebreakers.

[143] See Gordon W. STEAD, *ibid.,* at 152 and *Government Activities in the North, supra* note 141, at 233.

Continual research is carried on in such fields as hydrography, oceanography, glaciology, climatology and meteorology in order to obtain accurate ice forecasting. A central Ice Forecast Office in Halifax issues 30-day ice forecasts and 5-day ice forecasts for the Arctic and sub-Arctic; in addition, field ice forecast stations are set up temporarily at key points in the Arctic during the navigation season in order to provide short-range ice forecasts. In 1966, some 37 stations provided shore station ice reports during the navigation season. [144] Aerial ice reconnaissance is carried on from fixed-wing aircraft both before and during the shipping season; helicopters also provide convoys with short-range information on ice movement. With the data obtained from these various sources, the Meteorological Branch of the Canadian Department of Transport is able to publish an annual "Ice Summary and Analysis" describing Arctic ice conditions at 7 or 14 day intervals. This annual report contains a series of charts which indicate at a glance the ice conditions in a given area at a given time. Although ice conditions do vary from year to year, this is of considerable assistance for long term planning. Satellite photography is also used on a regular basis as an aid in ice forecasting.

As evidenced by the above, Canada is gradually developing the Northwest Passage into a reasonably safe maritime route. So far, it has been used by Canada alone and for local traffic only, except for a few experimental crossings by the United States. However, with the present volume of oil exploitation activities on the north slope of Alaska and in the Canadian Arctic Archipelago, it is very possible that the old Northwest Passage might eventually serve as a valuable commercial route to American and European markets.

2. WHAT BODIES OF WATER ARE USED BY THE NORTHWEST PASSAGE ?

In order to fully understand the geographical perspective of the Northwest Passage it is helpful to know something of the Canadian Arctic Archipelago. This archipelago is divided

---

[144]   See *supra* note 141, at 225.

into two main parts by the Parry Channel. The northern part of the archipelago is formed by the Queen Elizabeth Islands which cover an area of 167,769 square miles, [145] disregarding the small islands; the most northern and largest island of this group is Ellesmere (nearly as large as the United Kingdom), [146] which extends to 83°07′ North. The southern part of the archipelago includes all of the islands lying south of Parry Channel and north of Canada's mainland, covering an area of 331,786 square miles; the largest islands of this group are Banks and Victoria in the west, and Baffin island (nearly as large as France) [147] in the east.

Course of route — As indicated earlier, four lanes or channels have so far been developed, crossing from the Atlantic to the Pacific and vice versa: two northern lanes and two southern lanes (Figure 1). Of the southern lanes, one crosses the narrow Bellot Strait, and both go through somewhat difficult water areas south of Prince of Wales Island; a foreign ship would have to negotiate its way through a series of narrow and shallow straits around numerous small islands. These lanes would be unsuitable either for submarines or deep-draft surface ships. Of the northern lanes (Figure 3), one passes through M'Clure Strait north of Banks Island, and constitutes a difficult passage because of the permanent presence of polar ice in that strait; the other lane avoids M'Clure Strait by proceeding through Prince of Wales Strait, on the east side of Banks Island. This fourth lane is the best route of all and the one most likely to be used for international navigation; commencing in the east at Lancaster Sound, the route runs directly west through Barrow Strait and Viscount Melville Sound, then south-west through Prince of Wales Strait between Banks and Victoria Islands, and finally west again along the north coast of the mainland, toward Bering Strait. This is the Northwest Passage which really forms the subject of the present inquiry and which will now be described in detail.

---

[145] "Areas of Principal Islands", *Canada Year Book*, at 11 (1966).
[146] The area of Ellesmere Island is 82,119 sq. m., whereas the United Kingdom is 94,215.
[147] Baffin Island is 183,810 sq. m. in area, and France is 213,100.

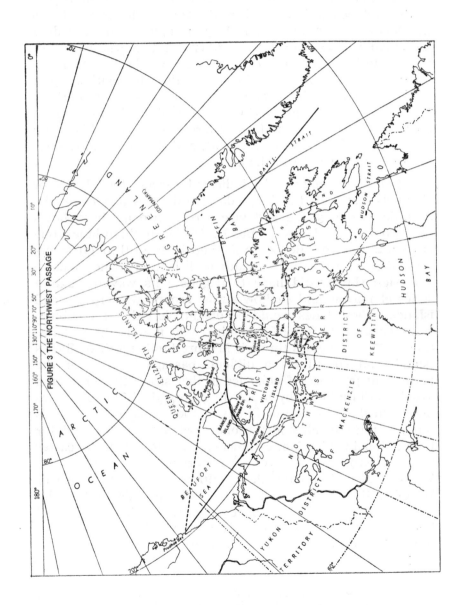

FIGURE 3 THE NORTHWEST PASSAGE

Nature of the route. — Lancaster Sound is a wide strait of at least 35 miles and remains so until it reaches Prince Leopold Island on the south side, where it narrows to about 25 miles. Barrow Strait is the only one of the four straits, forming the northernmost route of the Northwest Passage, with a small group of islands in the middle; the strait is narrowed to about 15 miles by the presence of Young Island on the south and Lowther Island on the north. The route then continues clear through Viscount Melville Sound and widens to more than 75 miles before reaching M'Clure Strait and turning southwest in Prince of Wales Strait. The northern entrance of this strait is over 11 miles wide, but it decreases to about 7 and is then divided by two small islands (Prince Royal) which leave passages of about 5 miles. The route then proceeds freely in a widening strait into Amundsen Gulf, which is over 50 miles wide.

Navigation conditions are generally good in the eastern half of the route but become less favourable when approaching M'Clure Strait; this strait usually remains choked throughout the season with ice coming from the Beaufort Sea. The navigation season is, therefore, reduced from over 3 months to about 2 months proceeding from east to west in Parry Channel. The Prince of Wales Strait is normally favourable, being protected from the ice by Banks Island. The ice conditions along the mainland coast depend essentially on the wind and ice movements in Beaufort Sea, but navigation is usually possible for at least two months; accordingly, the navigation season also lasts about two months throughout the Northwest Passage. [148]

It should be emphasized, however, that navigation conditions vary considerably from one year to another. For example, there was no ice in sight in Barrow Strait in the summer of 1960, whereas the same strait was choked with ice in 1963. [149] The type of ice will also vary from year to year; the normal ice cover is predominantly local winter ice, but

---

[148]   For a description of ice conditions in Canadian Arctic waters, see *Pilot of Arctic Canada*, Vol. I, 138-162 (2nd ed., 1970).
[149]   See Gordon W. STEAD, *supra* note 142, at 153.

significant amounts of polar ice will sometimes enter from either end of the Passage. This is particularly so at the western end, in M'Clure Strait and Byam Martin Channel north of Viscount Melville Sound. On this point the 1964 "Ice Analysis" is enlightening; it states: "Western Parry Channel remained congested throughout the summer for the first time since 1961 but in this area clearing is exceptional and congestion is normal. . . . The year 1964 provided further evidence to support the idea that Byam Martin Channel is the major source for polar ice found in Parry Channel." [150] Canadian icebreakers usually operate in the Arctic from mid-July to early October, extending the navigation season to almost four months.

It is evident from the foregoing that the waters of the Northwest Passage are navigable, and they are in fact being navigated. It is somewhat questionable, however, whether those waters are subject to the right of innocent passage in favour of foreign ships.

3. What is the Legal Status of the Northwest Passage ?

Keeping in mind the description of the Passage just given and the relevant principles of international law, let us examine Canadian legislation and government practice in order to determine what is the legal status of the waters involved.

Canada has not defined in any legislation the status of the waters of the Canadian Arctic Archipelago in general or those of the Northwest Passage in particular. Consequently, we must look at the Canadian maritime legislation of general application and at relevant government practice. This has manifested itself at the time of the two surface crossings by American ships which have taken place so far: one in 1957 and the other in 1969.

In April 1957, when it was announced that an American icebreaker and two hydrographic survey ships of the same

---

[150] DEP'T OF TRANSPORT, *Ice Summary and Analysis, Canadian Arctic,* at 72 (1964).

nationality would attempt to make an easterly crossing of the Northwest Passage, passing through Bellot Strait as had done the *St. Roch* in 1940-42, Prime Minister St. Laurent was asked "whether the Canadian government considers *these* waters to be Canadian territorial waters, and, if so, whether the United States government admits that such is the case ?" [151] The Prime Minister replied that the U.S. ships had complied with Canada's requirement that they obtain a waiver of the provisions of the Canada Shipping Act and that "the Canadian government considers that *these* are Canadian territorial waters". [152] It is difficult to tell from the context if "these waters" refer only to those of Bellot Strait or also to the waters of Lancaster and Viscount Melville sounds which had been mentioned by the Prime Minister just before the question was asked. If the exchange pertains to Bellot Strait only, the answer is perfectly accurate since this is a narrow strait 1½ miles wide. However, if it was meant to cover the waters of Lancaster and Viscount Melville sounds (and presumably Barrow Strait in between), the answer is of doubtful accuracy. Canada still claiming only the traditional three miles for territorial waters which it had inherited from Great Britain, [153] a tracing of those waters around Lowther and Young Islands in Barrow Strait would have left a strip of high seas of approximately 9 miles wide.

Barring any proof of historic title to the waters of the Northwest Passage, that was still the legal situation in 1969 when the proposed voyage of the U.S.S. *Manhattan* was announced. This announcement raised so many questions in the House of Commons that the Prime Minister felt obliged to make a "policy statement" on the whole question of "Canadian Sovereignty" in the Arctic. [154] Having regard to the

---

[151] *Can. H. C. Deb.*, Vol. III, at 3186 (6 April 1957); emphasis added.

[152] *Ibid.*, emphasis added.

[153] See The Customs Act of 1867, 31 Vict., c. 6 and The Territorial Waters Jurisdiction Act of 1878, 41-42 Vict., c. 73.

[154] See "Canadian Sovereignty statement respecting the Arctic Archipelago, the continental shelf and inland waters", *Can. H. C. Deb.*, at 8720 (15 May 1969).

importance of the statement, a substantial part of the text dealing with the Arctic waters is reproduced.

> With respect to the waters between the islands of Canada's Arctic archipelago, it is well known that in 1958 the then minister of Northern affairs stated the Canadian position as follows:
>
> The area to the north of Canada, including the islands and the waters between the islands and areas beyond, are looked upon as our own, and there is no doubt in the minds of this government, nor do I think was there in the minds of former governments of Canada, that this is national terrain.
>
> It is also known that not all countries would accept the view that the waters between the islands of the archipelago are internal waters over which Canada has full sovereignty. The contrary view is indeed that Canada's sovereignty extends only to the territorial sea around each island. [155]

The Prime Minister went on to say that the legal status of the waters was not in issue in the proposed transit, since the Canadian government had concurred in the passage, a Canadian icebreaker would assist the *Manhattan* and a Canadian government representative would be on board the *Manhattan* and act as technical adviser and coordinator of Canadian support for the operation. [156] As to the statement of the Prime Minister just quoted, it would seem to come very close to a declaration of "internal waters". However, a carefully prepared text such as this one should be strictly interpreted, and all it says specifically as to the Canadian position is that the waters in question "are looked upon as our own". The reference to "internal waters" is in relation to the possible opinion of other countries. This strict interpretation seems to be borne by a further statement made a few days later by the Prime Minister in answer to a question in the House of Commons:

> ... we are certainly not neglecting to consider the practical question of whether it will eventually be in Canada's inter-

---

155   *Ibid.*
156   *Ibid.*, at 8720-8721.

est to have these waters declared Canadian internal waters, rather than to encourage their use for commercial purposes. [157]

In other words, whatever their status, they would not be internal waters yet. As for the part of the Prime Minister's policy statement that "the contrary view is indeed that Canada's sovereignty extends only to the territorial sea around each island", it would seem to describe the well established position of the United States. And, since Canada still claimed only 3 miles of territorial sea [158] at the time of the *Manhattan* crossing, the ship would have remained on the high seas throughout if it had managed to negotiate M'Clure Strait. As it was, it had to traverse Canadian territorial waters by borrowing the narrow Prince of Wales Strait where there is an overlap of territorial waters even under the 3-mile rule. However, after the voyage of the *Manhattan*, Canada decided to extend its territorial waters from 3 to 12 miles. This decision raised three questions which will be examined presently: (1) what is the effect of a 12-mile territorial sea on the Northwest Passage ? (2) is the Northwest Passage an international strait ? (3) does the right of innocent passage still exist ?

(1) *What is the effect of a 12-mile territorial sea ?*

On April 17, 1970, the Secretary of State for External Affairs, the Honourable Mitchell Sharp, moved the second reading of *Bill C-203 to amend the Territorial Sea and Fishing Zones Act,* so as to extend the territorial waters of Canada from 3 to 12 nautical miles. The Minister explained the effect of the new 12-mile territorial sea limit with respect to the Northwest Passage in the following terms:

> Since the 12-mile territorial sea is well established in international law, the effect of this bill on the Northwest Passage is that under any sensible view of the law, Barrow

---

[157]   *Can. H. C. Deb.,* Vol. VIII, at 8826 (20 May 1969).

[158]   The traditional breadth of 3 miles was kept in the Territorial Sea and Fishing Zones Act of 1964; see 13, *Eliz. II, Statutes of Canada,* c. 22.

Strait, as well as the Prince of Wales Strait, are subject to complete Canadian sovereignty. [159]

What the Minister was saying in effect was that, the distance between Young and Lowther Islands in Barrow Strait being only 15 miles, there would now be an overlap of territorial waters at that juncture of the strait, thus forming a sort of "gateway" in the eastern section of the Northwest Passage, in addition to the existing "gateway" in Prince of Wales Strait. The term "gateway" was used by Mr. J. A. Beesley, Legal Adviser for the Department of External Affairs, when he described the legal implications, for the benefit of the Standing Committee on External Affairs and National Defence, in the following terms:

> This has implications for Barrow Strait, for example, where the 12-mile territorial sea has the effect of giving Canada sovereignty from shore to shore. To put it simply, we have undisputed control — undisputed in the legal sense — over two of the *gateways* to the Northwest Passage. [160]

With the coming into force of the new legislation, the validity of which is virtually impossible to challenge in international law considering the great number of states already subscribing to a territorial sea limit of 12 miles or more, it is no longer possible to speak of a strip of high seas throughout the Northwest Passage, when avoiding the Prince of Wales Strait and passing by M'Clure. [161]

Consequently, even if a tanker such as the *Manhattan* were to manage to negotiate the M'Clure Strait — which such a tanker is bound to do eventually — it would have to go through the territorial waters of Canada. In these circumstances, the coastal state may adopt measures to ensure that the passage of a foreign ship is an innocent one and is not prejudicial to its security. Indeed, if it is essential for the protection of its security, the coastal state may go so far as

---

[159]   See *Can. H. C. Deb.*, at 6015 (17 April 1970).
[160]   See *Standing Committee on External Affairs and National Defence, Minutes of Proceedings and Evidence,* No. 25, at 18; emphasis added (29 April 1970).
[161]   This was the present writer's opinion in 1968. See "Innocent Passage in the Arctic", 6 *C.Y.I.L.* 3, at 58 (1968).

to suspend temporarily the innocent passage of foreign ships. [162] Such suspension, however, could not be imposed by Canada if it should be found that the Northwest Passage is a strait that has been used for international navigation. [163] In other words, there could be no suspension of the right of innocent passage in the Northwest Passage, if the latter constitutes an international strait. This is the effect of the relevant provisions of the 1958 Territorial Sea Convention which, though not ratified by Canada, are generally considered as having become part of general international law.

(2) *Is the Northwest Passage an international strait ?*

The answer to the question whether or not the Northwest Passage may be regarded as an international strait depends on two sub-questions: is it used for international navigation, and does it connect one part of the high seas to another part of the high seas or the territorial sea of a foreign state. [164] The second sub-question will be examined in Part IV when studying the legal status of the Arctic Ocean but the first sub-question is examined immediately.

In its Note handed to the United States Government on April 16, 1970, Canada explained its position on this question in the following terms:

> The Canadian Government is aware of U.S.A. interest in ensuring freedom of transit through international straits, but *rejects any suggestion that the Northwest Passage is such an international strait . . . .* The Northwest Passage has not attained the status of an international strait by customary usage nor has it been defined as such by conventional international law. [165]

The same opinion was reiterated by Mr. J. A. Beesley, testifying before the Standing Committee on External Affairs

---

[162] See Article 16(3) of the *Convention on the Territorial Sea and the Contiguous Zone* (1958).

[163] *Ibid.,* Article 16(4).

[164] Those are the two conditions contained in Article 16(4), *ibid.*

[165] See "Summary of Canadian Note Handed to the United States Government on April 16, 1970", *Can. H. C. Deb.,* Appendix at 6028; emphasis added (17 April 1970).

and National Defence the following week. [166] One has to agree that the simple fact is that no convention or agreement of any kind has ever defined the Northwest Passage as an international strait. The only other way for the Northwest Passage to be classified as an international strait is to show that it is in fact used for international navigation. The use does not have to be extensive for the non-suspension provision to apply but there has to be some use. The examination which was made earlier of the known completed crossings of the Northwest Passage since Amundsen's first sailing in 1906 reveals that only seven of them have been made. The seven crossings may be recapitulated as follows:

(i) RCMP Schooner *St Roch* (1940-42): Amundsen's route east, except that it went through Bellot Strait and Prince Regent Inlet instead of Peel Sound;

(ii) RCMP Schooner *St Roch* (1944): Lancaster Sound, Barrow Strait, Viscount Melville Sound and Prince of Wales Strait;

(iii) HMCS *Labrador* (1954): same route as the *St Roch* in 1944;

(iv) USCGS *Spar, Bramble* and *Storis* (1957): same route as the *St Roch* in 1940-42;

(v) U.S.S. *Seadragon* (1960): following the Parry Channel (Lancaster Sound, Barrow Strait, Viscount Melville Sound and M'Clure Strait) and remaining underwater throughout, except for one surfacing at Resolute Bay:

(vi) U.S.S. *Manhattan* (1969): same route as the *St Roch* in 1944, for the return voyage as well;

(vii) C.S.S. *Hudson* (1970): Amundsen's route, except that it crossed Victoria Strait instead of going around King William Island through James Ross and Rae Straits.

Of those seven crossings, only numbers (iv), (v) and (vi) involved foreign ships and all of them American. Number (iv), the crossing of the three US Coast Guard icebreakers,

---

[166] See *supra* note 160, at 19.

was accomplished with the assistance of the Canadian naval icebreaker *Labrador*. Number (v) was a crossing by the USS *Seadragon*, a 2360-ton nuclear submarine, whose official orders were to "investigate the feasibility of a submarine passage through the Parry Channel". [167] It is the understanding of the writer that the passage was made with the consent and assistance of the Canadian government. Number (vi), the voyage of the *Manhattan*, was made with the full cooperation of the Canadian government and the assistance of the Canadian icebreaker *Macdonald*.

To sum up on the various crossings of the Northwest Passage, they have all been exploratory in nature and the only three made by foreign ships since Amundsen's discovery of the Passage have taken place with the acquiescence and assistance of Canada. Of those three, only the voyage of the *Manhattan* was by a commercial ship and it was strictly an experimental one. In these circumstances it is clear beyond doubt that the Northwest Passage has never been "a useful route for international maritime traffic" as the Corfu Channel had been and is not a strait "used for international navigation" envisaged by the 1958 Territorial Sea Convention. By the same token, it could not have acquired the status of an international strait by custom. This presupposes, by definition, a practice which has acquired force of law by long usage and acquiescence. This conclusion, [168] of course, does not mean that a foreign ship does not have the right of innocent passage in the Northwest Passage nor that Canada does not recognize such right.

(3) *Does the right of innocent passage still exist ?*

The general principle is that the right of innocent passage in a strait made up of territorial waters is as applicable

---

[167]   This is a quotation cited by its captain, G. P. STEELE, in *Seadragon under the Ice*, at 164 (1962).

[168]   Prof. J.-Y. MORIN, in his extensive study "Le progrès technique, la pollution et l'évolution récente du droit de la mer au Canada, particulièrement à l'égard de l'Arctique", also arrives at the conclusion that the Northwest Passage is not an international strait. See 8 *C.Y.I.L.* 158, at 219 (1970).

there as in ordinary territorial waters. To apply this principle to the Northwest Passage presumes, of course, that the waters of the Canadian Arctic Archipelago in general, and those of the Northwest Passage in particular, cannot be considered as having a more restrictive status than that of territorial waters. If Canada could establish proof of a historic title to those waters by the exercise of exclusive authority and control over a long period of time, accompanied by the acquiescence of foreign states, particularly those affected by the claim, the waters in question would then have the status of internal waters [169] and the right of innocent passage would not apply. Another method of giving those waters the status of internal waters would be to draw straight baselines around the whole of the Canadian Arctic Archipelago in order to delimit Canada's territorial waters, and this possibility will be examined in Part II. However, in this latter case, by virtue of Article 5 of the 1958 Territorial Sea Convention, the establishment of such straight baselines — even presuming their validity in international law — would not bar the right of innocent passage, if the waters in question were previously considered as part of the territorial sea or the high seas.

As for the Canadian Government's position on the right of innocent passage of foreign ships, it is quite clear: regardless of the exact status of the waters, innocent passage will be allowed. Both the Prime Minister and the Minister for External Affairs have so stated. Speaking in the debate on the speech from the throne in 1969, Prime Minister Trudeau had this to say:

> ... the government is studying its claims to the waters lying off the islands of the Arctic archipelago. To close off those waters and to deny passage to all foreign vessels in the name of Canadian sovereignty, as some commentators

---

[169] It is interesting to note that J. A. Beesley, legal adviser of Canada's External Affairs Department, is reported as mentioning the possibility of considering those waters not only as "internal" but also as "historic territorial waters" (see *supra* note 160). Prof. Morin similarly suggests that a foreign state, if excluded from the Passage and while admitting the historic character of the waters, might contend that they have been treated by Canada as territorial rather than internal waters (see *ibid.*, at 240-241).

have suggested, would be as senseless as placing barriers across the entrances to Halifax and Vancouver harbours. [170]

The Note of April 16, 1970, addressed to the United States at the time of the adoption of the Canadian Arctic Pollution Prevention legislation reiterates Canada's position on the question of passage: "The Canadian Government reiterates its determination to open up the Northwest Passage to safe navigation for the shipping of all nations subject, however, to necessary conditions required to protect the delicate ecological balance of the Canadian Arctic." [171] In other words, Canada insists that recognition of the right of innocent passage cannot preclude the coastal state from exercising pollution control in the waters being traversed. The Secretary of State for External Affairs made this very clear in the House of Commons:

> Certainly Canada cannot accept any right of innocent passage if that right is defined as precluding the right of the coastal state to control pollution in such waters. The law may be undeveloped on this question, but if that is the case, we propose to develop it. [172]

Canada's Legal Adviser for the Department of External Affairs expressed the same view in front of the Standing Committee on External Affairs and National Defence in the following terms:

> Canada has taken the position publicly that it does not consider that a passage through any body of water by a ship giving rise to a danger of pollution is an innocent passage. Such a ship is an inherently dangerous object. It represents a threat to the security of the state. [173]

Canada's position, therefore, is that the present provision that "[p]assage is innocent so long as it is not prejudicial to the peace, good order or security of the coastal state" [174] should be given a more restrictive interpretation than has

---

[170] See *Can. H. C. Deb.*, Vol. I, at 39 (1969).
[171] See *supra* note 165, at 6069.
[172] See *supra* note 159.
[173] See *supra* note 160, at 19.
[174] Article 14(4), *Convention on the Territorial Sea and the Contiguous Zone* (1958).

been traditionally the case. Surely this is a reasonable position to take in the light of the prevailing ice conditions in the Arctic and the consequent precautions which should be taken for the protection of the marine environment.

Summary of the legal situation

The main propositions which flow from the above study may be formulated as follows:

1. The Northwest Passage has never been used for international navigation and is not an international strait.

2. Canada's territorial waters now extending to 12 miles, there are two "gateways" of territorial waters in the Northwest Passage: a new one in Barrow Strait and the old one in Prince of Wales Strait.

3. There is a right of innocent passage in favour of all ships in the Northwest Passage, by virtue of general international law as it existed before, and as it has developed since, the Territorial Sea Convention of 1958.

4. Canada, as the coastal state, could suspend passage of foreign ships if it is essential to its security. This could include oil tankers not conforming to reasonable anti-pollution standards.

5. Warships may be expelled for refusing to comply with regulations made to insure the security of the coastal state.

PART II

Straight Baselines for the Canadian Arctic Archipelago

On May 15, 1969, when Prime Minister Trudeau made his "policy statement" in the House of Commons on Canadian sovereignty in the Arctic, he admitted that "not all countries would accept the view that the waters between the islands of the archipelago are internal waters over which Canada has full sovereignty". [1] He was then asked: "When will baseline co-ordinates be drawn around the rim of the Arctic archipelago to enclose it, and when will maps be issued so that it will be clear to other nations where Canadian boundaries are ?" [2] The above is typical of a number of questions asked to government ministers at the time of the *Manhattan* voyage in 1969 and of the adoption of the Arctic pollution prevention legislation in 1970. The questions seemed to presume that the government had already decided to draw straight baselines around the archipelago and indeed the pressure on the government to take steps in that direction was considerable. In December 1969, the Standing Committee of the House of Commons on Indian Affairs and Northern Development stated in its report that "the waters lying between the islands of the Arctic Archipelago have been, and are, subject to Canadian Sovereignty historically, geographically and geologically". [3] However, because of the prospect of oil tanker traffic, it considered it imperative "that the Government of Canada take whatever steps are necessary, consistent with international law, to assure recognition of Canadian Sovereignty by all vessels, surface and submarine, passing through the Arctic Archipelago". [4]

---

[1] See "Canadian Sovereignty statement respecting the Arctic Archipelago, the continental shelf and inland waters", *Can. H. C. Deb.*, at 8720 (15 May 1969).
[2] *Ibid.*, at 8729.
[3] Proceedings of *Standing Committee on Indian Affairs and Northern Development*, No. 1, at 6 (16 Dec. 1969).
[4] *Ibid.*, at 6-7.

The Standing Committee did not specify what steps "consistent with international law" the government could take to achieve this recognition. However, it seems that, basically, there can be only two ways that those waters could be given the status of internal waters: declare them historic waters or draw straight baselines around them. The second method, of course, does not necessarily exclude the first. Indeed, the best solution might be for Canada to draw straight baselines and invoke history as an element of support in justifying the baselines. Now, what exactly does the drawing of straight baselines around the archipelago imply in practical terms, with particular reference to the Northwest Passage ? It means drawing straight baselines across the entrance of Lancaster Sound (54 miles) on the east side, and Amundsen Gulf (93 miles) and M'Clure Strait (108 miles) in the west (Figure 4). Of course, not all countries subscribe to this method of tracing territorial waters around the islands of an archipelago. As the Prime Minister put it in his policy statement, "[t]he contrary view is indeed that Canada's sovereignty extends only to the territorial sea around each island". [5] It is interesting to note that "the contrary view" happens to coincide with that of the United States. However, the Prime Minister expressed his willingness to have such differences of opinion settled "with due regard for established principles of international law". [6] Indeed, international law has an important role to play in the ordinary peaceful settlement of such an issue. Although each state must decide how and when it will effect the delimitation of its territorial waters, such delimitation must be made in accordance with international law. More precisely, the act of delimitation is governed by domestic law but its international validity is governed by international law. This was fully recognized by the International Court of Justice in the *Fisheries Case,* in 1951. The relevant passage of the judgment reads as follows:

> The delimitation of sea areas has always an international aspect; it cannot be dependent merely upon the will

---

[5]   *Supra* note 1.
[6]   *Ibid.*

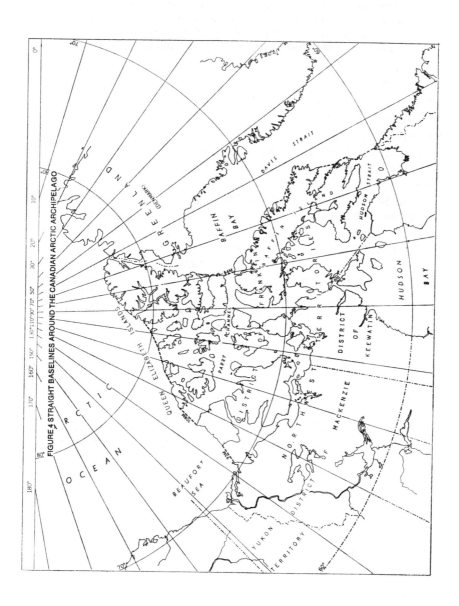

FIGURE 4 STRAIGHT BASELINES AROUND THE CANADIAN ARCTIC ARCHIPELAGO

of the coastal State as expressed in its municipal law. Although it is true that the act of delimitation is necessarily a unilateral act, because only the coastal State is competent to undertake it, the validity of the delimitation with regard to other States depends upon international law. [7]

The implementation of this basic proposition, however, is made difficult in this instance because of the uncertainty of the rules applicable to archipelagos. The International Law Commission studied the question and drafted a special article on groups of islands as far back as 1952; however, it eventually decided to delete the article completely from its draft, mainly because of disagreement on the breadth of territorial waters and the method of delimiting such waters. The Law of the Sea Conferences of 1958 and 1960 were not able to agree on a breadth of territorial waters, and left unresolved also the question of archipelagos as such. Nevertheless, the 1958 Convention on the Territorial Sea and the Contiguous Zone does have some application here, in that it contains provisions for the drawing of straight baselines where the coastline is deeply indented or where there is a fringe of islands along the coast. Although Canada has not yet ratified the Territorial Sea Convention, the applicable provisions are basically a codification of the principles formulated in the *Anglo-Norwegian Fisheries Case*. There are some slight differences between the two, however, and it might be advantageous for Canada to rely on the decision of the International Court; consequently, both the Convention and the *Fisheries Case* must be examined carefully. A brief review of the practice of states should also help in determining any possible trend in the application of straight baselines.

The present analysis will be made under the following headings: I — Distinction between coastal and oceanic archipelagos; II — Straight baselines for coastal archipelagos; III — Straight baselines for oceanic archipelagos; IV — State practice; V — Appraisal of the legal situation.

---

[7]   (1951) *I.C.J. Rep.*, at 132.

I. — DISTINCTION BETWEEN COASTAL AND OCEANIC ARCHIPELAGOS

Groups of islands are very varied in size and shape but they may be classified in two basic types, depending on whether they lie off the mainland or whether they are located in mid-ocean. In the first case, they are called coastal or off-shore archipelagos, whereas in the second instance they are referred to as outlying or oceanic archipelagos. It is important to distinguish between the two, since established rules of international law might apply only to one type of archipelago. In 1957, Mr. Jens Evensen of Norway prepared a paper, at the request of the Secretariat of the United Nations, on the question of the delimitation of the territorial waters of archipelagos, and formulated very useful definitions to which reference will be made here.

Coastal archipelagos are defined as "those situated so close to a mainland that they may reasonably be considered part and parcel thereof, forming more or less an outer coast-line from which it is natural to measure the marginal seas". [8] The typical example of such coastal archipelagos is the well known Norwegian "Skjaergaard". The number of insular formations making up the "Skjaergaard" (literally, rock rampart) is estimated by the Norwegian Government to be 120,000 and stretches all along the coast of the mainland. They are natural appendages of the coast and, in the words of the International Court, "what really constitutes the Norwegian coast line is the outer line of the 'skjaergaard'". [9] Other examples of such coastal archipelagos can be found off the coasts of Yugoslavia, Sweden, Iceland, Greenland, Finland, Alaska, the Soviet Union and Canada.

Oceanic archipelagos are those "groups of islands situated out in the ocean at such a distance from the coasts of firm land as to be considered as an independent whole rather than

---

[8] Jens EVENSEN, "Certain Legal Aspects Concerning the Delimitation of the Territorial Waters of Archipelagoes", U.N. Doc. A/CONF. 13/18 (Preparatory document No. 15), 289-302 (1957).

[9] (1951) *I.C.J. Rep.*, at 127.

forming part of the outer coastline of the mainland". [10] This mid-ocean type of archipelago has also been defined as being "a body of water studded with islands, rather than islands with waters". [11] In giving this description, Mr. Coquia had mainly in mind the Philippines but the description could be applied to most oceanic archipelagos. Such a definition brings out the importance of the water area and the close relationship between the water and the land in such a group of islands. The following may be cited as examples of oceanic archipelagos: the Faeroes (Denmark), Fiji, Philippines, Indonesia, Galapagos (Ecuador), Hawaii (United States), Spitzbergen (Norway) and Franz Josef Land (USSR).

The examples of archipelagos given so far are not too difficult to fit into the basic types of archipelagos defined, but the Canadian Arctic Archipelago under review presents considerable difficulty of categorization. Understandably perhaps then, the literature on the subject does not mention the important archipelagos lying north of the mainland of two major Arctic states, the USSR and Canada.

The Canadian Arctic Archipelago is divided into two main sections by a broad east-west waterway constituted by M'Clure Strait, Viscount Melville Sound, Barrow Strait and Lancaster Sound. To the north of this waterway is a large group of islands known as the Queen Elizabeth Islands, [12] covering an area of over 167,769 square miles [13] and, to the south, the numerous islands cover an area of 331,786 square miles excluding those of Hudson Bay and Strait. [14] The whole archipelago forms a network of channels connecting the Arctic Ocean and Beaufort Sea with Baffin Bay and Hudson Strait.

---

[10]   *Supra* note 8, at 290.

[11]   J. R. COQUIA, "The Territorial Waters of Archipelagoes", *Annuaire de l'Association des Anciens Auditeurs de l'Acamémie de Droit international de La Haye*, Vol. 30, 35, at 51 (1960).

[12]   In February 1954, the Minister of Northern Affairs, Jean Lesage, announced in the House of Commons that Her Majesty had graciously allowed her name to be given to this group of islands. See *Débats de la Chambre des Communes*, Vol. 96, No. 44, at 1914 (5 Feb. 1954).

[13]   See "Areas of Principal Islands", *Canada Year Book*, at 16 (1967).

[14]   *Ibid.*

The archipelago "contains some 16 major passages that range in width from 10 to 120 kilometers and in depth to over 700 meters". [15]

The most important passages are those running east and west and forming Lancaster Sound, Barrow Strait, Viscount Melville Sound and M'Clure Strait. This latter strait is usually choked with polar ice and, for that reason, the traditional route of the Northwest Passage avoids M'Clure Strait by using Prince of Wales Strait east of Banks Island. Geologically, there seems to be no doubt that all of these islands are located on the submerged plateau extending from the mainland and thus forming a unit with it. Geographically, the archipelago has been divided into sections, at least for description purposes. [16] Legally, however, the question arises as to whether these islands may be considered as constituting a single unit, justifying a uniform regime for the various bodies of water between them.

II. — STRAIGHT BASELINES FOR COASTAL ARCHIPELAGOS

1. The Importance of Baselines Generally

The proper fixing of a baseline is most important because it determines how far seaward a coastal state may exercise jurisdiction over a certain breadth of territorial waters beyond the baseline, as well as over the continental shelf which begins outside the territorial waters. It may also affect the extent of contiguous zones for purposes of customs, fiscal, immigration and sanitary regulations, since such zones may extend up to 12 miles "from the baseline from which the breadth of the territorial sea is measured". [17] The baseline of territorial waters has become significant also for the implementation

---

[15]   E. A. COLLIN, "The Waters of the Canadian Arctic Archipelago", *Proceedings of Arctic Basin Symposium,* at 128 (1963).
[16]   See the following: Patrick D. BAIRD, "Canadian Arctic Archipelago" in Kimble and Good (ed.) *Geography of the Northlands,* at 353 (1955); *Pilot of Arctic Canada,* Vol. I, at 1 (1965); and *Canada Year Book,* at 16 (1967).
[17]   Article 24, para. 2, of the 1958 Convention on the Territorial Sea and the Contiguous Zone.

of a new type of contiguous zone, namely the fishing zone. [18] This concept developed mainly because of the failure of the 1960 Law of the Sea Conference to agree on a uniform breadth of territorial waters. [19] Having regard to the important consequences of baselines, the 1958 Conference was careful to formulate strict rules for their applicability.

2.   THE GEOGRAPHY REQUIRED FOR STRAIGHT BASELINES

Article 3 of the Territorial Sea Convention specifies that "[e]xcept where otherwise provided in these articles, the normal baseline for measuring the breadth of the territorial sea is the low-water line along the coast as marked on large-scale charts officially recognized by the coastal State". It is obvious from this provision that baselines should follow the sinuosities of the coast, except in the special cases provided for in the Convention. There are four special cases covered: (1) across the mouth of a river flowing directly into the sea (Art. 13); (2) across the mouth of a bay when the closing or straight baseline does not exceed 24 miles, except for historic bays (Art. 7); (3) in deeply indented coasts (Art. 4); and (4) where there is a fringe of islands in the immediate vicinity of the coast (Art. 4).

The drawing of straight baselines across mouths of rivers and bays is not a new development in international law, but not so for the case of deeply indented coasts and coastal archipelagos. This latter use received official sanction for the first time in 1951, with the decision of the International Court of Justice in the *Fisheries Case*. Both the judgment of the Court and the Convention on the Territorial Sea make it quite clear that the use of straight baselines is a system of exception and is permissible only in cases where the peculiar geography of a coast warrants a departure from the normal rule of the low-water mark along the sinuosities of the coast. The Inter-

---

[18]   For an analysis of the legal nature of a contiguous zone, as envisaged by the 1958 Convention, see J.-Y. MORIN, "La zone de pêche exclusive du Canada", 1 *C.Y.I.L.*, at 82 (1964).
[19]   On the development of this concept, see A. E. GOTLIEB, "The Canadian Contribution to the Concept of a Fishing Zone in International Law", 2 *C.Y.I.L.*, at 55 (1964).

national Court described the type of coast which warranted such a departure in the following terms: "Where a coast is deeply indented and cut into, as is that of Eastern Finnmark, or where it is bordered by an archipelago such as the 'skjaergaard' along the western sector of the coast here in question, the baseline becomes independent of the low-water mark, and can only be determined by means of a geometric construction." [20] Those two types of exceptional coastlines described by the Court were retained by the Law of the Sea Conference in 1958 and included in Article 4 of the Convention. This article reads: "In localities where the coastline is deeply indented and cut into or if there is a fringe of islands along the coast in its immediate vicinity, the method of straight baselines joining appropriate points may be employed in drawing the baseline from which the breadth of the territorial sea is measured." As pointed out by Sir Gerald Fitzmaurice, the essential difference between the normal baseline and the straight baseline is that the latter is drawn *across water* whereas the former is drawn along the coast. [21]

For the Canadian Arctic islands under review, they must therefore be held to constitute "a fringe of islands along the coast in its immediate vicinity", before the straight baseline method becomes applicable.

3. Mode of Application of Straight Baselines

Once it has been decided that straight baselines are permissible because of the peculiar geography of the coast, certain criteria must be followed in the drawing of those baselines; otherwise, their international validity will be in jeopardy. The substance of those criteria were formulated by the International Court in 1951 and then incorporated in the Territorial Sea Convention. Article 4, paragraph 2 of the Convention covers the first two criteria and reads as follows:

> The drawing of such baselines must not depart to any
> appreciable extent from the general direction of the coast,

---

[20]   (1951) *I.C.J. Rep.*, at 128-129.
[21]   See FITZMAURICE, "The Law and the Procedure of the International Court of Justice, 1951-54: Points of Substantive Law", 31 *B.Y.I.L.* 371, at 388 (1954).

and the sea areas lying within the lines must be sufficiently
closely linked to the land domain to be subject to the regime
of internal waters (Art. 4, para. 2). [22]

It must be noted that these two criteria are of a geographical
nature and both of them are made mandatory in the drawing
of straight baselines.

The *first geographical criterion*, namely that straight baselines must not depart to any appreciable extent from the
general direction of the coast, lends itself to considerable
subjective judgment in its application; one must therefore
turn to the Court's decision in the *Fisheries Case* for guidance.
On the question of the degree of permissible departure from
the general direction of the coast, the Court stated that straight
baselines, "within reasonable limits, may depart from the
physical line of the coast". [23] In the *Fisheries Case* the Court
was faced with a specific problem in the application of that
criterion, when the United Kingdom challenged the delimitation of the Lopphavet Basin on the ground that it did not
respect the general direction of the coast. In such a case, the
Court said, "[o]ne cannot confine oneself to examining one
sector of the coast alone, except in a case of manifest abuse;
nor can one rely on the impression that may be gathered from
a large scale chart of this sector alone". [24] As a guide line,
therefore, when one has to determine if a straight baseline
has departed to any appreciable extent from the general direction of the coast, one ought to examine the coast as a whole
and not one sector of it only. The Court came to the conclusion that, with respect to the baseline being challenged, "the
divergence between the baseline and the land formations is
not such that it is a distortion of the general direction of the
Norwegian coast". [25] It is worthy of notice in this respect that

---

[22]   This article repeats practically verbatim the criteria formulated by the International Court. See (1951) *I.C.J. Rep.*, at 133.
[23]   This corrected passage of the Court's judgment was obtained
by the International Law Commission from the Registry of the Court
and can be found in (1956) *I.L.C. Yearbook* II, at 267. It appears also
in an *Erratum* published by the Court on October 22, 1956, and should
be inserted in the (1951) *I.C.J. Rep.*, English text, at 129.
[24]   (1951) *I.C.J. Rep.*, at 142.
[25]   *Ibid.*

one point on the Lopphavet baseline was 19 miles from the nearest point on land. [26] So, whilst the criterion of the general direction of the coast contains a great degree of subjective appreciation, it is possible to obtain guidance from the Court's judgment when applying the criterion to concrete situations.

The *second geographical criterion* formulated by the Court, and retained by the 1958 Convention, is that "the sea areas lying within the lines must be sufficiently closely linked to the land domain to be subject to the regime of internal waters" (Art. 4, para. 2). On the application of this requirement, which was taken literally from its judgment, the Court had this to say: "This idea, which is at the basis of the determination of the rules relating to bays, should be liberally applied in the case of a coast, the geographical configuration of which is as unusual as that of Norway." [27] At a previous point in its judgment the Court had specified that those sea areas did not have to be bays but it was "sufficient that they should be situated between the island formations of the 'Skjaergaard' *inter fauces terrarum*", [28] meaning literally "between the jaws of lands". The Court did apply this criterion quite liberally in the case of the Lopphavet Basin which is an extensive body of water dotted with large islands separated by inlets terminating the various fjords. It must be mentioned, however, that the Norwegian Government was also relying on a historic title to claim those waters as national or internal waters, and the Court did accept that the historic title relied upon was "clearly referable to the waters of Lopphavet". [29]

A *third geographical criterion*, made compulsory by the 1958 Convention, relates to the use of low-tide elevations in the drawing of baselines. The provision in question states that "[b]aselines shall not be drawn to and from low-tide elevations, unless lighthouses or similar installations which are permanently above sea level have been built on them" (Art. 4, para. 3). Otherwise, as pointed out by the International Law

---

26   II *Fisheries Case — I.C.J. Pleadings*, at 701 (1951).
27   (1951) *I.C.J. Rep.*, at 133.
28   *Ibid.*, at 130.
29   *Ibid.*, at 142.

Commission, "it would not be possible at high tide to sight the points of departure of the baselines". [30] Article 11 of the Convention defines a low-tide elevation as "a naturally-formed area of land which is surrounded by and above water at low-tide but submerged at high tide". These elevations are the same as what are perhaps more normally called "drying rocks" and "drying shoals", which are the terms used by the International Law Commission. The 1958 Convention permits the use of such low-tide elevations in the drawing of baselines, providing they have installations permanently above water such as lighthouses, whereas the International Law Commission had completely prohibited such use for the reason already given. [31] The International Court of Justice did not formulate any such criterion and, indeed, seems to have allowed Norway to use low-tide elevations even without lighthouses or similar installations.

Aside from the three compulsory criteria just reviewed, there is an additional and *optional criterion* : it is permissible to take into account regional economic interests in drawing certain particular baselines. Article 4, para. 4, of the 1958 Convention provides as follows:

> Where the method of straight baselines is applicable under the provisions of paragraph 1, account may be taken, in determining particular baselines, of economic interests peculiar to the region concerned, the reality and the importance of which are clearly evidenced by long usage.

It should be noted immediately that the reference to "long usage" should not be interpreted as constituting a separate legal basis for claiming what are commonly known as "historic waters". [32] In other words, the nature of this permissive criterion is strictly economic, and the only purpose of adducing

---

[30] "Commentary" to Article 5, para. 1, of the International Law Commission's draft, (1956) *I.L.C. Yearbook* II, at 268.

[31] See *ibid.,* at 267.

[32] This distinction is properly made by a number of writers. See in particular Richard YOUNG, "The Anglo-Norwegian Fisheries Case", 38 *Amer. Bar. Assoc. J.,* 243, at 244 (1952); and Jens EVENSEN "The Anglo-Norwegian Fisheries Case and its Legal Consequences", 46 *A.J.I.L.* 609, at 623-624 (1952).

evidence of "long usage" of certain water areas by the local population is to prove the reality and importance of the economic interests alleged to be peculiar to a certain region of the coast. That criterion was borrowed from the judgment of the International Court which applied the concept of economic interests to the part of the Norwegian coast already referred to, the Lopphavet Basin. In that particular instance, however, the Court seemed to be satisfied that Norway did possess a historic title to those waters; its conclusion was based partly on the fact that the Norwegian government had granted to one of its nationals exclusive fishing and whale hunting privileges as far back as the end of the seventeenth century. [33] In addition, the Court did find that fishing rights had been traditionally reserved to the local population because of an economic necessity. "Such rights", said the Court, "founded on the vital needs of the population and attested by very ancient and peaceful usage, may legitimately be taken into account in drawing a line which, moreover, appears to the Court to have been kept within the bounds of what is moderate and reasonable." [34] This idea of reasonableness, as a general and overriding consideration in determining the validity of straight baselines, was mentioned in a number of instances during the course of the Court's judgment. It follows from the foregoing that the only time it is permissible to go beyond geographical considerations in the drawing of a straight baseline is where it is necessary to protect the economic interests peculiar to the region concerned, which interests have become well established by long usage. Another problem relating to the use of straight baselines is the question of maximum length of such baselines.

4. LENGTH OF STRAIGHT BASELINES

The 1958 Convention makes no mention of any maximum length permissible for straight baselines, except for the 24-mile closing line in the case of bays. This does not indicate an omission on the part of the Conference delegates, nor does

---

[33] (1951) *I.C.J. Rep.*, at 142.
[34] *Ibid.*

it imply that the matter is of secondary importance. The question had already been considered by the International Court, but a maximum length was not retained as a criterion for determining the validity of straight baselines. In the case before it, the 47 baselines along the Norwegian coast varied greatly from a few hundred yards to some 44 miles. The United Kingdom had argued, by analogy to the old 10-mile rule for bays, that the maximum length for straight baselines should be 10 miles. Although the United Kingdom was able to point to the practice of a certain number of maritime states in support of its argument, the Court was not satisfied that the practice had materialized into a general rule of law. It rejected the argument in the following terms:

> In this connection, the practice of States does not justify the formulation of any general rule of law. The attempts that have been made to subject groups of islands or coastal archipelagoes to conditions analogous to the limitations concerning bays (distance between the islands not exceeding twice the breadth of the territorial waters, or ten or twelve sea miles), have not got beyond the stage of proposals. [35]

The Court added that a selection of straight baselines could be made in certain cases and the coastal state was in the best position to make that selection in accordance with the local conditions which it could best appraise. [36] It appears, therefore, that, having regard to the criteria previously discussed, it became unnecessary for the Court to fix a maximum length for straight baselines. In other words, if a straight baseline could be justified under the compulsory geographical criteria, and also perhaps under the optional criterion of an economic nature, such a line would be valid regardless of its length. Such was held to be the situation in the *Fisheries Case*, for the straight baseline across the Lopphavet Basin which, as pointed out by Waldock, was in effect a 62-mile line. [37]

---

[35] *Ibid.*, at 131.
[36] *Ibid.*
[37] WALDOCK, "The Anglo-Norwegian Fisheries Case", 28 *B.Y.I.L.* 114, at 146 (1951). The point made by the author is that the 44-mile line runs to an isolated submerging rock, and then runs a further 18 miles to another rock 3 and a half miles away from the next base point.

As for the water areas newly enclosed by straight baselines, it should be noticed that the 1958 Convention gave them only a qualified status of internal waters, which the International Court did not do. Article 5 of the Convention provides that "[w]here the establishment of a straight baseline . . . has the effect of enclosing as internal waters areas which previously had been considered as part of the territorial sea or of the high seas, a right of innocent passage . . . shall exist in those waters" (Art. 5, para. 2). The International Law Commission would have preserved that right only where the waters had normally been used for international traffic, [38] but the Conference delegates did not retain this suggested limitation. The right of innocent passage being preserved in that way, the question of a maximum permissible length for straight baselines becomes less important, at least theoretically. In practice, however, the coastal state might have a natural tendency to consider newly enclosed waters as being under the ordinary regime of internal waters and subject to its complete sovereignty. It would appear also that the question of the length of baselines acquires more importance in the case of outlying archipelagos, as will be seen later, since there is no mainland to which the islands can be linked.

5. SUMMARY OF THE LAW APPLICABLE TO COASTAL ARCHIPELAGOS

Except where otherwise indicated, the principles summarized hereunder exist by virtue of both the Convention on the Territorial Sea and customary law as interpreted in the *Fisheries Case*. Those principles may be formulated in seven propositions:

(1) Straight baselines may be used to join a fringe of islands along and in the immediate vicinity of a coast;

(2) Straight baselines must not depart to any unreasonable extent from the general direction of the coast;

---

[38]   See (1956) *I.L.C. Yearbook* II, at 267.

(3) The sea areas being enclosed must be sufficiently linked to the land domain to be subject to the regime of internal waters;

(4) Straight baselines must not be drawn to and from low-tide elevations, unless they have lighthouses or similar installations permanently above sea level (Convention only);

(5) The economic interests of a region may be considered in drawing particular baselines, providing such interests are clearly evidenced by long usage;

(6) There is no maximum length for straight baselines except for bays, in which case the closing line must not exceed 24 miles (Convention only, regarding bays);

(7) The waters enclosed by straight baselines are considered as internal waters, but the right of innocent passage continues to exist in water areas formerly considered as part of the territorial sea or of the high seas (Convention only, regarding innocent passage).

III. — STRAIGHT BASELINES FOR OCEANIC ARCHIPELAGOS

If the principles of law just discussed and summarized appear to be reasonably well established, it remains a question whether they are applicable to outlying archipelagos. The *Fisheries Case* was concerned only with a fringe of islands stretched along the coast of Norway, and the 1958 Convention on the Territorial Sea also confined itself to dealing with coastal archipelagos. Strictly speaking, therefore, the matter of outlying or mid-ocean archipelagos is still an open question. This does not mean, however, that no legal direction can be obtained from the *Fisheries Case* and the 1958 Convention. In the argument presented to the Court, the distinction between coastal and oceanic archipelagos was not always made and, indeed, it was argued by Norway that both types of archipelagos should be considered as units in the drawing of territorial waters. The Norwegian government stated in its counter-memorial: "L'unité juridique de l'archipel est admise même quand il s'agit d'archipels océaniques. A fortiori l'estelle quand il s'agit de complexes d'îles apparaissant comme l'accessoire de la côte." [39] The unity of archipelagos generally was not really contested by the United Kingdom; what it objected to strongly was the length of some of the baselines drawn by Norway. It must be admitted that this question seems to acquire more importance in outlying archipelagos, since there is no mainland to which the islands can be linked. It is no longer possible to speak of the islands constituting a mere extension of or appendage to the mainland. This does not mean, however, that some of the principles formulated by the Court are not of general application. Surely the fundamental requirement that there be a close relationship between the sea areas and the land formations is as applicable to outlying archipelagos as to coastal ones. Consequently, the islands of an outlying archipelago ought to be sufficiently close together to constitute a single unit, so as to permit a single belt of territorial waters. On this question of the principles applicable to outlying archipelagos, guidance may also be gained from the excellent paper already referred to and prepared by the Norwegian lawyer, Jens Evensen, on the eve of the 1958 Law of the Sea Conference. After a thorough study of state practice concerning outlying archipelagos he concluded that no uniform practice existed, and that one ought to look to the *Fisheries Case* for applicable principles. "The criteria here laid down by the Court", he said, "are equally applicable to outlying archipelagos and coastal archipelagos and the statements thus made are couched in general terms expressing basic principles of international law in this field." [40] It is the view of this writer that Mr. Evensen's statement is as applicable to-day as it was in 1957. No uniform state practice seems to have developed and the 1958 Conference left the question of outlying archipelagos unresolved. The only provision in the 1958 Convention which relates specifically to islands is article 10; it confines itself to defining an island and stating that "the territorial sea of an island is measured in accordance with the other provisions

---

[39] I *Fisheries Case — I.C.J. Pleadings,* at 495 (1951).
[40] Jens EVENSEN, *supra* note 5, at 300.

of these articles". The Conference did not retain the draft provision of the International Law Commission which stated that "every island has its own territorial sea". [41] In these circumstances, it is difficult to understand the interpretation given to Article 10 by A. L. Shalowitz, who concludes that, since the Conference took no decision on the question of groups of islands, "it must be assumed that each island of such a group will be governed by the rule laid down in paragraph 2, that is each will have its own territorial sea measured in the ordinary way according to the provisions of the Convention adopted, and are not to be enclosed by a series of straight baselines". [42] This must be considered as a somewhat spurious interpretation, and a more accurate view is surely that the 1958 Convention simply left the question unresolved. [43] This does not mean, however, that no assistance can be obtained from the criteria incorporated in the provisions of the Convention relating to coastal archipelagos. The reasoning by analogy with the *Fisheries Case* is now applicable with respect to the 1958 Convention. This is essentially the view of professor Sorensen who concludes that "the criteria laid down by art. 4 of the Geneva Convention do offer some guidance in the matter". [44]

Having regard to the absence of both customary and conventional rules, as well as uniform state practice, it is suggested that the International Court would in all likelihood look to its own pronouncements for direction if it had to adjudicate on the question of outlying archipelagos. Proceeding by analogy with the rules relating to coastal archipelagos, it is submitted that the following propositions are warranted:

1. Straight baselines may be used to join a group of islands lying in mid-ocean;

[41] (1956) *I.L.C. Yearbook* II, at 270.
[42] A. L. SHALOWITZ, *Shore and Sea Boundaries*, Vol. I, at 227 (1962).
[43] In support of this view, see Max SORENSEN, "The Territorial Sea of Archipelagos", 6 *Netherlands Int'l L. Rev.*, at 315 (1959).
[44] *Ibid.*, at 330.

2. Straight baselines must not depart to any unreasonable extent from the general direction of the perimeter of the archipelago;

3. The sea areas being enclosed must be sufficiently linked to the land domain of the archipelago to be subject to the regime of internal waters;

4. Straight baselines must not be drawn to and from low-tide elevations of the archipelago, unless they have light-houses or similar installations permanently above sea level;

5. The economic interests of a region of the archipelago may be considered in drawing particular baselines, providing such interests are clearly evidenced by long usage;

6. There is no maximum length for straight baselines except for bays, the closing line of which must not exceed 24 miles;

7. The waters enclosed by straight baselines are considered as internal waters, but the right of innocent passage continues to exist in water areas formerly considered as part of the territorial sea or of the high seas.

IV. — STATE PRACTICE RELATING TO ARCHIPELAGOS

In his excellent study of state practice prepared for the U.N. Secretariat prior to the 1958 Law of the Sea Conference, Jens Evensen came to the conclusion that "no hard and fast rules exist as to the delimitation of the territorial waters of archipelagos". [45] His conclusion applied to both types of archipelagos. The 1958 Territorial Sea Convention having dealt with coastal archipelagos only, Max Sorensen addressed himself to the problem of oceanic archipelagos and also found that the practice of states was far from being uniform. Since 1958, the use of straight baselines for both types of archipelagos has increased considerably and the average length of those baselines has also increased. In January 1971, Com-

---

[45] *Supra* note 8, at 301.

mander P. B. Beazley, of the British Admiralty Hydrographic Department, prepared the following:

"TABLE OF MAXIMUM STRAIGHT BASELINES" [46]

This table covers only those countries whose claims are known.

Country	Length (in miles)
1 — Albania	26
2 — Burma	222
3 — Canada	50
4 — Denmark	17
5 — Ecuador	147
6 — Faeroes	62
7 — Finland	8
8 — France	30
9 — Greenland	36
10 — Iceland	73
11 — Indonesia	123
12 — Ireland	25
13 — Malagasy	89
14 — Mauritania	79
15 — Mexico	34
16 — Mozambique	60
17 — Norway	45
18 — Philippines	140
19 — Portuguese Guinea	30
20 — Sweden	30
21 — Tanzania	44
22 — Turkey	22
23 — United Kingdom	40
24 — Yugoslavia	23
	1455

The length shown against each country in the above table represents the longest single baseline claimed. The total for the 24 countries being 1455, the average longest length is 61 miles. To be added shortly to this list will be Fiji, which proposes to "draw a base line in the form of a polygon around the outer extremity of low-water-mark of all of the islands

---

[46] P. B. BEAZLEY, "Territorial Sea Baselines", *International Hydrographic Rev.*, Vol. XLVIII, 143, at 145 (1971).

or drying reefs of the Fiji Group with the exception of the remoter islands, namely the Rotuma Group; the Ono-i-lau Group; the islands of Vatoa; and Conway Reef". [47] It would seem that its baselines might reach in the vicinity of 90 miles.

Since the drawing of straight baselines around the Arctic archipelago by Canada would affect some of the other Arctic states and since all of them could probably qualify to make use of them, their individual state practice should be examined briefly.

The *United States* does not accept the use of straight baselines to delimit territorial waters except in very few areas, "such as along the highly irregular and fragmented coasts of Yugoslavia, Norway, and Southern Chile". [48] It rejects the "archipelago concept" which would "box in" a group of islands by drawing a perimeter formed of straight baselines touching the outermost islands of the group and regards this type of straight baseline as "no more justified than a corresponding line along the mainland". [49] The attitude of the United States has been quite consistent in its restrictive delimitation of territorial waters around groups of islands. In 1947, the legal advice given by the State Department with respect to the territorial waters of the Pacific islands, formerly under Japanese mandate and transferred under the trusteeship of the United States after World War II, was that each island had its own belt of territorial waters. [50] In 1951, the United States sent a Note to Ecuador protesting against its "assertion of a claim to a single belt of territorial waters around the entire Colon Archipelago", as being contrary to international law. [51] In De-

---

[47] *Statement delivered by D. McLoughlin, Solicitor-General of Fiji* at the U.N. Seabed Committee meeting in Geneva, at 26 of typewritten text (July 1971).

[48] U.S. DEPT. OF STATE, "Sovereignty of the Sea", *Geographic Bull.*, No. 3, at 12 (April 1965).

[49] *Ibid.*, at 13.

[50] See Leonard C. MEEKER, "Territorial Waters of Former Japanese Mandated Islands", memorandum, M.S. Dept. of State (2 January 1947), file 894.0145/1-247, cited in 4 Whiteman, *Digest of Int'l L.*, at 281 (1965).

[51] See "Note, dated 7th June 1951 . . .", reproduced in 4 *Anglo-Norwegian Fisheries Case — I.C.J. Pleadings* 603, at 604 (1951).

cember 1957, the American Embassy in Djakarta delivered a Note of protest to the Indonesian government a few days after the latter had issued an announcement that all waters between the islands formed an integral part of the inland waters of Indonesia. [52] The United States sent a telegram of similar protest to the Philippines in January 1958, and repeated its protest at the 1958 Conference on the Law of the Sea. [53] Commenting on the 1960 Conference at which both Indonesia and the Philippines had reasserted their position, the Chairman of the United States delegation wrote that, on March 31 of that year, the nuclear-powered submarine "Triton passed submerged through waters within the Indonesian and Philippine archipelagos, which are claimed unilaterally by each of those nations as 'internal waters' although they include vast high seas areas". [54] He added that, since the right of innocent passage does not exist in such waters, it was for that reason that "we do not recognize the validity of this extensive and unilateral archipelago theory". [55] This refusal to accept the archipelago concept in drawing territorial waters is also followed by the United States with respect to Hawaii. Secretary of State Rusk wrote, in 1964, in answer to an inquiry by Attorney General Kennedy, that it was "the Department's position that each of the islands of the Hawaiian archipelago had its own territorial sea, three miles in breadth measured from low water mark on the coast of the island". [56] The United States could use straight baselines off the coast of Alaska but it has not done so and presumably still holds to its traditional policy.

The *Soviet Union* does not appear to have made use of straight baselines thus far, although it does have deeply indented areas and important groups of islands. Until 1971, its 1960 "Statute on the Protection of the State Border"

---

[52]   See 4 WHITEMAN, *Digest of Int'l L.*, at 284 (1965).
[53]   *Ibid.*, at 283-284.
[54]   Arthur H. DEAN, "The Second Geneva Conference on the Law of the Sea: The Fight for Freedom of the Seas", 54 *A.J.I.L.* 751, at 753 (1960).
[55]   *Ibid.*
[56]   Reproduced in 4 WHITEMAN, *Digest of Int'l L.*, at 281 (1965).

specified that the breadth of 12 miles of coastal sea waters was to be "computed from the line of lowest ebb-tide both on the mainland and also around islands, or from the line of the farthest extremity of internal sea waters of the USSR". [57] On June 10, 1971, the Soviet Union amended the 1960 Statute to read as follows:

> Coastal sea waters, twelve nautical miles in breadth, computed from the line of lowest ebb-tide both on the mainland and also around islands, or from the seaward line of internal sea waters of the USSR, *and in those localities where the coastline is deeply indented and cut into or if there is a fringe of islands along the coast in its immediate vicinity — from straight base lines joining appropriate points,* shall constitute the territorial waters of the USSR. The *geographic coordinates of the points through which the straight base lines pass for the purpose of computing the territorial waters of the USSR shall be confirmed in the procedure established by the Council of Ministers of the USSR.* In individual instances provided for by agreements of the USSR with other states, the breadth of territorial waters may be otherwise. [58]

To what extent the USSR intends to make use of straight baselines in future remains a question. It will be noticed that the amendment does not go any further than the provision of the Territorial Sea Convention in authorizing baselines, these being limited to deeply indented coasts and coastal archipelagos. This does not necessarily indicate, however, that the USSR is opposed to the system of straight baselines for oceanic archipelagos. Pravda reported on February 13, 1958, that the USSR formally recognized the Indonesian declaration of the previous December embodying the archipelago concept. [59]

Norway has led the way in the use of straight baselines by the enactment of its famous 1935 Royal Decree, approved by the International Court in 1951. It has not used straight

---

[57]   *Soviet Statutes and Decisions,* Vol. III, No. 4, at 10 (Summer 1967).

[58]   Wm. E. BUTLER, The Legal Regime of Russian Territorial Waters", 62 *A.J.I.L.* 51, at 63 (1968).

[59]   Wm. E. BUTLER, *The Soviet Union and the Law of the Sea,* at 48-49 (1971).

baselines around Svalbard, however, because of a provision in the 1920 Svalbard Treaty. Article 2 of the Treaty provides for equal fishing and hunting rights among the Parties within the islands specified and their territorial waters. [60]

Denmark has made a limited use of straight baselines so far in the delimitation of Greenland territorial waters, and the longest length is 36 miles. [61] It is currently studying the drawing of straight baselines for the delimitation of the territorial sea between Greeland and the Canadian Arctic islands, but the length of the baselines contemplated is not known to the writer. It would seem, however, that some parts of that coast might lend themselves to longer baselines.

Canada has provided for the use of straight baselines in its Territorial Sea and Fishing Zones Act of 1964, which enables the Executive to issue lists of geographical coordinates from which baselines may be determined. [62] So far Canada has promulgated two series of straight baselines: one for the east coast (except for an area facing the French islands of St. Pierre and Miquelon) in 1967 and one for the west coast in 1969. [63] The longest baseline used is 50 miles, across Notre Dame Bay, which has always been considered a historic bay. The question now arises as to whether it should use straight baselines in the Arctic.

V. — APPRAISAL OF THE LEGAL SITUATION FOR THE CANADIAN ARCTIC ARCHIPELAGO

1. A BRIEF DOCTRINAL REVIEW

The possibility of considering the waters of the Canadian Archipelago as internal waters and enclosing them with straight baselines has been a subject of discussion by Canadian and American scholars for a considerable time now. In 1958, Professor Maxwell Cohen, of McGill University, stated

---

60   This reason was confirmed to the writer in a reply from the Royal Norwegian Embassy in Ottawa on June 10, 1969.
61   See Table in BEAZLEY, *supra* note 46.
62   Sec. 5, s-s 1, 13 Eliz. II, *Statutes of Canada*, c. 22 (1964).
63   See *Orders in Council*, P.C. 1967, at 2025 of 26 October 1967, and P.C. 1969, at 1109 of 26 May 1969.

that the waters of the archipelago ought to be considered as "Canadian waters". Writing after the trans-Arctic cruise of the *Nautilus,* he expressed the following opinion:

> With respect to the various straits and bodies of water between the many islands of the Archipelago where American naval vessels traverse to-day, these must be treated as "Canadian waters" in the same sense that the International Court of Justice viewed the waters of the great Norwegian Archipelago as Norwegian "inland waters". . . [64]

He added, however, that innocent passage could be permitted: "Hence while 'innocent passage' may be permitted, the waters must be treated if not as wholly 'inland waters', certainly at the least as an extension of the idea of 'territorial waters', in some modified form." [65]

Ivan Head of the University of Alberta, writing in 1962 when he was in the Canadian Department of External Affairs, was less doubtful about the legal nature of those waters and the Canadian policy relating thereto. In reference to the archipelago, he wrote in the following terms:

> It does not lie astride any shipping routes. Canada regards the water between the islands as Canadian territorial waters, and this claim has been recognized by the United States. Prime Minister St. Laurent reported to the House of Commons in 1957 that United States vessels servicing D.F.W. line stations are required to apply to Canada for waivers of the provisions of the Canada Shipping Act before proceeding. [66]

It should be mentioned here that the DEW line is located below the Canadian archipelago and that its supply route is the southern branch of the Northwest Passage, the one first followed by Larsen in 1940-42 and borrowed by the three U.S. cutters in 1957. This is not the route, however, which a foreign ship would normally follow. In any case, if these are only "territorial" waters, the right of innocent passage would still exist. But Professor Head went on to suggest that those

---

[64] Maxwell COHEN, "Polar Ice and Arctic Sovereignty", 73 *Saturday Night,* No. 18, at 35 (30 August 1958).

[65] *Ibid.,* at 36.

[66] Ivan L. HEAD, "Canadian Claims to Territorial Sovereignty in the Arctic Regions", 9 *McGill L.J.* 201, at 218, (1962-1963).

waters might have the status of internal waters, which would normally bar the right of innocent passage. The relevant passage reads:

> The unitary appearance of the formation and, to a lesser extent, its location suggest support to a claim to these waters as internal waters. Surrounded on all sides by Canadian territory, they possess the character of Canadian waters. It is highly unlikely that uninterrupted surface passage from the Labrador Sea to either the Arctic Ocean or the Beaufort Sea, or vice versa, will ever be a reality. Future demands for the right of innocent passage through the archipelago are speculative to a degree. [67]

Of course, the Arctic oil discoveries could not be foreseen at the time of Mr. Head's writing in 1963 and the enclosure of the archipelago, which he considered permissible under the Territorial Sea Convention and the *Norwegian Fisheries* case, [68] could not affect the right of innocent passage at that time.

However, even after the oil discoveries at Prudhoe Bay established the probability of the Northwest Passage being used, legal commentators have regarded as possible the enclosure of the archipelago by straight baselines. Writing in 1970, Professor Morin, of the University of Montreal, considered that the cohesive character of the Canadian archipelago would permit its enclosure sooner or later, by a series of straight baselines. [69] He admitted however that, unless Canada could prove a historic title to those waters as being "internal", the right of innocent passage would probably apply under the Territorial Sea Convention. [70] Furthermore, the lengths of some of the baselines required would be longer than those presently found in the practice of states and Professor Morin suggested that it would be preferable for Canada to wait until its historic title had been consolidated. [71]

---

[67] *Ibid.*
[68] *Ibid.*, at 219.
[69] J.-Y. MORIN, "Le progrès technique, la pollution et l'évolution récente du droit de la mer au Canada, particulièrement à l'égard de l'Arctique", 8 *C.Y.I.L.* 158, at 240.
[70] *Ibid.*
[71] *Ibid.*, at 242.

Returning to the status of Canadian Arctic waters at the time of the adoption of the 1970 Arctic Waters Pollution Prevention Act, Professor Cohen expressed the view that it would have been risky for the Canadian Government to opt for the archipelago theory. He wrote in the following terms:

> It is clear that Canada might have opted for the high-risk total archipelago theory of jurisdiction as outlined in the *Norwegian Fisheries* case. This might have solved the problem of internal waters of the archipelago but it is not certain that Canada could have closed the Northwest Passage by the simple assertion of it as "internal waters". And because of the size of the archipelago and its division into a main northern group, north of the Passage, and a southern group, there might have been great difficulty in getting international acceptance of a pure archipelago claim as the basis of jurisdiction. [72]

In other words, Professor Cohen doubts that it would be acceptable on the international plane for Canada to draw straight baselines around its Arctic archipelago and thus close off the Northwest Passage.

Professor Reinhard, of the Dickson School of Law, expressed a somewhat different opinion. Although he felt that it would not be possible for Canada to encircle the archipelago with straight baselines under the criteria laid down in the *Fisheries Case* because it could not meet the test of economic interest evidenced by long usage, [73] he thought that the geographic factors were sufficiently met and concluded that straight baselines would be justified under the Territorial Sea Convention. His conclusion is:

> It is apparent that the Geneva Convention has attached more importance to the geographic configuration of the coastal state in question than to evidence of long economic usage. Therefore, since Canada qualifies on the other factors, as seen above, straight baselines may be drawn around the North American Archipelago and the waters of

---

[72] Maxwell COHEN, "The Arctic and the National Interest", 26 *Int'l J.* 52, at 80 (1970-71).

[73] Walter G. REINHARD, "International Law: Implications of the Opening of the Northwest Passage", 74 *Dickinson L. Rev.* 678, at 688-9 (1970).

the Northwest Passage may be called the internal waters
of Canada. It follows from the discussion of the applicability of the Convention that Canada would be able to
suspend innocent passage in these waters. If straight baselines are applied, the *Corfu Channel Case* is inapplicable
and innocent passage will also be suspended in the straits
which are part of the Northwest Passage. [74]

A conclusion similar to the above is reached by Professor
Dellapenna, of Willamette University. In a well-documented
article, in which he examines a number of ways for Canada
to protect its legitimate interests in Arctic waters, he concludes
that the archipelagic approach would be more acceptable
internationally than the present 100-mile pollution prevention
zone. His conclusion is as follows:

> The strait baselines (archipelagic) approach comes
> closest to achieving what contiguous zones achieve. It
> broadly asserts jurisdiction over the conventional surface
> navigation routes without sweeping far out into the Arctic
> Ocean. It particularly protects the most vulnerable area of
> the Canadian Arctic — the complex of islands and shallow,
> narrow seas off its north coast . . . . It would not spawn a
> new doctrinal basis for extreme claims in the sea. A system
> of straight baseline running along the outer edges of the
> Canadian mainland and islands as limited by the Conven-
> tion on the Territorial Sea would be a more reasonable, but
> still effective, solution to the Canadian anxiety over the
> Arctic environment and control of their national sea
> route. [75]

The present writer expressed the opinion in 1969, at a time
when Canada still claimed only 3 miles as territorial sea, that
two series of straight baselines could be drawn: one enclosing the islands south of Parry Channel with the mainland,
and the other around the Queen Elisabeth Islands north of
the channel. [76] This proposal preserved the existing strip of
high seas throughout Parry Channel. With Canada's extension of territorial waters from 3 to 12 miles in 1970, the strip

---

[74]   *Ibid.*, at 690.
[75]   Joseph W. DELLAPENNA, "Canadian Claims in Arctic Waters",
7 *Land and Water L. Rev.* 383, at 420 (1972).
[76]   Donat PHARAND, "The Waters of the Canadian Arctic Islands",
3 *Ottawa L. Rev.* 414, at 431-432 (1969).

of high seas has disappeared and no ship can now use the Northwest Passage without crossing Canada's territorial waters. In the light of this new and important consideration, it is proposed to re-examine the legal possibility for Canada to draw a single series of baselines around its Arctic archipelago.

2. A RE-EXAMINATION OF STRAIGHT BASELINES FOR THE CANADIAN ARCTIC ARCHIPELAGO

On the basis of the analysis made earlier on the use of straight baselines, three major questions must be answered: (1) Is the straight baseline system applicable ? (2) Would the baselines meet the compulsory criteria ? (3) Would the length of the baselines be acceptable ?

(1) *Is the straight baseline system applicable ?*

Under the Territorial Sea Convention, the applicability of straight baselines to the Canadian Arctic Archipelago would depend on whether that archipelago constitutes "a fringe of islands along the (northern) coast" of Canada and located "in its immediate vicinity" (Art. 4(4)). This provision is descriptive of the islands along the Norwegian coast as stated in the *Fisheries Case.* The test of the Convention would seem to be met by the southern section of the Canadian archipelago, in spite of the distance of Banks Island from the coast in the west and the presence of Hudson Bay (which is generally accepted as a historic bay) in the east, but the Queen Elisabeth group north of Parry Channel does pose a problem. It would be stretching the meaning of words unduly to say that it constitutes part of a fringe of islands along the northern coast of Canada, particularly if it is agreed that the latter runs in an east-west direction. [77] The fact remains, however, that the group in question does constitute a fairly cohesive unit, whose territorial waters now overlap those of the southern group. It is undoubtedly a projection of the southern group and the two are linked together by the same continental

---

[77]   For a contrary view, see REINHARD *supra* note 73, at 414.

shelf. Admittedly, these considerations do not change the triangular shape of the whole archipelago and the fact that the top group can hardly be considered simply as a fringe along Canada's northern coast. It is a quasi-oceanic unit, separated from the southern section by a long stretch of water about 50 miles wide, but linked with it by a group of smaller islands in Barrow Strait. It would seem that the straight base-line system is applicable to the Queen Elisabeth Islands in somewhat the same way as to ordinary oceanic archipelagos. However, because of the small islands in Barrow Strait linking the northern group to the southern one and causing an over-lap of territorial waters, the two may be considered as consti-tuting a single unit for the purpose of applying the straight baseline system. Of course, the applicability of straight base-lines could not rest solely on the rules relating to coastal archipelagos incorporated in the Territorial Sea Convention, but would depend in part on comparable rules applicable to oceanic archipelagos which may be formulated by analogy with those accepted for coastal archipelagos. Since Canada is not a Party to the Territorial Sea Convention, it is in a better position to borrow the practice of states and extend somewhat the application of the straight baseline system approved in the *Fisheries Case*. Once this question of applica-bility is resolved, the actual application of the system arises.

(2) *Would the baselines meet the compulsory criteria ?*

As seen earlier, both the Territorial Sea Convention and the *Fisheries Case* provide for the application of two geograph-ical criteria [78] of a compulsory character and one economic criterion of an optional nature. The latter is embodied in Article 4(4) of the Convention which stipulates that a state *may* take into account, in determining particular baselines, the economic interests peculiar to the region concerned when these are clearly evidenced by long usage. This optional crite-

---

[78]   There is a third criterion provided for in the Territorial Sea Convention, namely the requirement of lighthouses or similar installa-tions when low-tide elevations are used to draw baselines, but it is not of general application.

rion [79] is of uncertain application here and, therefore, the discussion will be limited to the two compulsory criteria of universal application: the general direction of the coast and the close link between land and sea areas.

The "general direction" criterion requires that straight baselines "must not depart to any appreciable extent from the general direction of the coast" (Art. 4(2)). This requirement is based on the judgment in the Fisheries Case which stated that, although straight baselines could depart, within reasonable limits, from the physical line of the coast, the divergence should not amount to a distortion of the general direction. If what really constitutes the Canadian coast line is the outer line of the archipelago [80] — which is a reasonable description when considering the whole archipelago as a unit — the baselines would definitely follow the general direction of the outer line of the archipelago.

The "close link" criterion requires that "the sea areas lying within the lines must be sufficiently closely linked to the land domain to be subject to the regime of internal waters" (Art. 4(2)). As stated in the Fisheries Case, "[t]he real question raised in the choice of base-lines is in effect whether certain sea areas lying within these lines are sufficiently closely linked to the land domain to be subject to the regime of internal waters". [81] Although the Court added that "[t]his idea ... should be liberally applied in the case of a coast, the geographical configuration of which is as unusual as that of Norway",[82] it is difficult to visualize how the sea areas of Parry Channel, averaging about 50 miles in width, can meet this requirement and be given the unqualified status of internal waters as in the Fisheries Case. It must be remembered, however, that those sea areas would not have that status under the Terri-

---

[79]   Both Reinhard (see supra note 73, at 688-9) and Dellapenna (see supra note 75, at 415-6) consider this criterion as compulsory under the Fisheries Case, but this would not appear to be supported by the judgment of the Court.

[80]   This is a paraphrase of the Court's judgment where it stated that "what really constitutes the Norwegian coast line is the outer line of the skjaergaard". See (1951) I.C.J. Rep., at 127.

[81]   (1951) I.C.J. Rep., at 133.

[82]   Ibid.

torial Sea Convention and would be subject to the right of innocent passage. In other words, Canada's control of access to those waters would be a qualified one and, for purposes of shipping through the Northwest Passage, the status of those waters would be more akin to that of territorial waters. Although Canada is not a Party to the Territorial Sea Convention and could conceivably argue that it would not be bound to recognize the innocent passage of foreign ships in those waters as a right, it has undertaken to do so.[83] Its major concern relates to the passage of oil tankers which it insists on regulating in order to protect the delicate Arctic ecology. In these circumstances, the basic reason for the "close rink" requirement — the resulting status of internal waters — is very considerably lessened and the application of the requirement should be correspondingly liberalized.

(3) *Would the length of the baselines be acceptable ?*

Three important baselines are involved here, since they affect the Northwest Passage. Two are located at the western end of the Archipelago, across Amundsen Gulf and M'Clure Strait, and the other, at the eastern end, across Lancaster Sound. Those straight baselines would be approximately 93, 108 and 54 miles long respectively. Those distances represent the actual breadth of the entrances in question. As seen earlier, no maximum length was laid down in the *Fisheries Case* or in the Territorial Sea Convention, and the practice of states since 1958 has shown a tendency toward increasingly long baselines. If a baseline otherwise conforms with the geographical criteria already discussed, its legality can hardly be questioned simply because of its length. As for the three baselines being examined, they would appear to meet the two basic geographical requirements and it is difficult to see how their length could be much different from that of the actual breadth of the entrances to those bodies of water.

---

[83] See in particular a strong statement by Prime Minister TRU-DEAU, in *Can. H. of C. Deb.*, Vol. I, at 39 (1969) and a written assurance in the Canadian Note sent to the United States at the time of the adoption of the Arctic Pollution Prevention Bill, reproduced in *Can. H. of C. Deb.*, Appendix at 6028 (17 April 1970).

Summary of the legal appraisal

The major propositions which may be formulated as a result of this analysis are the following:

1. Although divided into two main groups of islands on either side of Parry Channel, the Canadian Arctic Archipelago may be legally considered as forming a single unit; this is due mainly to

   a) the presence of several small islands in Barrow Strait creating a link between the two groups, and

   b) the overlap of territorial waters in Barrow Strait.

2. The straight baseline system is applicable to the Canadian Arctic Archipelago on the basis of

   a) the rules for coastal archipelagos found in the *Fisheries Case* and the Territorial Sea Convention, and

   b) rules for oceanic archipelagos formulated by analogy with those for coastal archipelagos.

3. The straight baselines envisaged meet the two compulsory criteria of universal application formulated in the *Fisheries Case* and incorporated in the Territorial Sea Convention:

   a) the "general direction" criterion is met by considering the outer line of the Canadian Arctic Archipelago as forming the northern coast line of Canada, relying on the *Fisheries Case;*

   b) the "close link" requirement should be considered as satisfied in spite of the large sea areas enclosed, on condition that the right of innocent passage is preserved in the Northwest Passage.

4. The length of the major baselines involved (across Amundsen Gulf, M'Clure Strait and Lancaster Sound) should be acceptable, since

a) no maximum length is provided for in the *Fisheries Case* or the Territorial Sea Convention;

b) the baselines otherwise comply with the compulsory geographical criteria, and

c) the baselines would represent the actual breadth of the entrances to the bodies of water in question.

PART III

Historic Waters in the Arctic

In the previous Parts the question of considering the waters of the Northeast and Northwest Passages as "historic waters" has been left open. This possibility has been advanced by certain writers in respect of both Passages and the legislation of the countries concerned lends itself to this possibility. The present Part will be devoted to a study of this question in the light of the relevant principles of international law. The question will be dealt with under the following headings: I — The Law of Historic Waters; II — Historic Waters in the Northeast Passage and III — Historic Waters in the Northwest Passage.

I. — THE LAW OF HISTORIC WATERS

1. THE CONCEPT OF HISTORIC WATERS

(1) *Nature*

In the *Fisheries Case* of 1951, the International Court of Justice had to deal with arguments based partly on the concept of historic waters. The Court gave the following definition: "By 'historic waters' are usually meant waters which are treated as internal waters but which would not have that character were it not for the existence of an historic title." [1] Such a historic title has been traditionally claimed in respect of certain bays and, indeed, the concept of historic waters is but an enlargement of the doctrine of historic bays which developed much earlier. [2] The doctrine of historic bays emerged gradually during the 19th century as the freedom of the high seas principle became established as a fundamental rule of International Maritime Law. The doctrine served as a protective measure for certain states having large bays closely

---

[1] (1951) *I.C.J. Rep.*, at 130.
[2] See *Memorandum prepared by the U.N. Secretariat on Historic Bays*, U.N. Doc. A/CONF. 13/1 (1957).

linked with the land and traditionally considered by those
states as part of national territory; they were often expressed
to be of vital importance from the economic and national
security standpoints. Consequently, the waters of those bays
were considered as internal or inland waters, and the territorial
sea was measured from a line drawn across the mouth of
such bays, in the same way as for smaller bays the entrance
of which did not exceed twice the breadth of territorial waters.
As the principles of law developed relating to the delimitation
of maritime areas, the idea of claiming bays on the basis of
a historic title was extended to other water areas adjacent to
the coast. The concept of historic waters, therefore, is a
regime of exception to the general rules of law relating to the
delimitation of the maritime domain of a state. Writers
generally agree that the concept of historic waters does constitute an exceptional regime.[3] The same view was presented to
the International Court by the United Kingdom in the *Fisheries
Case*.[4]

This exceptional nature of historic waters was contested
by Norway, at least in so far as its particular claim was concerned. It summarized its position as follows: "En résumé,
le titre historique, tel que le Gouvernement norvégien le con-
çoit et l'invoque dans le présent litige, n'a aucunement pour
rôle de légitimer une situation par ailleurs illégale, mais bien
de confirmer la validité de cette situation."[5] Professor Bourquin, who was one of the pleaders on behalf of Norway, has
expressed the similar view that, since there was no definite
rule of international customary law limiting the width of territorial bays to 10 miles, the concept of historic bays could no
longer be considered as an exception.[6] This view was a
defensible one concerning the nature of historic bays, as well

---

    3 See for instance the following: III GIDEL, *Le Droit Interna-
tional Public de la Mer*, at 651 (1934); FITZMAURICE, "The Law and
Procedure of the International Court of Justice 1951-1954; General Prin-
ciples and Sources of Law", 30 *B.Y.I.L.*, at 27-28 (1953); and Y. Z.
BLUM, *Historic Titles in International Law*, at 232-235 (1965).
    4 II *Fisheries Case* — *I.C.J. Pleadings*, at 302 (1951).
    5 III *Fisheries Case* — *I.C.J. Pleadings*, at 461 (1951).
    6 M. BOURQUIN, "Les baies historiques", in *Mélanges Georges
Sauser-Hall*, at 42-43 (1952).

as historic waters in general, before the 1958 Territorial Sea Convention, but this is no longer the case today. Indeed, the Convention embodies definite principles of law relating to the delimitation of the maritime domain and confirms historic titles to maritime areas as being exceptional in nature. Article 7 lays down provisions relating to the measurement of the closing line for bays, the maximum permissible length being 24 miles, and it specifies that those provisions "shall not apply to the so-called 'historic' bays . . ." [7] In the same way, Article 12 formulates a rule for the delimitation of territorial waters between opposite or adjacent states but it provides that "[t]he provisions of this paragraph shall not apply, however, where it is necessary by reason of *historic title* or other special circumstances to delimit the territorial seas of the two States in a way which is at variance with this provision". [8]

(2) *Relation with other concepts*

It has been pointed out that there are certain common features between the concept of historic waters or historic rights in general on the one hand, and the concepts of custom, prescription and occupation, on the other. [9] All of them presume that the resulting rights and titles have been preceded by two elements: a constant practice or exercise of state authority, and a toleration or acquiescence on the part of other states, particularly those directly concerned or affected by the practice in question. However, as properly pointed out by Norway in the *Fisheries Case,* the common features and process of development must not be exaggerated, for this could have important consequences on the burden of proof. For instance, acquisitive prescription generally gives the impression that there must be some adverse holding on the part of the claimant. This can hardly be the case when a state claims to have a historic title to a water area. Indeed, it is somewhat incompatible with the idea that the exercise of

---

[7]   Article 7, para. 6.

[8]   Article 12, para. 1; emphasis added.

[9]   See I. C. MacGibbon, "Customary International Law and Acquiescence", 33 *B.Y.I.L.* 114, at 119-121 (1957).

authority by the claimant state must have been peaceful.
Perhaps there is more affinity between the concept of historic
waters and that of occupation as a means of acquiring title
to territory. As stated by Lord Blackburn in a Privy Council
decision of 1877 relating to Conception Bay off the coast of
Newfoundland, "[I]t seems generally agreed that where the
configuration and dimensions of the bay are such as to shew
that the nation occupying the adjoining coasts also occupies
the bay it is part of the territory . . ." [10] It appears, therefore,
that the concept of historic waters draws from a number of
other related concepts concerning the acquisition of territorial
sovereignty and it is normal that it should be so, since a title
to a maritime domain is essentially the same as a title to a
territorial domain. There is an effective exercise of complete
sovereignty over both types of domain. Even the right of
innocent passage, which is preserved by the Territorial Sea
Convention when the establishment of straight baselines result
in converting part of the territorial sea or of the high seas
into internal waters, [11] is not safeguarded with respect to
historic waters. Naturally, a state may consent to allow innocent passage, although it is not legally bound to do so.

(3) *Present role of historic waters*

The 1958 Territorial Sea Convention has gone a long way
to obviate the necessity of claiming certain bays on the basis
of a historic title, by extending the permissible closing line to
24 miles. As mentioned by McDougal and Burke, the role of
historic bays has largely disappeared if the Territorial Sea
Convention can be considered as representing a general consensus regarding the maximum permissible closing line. [12]
Indeed, the 1958 Convention having been ratified by over 30
states including most of the major maritime Powers, it does
represent a general consensus of the international community
regarding the basic principles contained therein; consequently,

---

[10]   *The Direct United States Cable Co. Ltd.* v. *The Anglo-American
Telegraph Co. Ltd. et al.* (1877) 2 A.C. 394, at 419.
[11]   See Article 5, para. 2.
[12]   McDougal and Burke, *The Public Order of the Oceans*, at
357-358 (1962).

the concept of historic bay does have a more limited application than it formally did. This does not mean that the requirements for the establishment of a historic title to a maritime area have become more stringent, [13] but it does mean that, because of the extension of the permissible closing line to 24 miles, it is no longer necessary for states to rely on a historic title to claim a number of otherwise historic bays as internal waters. Furthermore, the same Convention permitting the use of straight baselines for deeply indented coasts enables states to enclose as internal waters large bodies of water, even though their entrances might exceed 24 miles, providing the geographical requirements described in Article 4 of the Convention are met. Canada has already taken advantage of her deeply indented coasts when delimiting its territorial sea and exclusive fishing zone off the east and west coasts. [14]

(4) *Status of historic waters*

It is now fairly well established that historic waters have the status of internal waters. Back in 1922, Sir Cecil Hurst made a study of this question with respect to bays and concluded that "[a]ll the waters lying inwards from this base line are national waters and form part of the national territory. They stand in all respects on precisely the same footing as the national territory." [15] In 1951 the United Kingdom argued in the *Fisheries Case* that, although Norway was entitled on historic ground to claim certain fjords and sunds as internal waters, it was only entitled to claim certain other bodies of water as territorial waters. The Court does not appear to have accepted that argument, at least as being applicable to Norway, since it held that all of the waters within the straight baselines regardless of their length were to be considered internal waters. It held specifically that ". . . the waters of the Vestfjord, as indeed the waters of all other Norwegian fjords, can

---

[13] See "Juridical Regime of Historic Waters, including Historic Bays", U.N. Doc. A/CONF. 4/143, at 13.
[14] See *Orders in Council* P.C. 1967, at 2025 of 26 October 1967, and P.C. 1969, at 1109 of 26 May 1969.
[15] Sir Cecil HURST, "The Territoriality of Bays", 3 *B.Y.I.L.* 42, at 54 (1923).

only be regarded as internal waters". [16] After this decision, some attempts were made by Fitzmaurice and Castberg to distinguish between two types of internal waters, one type which would be inland waters and another which would not be. [17] However, at its 1957 session, the Institute of International Law rejected the idea of so distinguishing internal waters, by adopting a compromise resolution which provided that a coastal state could continue to refuse access to foreign ships in its internal waters subject to acquired rights either by custom or by convention. [18] As for the 1958 Territorial Sea Convention, it does not expressly state that historic waters have the status of internal waters, but it does provide that the waters enclosed in a bay "shall be considered as internal waters" [19] and that waters claimed by "historic title" may affect the delimitation of the territorial seas between opposite or adjacent coasts. [20]

It must be mentioned, however, that the 1962 study by the United Nations' Secretariat concludes that the legal status of historic waters "would in principle depend on whether the sovereignty exercised in the particular case over the area by the claiming State and forming a basis for the claim, was sovereignty as over internal waters or sovereignty as over the territorial sea". [21] This conclusion is difficult to follow since it speaks of the exercise of sovereignty in both cases but with a different legal result. It would seem that the only logical consequence of the exercise of sovereignty, presumably unlimited sovereignty, must result in the waters falling within the regime of internal or inland waters.

2. REQUIREMENTS OF HISTORIC WATERS

The question of the legal prerequisites for the establishment of a historic title to water areas was left out completely

---

[16]   (1951) *I.C.J. Rep.*, at 142.
[17]   For a discussion of these attempts, see BLUM, *supra* note 3, at 303-307.
[18]   See text of the Resolution reproduced in BLUM, *ibid.*, at 307.
[19]   Article 7, para. 4.
[20]   Article 12, para. 1.
[21]   "Juridical Regime of Historic Waters, including Historic Bays", *supra* note 13, at 23.

of the 1958 Territorial Sea Convention. The only document which the Conference seemed to have from which to formulate principles relating to historic waters was the memorandum prepared by the United Nations' Secretariat. It was felt by Mr. François, the International Law Commission's special Rapporteur on the law of the sea, that the Conference did not have sufficient material at its disposal to lay down principles of law on the matter. He, therefore, suggested that the expression "historic bays" be inserted in the Convention and that, in the event of a dispute, the matter be interpreted by the Court. [22] The year following the Conference, the General Assembly adopted a resolution requesting the International Law Commission to undertake a study of the question of the juridical regime of historic waters, including historic bays. The Commission, in turn, asked the codification division of the Office of Legal Affairs of the U.N. Secretariat to prepare a study on the question in order to assist the Commission in eventually preparing draft articles incorporating the relevant legal principles. This study was done [23] and constitutes, along with the 1957 memorandum on historic bays, a very helpful source of information. These two documents review state practice, arbitral and judicial decisions, codification projects and the opinion of writers.

Upon reviewing the various pronouncements on the legal requirements for the establishment of a historic title to water areas, one is struck by the consensus which exists as to the essence of those requirements, but one is also equally impressed by the disagreement on matters of formal expression of those same requirements. The Japanese delegation submitted a proposal at the 1958 Conference which contained a definition of historic bays which could be applied to historic waters generally and which, in the writer's opinion, is as good a definition as can be found anywhere. The definition is as follows: "The term 'historic bays' means those bays over which coastal State or States have effectively exercised sover-

---

[22] See *U.N. Conference on the Law of the Sea,* Official Records, Vol. III, at 69, U.N. Doc. No. A/CONF. 13/39.

[23] See *supra* note 13, at 1.

eign rights continuously for a period of long standing, with explicit or implicit recognition of such practice by foreign States." [24] The Japanese delegation felt that the question of defining historic bays should not be left to arbtiral tribunals or courts when confronted with an actual dispute. It appears that the disagreement relates to the type of jurisdiction which the coastal state must exercise as well as to the time at which recognition or acquiescence on the part of foreign states must be shown. In any event, there is a general consensus that two basic requirements must be met: the exercise of authority by the coastal state and the acquiescence by foreign states. In addition, the coastal state may strengthen its claim by showing that its vital interests are involved.

(1) *Exercise of authority by the coastal state*

Nature of authority. — Since a claim to historic waters is one over a maritime area which the coastal state considers as part of its national domain, the type of jurisdiction exercised should have the same basic characteristics as the jurisdiction being exercised on the rest of its national domain. More precisely, the coastal state must exercise an effective control over the maritime area being claimed to the exclusion of all other states from that area. Naturally, the effectiveness of control will vary depending on a number of factors such as the size of the area, its remoteness, the degree of its use and so on. The coastal state must be in a position to show that it took whatever action was necessary to assert and maintain its authority and control over the area in question. As to the type of evidence which must be adduced, Gidel states that the exclusion from these areas of foreign vessels or their subjection to rules imposed by the coastal state which exceed the normal scope of regulations made in the interests of navigation, would obviously be acts affording convincing evidence of the state's intent. [25] The learned author is careful, however, to point out that those are not the only acts of authority which constitute evidence of the exercise of sovereignty by the coastal

---

24   Reproduced in (1962) *I.L.C. Yearbook*, Vol. II, at 3.
25   See GIDEL, *supra* note 3, at 633.

state. Indeed, normally, the physical act of excluding foreign vessels is preceded by national legislation which provides for such exclusion. In the case of Norway in 1951, she was in a position to point to a number of laws, regulations, administrative measures and judicial decisions in support of her claim. But, as pointed out by Bourquin, the intent of the state must be expressed by deeds and not merely by proclamations. [26] Naturally, if the laws and regulations of the coastal state are never challenged, no special action will be necessary on the part of the coastal state. But, if they are challenged, the coastal state will have to meet that challenge with whatever action is necessary to maintain the effective control needed to support a claim of sovereignty.

Duration of activities. — Somewhat as for the formation of a custom, it is impossible to determine in advance how long the exercise of authority must last before it materializes into a historic title. A great variety of terms is employed on the description of the length of time required for a usage or exercise of authority to have legal effect. The more common expressions used are "well established usage" and "immemorial usage". The exact period of time which must elapse will of course vary from one case to another. This will depend on a number of factors such as the degree of the change being effected, the attitude of other states and the political strength of the claimant state. In the case of historic bays, a longer period of time might be required. This appears to be the opinion of Professor Bourquin when he states that "[L]'usage dont l'État se prévaut en pareil cas, remonte au plus lointain passé. C'est un usage immémorial, au sens propre du mot." [27] In 1951, Norway was able to prove that she had applied the same system of delimitation consistently and without interruption for some 80 years before the dispute arose. [28] However, as in the case of an international custom, the period of time might be comparatively short for the acquisition of a historic title. On this question of the lapse of time required,

---

[26]   M. BOURQUIN, *supra* note 6, at 43.

[27]   M. BOURQUIN, *ibid.*, at 49.

[28]   See (1951) *I.C.J. Rep.*, at 138.

MacGibbon has expressed a very accurate opinion in the following terms:

> The passage of considerable period of time is an essential element in the growth of prescriptive and historic rights, the presumption of general or particular acceptance which may be raised by absence of protest being strengthened in proportion to the length of time silence persists. [29]

In other words, the period of time will depend considerably on the attitude of other states, particularly those directly affected. In order for those states to express their reaction they must of course be aware of the activities of the claimant's state.

Notoriety of activities. — Although formal notification on the part of the claimant's state is not generally required, it certainly facilitates proof; this is particularly so if the maritime area being claimed as historic waters happens to be located in remote and somewhat inaccessible parts of the globe such as the Arctic regions. In any event, the exercise of sovereignty by the coastal state must be of such a notoriety that knowledge on the part of interested states may be imputed. In the *Fisheries Case,* the United Kingdom had argued that the Norwegian system of delimitation did not possess the degree of notoriety required and, indeed, the United Kingdom seemed to have been unaware of some of the relevant Norwegian legislative enactments. However, the Court refused to accept this view and held that "[t]he United Kingdom could not have been ignorant of the Decree of 1869 which had at once provoked a request for explanations by the French Government". [30] It is interesting to note that judges McNair and Read did not go along with the majority of the Court in attributing constructive knowledge to the United Kingdom. [31]

(2) *Acquiescence by foreign states*

Meaning of acquiescence. — Everybody agrees that the attitude of foreign states is most important in the process of

---

[29]   I. C. MACGIBBON, "Customary International Law and Acquiescence", 33 *B.Y.I.L.* 114, at 120.

[30]   (1951) *I.C.J. Rep.,* at 139.

[31]   See McNAIR, (1951) *I.C.J. Rep.,* at 180, and READ, *ibid.,* at 194.

development of historic rights, and that some form of acquiescence is necessary before the claimant state can be said to have acquired any sovereign right in its favour and against the others. However, there is some disagreement as to the form which the acquiescence should take. The opinions seem to be divided into two groups, depending on the view which is taken of the nature of historic rights. Those who consider historic rights as an exception to the general rules relating to the acquisition of sovereignty take a stricter view of acquiescence. They seem to consider acquiescence as a form of consent or recognition of the sovereignty of the coastal state over certain maritime areas, and this recognition or consent must come from those states that are affected by the claim in question. The other group maintains that silence or the absence of protest on the part of the other states is sufficient for the exercise of sovereignty by the claimant coastal state to result in a historic title. This difference of opinion, however, is not as serious as it would appear to be on the surface, since those groups are quite close together when it comes to the matter of proving the acquiescence. The first group, represented by Fitzmaurice, admits that acquiescence need not take the form of a positive act on the part of the foreign states and that the role of the theory of historic rights is to create "a presumption of acquiescence arising from the facts of the case and from the inaction and toleration of States". [32] The other group, represented by Professor Bourquin, maintains that while it is wrong to say that the acquiescence of these states is required, it is true that if their reactions interfere with the peaceful and continuous exercise of sovereignty, no historic title can be formed. [33]

This difference of approach as to the exact form which the reaction of foreign states should take was also evident in the *Fisheries Case* of 1951. While admitting that the reaction of foreign states constitutes a very important element in the formation of a historic title which must be peaceful and con-

---

[32] FITZMAURICE, "The Law and Procedure of the International Court of Justice 1951-1954; General Principles and Sources of Law", 30 *B.Y.I.L.* 1, at 30.
[33] See BOURQUIN, *supra* note 6, at 46.

tinuous, the Norwegian Government rejected the view of the United Kingdom that ". . . le titre historique aurait pour seul fondement l'acquiescement des autres États et se confondrait ainsi, substantiellement, avec l'institution juridique de la reconnaissance". [34] The Norwegian Government went on to say that it considered the absence of reaction on the part of foreign states as being sufficient to confirm the peaceful and continuous character of the usage. [35] The Court seemed to accept the Norwegian argument when it stated that "[t]he general toleration of foreign States with regard to the Norwegian Practice is an unchallenged fact". [36] Having found as a fact that the Norwegian practice had met with the general toleration of foreign states, the Court went on to hold that Norway was entitled to enforce her practice against the United Kingdom. The Court stated in particular:

> The notoriety of the facts, the general toleration of the international community, Great Britain's position in the North Sea, her own interest in the question, and her prolonged abstention would in any case warrant Norway's enforcement of her system against the United Kingdom. [37]

It would thus appear from the judgment of the Court that a general toleration or the absence of protest on the part of foreign states is sufficient to create a historic title. In other words, there is at least a very strong presumption of acquiescence which results from the absence of protest during a long period of time. This presumption would appear to be almost impossible to rebut.

Effective protest. — An effective protest on the part of foreign states might serve to rebut the presumption of acquiescence which would otherwise arise. The protest, however, must be a real one, and it must usually be followed by some more forceful steps by the protesting state in order to prevent the formation of a historic title. The protest must be a real one in the sense that the mere raising of an objection in an

---

34   III *Fisheries Case* — *I.C.J. Pleadings,* at 462 (1951).
35   See *ibid.*
36   (1951) *I.C.J. Rep.,* at 138.
37   *Ibid.,* at 139.

indirect way would not suffice. For instance, in the *Fisheries Case,* the Court held that the negotiations between the Norwegian and the United Kingdom Governments, which followed the 1911 incident when a British trawler was seized and condemned for having violated the fishing limit of Norway, did not suffice to constitute an effective protest. Those discussions related to the two questions: the 4-mile breath of territorial sea and Norway's sovereignty over Varangerfjord. In the opinion of the Court, those two questions "were unconnected with the position of baselines" and therefore could not be considered as a formal protest. The Court went on to specify: "It would appear that it was only in its memorandum of July 27th, 1933, that the United Kingdom made a formal and definite protest on this point." [38] It would therefore seem from the foregoing that a formal objection on the specific points at issue is necessary before it can constitute a valid protest. Fitzmaurice does not appear to be quite that strict as to the form which a valid protest may take when he states:

> Apart from the ordinary case of a diplomatic protest, or a proposal for reference to adjudication, the same effect could be achieved by a public statement denying the prescribing country's right, by resistance to the *enforcement* of the claim or by counter-action of some kind. [39]

Presuming that a valid protest has been made, this might suffice for a while to prevent the period of time from starting to run, but it usually must be followed by some more forceful action on the part of the protesting state. If such a state is really concerned about the possibility of a historic right materializing, it ought to take all permissible means at its disposal to prevent the practice or exercise of authority in question from developing itself into a historic title. As stated by Blum, "[t]hese means will usually comprise the active prosecution of the objection through diplomatic negotiations, the arrangement of some kind of *modus vivendi,* or the seeking of a solution by enquiry, mediation or conciliation". [40] In addition to these possibilities, a state could of course bring the matter

---

[38] (1951) *I.C.J. Rep.,* at 138.
[39] FITZMAURICE, *supra* note 32, at 42, Footnote 1.
[40] Y. Z. BLUM, *supra* note 3, at 162.

to the forum of the United Nations, particularly if the dispute threatens international peace and security. In so far as the possibility of seeking a judicial settlement is concerned, the protesting state might be unable to invoke this mode of settlement if the claimant state has not recognized the jurisdiction of the International Court or has continuously refused in the past to submit disputes to arbitration. Such is the case for the Soviet Union and it would probably be pointless for the United States, for instance, to attempt an arbitral or judicial settlement of the question of whether the Northern Sea route or Northeast Passage should be opened to international navigation. Naturally the degree of effectiveness of a protest will depend on a number of factors such as the interest of the protesting state, its geographical situation, its political strength, and the fact that it is or is not the sole protestor. In the *Fisheries Case* of 1951, the United Kingdom argued that "the protest of a single State . . . is effective to prevent the establishment of a . . . title precisely to the extent that the State takes all necessary and reasonable steps to prosecute all available means of redressing the infringement of its rights". [41] This is not the consensus of writers, [42] and the Court did not seem to accept the argument of the United Kingdom. The Court agreed that the United Kingdom had made a formal protest in 1933, but it did not find this protest by a single state as sufficient to prevent a historic consolidation of the Norwegian practice. The Court stated in particular:

> . . . that even before the dispute arose, this method had been consolidated by a constant and sufficiently long practice, in the face of which the attitude of governments bears witness to the fact that they did not consider it to be contrary to international law. [43]

(3) *Vital interests of the coastal state*

When considering the question of the establishment of a historic title to water areas, particularly bays or gulfs, the

---

41   II *Fisheries Case* — *I.C.J. Pleadings,* at 654 (1951).
42   See in particular GIDEL, *supra* note 3, at 634, and BOURQUIN, *supra* note 6, at 47-48.
43   (1951) *I.C.J. Rep.,* at 139.

matter of vital interests often arises. Coastal states will usually buttress their claim to a historic bay with considerations of geography, economics and national security. This was done, for instance, by the Soviet Union in 1957 in the case of the Bay of Peter the Great, when it invoked the special geographical configuration of that bay as well as its special economic and defence significance. Although some writers would prefer to treat the question of vital interests as a basis for a claim outside of the historic title, [44] the great majority of authorities, including arbitral and judicial tribunals, deal with the question of vital interests along with the requirements for the establishment of a historic title. For instance, Dr. Drago, in his dissenting opinion in the *North Atlantic Coast Fisheries Arbitration* of 1910, quoted with approval from Westlake who maintained that certain bays belong to the coastal state "when such country has asserted its sovereignty over them, and particular circumstances such as geographical configuration, immemorial usage and above all, the requirements of self-defence, justify such a pretention". [45] The vital interest factor was given consideration and weight by the International Court in the *Fisheries Case*, particularly with respect to the geographic and economic aspects; both parties were otherwise on excellent terms and there was no question of Norway's national security being threatened. However, the importance of the peculiar geography of Norway permeates throughout the whole judgment of the Court. Even when discussing the strictly historic aspect of Norway's claim, the Court emphasized that the Norwegian system "was imposed by the peculiar geography of the Norwegian coast". [46] The Court also referred to the regional economic interests which

---

[44]   See M. BOURQUIN, *supra* note 6, at 51, where he states: "Le 'titre historique' est une chose; l'intérêt vital' en est une autre."

[45]   L. M. DRAGO, Dissenting Opinion in the *North Atlantic Coast Fisheries Case, Scott's Hague Court Reports* 195, at 200 (1961). It must be noted that the majority opinion also admitted the importance of the vital interest factor when it stated: "[T]hus conditions of national and territorial integrity, of defense, of commerce and of industry are all vitally concerned with the control of the bays penetrating the national coast line. This interest varies, speaking generally in proportion to the penetration inland of the Bay." See ID., 141, at 183.

[46]   (1951) *I.C.J. Rep.*, at 139.

had been established by long usage in favour of the coastal fishermen of Norway. The question of defence interests or national security in the case of bays is developed by Mitchell Strohl, a commander in the U.S. Navy, in his book on the International Law of Bays. In his special study of the status of Hudson Bay he comes to the conclusion that Hudson Bay is a potential area for the operation of submarines. [47] He states:

> With its tremendous area and location it constitutes a real problem for anti-submarine defense. For this reason Canada may be expected to see Hudson Bay as being more intimately connected with her national security than in times past. If Hudson Bay remains a part of Canadian internal waters, then Canada can, by international law, forbid the entry of foreign warships including submarines. This does not make an intruding submarine any easier to find, but it does permit Canada to take forceful and positive measures against such craft if their presence is detected. [48]

A similar reasoning could be made with respect to the waters of the Canadian Arctic Archipelago and it is very possible that Prime Minister Trudeau was making such reasoning when he made his formal statement on April 3, 1969 relating to Canada's defence policy. He might have been thinking particularly about the Arctic regions when he stated that one of the roles of Canada's armed forces was to insure "the surveillance of our own territory and coastlines, i.e. the protection of our sovereignty". [49] Indeed, a few months later, in his statement in the House of Commons relating to the Arctic regions in general and to the Arctic waters in particular, he stated that "[T]he Canadian Armed Forces carry out continuous surveillance activities". [50]

3. THE BURDEN OF PROVING HISTORIC WATERS

There appears to be a general consensus that the onus of proving the existence of a historic title to certain maritime

---

[47]   See M. P. STROHL, *The International Law of Bays*, at 250 (1963).

[48]   *Ibid.* The word "against" was inserted by the writer.

[49]   See "A Defence Policy for Canada", *Statements and Speeches*, No. 69/7 (1969).

[50]   See 114 *Can. H. C. Deb.*, at 39 (1969).

areas rests with the coastal state making such a claim. The 1930 Hague Codification Conference in its Basis Discussion No. 8, expressed the view that, if by usage a bay was under the exclusive authority of the coastal state, "the onus of proving such usage is upon the coastal State". [51] Gidel expressed the same view when he stated: "En ce qui concerne le fardeau de la preuve, il pèse sur l'État qui prétend attribuer à des espaces maritimes proches de ses côtes le caractère, qu'ils n'auraient pas normalement, d'eaux intérieures." [52] In the *Fisheries Case* of 1951, both the United Kingdom and Norway agreed that the burden of proof rested with the party claiming an exceptional right but the parties disagreed as to the scope of the burden of proof. In its counter-memorial the Norwegian Government stated that "the usage must be proved by the State which invokes it". [53] But Norway went on to say that it disagreed with the United Kingdom concerning the conditions of proof and the nature of the elements of proof to be produced. [54] The United Kingdom agreed "that the burden of proof lies upon the State which invokes the historic title". [55] It added that "[t]he role of the historic element being to validate what is an exception to general rules and therefore intrinsically invalid, it is natural that the burden of proof should so emphatically be placed upon the coastal State . . ." [56] Norway did not agree that she had such a heavy burden of proof since in her opinion the method of delimitation in question did not constitute an exception to the general rules. On this point it stated:

> En résumé, le titre historique, tel que le Gouvernement norvégien le conçoit et l'invoque dans le présent litige, n'a aucunement pour rôle de légitimer une situation par ailleurs illégale, mais bien de confirmer la validité de cette situation. [57]

---

[51] Acts of the Conference for the Codification of International Law, Vol. III: Meetings of the Second Committee, at 179, reproduced in U.N. Doc. A/CONF. 4/143 (1962).
[52] GIDEL, *supra* note 3, at 632.
[53] I *Fisheries Case — I.C.J. Pleadings,* at 566 (1951).
[54] *Ibid.*
[55] II *Fisheries Case — I.C.J. Pleadings,* at 645 (1951).
[56] *Ibid.,* at 646.
[57] III *Fisheries Case — I.C.J. Pleadings,* at 461 (1951).

The Court itself did not express any definite opinion as to the general burden of proof in the case of a historic title. However, it did define the historic title as being a regime of exception and consequently, Norway having admitted that in such a case the burden did rest with the claimant, the Court must have been satisfied that Norway did in fact discharge the general onus of proof which rested with it. Mr. Blum, who made a study of this question, comes to the following conclusion:

> It is submitted that, owing to the exceptional character of an historic claim and its deviation from the general rules of customary law, the burden of proof in such cases falls on the State which claims such a title in its favour to prove all those facts which, in its opinion, support the exceptional claim, irrespective of whether the legal proceedings had been instituted by the party alleging such a title or by a party denying the acquisition by its opponent of an historic title. [58]

This conclusion appears to the writer to be quite sound and it is fully agreed with.

Summarizing this examination of the question of historic waters in international law, the following propositions are submitted:

1. The concept of historic waters constitutes a regime of exception to the general rules of law relating to the delimitation of the maritime domain of a state.

2. The role of historic waters has largely disappeared since the advent of the 1958 Territorial Sea Convention, which extends to 24 miles the permissible closing line for bays, and permits the use of straight baselines for deeply indented coast to enclose as internal waters large water areas with possible entrances of over 24 miles.

3. Historic waters have the status of internal waters and innocent passage does not exist as of right.

4. Two basic requirements are necessary to support a claim to historic waters: 1) the exercise of exclusive authority

---

[58]   Y. Z. BLUM, *supra* note 3, at 232.

and control by the coastal state over a long period of time; 2) acquiescence by foreign states, particularly those affected by the claim in question.

5. A state may buttress its claim to historic waters by showing that its vital interests are at stake; considerations of geography, economics and national security may be invoked.

6. The burden of proving the existence of a historic title to certain water areas rests with the state making such a claim.

The practical and rather difficult question now is: do the waters of the Northwest and Northeast Passages meet the requirements just formulated.

II. — HISTORIC WATERS IN THE NORTHEAST PASSAGE

The possibility of the Siberian seas being considered as historic waters of the Soviet Union is evidenced by at least two or three facts. In the first place, the laws of the USSR define its "internal sea waters" as including the following: "waters of bays, inlets, coves, and estuaries, seas and straits, historically belonging to the USSR". [59] This legislative enactment might have been the basis for its reported objection in an exchange of notes with the United States prior to the latter's announced oceanographic research voyage in the Northeast Passage in 1965. [60] In the second place, it might also be significant that in 1957 the Soviet Union adopted a decree declaring the waters of Peter the Great Bay to be internal waters with a closing line of 108 miles. In its reply to a note of protest from the United States, the Soviet Government explained that those waters "are historically waters of the Soviet Union by force of the special geographic conditions of that bay and its special economic and defense significance". [61] The

[59] Article 4(c), "Statute on the Protection of the State Border of Soviet Socialist Republics", *Soviet Statutes and Decisions*, at 10-11 (Summer 1967).

[60] See Wm. E. BUTLER, *The Soviet Union and the Law of the Sea*, at 114 (1971).

[61] See 4 WHITEMAN, *Digest of Int'l Law*, at 255 (1965).

rest of the Soviet note emphasized the historical rights of the USSR to the waters of that bay which, it alleged, had been recognized as being formed of internal waters for more than half a century. It is interesting to note in passing that the historical basis is supported by the well known doctrine of "vital interests". A third indication of possible relevance is the fact that Soviet jurists are virtually unanimous in their opinion that the Siberian seas are internal waters. This opinion is reported in a textbook on international law, edited by Professor Kozhevnikov, where it is stated:

> Soviet jurists rightly consider the Siberian seas which are akin to gulfs (Kara Sea, Laptev Sea, East Siberian Sea and Chukotsk Sea) as Soviet internal waters. These seas, which in effect constitute gulfs and which are of exceptional economic and strategic importance to the Soviet Union, have over a prolonged period of history been used by Russian seafarers. [62]

A number of Soviet jurists have also interpreted the sector theory as giving the Soviet Union sovereignty over all of the maritime area covered by its sector. In these circumstances, we shall examine the possibiltiy for the Soviet Union to make a valid claim to the water areas traversed by the Northeast Passage on the basis of its maritime activities or its use of the sector theory.

1. MARITIME ACTIVITIES

A preliminary examination of state activities in the Siberian Seas would indicate that they may be conveniently classified into three periods: pre-1917, 1917 to the end of World War II and post World War II. The *pre-1917* activities may be characterized as the discovery period. The British and the Scandinavians were anxious to discover a Northeast Passage for commercial purposes and ships were commissioned to search for a passage and for new lands. Starting with the Willoughby-Chancellor expedition in 1553 in the Kara Sea, [63] the only indication during this period that Russia

---

[62]   F. I. KOZHEVNIKOV (ed.), *International Law*, at 206 (1961).
[63]   See M. MITCHELL, *The Maritime History of Russia* 848-1948, at 92 (1949).

was opposed to the presence of foreign ships was the Ukaz of 1619 which excluded foreign ships from the Kara Sea. [64] However, this decree could not have been enforced for long, if it ever was, having regard to the numerous expeditions to the Kara Sea in the middle of the 17th and throughout the 18th and 19th centuries. Indeed, in 1896, an English Company was formed for Arctic trading purposes and it even established an agency on the Yenesei River. The Russian Government of the time was so gratified with the British efforts in creating a regular maritime service to Siberia that it "reduced by one half all the customs dues on the English goods, and granted the company various mining concessions". [65] The author of the Maritime History of Russia adds that "[i]n 1905 a fleet of twenty-two ships reached the Yenesei by the Northern Sea Route, and all the vessels returned safely to their western destinations". [66] It should be recalled that it was during this period, in 1878-1879, that the Northeast Passage was crossed for the first time by the Swedish captain, A. E. Nordenskiöld, from the Atlantic to the Pacific. The second successful crossing did not occur until 1914-1915, when it was sailed in the reverse direction by the Russian Boris Vilkitski.

The second period, from 1917 to the end of World War II, is characterized by intense efforts on the part of the Soviet Union to develop the Northeast Passage and transform it into a regular shipping route for the exploitation of its northern natural resources. Except for Amundsen's crossing of the Northeast Passage in 1918-1920, the Soviet Union seem to have been the only country during this period engaged in maritime activities in the Siberian seas. In 1932, the Northeast Passage was crossed in one season by the icebreaker *Sibiriakov*, navigating from Murmansk to Vladivostok. [67] The following year the same feat was nearly accomplished by the *Cheliuskin*, but the ship was crushed in the ice when it was

---

[64] This Ukaz is referred to by S. A. VYSHNYEPOLSKY in "The Problems of a System of Law for the Arctic Regions", *Soviet Press Translations*, Vol. 7, No. 18, at 372 (15 Oct. 1972).
[65] M. MITCHELL, *supra* note 63, at 104.
[66] *Ibid.*
[67] *Ibid.*, at 108.

practically in sight of Bering Strait and had to be abandoned. [68]
In 1934, the Canadian-built icebreaker *Litke* (originally known
as *Canada*), named after Admiral Litke who had met the coast
of Novaya Zemlya in his voyages in 1821 to 1824, left Vladivostok in June and reached Murmansk in September, thus
becoming the first ship to make a one season crossing from
east to west. [69] In 1935, the Northern Sea Route was traversed both ways in the same year by cargo ships. [70]

The Post World War II period has witnessed considerable
activities in the Siberian Seas, as well as the Arctic Ocean
properly so-called, by the Soviet Union. This was accomplished
mainly by icebreakers and drifting ice stations. The Soviet
Union, however, was not the only country during the present
period to carry on activities in the Siberian seas. Consequently,
the attitude of the USSR with respect to the presence of foreign
ships in those seas should be examined. The *Barents Sea,*
named after the Dutchman William Barents who discovered
it, does not appear to have ever been claimed as a Russian
sea. The USSR did not object in August 1967 to the fact that
U.S. icebreakers were present in that sea. Furthermore, Norway borders on the Barents Sea and uses it regularly. It is
worth noting, however, that the USSR is reported to have
carried on naval manoeuvres in that sea to test new weapons
during 1961 and 1962. [71] The Ministry of Defence issued a
statement giving the geographic coordinates and warned of
the dangers for both maritime and aerial navigation. The
dangerous manoeuvres zone covered the western part of the
Kara Sea, from east meridian 77° as far west in the Barents
Sea as the east meridian 35°30'; [72] Norway's protests that
those manoeuvres interfered with freedom of navigation and
fishing were ignored by the Soviet Government. However,
Soviet foreign minister Gromyko, while on visit to Oslo in 1963,
is reported to have said that the interests of Norwegian

---

[68]   *Ibid.,* at 105.
[69]   *Ibid.,* at 261.
[70]   *Ibid.,* at 262.
[71]   See ROUSSEAU, "Chronique des faits internationaux", *Revue
générale de droit international public,* 399-404 (1963).
[72]   See Map, *ibid.,* at 402.

fishermen would be taken into account as much as possible in future. [73] The fact remains, however, that the Barents Sea has never been claimed by the USSR as historic waters, not even by Soviet writers.

The Kara, Laptev, East Siberian and Chukchi Seas present a different picture. The USSR has never officially claimed these seas as historic waters, but Soviet writers have. The strongest proponent of this claim is probably Vyshnyepolsky; he maintains that these "purely Arctic seas" are not subject to the principle of the freedom of the high seas, since navigation is impossible without special assistance and that, in any event, they are historic Russian seas. They are described as seas of the gulf-type, such as Hudson Bay, and reference is made to Marten's writings and to the Great Soviet Encyclopedia in support of this claim. With respect to the Northern Sea Route, Vyshnyepolsky asserts categorically: "The Northern Sea Route passing through the purely Arctic seas of the Soviet polar sector is our historic national sea route, created by the stubborn labors of the Russian people over a period of several centuries." [74] Soviet jurists generally are also reported to consider these four seas as constituting internal waters on the basis of history. [75] It is interesting to note that Soviet jurists interpret the decision of the International Court in the *Anglo-Norwegian Fisheries Case* as supporting their claim to consider those seas as internal waters. The passage continues:

> This point of view corresponds to international practice and is in line with the Judgment of the International Court of Justice of December 18, 1951 in the case of the Anglo-Norwegian dispute, in which, as already noted, the sea route along the Norwegian coast was held to be Norwegian internal waters, having been marked for navigation by Norway. [76]

If the intention is to compare the Northern Sea Route to the Indrelia route, the passages of which are confined to the Nor-

---

[73] *Ibid.*, at 404.
[74] S. A. VYSHNYEPOLSKY, *supra* note 64, at 374.
[75] See KOZHEVNIKOV, *supra* note 62, and BUTLER, *supra* note 60, at 106.
[76] KOZHEVNIKOV, *ibid.*

wegian Skjaergaard and seldom exceed 8 miles in width, such an interpretation would not even seem justified.

The attitude of the Soviet Government itself toward the status of the four seas under consideration has not been as severe as that of its legal writers. In 1965, the *Northwind* spent nearly two months in the Kara Sea; it took oceanographic readings throughout its voyage, and made 160 stations from which it collected water samples all over that sea, including the southern part between Novaya Zemlya and the coast. [77] A Soviet destroyer kept the ship under surveillance, but it never actually interfered. The Soviets are reported to have objected, however, to the bottom-coring program carried out by the *Northwind*, as being contrary to the 1958 Geneva Convention on the Continental Shelf. [78] It must be conceded here that the USSR, as the coastal state, possesses the exclusive right to explore the continental shelf and, therefore, had some apparent basis of protest. The legal status of the superjacent waters as high seas is, of course, preserved by the Convention and the Soviet Union seems to have respected that status. In 1967, U.S. icebreakers spent seven weeks exploring the Kara Sea a second time, after they had been refused permission to go through the Vilkitsky Straits; Captain Benkert of the *Eastwind* is quoted as saying: "We put in a profitable seven weeks in the Kara Sea and made a very complete oceanographic survey of the entire sea, which had only been partially surveyed before by United States vessels." [79] There is no report of interference during that time. The United States has also carried on a considerable amount of oceanographic research in the Chukchi Sea, the eastern portion of which crosses the Alaskan boundary line. In the summer of 1947, the U.S. *Boarfish* (SS-327) conducted experiments in under-ice dives in the Chukchi Sea; [80] the following summer, further experiments in diving and surfacing in ice

---

[77]   See R. PETROW, *Across the Top of Russia,* at 344-345 (1967), for a map showing the location and number of stations made by the *Northwind.*

[78]   *Ibid.,* at 351.

[79]   *The Polar Times,* at 13 (Dec. 1967).

[80]   "Submarines in the Arctic", *U.S. Naval Institute Proceedings,* Vol. 87, No. 10, 58-65 (Oct. 1961).

were carried out by the USS *Carp* (SS-338). [81] In July 1958, the *Nautilus* went through a considerable part of the Chukchi Sea before turning back because of the shallow waters and the thickness of the under-sea ice. [82] These activities on the part of the United States are known to the Soviet Union and acknowledged by its scientists. A descriptive note of the Chukchi Sea, written jointly by a member of the Soviet Institute of Oceanography and a member of the Lamont Geological Observatory of Columbia, states that "[s]ince the Second World War, both the U.S. and USSR have sponsored a number of oceanographic research expeditions to the Chukchi Sea". [83]

But the United States activities have not been confined to the Arctic seas at either end of the Northern Sea Route. A report entitled "United States Activities in Waters North of the USSR, 1962 to 1965", appearing in the Polar Record of September 1966, summarizes those activities. The report based on information supplied by N. A. Ostenso of the Geophysical and Polar Research Center, University of Wisconsin, shows that oceanographic surveys were carried out by the U.S. Coast Guard icebreaker *Northwind* and the USS *Burton Island* throughout these four Arctic seas. [84]

It would appear from the evidence just examined that the USSR would have a very difficult task to discharge the burden of proving that some of the Siberian seas constitute historic waters. Indeed, it would have to show that it has exercised exclusive control over those seas and that foreign states, in particular the United States, have manifested an acquiescence in this control.

2. THE SECTOR THEORY

A good deal of writing has already taken place about the application of the sector theory to the Soviet Arctic [85] and the

---

81 *Ibid.*
82 See Wm. R. ANDERSON, *Nautilus 90°North*, at 166 (1959).
83 *Encyclopedia of Oceanography*, Vol. I, at 192 (1966).
84 *Polar Record*, Vol. 13, No. 84, at 305 (Sept. 1966).
85 See in particular the following: W. L. LAKHTINE, *Rights over the Arctic* (in Russian), Moscow (1928), with diplomatic notes of 1916 and 1924 (in French) in appendix; W. L. LAKHTINE, "Rights over the

purpose of this brief survey is only to determine to what extent and in what way the theory in question has been applied by the USSR. In its diplomatic notes of 20 September 1916 and 4 November 1924 sent to the United States, the Soviet Government claimed sovereignty over the islands north of its coast, including those north of Siberia which constituted, in the words of the Note of 1916, "une extension vers le nord de la plateforme continentale de la Sibérie". [86] The 1924 Note referred to the 1867 Treaty between the USSR and the United States as laying down the boundary west of which the United States "se sont engagés de ne formuler aucune revendication". [87] It will be recalled that this is the treaty which stipulates that the line of demarcation "se prolonge en ligne directe, sans borne, vers le Nord jusqu'à la Mer Glaciale". [88] It appears therefore from the above that the Soviet Union already considered the 1867 treaty as defining one of the boundaries of its sector. On April 15, 1926, the Presidium of the Central Executive Committee adopted a decree defining both boundaries:

> All *lands and islands* situated in the Arctic to the North, between the coastline of the USSR and the North Pole, both already discovered and those which may be

Arctic", 24 *A.J.I.L.*, 703-717 (1930); G. SMEDAL, *De l'acquisition de souveraineté sur les territoires polaires*, Paris (1932), at 85-115; T. A. TARACOUZIO, *Soviets in the Arctic* (1938); E. PLISCHKE, *Jurisdiction in the Polar Regions* (A study of juridical principles governing the original acquisition of polar territory in the Arctic with special reference to the sector principle), Ph.D. dissertation submitted to the Faculty of Clark University, Worcester, Massachusetts (1943); G. W. SMITH, *The Historical and Legal Background of Canada's Arctic Claims*, Ph.D. dissertation submitted to the Faculty of Political Science, Columbia University (1952); C. M. FRANKLIN and V. C. McCLINTOCK, "The Territorial Claims of Nations in the Arctic: an Appraisal", 5 *Oklahoma L. Rev.* 37, at 42-48 (1952); D. PHARAND, *La théorie des secteurs dans l'Artique à l'égard du droit international* (unpublished), Paris (1955); I. L. HEAD, "Canadian Claims to Territorial Sovereignty in the Arctic Regions", 9 *McGill L. J.* 200, at 206-210 (1962-63); W. H. McCONNEL, "The Legal Regime of Archipelagoes", 35 *Sask. L. Rev.* 121, at 129-140 (1971-72).

[86]   See Note of 20 September 1916 in Appendix to W. L. LAKHTINE, *Rights over the Arctic* (in Russian), Moscow (1928).

[87]   See *ibid.*

[88]   See Article 1, Traité pour la cession de l'Amérique russe aux Etats-Unis, signé à Washington le 30 mars 1867, *Recueil de Martens*, N.R., 2ᵉ Série, Vol. 1, at 39.

discovered in the future, which at the time of the publication of the present decree are not recognized by the Government of the USSR as the territory of any foreign State, are (hereby) declared territory of the Union, (namely in the area) between the meridian 32°4′35″ longitude . . . and the meridian 168°49′30″ longitude . . . . [89]

It will be noted that the sector theory incorporated in the decree just quoted does not mention water areas but confines itself to claiming "lands and islands". A number of Soviet jurists, however, have given a very extensive interpretation to this decree so as to include all maritime areas within the sector. Among them are the following: Korovin in 1926, [90] Sigrist in 1928, [91] Lakhtine in 1928, [92] and Vyshnyepolsky in 1952. [93] Lakhtine not only suggested that the Soviet sector be interpreted so as to cover water areas, but he systematized the sector and suggested that the Arctic regions be divided into 6 sectors (Figure 5). [94] In spite of this doctrinal support for a wide interpretation of the sector theory for about 25 years following the adoption of the decree, two facts are important to note in this connection. In the first place, the international law textbook, edited by Professor Kozhevnikov in 1961 and published under the auspices of the Academy of Sciences of the USSR, confines the application of the polar sector to lands and islands. [95] Secondly, no Soviet Government has ever officially invoked the sector theory in support of a claim over maritime areas. Indeed, it is quite obvious that the 1926 decree was intended specifically to buttress its claim to Wrangel and Herald Islands. The first one had been occupied by

---

[89] HUDSON, *Cases on International Law*, at 220 (1951); emphasis added.
[90] See T. A. TARACOUZIO, *Soviets in the Arctic*, at 348 (1938).
[91] *Ibid.*, at 349.
[92] W. L. LAKHTINE, "La voie aérienne arctique et l'état juridique des territoires polaires septentrionaux", 13 *Revue de droit aérien* 532, at 549-551 (1929), and "Rights over the Arctic", 24 *A.J.I.L.*, at 703 (1930).
[93] S. A. VYSHNYEPOLSKY, *supra* note 64, at 371. See also a Comment on Vyshnyepolsky's views by W. W. KULSKI in 49 *A.J.I.L.*, at 130-133 (1953).
[94] W. L. LAKHTINE, "La voie arctique et l'état juridique des territoires polaires septentrionaux", 13 *Revue de droit aérien* 532, at 554-556 (1929) and "Rights over the Arctic", 24 *A.J.I.L.* 703, at 715-716 (1930).
[95] F. I. KOZHEVNIKOV (ed.), *supra* note 62, at 190-191.

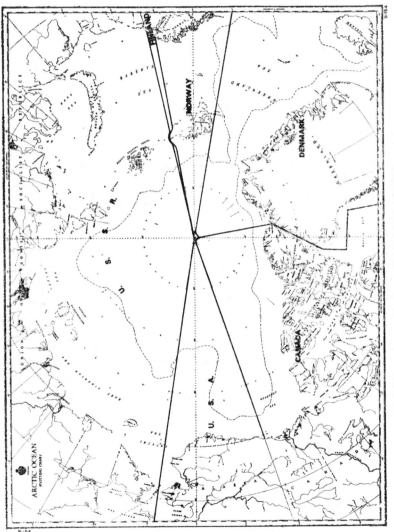

FIGURE 5   THE SECTOR THEORY AS PROPOSED BY V.L. LAKHTINE

a Canadian expedition headed by Stefansson from September 1921 to May 1924, and then by an American and 12 Esquimos from Alaska. On August 24, 1924, the *Red October* took possession of the island, made the occupants prisoners, put up the Red flag in replacement of the Union Jack which was still flying and installed a small Soviet colony. [96] As for Herald Island, it was found inoccupied by a group of Americans in September 1926 and they took possession of the island in the name of the United States. In due course the Soviet Union established its full and exclusive control over these two islands so that an insistance on the sector theory became unnecessary. However, even assuming for a moment that the sector theory could serve as a proper basis in international law for the acquisition of territorial sovereignty — an assumption with which this writer does not agree — [97] such sovereignty could not extend in this instance to the water areas. Not only would it be contrary to the basic concepts of the law of the sea but it would go beyond the specific claim to "lands and islands" clearly expressed in the 1926 decree and made even clearer by the events immediately preceding the decree.

CONCLUSION ON THE NORTHEAST PASSAGE

The above examination of the maritime activities and the use of the sector theory by the Soviet Union leads to the conclusion that it would be most difficult, if not impossible, for it to prove that the seas and straits traversed by the Northeast Passage meet the stringent requirements of historic waters. A similar conclusion has been reached by Professor Butler who has examined relevant Soviet legislation and writings. His conclusion is the following:

> The voyages of American icebreakers into those seas since 1964 have confirmed that as a matter of state practice the USSR treats the polar seas as open seas. Although Soviet international lawyers would assimilate the region into the regime of historic internal waters, this has not

---

[96] For a full account of this incident, see V. STEFANSSON, *The Adventure of Wrangel Island,* London (1925).

[97] See D. PHARAND, *La théorie des secteurs dans l'Arctique à l'égard du droit international,* at 47-149 (unpublished), Paris (1955).

been accomplished in either international law or Soviet
legislation. It would now appear that Soviet jurists may be
significantly revising their doctrine of historic waters to
bring them into accord with existing legislation. [98]

The above passage would seem to imply that proof of historic
waters could definitely not be made, and this might very well
be the case. To express a definite view would require a historical study of all relevant archival and governmental documents, most of which would be in the Soviet Union and some
of which inaccessible to the public.

III. — HISTORIC WATERS IN THE NORTHWEST PASSAGE

Canadian laws do not make any express reference to
historic waters. However, the definition of internal waters is
sufficiently wide to include historic waters. *The Territorial
Sea and Fishing Zones Act* of 1964 contains the following
provision: "The internal waters of Canada include any areas
of the sea that are on the landward side of the baselines of the
Territorial Sea of Canada." [99] In the first place, the definition
is not an exhaustive one and could very well include water
areas not specifically mentioned; and, in the second place,
it is possible that all of the waters within the Canadian Arctic
Archipelago might be considered as coming within the "landward side of the baselines of the territorial sea of Canada".
This would be the case if the Canadian Archipelago were
considered as a single unit and straight baselines were drawn
around the outermost edges so as to serve to delimit one single
belt of territorial sea around the entire archipelago. It might
also be appropriate to recall here that Canada already considers as historic waters those of Hudson Bay and of other
bays of considerable size along the coasts of Newfoundland
and Nova Scotia. More significant is the fact that, at the time
of the *Manhattan* crossing of the Northwest Passage in 1969,
the Prime Minister spoke in the House of Commons on the
status of the Canadian Arctic Archipelago in such a way as
to indicate that Canada might be relying on a historic title

---

[98] Wm. E. BUTLER, *supra* note 60, at 115.
[99] Section 3(2), 13 *Eliz. II, Statutes of Canada*, c. 22 (1964).

to claim jurisdiction over the Arctic waters. The statement is part of a prepared address on the Speech from the Throne and is reproduced here.

> Canadian activities in the northern reaches of this continent have been far-flung but pronounced for many years, to the exclusion of the activities of any other government. The Royal Canadian Mounted Police patrols and administers justice in these regions on land and ice, in the air and *in the waters*. The Canadian Armed Forces carry out continuous surveillance activities; Canadian postal services, health services and communications networks criss-cross these territories to serve those who live and work there. Among these persons are the Canadian Eskimos, who pursue their food and conduct their activities over the icy wastes without heed to whether that ice is supported by land or by water. In all these activities, and in others, ranging from geophysical explorations to the distribution of family allowance cheques, Arctic North America has, for 450 years, progressively become the Canadian Arctic. [100]

This statement by the Prime Minister, followed six months later by the Arctic pollution prevention legislation, gained the support of some commentators. It is stated that the various activities of Canada, coupled with the sector theory, could enable it to make a case either immediately [101] or eventually. [102] One commentator has gone so far as to make the following submission:

> It is submitted that, in the light of the Canadian administrative and other activities in the area, the absence of any concrete claim of opposition by any other State — pace the situation that has now arisen — sufficient time has enured for Canadian sovereignty over the entire Canadian Arctic as far as the Pole, and embracing land, islands, sea and pack-ice, to have become a fact in law. Had any question arisen, say, five years before the Manhattan effort,

---

[100]   See *Can. H. C. Deb.*, Vol. I, at 39-40 (24 Oct. 1969).

[101]   R. W. KONAN, "The *Manhattan*'s Arctic Conquest and Canada's Response in Legal Diplomacy", 3 *Cornell Int'l L. J.* 188, at 196-199 (1970).

[102]   J.-Y. MORIN, "Le progrès technique, la pollution et l'évolution récente du droit de la mer au Canada, particulièrement à l'égard de l'Arctique", 8 *C.Y.I.L.* 158, at 240-242 (1970).

there is little doubt that the world at large would have
recognized Canada's historic title to the whole area. [103]

That is quite a strong submission and it seems to this writer
that it would be necessary to study the relevant archival and
governmental documents (British and Canadian) before forming a definite opinion as to whether Canada could make a
case of historic title to the waters of its Arctic archipelago.
The present purpose is limited to making a brief analysis of
the maritime activities of Canada in the Arctic and of its use
of the sector theory, in the hope of forming a preliminary
opinion on this very complex question.

1. MARITIME ACTIVITIES [104]

The maritime activities in the Canadian Arctic which
Canada could invoke in support of a claim of historic waters
may be grouped into two periods: from 1576 to 1880 and
from 1881 to the present.

The first period runs from the year of the first voyage
made by Martin Frobisher in search for the Northwest Passage
in 1576 to the year of the transfer of all British possessions
in North America not already belonging to Canada or Newfoundland by Imperial Order in Council of July 31, 1880.
During this period, some 49 British expeditions were carried
out in the Canadian Arctic, [105] most of them in search of the
Northwest Passage or of the missing men of the last expedi-

---

[103]   L. C. GREEN, *"Canada and Arctic Sovereignty"*, 48 *Can. Bar
Rev.* 740, at 760 (1970); emphasis already in text.
[104]   The main sources used for this section are the following:
Pilot of Arctic Canada, Vol. I (2nd ed., 1970) published under the
authority of the Government of Canada, by the Canadian Hydrographic
Service; *A Historical Summary of Maritime Exploration in the Canadian
Arctic and Its Relevance in Connection with Subsequent and Recent
Sovereignty Issues,* a manuscript of 34 pages prepared by Gordon W.
Smith for publication in the Proceedings of the International Commis-
sion of Maritime History, meeting in conjunction with the Thirteenth
Congress of the International Committee for Historical Sciences in
Moscow, August 1970; and *Geographical Discovery and Exploration in
the Queen Elizabeth Islands,* by Andrew Taylor, published by the Depart-
ment of Mines and Technical Surveys, Ottawa (1955).
[105]   See *Documents concerning Canadian Sovereignty in the Arctic,*
Library of the Department of Indian Affairs and Northern Development, Ottawa.

tion of Sir John Franklin who had perished in 1846 when caught in the ice northwest of King William Island. During the same period there were only 8 American expeditions and one Danish. [106] The American expeditions had for objective, except for a few in search of Franklin's men, the reaching of the North Pole by navigating through Kennedy and Robeson Channels between Ellesmere Island and Greenland. It was during this period that Lieut. W. E. Parry sailed in the Northwest Passage some 630 miles as far as M'Clure Strait in his first voyage of 1819-1820. [107] He was followed by Capt. Henry Kellett who reached Mercy Bay north of Banks Island and nearly half-way through M'Clure Strait, during his voyage of 1852-1854. [108] The famous M'Clure Strait was finally crossed in an easterly direction by M'Clure, who made it — albeit on foot — from Mercy Bay, where he had abandoned his ship, to Viscount Melville Sound. It was for this feat of crossing the last link of one of the routes of the Northwest Passage that M'Clure and his crew were awarded the British Admiralty prize. [109] The British explorers of this period laid claims to lands and islands which they discovered or explored and which served as a basis for the transfer of title to Canada in 1880.

The second period runs from 1880 to the present and, with a few exceptions, is characterized by Canadian expeditions whose primary purpose was to consolidate the title to the lands and islands obtained from Great Britain, and to insure Canadian control over those transferred possessions. The exceptions mentioned refer to three events: the sailing of the Northwest Passage by Amundsen in 1903-06, Denmark's question of Canadian sovereignty on Ellesmere Island in 1920, and the recognition by Norway of Canada's title to the Sverdrup Islands in 1930. The sailing of the Northwest Passage by Amundsen of Norway, through what has become one of the two southern routes of the Passage, was limited in

---

[106] *Ibid.*
[107] A. TAYLOR, *Geographical Discovery and Exploration in the Queen Elizabeth Islands,* at 28 (1955).
[108] *Ibid.,* see Map, at 50.
[109] CANADIAN HYDROGRAPHIC SERVICE, *Pilot of Arctic Canada,* Vol. I, at 61-62 (2nd ed., 1970).

its objective to succeeding a complete crossing for the first time. It resulted in no claim whatever on the part of Amundsen or Norway. The questioning by Denmark of Canada's sovereignty over the east part of Ellesmere Island in 1920 arose after the Canadian Government wrote to Denmark asking it to restrain Greenland Eskimos from killing musk-ox on Ellesmere. The reply of the Danish Government included a letter signed by the explorer Knud Rasmussen stating that the region in question was "No Man's Land". [110] This resulted in a strong protest being transmitted by the Governor General to the Secretary of State for the Colonies against the assertion by Denmark. It seems that this protest put an end to the matter and no reply was ever received from Denmark. As for the recognition by Norway of Canada's title to Sverdrup Islands (Axel Heiberg and the Ringness Islands), the exchange of Notes settled the matter in a definitive manner and related solely to land. [111] Some of the Canadian expeditions, such as those of Stefansson in 1913-1918, resulted in the discovery of new islands, but the rest were in the nature of patrol and surveillance. The more important ones in this regard have been the expeditions of Low, in command of the *Neptune* in 1903-1904 and of Bernier, in command of the *Arctic* from 1901 to 1906.

The purpose of the Low expedition is summed up in Pilot of Arctic Canada in the following terms:

> In September 1880, Great Britain transferred to Canada her sovereignty rights in the Canadian Arctic, but it was not until 1903 that Canada took active steps to assert these rights in high altitudes. In that year, A. P. Low of the Geological Survey of Canada was sent north from Halifax in command of the *Neptune,* "to patrol the waters of Hudson Bay and those adjacent to the eastern Arctic Islands; also to aid in the establishment on the adjoining shores of permanent stations for the collection of customs, the ad-

---

110   See *Report of Advisory Technical Board on the Question of Canadian Sovereignty in the Arctic*, Public Archives of Canada, at 2A-3A (1920).

111   See Exchange of Notes between Canada and Norway, *Canada Treaty Series,* No. 17 (1930).

ministration of justice and the enforcement of law as in other parts of the Dominion". [112]

Although the instructions specify that the expedition is to patrol "the waters", it is obvious from the context that the main purpose of such patrol was to assert its sovereignty over the territory and islands transferred to it by Great Britain. This is confirmed by Andrew Taylor, writing a summary of the Arctic expeditions for the government of Canada, who states clearly: "The primary purpose of the voyage was to 'plant the flag' in numerous localities throughout the Arctic; it was the signature of Canada's growing interest in the islands, sovereignty over some of which was being contested by Norway on the basis of the work of Sverdrup and Amundsen." [113] However, it is a fact that whalers had been operating in the Arctic waters, particularly in Hudson Bay, Davis Strait and Lancaster Sound, so that Low might have kept an eye open for them while he patrolled those waters.

As for the three Bernier expeditions of 1906-1907, 1908-1909 and 1910-1911, Capt. Bernier sailed as far as Melville Island on his first voyage, reached Mercy Bay in M'Clure Strait on the second and not quite as far in M'Clure Strait on the third. Here again the main purpose of Bernier's voyages was to assert Canada's sovereignty over the Arctic islands and to cross the Northwest Passage if possible. [114] During his last voyage, Bernier laid a plaque on Melville Island commemorating the taking of possession for Canada of the whole Arctic archipelago. After the Low and Bernier expeditions, Canada instituted the regular Eastern Arctic Patrol in 1922, then the RCMP patrols which extended over most of the Arctic islands by 1929.

The above brief summary of the maritime activities of the British and Canadian expeditions would seem to present very little evidence that their purpose was to lay claim to water areas or to exercise exclusive control over them. This was essentially the conclusion reached by Dr. Gordon Smith

---

[112]   *Supra* note 109, at 71.
[113]   *Supra* note 107, at 112.
[114]   For a summary of Capt. Bernier's voyages, see *ibid.*, at 113-120.

who, after making a review of all expeditions in the Canadian Arctic, makes the following statement relating to the explorers:

> ... they were concerned with land, not water; and it is conspicuous that whenever claims were made these claims were for the most part specifically to land. It is equally apparent that both Great Britain and Canada at the time of the transfer of 1880, and Canada during the years thereafter when she was trying to establish her sovereignty, were also concerned essentially with the islands themselves. It is only in comparatively recent years that issues involving arctic waters have come to the fore. [115]

In the light of this brief survey it would appear difficult for Canada to make a case of historic waters. However, she might be able to find support in her application of the sector theory and this will now be examined.

2. THE SECTOR THEORY

The first indication of Canada's practice relating to its boundaries in the Arctic regions appears on a map of Canada, published by the Department of the Interior in 1904, entitled "Explorations in Northern Canada and adjacent portions of Greenland and Alaska". [116] That map showed the western boundary of Canada as being the 141st meridian of west longitude extending to the North Pole, and the eastern boundary as being the 60th meridian of west longitude extending also to the Pole and beginning at a point north of the 78th parallel between Ellesmere Island and Greenland. Interestingly enough, virtually all subsequent maps of the Arctic regions published by Canada showed those same meridians as international "boundaries". [117] The practice was continued in 1952

---

[115]   Gordon W. SMITH, *supra* note 104, at 26.
[116]   This appears to be the real origin of the Sector Theory rather than the intervention of Senator Poirier on February 20, 1907. However, in 1956, the Hon. Jean Lesage stated the relevant year to be 1903 rather than 1904. He also added that "it was not to show the boundaries of Canada. It was to show the lines within which the lands and the territorial waters around those lands were claimed by Canada ...", 98 *Can. H. C. Deb.*, No. 143, at 6358 (1956).
[117]   See in particular the following maps which are kept in the Public Archives at Ottawa: *Atlas of Canada No. 1 — Territorial Divisions* (1906); *Map of the Northwest Territories* (1924); *Map of the*

when, for the first time, the government published a map of Canada for the general public showing all of the Arctic regions, and the practice still continues to-day. It is not known why the sector in question is still shown on Canadian maps, unless it is to support a claim to water areas, for there has not been any serious question about Canada's sovereignty over any of the Arctic islands since Norway recognized that sovereignty over the Sverdrup Islands in 1930. In its Note of August 8, 1930, Norway emphasized "that their recognizance of the sovereignty of His Britannic Majesty over these islands is in no way based on any sanction whatever of what is named 'the sector principle'" [118] and there appears to be no doubt that the original intent behind the sector shown on the early maps starting in 1904 was to buttress Canada's claim to all the islands within that sector. More specifically it was to lend support to the expeditions of A. P. Low and of Capt. J. E. Bernier. The latter unveiled and deposited a plaque at Parry's Rock, on July 1, 1909, bearing the inscription:

> This Memorial is erected today to commemorate the taking possession for the DOMINION OF CANADA of the whole ARCTIC ARCHIPELAGO lying to the north of America from long. 60°W. to 141°W. up to latitude 90°N. Winter Har. Melville Island. CCS Arctic. July 1st 1909. J. E. Bernier. Commander. [119]

As explained by Captain Bernier himself, the purpose of this official taking of possession was to re-affirm Canada's sovereignty over the territory transferred to Canada by Great Britain in 1880. His own account of the ceremony reads:

> I briefly referred to the important event in connection with the granting to Canada by the Imperial government on September 1st, 1880, all the British *territory* in the northern waters of the continent of America and *Arctic Ocean*, from 60 degrees west longitude to 141 degrees west

---

Northwest Territories (1929); and *Map of the Northwest Territories and the Yukon* (1939) showing the "Arctic Islands Preserve" going up to the Pole.

[118] See *supra* note 111.

[119] See Photograph of plaque in J. E. BERNIER, *Master Mariner and Arctic Explorer,* at 128 (1939).

longitude, and as far north as 90 degrees, that is to say to
the North Pole. [120]

The Imperial Order-in-Council of July 31, 1880, referred to
by Bernier, transferred "all British territories and possessions
in North America, not already included within the Dominion
of Canada, and all islands adjacent to any of such territories
or possessions . . . with the exception of the Colony of Newfoundland and its dependencies". [121] The Order did not say
anything about territory in the Arctic Ocean, so Captain Bernier felt apparently that his reaffirmation of possession should
cover any such possible territory. The same possibility was
in the mind of the Minister of the Interior in 1925 when he
gave support to the sector theory.

On June 1, 1925, the Canadian Government introduced a
bill in the House of Commons amending the Northwest Territories Act to provide for the issuing of licences to scientists
and explorers wishing to enter the territories. The legislative
amendment was aimed specifically at the Byrd-MacMillan
Arctic hydroplane expedition, the purpose of which was to
verify rumours as to the existence of land in the Arctic Ocean
north of Canada. Rumours had circulated for years about
the possible existence of "Crocker Land" which Commander
Peary thought he had seen in the Arctic Ocean. [122] The
Honourable Charles Stewart, the Minister of the Interior who
moved second reading of the Bill, made quite clear that what
the government wanted to insure was sovereignty over land
within the "Canadian" sector. What follows is the exchange
which took place on this point:

> Mr. STEWART: Here we are getting after men like
> MacMillan and Doctor Amundsen, men who are going in
> presumably for exploration purposes, but possibly there may
> arise a question as to the sovereignty over some *land they
> may discover* in the northern portion of Canada, and we
> claim all that portion.

---

[120] *Ibid.*, at 344; emphasis added.
[121] *The Canada Gazette*, Vol. XIV, No. 15 (9 Oct. 1880).
[122] See D. H. DINWOODIE, "Arctic Controversy: the 1925 Byrd-
MacMillan Expedition Example", 53 *Canadian Historical Review* 51, at
52 and 59 (1972).

Mr. BROWN: We claim right up to the Pole.

Mr. STEWART: Yes, right up to the North Pole. [123]

On June 10th, when asked specifically about the Byrd-Mac-Millan expedition and precautions taken by Canada to protect its rights in the Arctic, the Minister gave the following answer:

> Indeed, I made the statement in the House the other evening that we claimed all the *territory* lying between meridians 60 and 141. This afternoon when dealing with the estimates of the Department of the Interior I propose to bring down a map to make it clear what precautions we are taking to establish ourselves in that *territory* . . . [124]

It should be obvious from what precedes that Canada was giving official support to the sector theory to assist in establishing her claim to territory of which she did not have quite full control or which she thought was perhaps yet undiscovered but contiguous to her northern coast and within the sector in question.

In 1926, a federal Order-in-Council established three preserves, one of which was the Arctic Islands Preserve. The descriptions reads. "Comprising all that tract of *land* which may be described as follows: [then follows a description which includes the sector between meridians 60 and 141]." [125] The Order prohibited persons, other than native born Indian and Eskimos and except with the permission of the R.C.M.P. Commissioner from hunting, trapping and trading in the areas in question. As may be seen from the description, there is no mention of water in the Order in question. The next pronouncement in the House of Commons on the sector theory came in 1938. When being asked if there was international recognition that Canada had "a sort of sovereignty over the triangle" in question, the Minister of Mines and Resources, Mr. Crerar, gave the following reply:

> Yes. What is known as the sector principle, in the determination of these areas is now very generally recog-

---

[123]   *Can. H. C. Deb.*, Vol. IV, at 3773 (1 June 1925); emphasis added.

[124]   *Ibid.*, at 4069 (10 June 1965); emphasis added.

[125]   Order in Council P.C. 1146 (19 July 1926); emphasis added.

> nized, and on the basis of that principle as well as our
> sovereignty extends right to the pole within the limits of
> the sector. My own view is that our supremacy there is
> established to a point where it could not be successfully
> challenged by any other country. [126]

The statement is broad enough to cover water as well as land,
but an examination of the whole exchange seems to indicate
that the members of Parliament and the Minister were thinking of land and islands, and not of water. Indeed, a specific
question was put on that occasion as to the sovereignty over
Wrangel Island.

In 1953, when moving second reading of the bill creating
a Department of Northern Affairs, Prime Minister St.-Laurent
made a fairly lengthy statement about the importance of
Canada's northern territories. After referring to the fact that
those territories were situated between the USSR and the
United States, he made the following statement: "We must
leave no doubt about our active occupation and exercise of
our sovereignty in these northern *lands* right up to the pole." [127]
It is quite obvious from a reading of the whole speech that
the Prime Minister had nothing else in mind but land. The
fact that there are no "lands right up to the pole" is no reason
to assume that he was talking about water and ice. There is
absolutely no reference to water or ice in the speech, but the
expressions "lands", "territories", "northern lands" and "northern territories" recur throughout. It seems that the Prime
Minister might have been carried away in his description of
the northern frontier, for he referred to "Quebec, which
reaches almost up to the north pole with its extended boundaries". [128] However, if this speech left any doubt as to whether
Canada claimed sovereignty over the ice and water areas,
such doubt was removed a few years later. In 1956, the
Honourable Jean Lesage, Minister of the new Department of
Northern Affairs, made the following statement, in answer to

---

[126]   *Can. H. C. Deb.*, Vol. III, at 3081 (1938).
[127]   96 *Can. H. C. Deb.*, Vol. I, at 700 (1953); reprinted in 6
External Affairs, at 16 (1954).
[128]   *Ibid.*, at 698.

a question about the "ownership of the ice cap north of the land area":

> We have never subscribed to the sector theory in application to the ice. We are content that our sovereignty exists over all the Arctic Islands .... To our mind the sea, be it frozen or in its natural liquid state, is the sea; and our sovereignty exists over the lands and over our territorial waters. [129]

The Minister then went on to emphasize that the "ice cap" in international law is high seas: "It is the high sea in frozen form. The ordinary laws of the high sea apply to high seas whether they be in liquid or frozen form." [130]

In 1957, after a change of government, former Minister Jean Lesage put the following question which was indirectly related to the sector theory: "Are the waters of the Arctic ocean north of the Arctic archipelago up to the north pole, in the so-called Canadian sector, Canadian waters ?" [131] The answer read by the new Minister, the Honourable Alvin Hamilton, was as follows:

> Mr. Speaker, the answer is that all the islands north of the mainland of Canada which comprise the Canadian Arctic archipelago are of course part of Canada. North of the limits of the archipelago, however, the position is complicated by unusual physical features. The Arctic ocean is covered for the most part of the year with polar pack ice having an average thickness of about eight feet. Leads of water do open up as a result of the pack ice being in continuous motion, but for practical purposes it might be said for the most part to be a permanently frozen sea. It will be seen, then, that the Arctic ocean north of the archipelago is not open water nor has it the stable qualities of land. Consequently the ordinary rules of international law may or may not have application. [132]

The least that can be said about this answer is that it is noncommittal. It cannot be considered as an application of the sector theory to ice or water.

---

[129] *Can. H. C. Deb.*, Vol. VII, at 6955 (1956).
[130] *Ibid.*, at 6956.
[131] *Can. H. C. Deb.*, at 1559 (1957).
[132] *Ibid.*

In 1958, Prime Minister Diefenbaker made a statement on the question of Canada's sovereignty in the Arctic which seemed to presuppose a reliance on the sector theory. When asked by the Leader of the Opposition, Mr. Pearson, what procedures had to be observed by Canadians visiting United States defence installations in the Canadian Arctic, he gave the following reply:

> When I became Prime Minister one of my first acts was to have this question looked into in detail, with a view to assuring that while we co-operate in defence willingly and freely, in no way shall our sovereignty be impeded or interfered with; and further than that, that everything that could possibly be done should be done to assure that our sovereignty to the North pole be asserted, and continually asserted, by Canada. [133]

This answer is not altogether free from ambiguity, since the defence installations in question were definitely located on land. Consequently, the sovereignty being asserted did not relate to water areas.

In 1964, the Minister of Northern Affairs was asked to assure the house "that the government of the United States recognizes Canada's title to all *islands* north of the mainland up to the north pole ?" [134] The Hon. Arthur Laing replied: "For some years now the present government and the previous governments have asserted our sovereignty over the *islands* extending northward [then follows a description of the sector] . . ." [135] This statement definitely invoked the sector theory, but only to circumscribe the northern islands over which Canada asserted sovereignty. This was the position taken also in a 1964 publication of the Canadian Government, entitled "The Boundaries of Canada, its Provinces and Territories", which contains numerous maps showing the sector right up to the Pole. [136] However, having referred to the statements of

---

[133] *Can. H. C. Deb.*, at 3652 (1958).
[134] *Can. H. C. Deb.*, Vol. VII, at 7657 (1964); emphasis added.
[135] *Ibid.*, emphasis added.
[136] Norman L. NICHOLSON, *The Boundaries of Canada, its Provinces and Territories*, at 42, published by the Department of Mines and Technical Surveys (1964).

the Hon. Stewart in 1925 and of the Right Hon. St.-Laurent in 1953, the following comment is made:

> Lines delimiting the sector have subsequently appeared on political maps of Canada published by the Federal Government. These it is presumed, however, should merely be regarded as lines of allocation, which are delimited through the high seas or unexplored areas for the purpose of allocating lands without conveying sovereignty over the high seas. [137]

The sector theory was then left dormant until awakened by the Right Hon. Diefenbaker in 1969, when he asked Prime Minister Trudeau: "Does the Prime Minister accept the sector principle, and if he does, and if that is still the policy of the government of Canada, then waterways are in the same position as islands and other lands ?" [138]

The reply given by the Prime Minister was:

> Mr. Speaker, I do not have the same understanding of this as the right hon. gentleman. I believe the sector theory applies to the seabed and the shelf. It does not apply to the waters. The continental shelf is of course under Canadian sovereignty — this is the seabed, but not the waters over the shelf. [139]

He added later on, in the same exchange: "My assertion of the sector theory would apply to the seabed, not to the waters or ice." [140] It is therefore quite clear that the Trudeau government does not subscribe to the sector theory to claim sovereignty over water and ice. Indeed, the evidence just examined would indicate that the sector theory never did receive specific application to water and ice areas by the responsible ministers or the Prime Ministers of Canada. [141]

---

[137] *Ibid.*, at 44.
[138] *Can. H. C. Deb.*, Vol. VI, at 6396 (1969).
[139] *Ibid.*
[140] *Ibid.*
[141] The only Prime Minister who defined the Canadian Arctic as including "the frozen sea north of the mainland between the meridians of its east and west boundaries, extended to the North Pole", is Pearson. He did not make that statement as Prime Minister, but did so when he wrote an article in his personal capacity at the time he was Canadian ambassador to the United States. See L. B. PEARSON, "Canada Looks Down North", 24 *Foreign Affairs* 638 (1946).

CONCLUSION ON THE NORTHWEST PASSAGE

The above survey of Canada's maritime activities in the Arctic and its use of the sector theory in relation to water areas in that region is admittedly quite insufficient to form a definite opinion as to whether Canada could claim the waters of the Canadian Arctic Archipelago as historic waters. This would require a complete study of all relevant archival and governmental documents, both British and Canadian, going back some four hundred years. It would appear, however, on the basis of the present study, that Canada might have considerable difficulty in establishing the two basic requirements for a historic title, namely: the assertion and exercise of exclusive jurisdiction for a long period of time and the acquiescence by foreign states in that jurisdiction. Reliance on the sector theory would be particularly difficult, since at least two Arctic states have expressed opposition to the theory in question. In 1930, when Norway recognized Canada's sovereignty over the Sverdrup Islands, it did so with the express *caveat* that its recognition was "in no way based on any sanction whatever of what is named 'the sector principle' ". [142] As for the United States, they have expressed their opposition to the application of the sector theory to the Arctic as well as the Antarctic. In 1929, when someone suggested that the Arctic should be partitioned into five national sectors, the Secretary of the Navy expressed his disapproval and stated, in particular, that the proposed sector division "is in effect a claim of sovereignty over high seas, which are universally recognized as free to all nations, and is a novel attempt to create artificially a closed sea and thereby infringe the rights of all nations to the free use of this area". [143] The United States' position on the sector theory was reiterated in 1959, before Lt. Cmdr. C. Fry left for the North Pole with the nuclear submarine *Skate*. The letter addressed to him by the Assistant Legal Adviser of the State Department specified that ". . . the United States has not recognized (the so-called 'Sector Prin-

---

142   CANADA, *Treaty Series* 1930, No. 17 (1931).
143   Letter from the Secretary of the Navy (Adams) to the Secretary of State (Stimson), 23 Sept. 1929, M.S. Department of State, file 800.014 Arctic/26, quoted in 1 HACKWORTH, *Digest of Int'l Law*, at 463-4 (1940).

ciple') as a valid principle for claiming jurisdiction"; [144] it seems clear that the jurisdiction in question related to the Arctic Ocean. Further evidence of the American opposition to the sector theory is found in an official interpretation of the U.S.-Russian boundary convention of 1867, given by the State Department in 1965. Since that convention has been invoked, mainly by Soviet jurists, as a legal basis for dividing the Ocean into sectors, the full passage of the Department's interpretation is reproduced here:

> It should be noted that the original Convention language stated that the line "proceeds thence due north, without limitation, into the same Frozen Ocean." Since the United States does not support so-called "sector claims" in the polar regions, the northernmost point for the representation of the Convention line was agreed to be 72°00′N. Furthermore, in keeping with the policy that the line does not constitute a boundary, the standard symbol for the representation of an international boundary should never be used. Furthermore, labelling of the line as "U.S.-Russia Convention of 1867" is recommended. [145]

This interpretation is consistent with the view that most lines drawn in water areas in boundary treaties "are not boundaries between waters under the jurisdiction of the contracting parties, but a cartographic device to simplify description of land areas involved . . . ." [146] The basis for fixing 72°00′N. as the northernmost point is not mentioned, but a study of the map shows that the point is just north of Wrangel and Herald islands on the Soviet side of the boundary line.

Consonant with this position, the United States did not hesitate to exercise criminal jurisdiction in 1970, when a homicide took place on Ice Island T-3 located within the "Canadian" sector north of the Canadian Arctic Archipelago. [147] True, the opposition to the sector theory manifested thus far

---

[144]   See 2 WHITEMAN, *Digest of Int'l Law,* at 1268 (1963).

[145]   U.S. DEPARTMENT OF STATE (Bureau of Intelligence and Research), *International Boundary Study No. 14 (Revised),* (1 October 1965).

[146]   S. W. BOGGS, "Delimitation of Seaward Areas under National Jurisdiction", 45 *A.J.I.L.* 240, Note 2, (1951).

[147]   See *infra* Part V, section III, "The Escamilla Case".

has been a general one and did not relate specifically to the application of the theory to the waters of the Canadian Arctic Archipelago only. However, the disapproval of the theory was originally directed at its application to the islands of the archipelago and there is no apparent reason to suppose that the same disapproval would not hold when the theory is applied to the waters between the islands. [148]

---

[148] It is interesting to note, however, that Professor Morin believes that the sector theory, though not valid to claim jurisdiction over the Arctic Ocean, could be invoked in respect of the waters of the archipelago. See J.-Y. MORIN, "Le progrès technique, la pollution et l'évolution récente du droit de la mer au Canada, particulièrement à l'égard de l'Arctique", 8 C.Y.I.L. 158, at 240 (1970).

PART IV

Freedom of the Seas in the Arctic Ocean

When the rules of international law relating to the high seas were codified in 1958, the term "high seas" was defined in the Convention on the High Seas as meaning "all parts of the sea that are not included in the territorial sea or in the internal waters of a state" (Art. 1). The provisions of the Convention are stated to be generally declaratory of established principles of international law and they are of general application. This does not mean, however, that all states and international lawyers agree as to its application to all seas. Furthermore, no reference to the Arctic Ocean can be found in the deliberations of the International Law Commission, nor in those of the Geneva Conference of 1958. One may, therefore, wonder if the Arctic Ocean does really come within the scope of the Convention; there is no doubt that it does pose a problem of definition because of the presence of ice and, consequently, some writers and commentators have suggested that the principle of the freedom of the seas is not applicable. The answer will depend mainly on the possibility of navigation, since this is the underlying reason for the very existence of the principle involved, and on the attitude of the Arctic states themselves. Consequently, this subject will be treated under the following headings: I — the problem viewed by writers; II — a physical description of the Arctic Ocean; III — the possibility of navigation; and IV — the attitude of Arctic states and the legal status of the Arctic Ocean.

I. — THE PROBLEM VIEWED BY WRITERS

In discussing the legal status of the Arctic Ocean, international lawyers have characterized the presence of ice in various ways: immobile ice, "territoire glaciaire", permanent ice, "glaces éternelles", polar ice cap, quasi-land, quasi-fixed mass, and so on. These expressions have been taken from the writings of those who maintain that the principle of freedom of the seas is not applicable to the Arctic Ocean. Some have even asserted that territorial acquisition is possible over ice in somewhat the same way as over land, while others have contended that the adjacent Arctic states ought to exercise at least some form of national jurisdiction and control.

In 1904, Rolland discussed the legal status of coastal ice, beyond the territorial waters of Alaska, on which a gambling house had been established so as to escape the territorial application of American gambling laws. He obviously considered the ice in question to be permanent, since he specified: "Nous ne nous occupons actuellement que des glaces qui ne disparaissent point." [1] Such permanent and immobile coastal ice was regarded as a mere extension of the land, and he characterized it as "territoire glaciaire"; logically enough, he felt that the coastal state had complete territorial jurisdiction over such ice, since there had been acquisition by accession. In fairness to Rolland, it must be conceded that little was known about the real nature of the ice in the Arctic Ocean at that time. Given the assumption that the ice in question was permanent, Rolland's legal reasoning was perfectly acceptable; but the fact is that the ice north of Alaska is far from being permanent, and the waters are quite navigable for about three months of the year.

An opinion which went much beyond that of Rolland was subsequently expressed by Waultrin, who seemed to have proceeded on the assumption that the whole of the Arctic Ocean could be assimilated to land. [2] In 1925, Fauchille still apparently believed that permanent ice existed at the North Pole, and he adopted Rolland's characterization of "territoire glaciaire". He was accordingly of the opinion that the polar regions were susceptible of appropriation by the traditional mode of occupation; [3] he did concede, however, that it would be an occupation by exploitation rather than by habitation.

---

[1]   L. ROLLAND, "Maison de jeu établie sur les glaces au delà de la limite des eaux territoriales", *Revue générale de droit international public,* at 342 (1904).
[2]   René WAULTRIN, "Le problème de la souveraineté des pôles", *Revue générale de droit international public,* at 649 (1909).
[3]   FAUCHILLE, I *Traité de Droit international public,* at 16-17 and 652-653 (1925).

The following year, Professor Korovin wrote that the 1926 Decree of the USSR, claiming sovereignty over lands and islands north of its territory, ought to be interpreted as including "ice formation and the seas surrounding them". [4] Sigrist followed with a similar view when he said: "We refuse to admit any legal difference between frozen land and immobile ice . . ." [5] Verdross was apparently of the same opinion when he asserted that the principle of effective occupation was also applicable to what he described as "territoires glaciaires constitués d'eau devenue solide par les glaces éternelles qui la recouvrent". [6] Lakhtine, who systematized the sector theory, also maintained that "floating ice should be assimilated legally to open polar seas, whilst ice formations that are more or less immovable should enjoy a legal status equivalent to polar territory". [7] As late as 1935, Genet argued that not only were the floating icebergs susceptible of acquisition by occupation but so were the frozen areas of the Poles which have all of the characteristics of territory. [8]

In 1945, Professor Hyde devoted a considerable number of pages to the question of the "Acquisition of Sovereignty over Polar Areas"; [9] he asserted flatly that "whether the polar areas as such may be subjected to rights of sovereignty appears no longer to be a moot question. States are in fact asserting that they may be; and that is decisive." [10] One might at first think that Hyde had mainly in mind the Antarctic continent, but he made it quite clear later that his statement was meant to encompass the Arctic regions, including water areas covered with ice. "It is not apparent", he stated, "why the character

---

[4] KOROVIN, "S.S.S.R. i Poliarnye Zemli", 3 *Sovetskoye Pravo*, at 45-46 (1926), cited by TARACOUZIO, in *Soviets in the Arctic*, at 348 (1938).

[5] SIGRIST, "Rabochii Sud", at 984 (1928), cited by Taracouzio, *supra* note 4.

[6] VERDROSS, "Règles générales du Droit international de la paix", 30 *Recueil des Cours*, at 368 (1929).

[7] LAKHTINE, "Rights over the Arctic", 24 *A.J.I.L.*, at 712 (1930).

[8] R. GENEST, "Notes sur l'acquisition par occupation et le droit des gens traditionnel", 15 *Revue de droit international et de législation comparée*, at 436 (1934).

[9] HYDE, I *International Law*, at 347-355 (1945).

[10] *Ibid.*, at 347.

of the substance which constituted the habitual surface above that level (of the sea) or its lack of permanent connection with what is immovable, should necessarily be decisive of the susceptibility to a claim of sovereignty of the area concerned."[11] In other words, sovereignty could be claimed over ice, even when not attached to land. In a footnote at this point, Hyde refers to a statement made by a State Department official in 1937 to the effect that sovereignty could not be claimed over areas in the North Pole region since there was "nothing but open sea, filled most of the time with large ice floes". [12] Professor Hyde gave two reasons for assimilating ice to land: first, the surface is "sufficiently solid to enable man to pursue his occupations thereon"; and second, "its solidity and permanence constitutes in itself a barrier to navigation as it is normally enjoyed in the open sea". [13] These are serious reasons and their validity will be examined during the course of this study.

In 1958 Professor Maxwell Cohen conceded that the Beaufort Sea and Western Arctic Ocean were high seas but felt that, for the greater part, the "polar ice cap" constituted "a quasi-fixed mass equivalent in its usefulness for bases and for temporary habitation to the northernmost lands of the Arctic themselves". [14] Cohen emphasized that "this ice cap represents a kind of quasi-land for all purposes of peaceful or military use"; [15] consequently, he contended that Canada ought to assert jurisdiction over its sector of the "ice cap" as well as over the waters beneath. In 1961, a law specialist in the U.S. Navy Department contended that the Arctic "ice pack" was "subject to occupation and usage very similar to that of certain land areas". [16] He concluded by suggesting that the United States ought to give horizontal recognition to the sector theory covering the "ice pack", but continue to consider the

---

11   *Ibid.*, at 348.
12   *Ibid.*, at 348, note 5.
13   *Ibid.*, at 348.
14   Maxwell COHEN, "Polar Ice and Arctic Sovereignty", 73 *Saturday Night*, No. 18, at 36 (30 Aug. 1958).
15   *Ibid.*
16   Ben PARTRIDGE, "The White Shelf: A Study of Arctic Ice Jurisdiction", 87 *U.S. Naval Institute Proceedings*, No. 9, at 55 (1961).

air space above and seas below as being free for use by all nations. The relevant passage reads as follows:

> Since there appears to be no logically defensible basis for blindly continuing to maintain that the Arctic ice pack is not in any respect subject to any form of national sovereignty, it would appear proper, reasonable, and in consonance with our national interests for the United States to recognize the validity of the sector principle of Arctic sovereignty, but to limit such recognition to the horizontal strata of the permanent polar ice pack. The seas below (the low seas, if you wish), the air space above the Arctic ice pack, and the adjacent open ocean areas are clearly navigable and should continue to be considered res communis for the use of the trade and commerce of all nations. [17]

Partridge's idea is original and provides a simple solution to the problem; its possible implementation becomes very doubtful, however, when the physical characteristics of the "ice pack" are examined.

As recently as 1970, Professor Douglas Johnston described the Arctic Ocean in the following terms:

> The Arctic Ocean is largely hypothetical, a peculiar combination of hypothetical waters and hypothetical islands, the distinction mostly covered over by large masses of ice. If international lawyers are prepared to give full weight to the ice factor in the treatment of sovereignty claims to hypothetical islands, they should be ready to question the mechanical application of the freedom of the high seas to hypothetical waters. [18]

It should not be concluded from the above that the majority of writers do not view the Arctic Ocean as high seas or believe in the possibility of acquiring sovereignty over the pack ice. Indeed, the opposite is perhaps true. Even after Commander Peary was able to reach the North Pole on foot,

---

[17] *Ibid.*, at 57.

[18] D. M. JOHNSTON, "The Arctic Marine Environment: A Managerial Perspective", in L. M. Alexander (ed.), *Proceedings of the Fifth Conference of the Law of the Sea Institute,* at 315 (1970).

Scott [19] and Balch [20] maintained that acquisition of sovereignty ought not to apply to moving ice. They were followed by Clute, a Canadian lawyer, who was quite emphatic that "the term 'freedom of the open sea' is as applicable to the Arctic as to the Atlantic, Pacific or Indian Oceans". [21] Subsequent authors, who have studied the question and maintained that the character of "high seas" applies to the Arctic Ocean, include Smedal, [22] Vallaux, [23] Taracouzio, [24] McKitterick, [25] Dollot, [26] Svarlien, [27] Frazier, [28] Head, [29] Mouton [30] and Morin [31].

This brief review of opinion indicates that international lawyers are somewhat divided as to the legal status of the Arctic Ocean, and it would appear that the division of opinion is partially caused by differing appreciations of the nature of that ocean. An inquiry into the physical reality of the Arctic Ocean should be helpful in determining what should be its legal regime.

---

[19]   J. B. SCOTT, "Arctic Exploration and International Law", 3 *A.J.I.L.* 928-941, at 928 (1909).
[20]   T. W. BALCH, "The Arctic and Antarctic Regions and the Law of Nations", 4 *A.J.I.L.* 265-275, at 266 (1910).
[21]   A. R. CLUTE, "The Ownership of the North Pole", *Can. Bar Rev.* 19-26, at 21 (1927).
[22]   Gustav SMEDAL, *De l'Acquisition de souveraineté sur les territoires polaires* (translation), at 44 (1932).
[23]   C. VALLAUX, "Droit et prétentions politiques sur les régions polaires", *Affaires Etrangères,* 14-33, at 26 (1932).
[24]   TARACOUZIO, *Soviets in the Arctic,* at 359 (1938).
[25]   T. E. M. McKITTERICK, "The Validity of Territorial and Other Claims in Polar Regions", 21 *J. of the Soc. of Comp. Leg.* 89-97, at 95 (1939).
[26]   René DOLLOT, "Le Droit international des espaces polaires", 75 *Recueil des Cours,* 118-200, at 125 (1949, II).
[27]   Oscar SVARLIEN, "The Legal Status of the Arctic", *Proc. Amer. Soc. Int'l L.* 136-143, at 142 (1958); by the same author, "The Sector Principle in Law and Practice", *The Polar Record,* No. 66, 248-263, at 257 and 261 (1960).
[28]   Cmdr. Paul FRAZIER, USN, in *Proc. Amer. Soc. Int'l L.,* at 164 (1958).
[29]   Ivan L. HEAD, "Canadian Claims to Territorial Sovereignty in the Arctic Regions", 9 *McGill L.J.,* 200-226, at 223-224 (1962-1963).
[30]   M. W. MOUTON, "The International Regime of the Polar Regions", 107 *Recueil des Cours,* at 201 (1962, III).
[31]   J. Y. MORIN, "Le progrès technique, la pollution et l'évolution récente du droit de la mer au Canada, particulièrement à l'égard de l'Arctique", 8 *C.Y.I.L.* 158, at 238 (1970).

II. — PHYSICAL DESCRIPTION OF THE ARCTIC OCEAN

The Polar regions, the Arctic and the Antarctic, have sometimes been treated together when discussing the applicability of legal principles to certain national claims over those regions. It is submitted, however, that the two regions in question are sufficiently different to warrant completely separate treatment. Not only are the Arctic and the Antarctic located at opposite ends of our planet, but they are essentially opposite in their very nature: whereas the Antarctic is a continent surrounded by a vast maritime belt, the Arctic is an ocean surrounded by a vast and nearly continuous continental belt. The North Pole rests on 4300 meters of water[32] covered by moving ice about 3 meters thick, whereas the South Pole rests on nearly 3300 meters of land covered by a solid ice cap which may be 1500 meters thick. By way of further contrast, it might also be mentioned that the Antarctic is about twice as cold as the Arctic. [33]

The Arctic Ocean has remained a great mystery until recent times, but the last two decades have witnessed very considerable progress: the unknown ocean has become one of the most studied in the world and is gradually revealing its secrets to scientists. Some of the data obtained will be mentioned here, since they constitute relevant facts to be considered when examining the possibility of exercising the various freedoms of the high seas. Thus, the water masses and the pack ice become important considerations.

1. THE WATER MASSES

The water masses under the ice cover are basically the same as in any other ocean. True there is an undersea mountain extending from the New Siberian Islands to Ellesmere

---

[32] M. M. DE LEEUW, "New Canadian Bathymetric Charts of the Western Arctic Ocean", 14 *Deep Sea Research*, at 501 (Oct. 1967).

[33] A temperature of −105°F. was recorded at the South Pole during the International Geophysical Year of 1957-58, whereas it very seldom gets below −50°F. in the Arctic; see E. R. POUNDER, *The Physics of Ice*, at 31 (1965). In August 1958, the captain of the *Nautilus* recorded the water temperature precisely at the North Pole at 32.4°F.; see Wm. R. ANDERSON, *Nautilus 90° North*, at 224 (1959).

Island, and the sea floor reveals a physiographic complex of basins and ridges, but there is nonetheless a displacement of water masses as in other oceans, although probably to a lesser degree. There are three main water masses, the divisions of which are based essentially on temperature differences.

The surface layer (Arctic water), going to a depth of about 200 meters, registers a variable temperature "from −1.4°C at the end of summer to −1.7°C at the end of winter". [34] As a result of the melting and freezing of the pack ice, the surface layer is said to be "the most variable of the water masses". [35] The phenomenon is described as follows: "With the summer melt, warm water of low salinity will often form an irregular layer less than 1 meter thick beneath the ice pack. This melt water mixes downward with agitation of the ice pack and eventually re-freezes in winter." [36] Within this surface water mass may be inserted a thin interlayer of Pacific waters which comes into the Arctic Basin from the Bering Strait. This quantity of warm water (−0.7°C) is so small, however, that it does not appreciably affect the temperature of the Arctic water.

The middle layer (Atlantic water) extends to a depth of about 900 meters and is the warmest of the three water masses, "with a temperature above 0°C and occasionally as high as +1°C". [37]

The bottom layer, going down to the ocean floor, is generally colder than the middle layer; the temperature on the Atlantic side of the Lomonosov ridge is −0.70° to −0.80°C, whereas it is −0.30° to −0.40°C on the Pacific side.

The water masses of the Arctic Ocean also affect those of adjacent seas. [38] There is a small inflow of surface water from the Bering Sea, and a considerable inflow of Atlantic

---

[34]   I FAIRBRIDGE, *Encyclopedia of Oceanography*, at 53 (1966).
[35]   *Ibid.*
[36]   *Ibid.*
[37]   *Ibid.*
[38]   For a description of the water budget of the Arctic Ocean, see Hakon MOSBY, in *Proceedings of the Arctic Basin Symposium*, at 70-76 (1963).

and bottom water from the Norwegian Sea. The outflow of water is mainly through the East Greenland Current which accounts for nearly two-thirds of the total outflow; most of the balance of the outflow takes place through the Canadian archipelago and Robeson Channel between Ellesmere Island and Greenland. This communication of water masses, accompanied by current and wind, affects the ice on top, as will presently be seen.

2. THE PACK ICE

The pack ice consists of ice floes averaging about 3 meters thick and covering approximately 90% of the Arctic Ocean; the floes or fragments of ice are generally in close contact. However, the ice within the pack is not compact, uniform, permanent or immobile.

The ice is not compact. — The misnomer "ice cap", or even the more accurate expression "pack ice", would seem to indicate that the ice is compact in nature, but this is not the case. The ice floes are neither firmly packed nor joined together but are separated by a number of leads or polynyas, which resemble lakes of open water. Burkhanov, of the Northern Sea Route Authority of the USSR, gives the following description of the Arctic pack ice:

> The ice-cover of the Central Arctic is not a continuous massif of old ice. On the contrary, the ice is inhomogeneous. It consists of icefields and fragments of different thickness and age, with open leads between all the mobile floes, no matter what their thickness, degree of hummocking, geographical position, or season of the year. [39]

The presence of large leads in the pack ice, even in the vicinity of the North Pole, is amply confirmed by the captain of the *Skate,* who described the surfacing of his submarine in August 1958 in the following terms:

> Only 40 miles from the North Pole we found the largest polynya of our cruise — nearly half a mile in diameter.

---

[39] V. F. BURKHANOV, "Soviet Arctic Research", translated from *Priroda* 5, at 21-30 (1957) by E. R. Hope, Defence Research Board of Canada, T 265 R (Nov. 1957).

> We surfaced in it easily, with the feeling of release from
> unbearable confinement. It was clear that the North Pole
> area did have some large lakes after all. [40]

These leads tend to freeze over but the thickness of the ice
does not prevent surfacing by nuclear submarines such as the
Skate. In 1959, for the first time in history, a submarine
surfaced at the North Pole in the middle of winter; in fact,
the *Skate* surfaced twice in March of that year. "The lead",
said Cmdr. Calvert, "was narrow and heavily hummocked on
either side, wandering into the blowing snow like a meander-
ing creek for the quarter of a mile or so I could see." [41] This
description shows that, even in winter, large openings may be
found within the Arctic pack. In April 1967, an 8-man expedition, trying to reach the North Pole by skimobile, was stopped
for five days by a big lead north of Ellesmere Island; they
finally crossed it after it had frozen over to a depth of a few
inches. [42] The visual ice reconnaissance flights, carried out
practically on a year-round basis by the United States, make
it possible to estimate the size and frequency of water openings
in the pack ice; [43] these water openings account for roughly
10% of the surface and are so numerous in summer that the
Arctic Ocean really becomes marine in character. In the words
of Horace Wilson, a Canadian meteorologist, "[d]uring the
summer, when the Arctic pack is broken into floes, the Arctic
Ocean becomes dominantly marine in character with a highly
absorbent surface . . ." [44]

---

[40]   Cmdr. James CALVERT, USN, *Surface at the Pole*, at 127
(1960).

[41]   *Ibid.*, at 182.

[42]   See "Destination North Pole", *CBC Special Report*, 7 February
1968. The expedition, led by Ralph S. Plaisted, travelled some 216 miles
in 37 days but had to abandon at 83°36′N., 384 miles from the Pole.
Finally, the Plaisted Expedition reached the North Pole on 19 April
1968, after covering 413 nautical miles from its base camp at Ward
Hunt Island; the expedition had taken 44 days and driven 825 statute
miles in snowmobiles. See *Newsletter of Arctic Institute of North America*, No. 4, at 4 (June 1968).

[43]   See W. I. WITTMANN of U.S. Oceanographic Office, in *Proceedings of the Arctic Basin Symposium*, at 228 (1963).

[44]   Horace P. WILSON, "Notes on Arctic Weather", *ibid.*, at 257
(1963).

The ice is neither uniform nor permanent. — Although the average thickness of ice floes throughout the pack is about 3 meters, the thickness of individual ice floes may vary considerably, depending on a number of factors such as location, temperature and wind. Dr. E. R. Pounder, director of the McGill Ice Research Project, puts it thus: "There are, of course, considerable variations from the average thickness of 3.5 m. quoted, because of climatic conditions, effect of rafting, and so on — ice floes over 5 m thick are found frequently." [45] This is particularly the case with the hummocked type of ice floe which is caused by fracturing and pressure ridging, due to the action of strong current and wind. But the thickness of an individual ice floe is normally the result of a process of accretion and ablation. Observations have shown that melting and freezing takes place both at the top and the bottom of the ice; in summer, there is ablation by melting of the upper surface and, in winter, there is accretion of the lower surface by freezing. Dr. Untersteiner shows how, in normal conditions, an individual ice floe attains an equilibrium thickness during the course of a year. [46] The process is repeated every year, and the ice is thereby not only rejuvenated but renewed periodically; consequently, it is not possible to speak of permanent ice or to estimate its age by density. The floes of the pack ice are more than a year old but they are far from being permanent ice; the most that can be said about permanency is that there exists an area in the Arctic Ocean where ice is permanently present. The outer rim of that area is normally referred to as the "approximate limit of permanent polar ice" or "approximate limit of pack ice in August". Furthermore, any discussion of permanency, density and age of the ice must also take into account the possibility of ice floes being crushed on the spot or drifting away outside the Arctic Ocean. The possibility of an ice floe being crushed on the spot appeared very real indeed to Bjorn Staib, who tried to reach the North Pole on skis and dog sled in 1964. Explaining how his expedition had been forced to retreat by an "icequake" at 86°31′N.,

---

[45]   E. R. POUNDER, *The Physics of Ice,* at 29 (1965).
[46]   See *supra* note 43, at 220 (1963), where Dr. N. Untersteiner of the University of Vienna describes the ice budget of the Arctic Ocean.

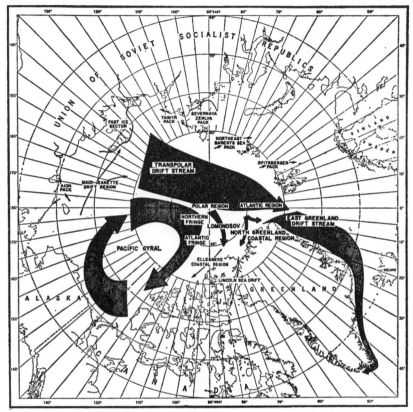

Reproduced from Proceedings of the Arctic Basin Symposium, at 92 (1963),
published by the Arctic Institute of North America.

FIGURE 6.   MAJOR DRIFTS OF POLAR ICE (Dunbar and Wittman, 1963).

he wrote: "Our floe, no more than 60 by 100 feet, clearly was
going. The edges had crumbled badly, and the tilting continued. Once it slipped down among the neighbouring blocks,
it would be ground to porridge in an instant." [47] The other possibility, that of drifting out of the Arctic Ocean and melting
away completely, is also very real because of the mobility of
the ice.

The ice is actually mobile. — The ice floes are not only
in constant motion locally but also move around all over the

---

[47]   B. O. STAIB, "North toward the Pole on Skis", 127 *National
Geographic Magazine*, at 254 (1965).

Arctic Ocean, a considerable proportion being carried outside completely. The ice circulation pattern of the Arctic Ocean is characterized by two basic or dominant movements or drifts. The more important one is the *transpolar drift* (Figure 6), which carries ice from the general area of the East Siberian Sea, passing across the North Pole itself and continuing between Spitzbergen and Greenland; [48] the other major ice circulation follows an anticyclonic or clockwise movement north of Alaska and the Canadian Arctic Archipelago, and is called the Pacific gyral. These two main circulation movements are not absolutely constant and independent from each other, and there are numerous local circulation patterns which keep the ice floes in constant movement. Ice drift depends mainly on wind but also on current, as well as the type of ice in the immediate vicinity and the number and size of leads; consequently ice floes and ice islands do not always follow the patterns of circulation expected of them. Most of the ice export takes place through the Greenland Sea, but an appreciable amount goes through the numerous sounds of the Canadian archipelago. The rate of speed at which the Arctic ice floes move has been estimated by the drifting stations as varying between 1.2 to 4.0 nautical miles per day. [49] The whole question of ice movement in the Arctic Ocean has been the subject of intense study by the Soviet and the American drifting stations. The activities of those stations will now be reviewed briefly in discussing the possibility of navigation.

III. — THE POSSIBILITY OF NAVIGATION

Three types of navigation will be discussed: 1 — drift surface navigation, 2 — subsurface navigation, and 3 — conventional surface navigation.

1. DRIFT SURFACE NAVIGATION

This type of surface navigation is accomplished by drifting either in an ice-bound vessel or on an ice floe (or ice island),

---

[48]   See DUNBAR and WITTMANN, "Some Features of Ice Movement in the Arctic Basin", *supra* note 43, at 90 (1963). This article describes the ice circulation patterns, the speed of drift and the factors affecting ice movement.
    [49]   *Ibid.*, at 93.

the aim of such unconventional navigation being essentially scientific. So far, it has served for the study of ice movements and currents in the Arctic Ocean, for meteorological and oceanographic observations, and for geophysical investigation of the ocean floor.

(1) Drifting ship stations

The idea of investigating the pattern of ice movement in the Arctic by setting up drifting stations is quite old. In 1893, Nansen was the first to organize a successful drifting station by letting his specially-made ship, the *Fram*, drift in pack ice from the Laptev Sea across the Arctic Ocean right up to Spitzbergen. [50] This voyage, which lasted 35 months, proved that there was a strong transpolar drift stream on the Russian side of the Pole in the direction of the Greenland Sea.

In 1922, [51] having already succeeded in navigating the passages on either side of the North Pole, Amundsen decided to explore unknown parts of the Arctic Ocean and spent two years drifting aboard the *Maud*, a ship designed after the rounded hull concept of the *Fram*. He started on the west coast of Alaska, crossing the Chukchi Sea north of Wrangel Island and ending at the New Siberian Islands.

A Soviet ship, the *Sedov*, was the only other ship organized as a drifting station. This was done in 1937, after it became ice-bound in the Laptev Sea. It drifted for over two years across the Arctic Ocean, following roughly the same path

---

[50]   For a map of the major drifts of vessels and ice islands until 1958 see *Oceanographic Atlas of the Polar Seas*, Part II, Arctic, at 13 (1958). Nansen had concluded that there was a transpolar current, after the relics of the *Jeannette* were found off the coast of Greenland. The *Jeannette* became ice-bound in the Chukchi Sea and drifted north of the East Siberian Sea, where it was crushed by the ice. Nansen avoided this danger by designing a rounded hull which forced the ice floes to deflect downward beneath the keel and raised the ship instead of crushing it.

[51]   Before 1922, there were two other drift ships: the *Karluk* and the *St. Anna*. The *Karluk* was beset by ice north of Alaska in 1913 and drifted westward as far as Herald Island in the Chukchi Sea, where it was crushed. In the same year, the *St. Anna* drifted from the southern portion of Kara Sea northward, around Novaya Zemlya, as far as Franz Josef Land.

as that of the *Fram*, terminating its voyage close to Spitzbergen. Nansen's transpolar drift theory was thus definitely confirmed.

For a number of years the U.S. Navy planned to embed a ship in the polar ice of the Arctic Ocean and studied the best place to launch it, having regard to the drift paths followed by previous drift ships and ice stations. [52] The launching has not yet taken place, however, and the present status of the project is unknown to the writer.

(2) *Drifting ice stations*

The USSR and the United States have been actively engaged in drift surface navigation on ice stations for a long time. The history of the Soviet drifting stations covers more than twenty-five years, during which time Soviet scientists have collected information from most of the Arctic Ocean; they have manned over 20 such ice ships so far, and have covered more than 50,000 kilometers. The first drifting ice station was established on May 21, 1937 by I. D. Papanine who was dropped on an ice floe, along with three compatriots, at 89°55′N. and 78°40′W., close to the North Pole; the station drifted for 274 days before Papanine and his men were picked up by the Soviet ship *Murman* in the Greenland Sea. In 1962, Gordienko, of the Soviet Arctic and Antarctic Research Institute, summarized the activities of the ice stations during their twenty-five years of operation. His table entitled "Data on Drifting Scientific Stations in the Arctic Basin up to April 1, 1962" [53] gives the following information for the first 10 stations: the duration of the drift, the distance covered by the drift, and the rate of the drift per day. The second drift station was not launched until 1950 and the third one until 1954; since then, however, it seems that the Soviets have launched one every year. Gordienko has also prepared a map showing the drift course followed by the first 10 Soviet stations. [54]

---

[52]   See W. I. WITTMANN et al., *Proposed Arctic Drift Ship Station Study*, Report No. 19-61, UNPUBLISHED MANUSCRIPT (June 1965).
[53]   See N. A. OSTENSO (ed.), *Problems of the Arctic and Antarctic No. 11*, Leningrad (1962); English translation, at b-4 (1966).
[54]   *Ibid.*, at b-7, for map entitled "Drift course of Soviet 'North Pole' stations" (1937-1962).

American drifting stations have been operating in the Arctic Ocean since 1952. The U.S. Air Force had spotted the first ice island five years earlier but did not accupy it until April 1952; known as T-3, or Fletcher's Ice Island, [55] it has been drifting ever since except for a year and a half when it was grounded north of Alaska. The Americans have operated at least seven drifting ice stations, two of which were ice islands, and five ordinary ice floes.

In 1966, Louis O. Quam, Director of the Earth Sciences Division of the U.S. Naval Research Office, made a review of the research arctivities carried on by American scientists on drifting ice stations; he shows the drift paths followed by the two major stations, both of which were ice islands. [56] Fletcher's Ice Island, first spotted in 1947 north of the Canadian archipelago, has drifted 2½ times around the "Pacific Gyral" in 20 years; the ice island is still operated as a drift station and, in 1967, some 40 scientists and technicians were reported working on the island. [57] The other station, Arlis II, was operated continuously for four years but had to be abandoned when it drifted into the Greenland Sea; it had covered more than 4300 nautical miles during its drift across the Arctic Ocean. [58]

It should be noted that these drift stations are being operated by the U.S. Office of Naval Research through the Arctic Research Laboratory at Point Barrow, Alaska. Mr. Quam explains the main purpose of this research program as follows:

> The Navy scientists sought two important benefits from research in the Arctic Ocean: (1) to develop a method for forecasting the extent, character, and movement of the pack ice, which severely hampered passage of the ships

---

[55]   "T-3" indicates that it was the third target (ice island) spotted by radar. Lt.-Col. J. O. Fletcher was the Air Force officer in charge of the first group to land on and occupy the ice island.

[56]   See map in *Naval Research reviews*, at 13 (Oct. 1966).

[57]   The *Polar Times*, at 12 (Dec. 1967).

[58]   For a review of the activities on and the drift paths of ice islands T-3 and Arlis II, see John F. SCHINDLER, "The Impact of Ice Islands — The Story of Arlis II and Fletcher's Ice Island, T-3, since 1962", in John E. SATER (Coord. by), *Arctic Drifting Stations* 49-78 (1968).

that resupplied the Naval Petroleum Reserve camp and (2) to explore the possibility of utilizing submarines in the deep Arctic Basin. [59]

In other words, the idea was to develop surface and sub-surface navigation in the Arctic Ocean. We shall now see to what extent those types of navigation are possible.

2. SUB-SURFACE NAVIGATION

For the moment, the future of the Arctic Ocean appears to belong to the submarine. At the beginning of this century explorers Stefansson and Wilkins foresaw the use of sub-marines in the Arctic Ocean, but it wasn't until recent years that events proved the accuracy of their foresight. In 1931, Sir Hubert Wilkins succeeded in making a dive under the ice floes with his little *Nautilus*, but the ice drill became jammed and he had to abandon the project of making a cruise to the Pole; it was far from being an adequate submarine for under-ice navigation. Shortly after World War II, the United States commenced under-ice experiments in the Arctic, first in Kane Basin, then in the Chuckchi Sea and in the Beaufort Sea. In 1957, the U.S.S. *Nautilus* attempted to reach the North Pole by way of the Greenland Sea, but had to turn back at 87° North when her gyrocompasses ceased to function. In August 1958, however, the *Nautilus* cruised without difficulty across the Arctic Ocean from the Bering Sea to the Greenland Sea, passing beneath the geographic North Pole. In the words of her captain, "[s]he had blazed a new submerged Northwest Passage, vastly decreasing the sea-travel time for nuclear submarines from the Pacific to the Atlantic, one that could be used even if the Panama Canal were closed". [60] And he adds quite appropriately: "When and if nuclear-powered cargo submarines are built, the new route would cut 4,900 miles and thirteen days off the route from Japan to Europe." [61]

---

[59] Louis O. QUAM, "Arctic Basin Research", *Naval Research reviews*, at 2-3 (Oct. 1966). For a complete history of the activities of the Naval Arctic Research Laboratory at Point Barrow, Alaska, see REED and RONHOVDE, *Arctic Laboratory*, 748 pages, Arctic Institute of North America (1971).

[60] Wm. R. ANDERSON, *Nautilus 90° North*, at 224 (1959).

[61] *Ibid.*

Although the crossing of the *Nautilus* was described by Cmdr. Anderson as "the most Top Secret peacetime naval operation in history", [62] the U.S. government did think of the non-military aspects; the Presidential Unit Citation awarded to the ship read in part as follows: "This voyage opens the possibility of a *new commercial seaway, a Northwest Passage,* between the major oceans of the world. Nuclear powered cargo submarines may, in the future, use this route to the advantage of world trade." [63]

The first Arctic Ocean crossing by the *Nautilus* was followed very closely by that of the *Skate*, in August 1958, and then again by the same ship in March 1960. Not only did the *Skate* prove that submarine navigation was quite feasible in the Arctic Ocean, but it found that leads were numerous enough to surface, even in the middle of winter. [64] The leads were in fact so large that the captain of the *Skate* was surprised when he saw the ice creeping up the sides of his ship. "This was the fifteenth time", he wrote, "we had surfaced in the Arctic Ocean and also the first we couldn't submerge easily and quickly." [65]

In 1960, the U.S.S. *Sargo* further tested the feasibility of winter submarine navigation; she carried out a 31-day cruise under the ice of the Arctic Basin during January and February. During the trip to the North Pole and back, she surfaced twenty times, and twice through ice three feet thick. [66] In the fall of the same year, the U.S.S. *Seadragon* made history by crossing the old Northwest Passage from east to west via the Parry Channel throughout, and then added a quick trip to the North Pole for good measure. In the words of the *Seadragon's* captain, "all of the Arctic is now open to navigation by any nation having nuclear submarines". [67] The United Kingdom proved this when its submarine H.M.S. *Dreadnought*

---

62   ANDERSON, *Nautilus 90° North*, at 106 (1959).
63   Quoted by ANDERSON, *ibid.*, at 238.
64   See CALVERT, *supra* note 40, at 182.
65   *Ibid.*, at 204.
66   See *The Polar Record*, No. 66, at 279 (1960).
67   James T. STRONG, "The openings of the Arctic Ocean", *U.S. Naval Institute Proceedings*, Vol. 87, No. 10, at 63 (Oct. 1961).

made a trip to the North Pole in March 1971. There are, of course, certain problems involved in operating submarines under ice, but these are gradually being solved. Submarine research is being carried on constantly and with imagination; a miniature Arctic Ocean has been devised in San Diego, California, "where sea ice is grown under controlled conditions and its resulting physical properties can be studied in relation to the controlled conditions". [68] This kind of laboratory experimentation, coupled with all of the field research pursued in the Arctic Ocean itself, [69] is perfecting submarine navigation to the point where its use may become quite feasible for international commerce. At the moment, a number of feasibility and cost studies are being carried out, with a view to using giant submarine tankers to transport oil, not only through the Northwest Passage to the American east coast, but also through the Arctic Ocean itself to Western Europe. [70] With the improvement of submarine hull design, the development of better under-ice sonar and the ever-increasing knowledge of the Arctic basin, it is not impossible to envisage the use of the giant submarine tanker as the principal means of transporting petroleum products from the Arctic.

3. Conventional Surface Navigation

Conventional surface navigation in the peripheral seas of the Arctic Ocean has been practised for a long time, but it has always been hampered by the presence of ice. Nevertheless, significant northings have been attained, particularly

---

[68] Waldo Lyon, "The Submarine and the Arctic Ocean", *The Polar Record*, No. 75, at 704 (1963).
[69] More than 100 scientists are reportedly gathering data from two ice stations in order to build a mathematical model of the Arctic basin. The project is a joint one between the Office of Naval Research and the National Science Foundation. It will study the whole Arctic Ocean system, with particular reference to the interaction of the water with the undersurface of the ice and that of the ice surface with the air. See "Mapping Arctic model" in the *Montreal Star,* 27 March 1972 (Final edition) at 55. See also J. O. Fletcher, "Probing the Secrets of Arctic Ice", *Naval Research reviews* 9-24 (Mar. 1971).
[70] See, for instance, "Polar Route for Supertankers", *Oilweek* 14-16 (25 Nov. 1968). It might prove difficult, however, to use giant submarine tankers in the Northwest Passage because of the rather shallow waters in Barrow Strait.

in the Chuckchi and Beaufort Seas. [71] In more recent years, with the development of modern icebreakers, conventional surface navigation has been reaching further and further into the pack ice. Ships of the USSR use the Northern Sea Route, crossing the five seas bordering the Arctic Basin itself for at least three months of the year. In 1956, the diesel M V *Ob* made a high latitude seaborne expedition in the Greenland Sea: on July 26, it is reported to have reached 83° N. [72] In 1961, the nuclear-powered icebreaker *Lenin* completed a high latitude expedition of some 8153 miles, 5669 of which was through ice. [73] The course followed was about the same as that of the *Jeannette* in 1879-1881 and of the *Maud* in 1922-1924; there was one very important difference, however: the *Lenin* was in full control of its movements, whereas the other ships were prisoners of the ice. During that cruise the *Lenin* reached 81°30′N. in the Laptev Sea; she did not proceed further north because "further penetration north was not within the program of the expedition". [74] Summing up the results of the expedition, Maksutov writes:

> The most important results of the expedition were the demonstration of the feasibility of establishing "North Pole" drifting stations in high latitudes late in fall by means of an icebreaker, and the possibility of navigation in the Central Arctic during periods of ice formation and during the polar night. [75]

This "possibility of navigation in the Central Arctic" is all the more significant because the voyage took place from September 29th to November 22nd, after the normal navigation season.

American icebreakers, although not yet nuclear-powered, have also shown the feasibility of high latitude navigation in the Arctic Ocean. In September 1965, the *Northwind* reached

---

[71]   See Table in W. I. WITTMANN et al., *supra* note 52, at 10. It shows the latitude reached by 23 ships of various types from 1849 to 1961.

[72]   See V. F. BURKHANOV, *supra* note 39, at 12.

[73]   D. D. MAKSUTOV, "High-Latitude Expedition of the Nuclear-Powered Icebreaker Lenin", in OSTENSO, *supra* note 53, at n-2 & 6.

[74]   *Ibid.*, at n-5.

[75]   *Ibid.*, at n-6 & 7.

latitude 81°37.7′ North, rounding the northern tip of Severnaya Zemlya, without hitting any ice. [76] She did not proceed further north because it was desired to make the return trip by the Northeast Passage. [77] Two years later, the same ship did get deep into the pack ice north of Alaska by proceeding as far as 79°25.5′ North, before being stopped by a broken propeller in ice eight feet thick; [78] she was then rescued by the Canadian icebreaker *John A. Macdonald.*

Japan is another country which is in the forefront of building modern icebreakers; its 320-foot *Fuji,* with a displacement capacity of 8,566 tons, has air-conditioned quarters, three helicopters with hangar and maintenance facilities, antiroll devices, rudder and propeller protection, and 20 per cent more icebreaking ability than U.S. Wind-class icebreakers.[79] Japan has gained considerable experience in her many expeditions in the Antarctic, and has shown an interest in navigating the Arctic Ocean; indeed, there are reports that she once discussed with the USSR the possibility of using the Northern Sea Route. [80]

Canada also has been active in the development of efficient icebreakers. In 1964, the heavy icebreaker C.C.G. *Labrador* set a Canadian record by reaching 81°45′ North into Robeson Channel between Ellesmere Island and Greenland. In 1971, another Canadian icebreaker was reported to have established a new record for Canada by attaining 82°56′N. in the same channel.

With the development of ice-strengthened ships such as the *Manhattan,* which was able to traverse the greater part

---

[76]   Richard PETROW, *Across the Top of Russia,* at 339 (1967).
[77]   The message sent by the *Northwind* read in part "Thirty miles of clear water over top of Severnaya Zemlya. Passage clear for a transit eastward", PETROW, *ibid.,* at 336. Unfortunately, she did not obtain permission for such transit, and had to return via the Atlantic.
[78]   See *The Polar Times,* at 21 (Dec. 1967). The question of propeller damage by ice has received special attention in a study on the effectiveness of American icebreakers, where the author makes specific recommendations for their improvement. See Capt. E. A. McDONALD, "Our Icebreakers are not good enough", *The Polar Times,* 16-20 (June 1966).
[79]   Described by Capt. McDONALD, *ibid.*
[80]   See *The Polar Times,* at 30 (June 1967).

of the western end of the Northwest Passage where a good deal of polar ice was met, it is certainly possible that an improved design of such a ship could also negotiate the Arctic Ocean itself. As pointed out by Captain Maybourn in relation to the Northwest Passage, "[a]t its most severe this ice is comparable to the ice of the polar pack and, indeed, the western most 500 miles or so are through a section of the polar pack". [81] Captain Maybourn concludes his article on the problems of operating large ships in the Arctic by saying:

> Once navigation is established along the North-West Passage route it can only be a matter of time before the logic of opening routes across the pole to Europe, or from Baffin Island's rich iron ore mines to Japan through the Bering Strait, is accepted. [82]

Surface navigation in the Arctic is being made more and more feasible, not only by the development of better icebreakers and ice-strengthened ships, but also by a warming trend in the Arctic temperature resulting in a noticeable retreat of the pack ice. A scientific writer for Tass reported in 1959 that, according to tests made by the Leningrad Oceanological Institute, "the North Pole is getting warmer after ten centuries of cooling off". [83] A similar observation had been made previously in a study of climate evolution, where the author compared the average thickness of Arctic polar ice at the time of the drift of the *Fram* in 1893-1896 with that reported during the drift of the *Sedov* in 1937-1940; [84] he found that the thickness had diminished by nearly 50%. This warming trend is general in the earth's atmosphere but seems to be more evident in the Arctic than it is in the Antarctic. Dr. H. E. Landsberg, Director of the U.S. Weather Bureau's Office of Climatology, is reported to have said that,

---

[81]   R. MAYBOURN (Capt.), "Problems of Operating Large Ships in the Arctic", 24 *The Journal* (The Institute of Navigation) 135, at 142 (1971).
[82]   *Ibid.*
[83]   *The Polar Times*, at 12 (June 1959).
[84]   J. S. ACTURUS, "Evolution du Climat: conséquences humaines", *France Illustration*, at 65 (July 1949). For a good study on the relationship between climate and ice, see H. W. AHLMAN, "Glaciological research on the North Atlantic coasts", *Roy. Geogr. Soc. Ser.*, No. 1 (1948).

in the Arctic, "there is substantial physical evidence as well as temperature figures to support the warming trend theory". [85] A study on the climate of the Canadian Arctic shows that the popular concept of the Arctic as a place of perpetual and forbidding cold is not quite accurate; as pointed out by Mr. Thompson, "record low temperatures of $-55°F.$ to $-60°F.$ at most Arctic stations are not as low as the North American record of $-81°F.$ reported at Snag in the Yukon, or even the $-70°F.$ to $-75°F.$ temperatures that have been reported at a few northern locations in the western provinces and Ontario". [86]

The exact interaction between the ice and the air is still being studied, but scientists seem to agree that the warming trend of the atmosphere and of the hydrosphere has contributed to a noticeable regression of the pack ice. The trend may be cyclic rather than permanent, however, and some physical scientists have thought of helping nature to accelerate the melting of polar ice in the Arctic. Since 1948, Soviet scientists have put forward a number of schemes to raise the temperature of the waters in the Arctic Basin. [87] An early scheme provided for a 55-mile dam across the Bering Strait and the pumping of warm waters from the Pacific into the Arctic Basin by means of an atomic power station, thus creating an artificial Gulf Stream. This would raise the temperature of the waters of the Arctic Basin, increase their salinity and thus reduce or possibly remove altogether the ice cover from the Arctic Ocean. This result could also be obtained by injecting heat and CO_2 into the atmosphere. The following passage taken from a Study on Man's Impact on Climate is very revealing:

> There is a distinct possibility — according to some a probability — that a temperature rise associated with the

---

[85] *The Polar Times,* at 12 (June 1959).

[86] H. A. THOMPSON, "The Climate of the Canadian Arctic", in *Canada Year Book* 55-74, at 57 (1967).

[87] For literature on these schemes, see the following: L. G. TOPORKOV, "Is it possible to remove the ice cover of the Northern Arctic Ocean", *Priorda,* No. 11, 93-97 (Nov. 1961), translated by U.S. Air Force, Cambridge Research Lab. (1964); L. K. COACHMAN et al., "On the water exchange through Bering Strait", in *Limnology and Oceanography,*

anticipated injections of heat and CO_2 into the atmosphere in the next century would result in the summer melting of arctic ice. The mean lifetime of arctic sea ice is less than 10 years, and it is possible that the transition from ice-covered to an ice-free ocean would occur quite suddenly — within a few years. [88]

It seems quite probable that such schemes could be carried out but it is conceivable that an ice-free Arctic Ocean might have a significant effect on the climate of the northern hemisphere and possibly the whole globe. In 1965, the Rand Corporation published a study in which it evaluated "the heat balance of the Earth's surface and the atmosphere in the Arctic under present conditions and, also, for an assumed ice-free ocean"; [89] the study points to the need of more input data before the prevailing hypotheses concerning the results may be proved or disproved. Intensive study of the Arctic Basin is to be continued, and the data will be fed to computers with greater capacity in order to obtain more accurate answers.

The foregoing should be sufficient to show that, in spite of the presence of ice, navigation in the Arctic Ocean is possible and is in fact taking place, although to a limited extent. There is no telling how soon this limited degree of navigation may increase with the development of science and technology, particularly if scientific cooperation between the Soviets and the Americans intensifies. [90]

IV. — THE ARCTIC STATES AND THE STATUS OF THE ARCTIC OCEAN

The practice of states has always played an important role in the evolution of international law, and the crystallisa-

---

Vol. II, No. 1, 44-59 (Jan. 1966); and M. J. DUNBAR, *Second Report on the Bering Strait Dam*, Dept. of Northern Affairs and National Resources (1962).

[88]   See *Inadvertent Climate Modification, Report of the Study of Man's Impact on Climate* (SMIC), M.I.T. Press, at 160 (1971).

[89]   GLACIOLOGY PANEL, "Glaciology in the Arctic", *Transactions of the American Geophysical Union*, Vol. 48, No. 2, at 760 (1967).

[90]   A number of Agreements were concluded in May 1972 when President Nixon visited the USSR, some of which provide for scientific cooperation in various fields such as environmental protection, including marine pollution. See "Agreement on Environmental Protection" reproduced in 66 *Dep't State Bull.*, No. 1722, at 921 (26 June 1972).

tion of such practice into principles of law will often depend on the importance of the states involved. To use the imagery of Charles de Visscher in his discussion of the importance of power in the formation of rules of international law, [91] some states are heavier than others and will thus mark the path of their practice in a more definite and permanent way. So that, if the state practice of both the United States and the Soviet Union were to indicate that they do not consider the freedom of the seas applicable to the Arctic Ocean, their practice might constitute an effective limitation on that fundamental principle of international law. This does not mean that the attitude of the other Arctic states is not important, but it is necessarily less so; their attitude could increase or decrease the importance of a practice followed by either of the two great Powers or by both, but would hardly change the actual course of such a practice.

1. THE ATTITUDE OF THE ARCTIC STATES

The United States

The United States has followed a consistent policy with regard to the Polar regions: it has made no claim for itself and it has recognized none for others. This is particularly true with respect to the Arctic pack ice, although it was a U.S. naval officer who first hoisted the national ensign of the United States at the North Pole. When Admiral Peary formally took possession of the entire region in the name of the President, the United States refused to claim jurisdiction over the pack ice. There was interest in acquiring new lands if some could be found in the Arctic Ocean, [92] but the United States did not wish to make claims of sovereignty over the ocean. That has been the official position consistently followed by Washington.

---

[91]   Charles DE VISSCHER, *Théories et Réalités en Droit international public* 177-198 (1955).

[92]   In 1924, Mr. Denby, Secretary of the Navy, stated that it was "highly desirable that if there is in that region land, either habitable or not, it should be the property of the United States . . ." See *Hearing on House Resolution* 149, concerning contemplated flight of the *Shenandoah* to the North Pole Regions; Committee on Naval Affairs, House of Representatives, 1924, 452-453, quoted by HYDE, I *International Law*, at 353, n. 1 (1945).

In 1929, when the U.S. State Department asked the Navy for its opinion on the idea of calling a conference to partition the Arctic into five national sectors, the response was negative. Admiral Adams, Secretary of the Navy, stated in his reply that such partitioning "is in effect a claim of sovereignty over high seas, which are universally recognized as free to all nations, and is a novel attempt to create artificially a closed sea and thereby infringe the rights of all nations to the free use of this area". [93] In 1937, State Department officials were quoted as saying that "no question of sovereignty over the area about the North Pole has ever arisen because there is no land there". [94] In 1961, Cmdr. Partridge, from the Executive Office of the Secretary of the Navy, related the cruise of the *Nautilus* to government policy in the following terms:

> ... the Nautilus cruise appears to furnish support for the official position of the United States that the Arctic Sea should be considered as the *high seas* under international law and therefore open to the free use of all the maritime nations of the world and not subject to claims of territorial sovereignty by any individual nation. [95]

In addition to the evidence just presented, the proof that Washington regards the Arctic Ocean as any other ocean is the extent of its activities there for the last twenty years or more; U.S. submarines, icebreakers, aircraft and scientists on drifting ice stations have been a constant reminder that it considers the area as high seas open to all nations.

The Soviet Union

Although Soviet jurists such as Sigrist, Lakhtine and Korovin have interpreted the sector theory to include ice formations within the sector, the government of the USSR does not appear to have subscribed to such an extensive interpretation. True, most of its research has been done on the Soviet side of the Pole but, since it is impossible to control ice stations,

---

93   HACKWORTH, I *Digest of Int'l L.*, at 464 (1940).
94   HYDE, I *International Law*, at 348, n. 5.
95   Ben PARTRIDGE, "The White Shelf: A Study of Arctic Ice Jurisdiction", 87 *U.S. Naval Institute Proceedings*, No. 9, at 51 (Sept. 1961); emphasis added.

they sometimes take unexpected courses; consequently, a number of Soviet ice stations have drifted well outside the Soviet sector. However, much more significant is the fact that the USSR has established a number of stations well within the American sector north of Alaska. Such was the case with North Pole 2 which was not only set up within that sector, but remained so throughout its year of operation. North Pole 3 crossed the northern portion of both the American and Canadian sectors in an easterly drift; and at least three other stations (North Poles 7, 8 and 9)[96] were installed on ice floes within the American sector. Another indication of the official attitude of the Soviet Union is the great number of high latitude airborne expeditions over most of the Arctic Ocean; a map published in 1957 by a senior officer of the Northern Sea Route Authority indicates the extent of those expeditions up to that time.[97] It should also be recalled at this point that, in August 1967, the Soviet Union did not really object to or interfere with the presence of the U.S. icebreakers in the seas north of her coast, until they tried to borrow the Vilkitsky Strait which it considers as territorial waters.[98]

Canada

Canada's official attitude toward the status of the Arctic waters, including the Arctic Ocean, has not been altogether clear. Over the years, numerous statements have been made by ministers in the House of Commons relating to the meaning of and support for the sector theory which extends to the North Pole across the Arctic Ocean.[99] It would appear from an examination of those statements that responsible ministers never meant to invoke the theory in question to claim jurisdiction over water and ice areas of the Arctic. Prime Minister

---

[96]   All relevant coordinates are given by GORDIENKO in his Table entitled "Data on Drifting Scientific Stations in the Arctic Basin up to April 1, 1962", in OSTENSO, *supra* note 53.

[97]   See V. F. BURKHANOV, *supra* note 39, at 12.

[98]   For an account of this incident, see D. PHARAND, "Soviet Union Warns United States Against Use of Northeast Passage", 62 *A.J.I.L.* 927-935 (1968).

[99]   See "The Sector Theory" under "Historic Waters in the Northwest Passage" in *Part III — Historic Waters in the Arctic, supra.*

Trudeau would not even apply the sector theory to the waters and ice of the waterways within the Canadian Arctic Archipelago. [100] A fortiori, it would seem, the Canadian Government would not invoke the same theory to support a claim to the Arctic Ocean between the Arctic archipelago and the North Pole. In these circumstances, it is somewhat surprising that the official maps prepared and issued by the Government continue to show the "boundary" lines of Canada as extending to the North Pole. [101] In apparent support of these lines, the "Physical Geography" section of the Canada Year Book states that "[i]n latitude it (Canada) stretches from Middle Island in Lake Erie, at 41°41′N. to the North Pole"; [102] and that section is indicated as having been revised by the Geographical Branch of the Department of Energy, Mines and Resources. [103] On the other hand, there is some evidence in that same Year Book that the projected boundary lines and the geographical description referred to might not be significant. For the first time, in the 1967 edition, there appears an article on the "Growth of Geographical Knowledge of Canada" which sheds some light on the subject. It contains the following passage:

> The seaward extent of Canadian sovereignty in the Far North has been less than precisely known. Canadian maps have customarily shown lines extending from the easterly and westerly limits of the country along the 60th and 141st lines of longitude as far as the North Pole, with the declared intention of claiming any new lands that may be found within these limits. In view of the advanced state of geographical knowledge in the Arctic today, the lines are probably no longer significant. [104]

The author of the above article, written for the Canadian Government, is Dr. Trevor Lloyd, noted geographer and professor at McGill University. Dr. Lloyd was even more definite on the lack of significance of those projected boundary lines

---

[100]   *Can. H. C. Deb.*, at 6396 (10 March 1969).
[101]   See the Political Map of Canada inserted in the back-cover pocket of the 1967 *Canada Year Book* and indicated as being "compiled and drawn by the Department of Energy, Mines and Resources for the Canada Year Book, Dominion Bureau of Statistics".
[102]   *Canada Year Book*, at 7 (1967).
[103]   *Ibid.*
[104]   *Ibid.*, at 2.

a few years earlier, when he wrote: "they cannot mean that a formal claim is made to the sea, the floating ice or even the sea floor far beneath." [105] He expressed the very definite opinion then that "[t]he recognized limit of Canadian sovereignty in the far north extends as it does elsewhere three miles offshore, except that claims may now be made to mineral rights in the continental shelf". [106] It is not suggested that these latter statements on the part of Dr. Lloyd must be associated with government policy; they are quoted here because they appear to represent a fuller expression of his opinion on the question. It is suggested, however, that the Government of Canada could hardly disassociate itself completely from what Dr. Lloyd has written at its request and which it has published in the Canada Year Book as part of the physical description of Canada.

Whatever might be the intent behind Canada's continuing practice to show a polar sector on its maps, it would seem reasonably clear that it is not in support of a claim to sovereignty and, indeed, the sector theory *per se* can find no such basis in international law. However, Canada has recently questioned the legal status of the Arctic Ocean — or at least part of that ocean — as high seas. On April 15, 1970, Prime Minister Trudeau, speaking to the Annual Meeting of the Canadian Press on Canada's fight against pollution, stated that "[o]nly by an examination conceptually removed from reality can Beaufort Sea be described as 'high sea' ". [107] The next day Canada sent a Note to the United States which contained the following statement relating to the freedom of the high seas in the Arctic:

> It is idle ... to talk of freedom of the high seas with respect to an area, large parts of which are covered with ice throughout the year, other parts of which are covered with ice most of each year, and where the local inhabitants use the frozen sea as an extension of the land to travel over it by dogsled and snowmobile far more than they can use it

---

[105]   Trevor LLOYD, "Canada's Northland", 66 *Queen's Quarterly* 529, at 532 (1959-1960).

[106]   *Ibid.*

[107]   P. E. TRUDEAU (Rt. Hon.), "Canada Leads the Fight Against Pollution", *Statements and Speeches*, No. 70/3, at 4 (1970).

as water. While the Canadian Government is determined
to open up the Northwest Passage to safe navigation, it
cannot accept the suggestion that the Northwest Passage
constitutes high seas. [108]

If the "area" in question is the one defined by the Arctic Waters
Pollution Prevention Act as "Arctic waters", then it includes
part of the Beaufort Sea. However, it is possible that the passage just quoted relates only to the waters of the Northwest
Passage itself between the Canadian Arctic Islands, or perhaps
the statement is meant to refer to both bodies of water. In any
event, the legal adviser J. A. Beesley, speaking a few days later
to the Standing Committee on External Affairs and National
Defence, referred specifically to both the Arctic Ocean and the
Beaufort Sea. In discussing the question of whether or not the
Northwest Passage could be considered as an international
strait, he made the following statement:

> The conventional law does not settle the question one
> way or the other because it talks about joining two bodies
> of the high seas, as I think one would have to stretch the
> definition rather widely to refer to the Beaufort Sea or the
> Arctic Ocean as a high sea because much of them are
> covered with ice during most of the year. [109]

Mr. Beesley amplified on Canada's view of the Arctic waters
in April 1971 in his statement at the Ditchley Conference.
Having stated that "the Arctic waters and ice do not constitute high seas to which the traditional freedoms apply",
he specified that "[s]o far as Canada is concerned, the
special characteristics of the Arctic waters and ice combine
to give them a *special status — however defined —* which
implies special rights and responsibilities for the Arctic coastal
states". [110] It would seem that the "Arctic waters" envisaged
here did include the Arctic Ocean as well as the Beaufort Sea,

---

[108]   *Can. H. C. Deb.*, 6028 (17 April 1970).

[109]   J. A. BEESLEY, in *Standing Committee on External Affairs and
National Defence, Minutes of Proceedings and Evidence*, No. 25, at 19-
20 (29 April 1970).

[110]   See J. A. BEESLEY, "Rights and Responsibilities of Arctic
Coastal States: The Canadian View", published in 3 *J. Mar. L. & Com.*
1 at 3 (1971), and in *The Arctic Circular*, Vol. 22, No. 22, 98-110 (1972);
emphasis added.

since specific reference had been made to them before the passage just quoted.

Trying to sum up the Canadian position toward the Arctic Ocean, it seems to be this: Canada makes no claim to sovereignty over any sector but it claims that the waters of the Arctic Ocean have a special undefined status because of the presence of ice and do not qualify as high seas.

Norway and Denmark

Norway and Denmark have not had much occasion to manifest their official attitude toward the status of the Arctic Ocean in recent years, but their history would indicate that they regard it as being open to all nations. It was a Norwegian explorer, Nansen, who became the first to cross the Arctic Ocean in 1893-1896. Norway has had a long and successful history of Arctic exploration and she has administered the archipelago of Spitzbergen, at the very edge of the Arctic Ocean, ever since her sovereignty was recognized by treaty in 1920. She has never recognized any form of sector theory in the Arctic; on the contrary, the Norwegian Government expressed a categorical reservation on the matter in a Diplomatic Note to Canada in 1930. While recognizing Canada's sovereignty over the Sverdrup Islands, it emphasized that this recognition was "in no way based on any sanction whatever of what is named 'the sector principle' ". [111] Furthermore, Norway does not appear to have ever objected to the seaborne and airborne activities carried on in the Arctic Ocean north of her territory of Spitzbergen. It should also be added that the Norwegian Polar Institute has always been, and still is, active in polar research activities, including the Arctic Ocean.

As in the case of Norway, Denmark has had a long history of Arctic exploration and, ever since 1932 when sovereignty over Eastern Greenland was decided in her favour, her territory has bordered the Arctic Ocean itself. The northern tip of that great land, four times the size of France, reaches close to 84° N. and constitutes the northernmost point of land

---

[111] HACKWORTH, 1 *Digest Int'l L.*, at 463 (1940).

in all of the Arctic regions. Denmark has never invoked the sector theory to support her claims to Arctic territory, although she could have done so with respect to the eastern part of Ellesmere Island, [112] and has never made any claim to that part of the Arctic Ocean north of Greenland. On the contrary, her cooperative attitude would indicate that she regards it as any other ocean. It was from Thule base in Greenland, for instance, that the U.S. Air Force supplied its personnel on ice island T-3 during part of 1953. [113] Denmark also participated, through the Scandinavian Airlines, in the pioneering of trans-polar civil aviation. Finally, it is worth mentioning that the Danish Arctic Institute, located in Copenhagen, is well recognized for its research activities not only relating to Greenland but to the Arctic regions generally.

2. THE LEGAL STATUS OF THE ARCTIC OCEAN

As indicated at the beginning, it is submitted that the legal status of the Arctic Ocean should depend primarily on two factors: the possibility of exercising the freedoms of the seas and the attitude of the Arctic states whose territories form a sort of continental belt around it.

As for the possibility of exercising the freedoms of the seas, the first and foremost freedom is being exercised to a substantial degree: navigation is now an accomplished fact in so far as subsurface navigation is concerned, and there are indications that conventional surface navigation will become a fact in the fairly near future. In other words, the main basis for the very existence of the principle of freedom of the seas is unquestionably present. Another important freedom is the right to fly over the seas; this freedom is being pursued over all of the surface of the Arctic Ocean. The other two freedoms expressly mentioned in the Convention on the High Seas are the "freedom of fishing" and the "freedom to lay submarine

---

[112] Denmark's claim to Ellesmere Island was based on Rasmussen's expeditions and not in any way on its location partially within (about 15 degrees) the Greenland or Danish Sector.

[113] See *Greenland,* published by the Danish Ministry of Foreign Affairs, at 170-171 (3rd ed. 1961).

cables and pipelines" (Art. 2). Fishing is not being practised in the Arctic Ocean but this does not mean that fish are completely absent; the commander of the *Skate* reports that, at less than 300 miles from the North Pole, the television screen, used to observe the bottom of the ice, became suddenly "flooded with fish". [114] The quantity of fish in the Arctic Ocean is small, however, due to the low temperature of most of the water masses. As for animal life at the bottom of the ocean floor, present knowledge is still inadequate [115] but it may possibly be more plentiful than has been traditionally suspected. [116] The laying of submarine cables and pipelines has not yet come about but, with the increasing knowledge of the sea floor of the Arctic Ocean, that possibility certainly exists; need and cooperation among nations will determine the future use of that freedom. There is a fifth freedom which is not specified in the Convention but which exists nevertheless: it is the "freedom to undertake scientific research on the high seas". [117] This freedom, which has been the object of debate in the U.N. Sea-bed Committee, is in fact exercised by the Arctic states, particularly by the United States and the Soviet Union from their drifting stations.

Coming to the attitude of the Arctic states as to the status of the Arctic Ocean, only Canada has expressed doubt in recent years in recognizing those waters as high seas. Its reservation is based on the fact that ice is permanently present and, as a result, it claims that the Arctic Ocean should have a special status. It has not spelled out what this special status ought to be and the other Arctic states have not supported the idea. On the contrary, the United States has strongly objected to the adoption of the Arctic Waters Pollution Pre-

---

[114]   James CALVERT, *supra* note 40, at 171.
[115]   See R. J. MENZIES, "The Abyssal Fauna of the Sea Floor of the Arctic Ocean", in *Proceedings of the Arctic Basin Symposium*, 46-65 (1963).
[116]   See K. HUNKINS et al, "The Floor of the Arctic Ocean in Photographs", 23 *Arctic* at 175 (1970), where the authors report that their photographs showed evidence of animal life on both the ridges and the basins of the Arctic Ocean.
[117]   Commentary to Article 27 of the I.L.C. Draft, which draft provision became Article 2 of the Convention on the High Seas (1956) *I.L.C. Yearbook* II, at 278.

vention Bill by Canada in 1970, on the grounds that it represented a unilateral extension of jurisdiction on the "high seas" and that its implementation would affect "the right to freedom of the seas in large areas of the high seas". [118] In these circumstances, it is difficult to see how the attitude of one state can affect the degree of recognition as high seas accorded to the Arctic Ocean by the others, particularly by the United States and the Soviet Union.

CONCLUSION

The foregoing analysis reveals that it is possible for states to exercise all of the freedoms of the seas in the Arctic Ocean. True, some of those freedoms are not yet exercised fully or at all, but it is only because the need has not arisen or the relevant knowledge and technology have not developed to a sufficient degree. A close and realistic look at the physical nature of the Arctic Ocean shows that it is not possible to assimilate the pack ice to land. The assertion that the pack ice will permit man to pursue his normal occupations thereon is not tenable. In spite of the most modern equipment and of financial support by their Governments, the special occupation by scientists of thick ice floes can only be temporary and, even then, it is precarious and often dangerous. The other suggestion permitting horizontal sovereignty over the pack ice, is not really tenable either. With the displacement of ice floes which continually takes place in various parts of the Arctic Ocean, that which is being appropriated (the pack ice) would also be continually changing; ice floes under the sovereignty of one state to-day could come under the sovereignty of another state to-morrow. Territorial sovereignty cannot be considered horizontally, if it is to have the stability and permanence needed for the proper exercise of exclusive jurisdiction; the entire concept of territorial integrity would be shattered and it would hinder rather than help the maintenance of peaceful relations between states. This rejection of the ice-is-land theory does

---

[118] See "U.S. Press Release on Canada's Claim to Jurisdiction over Arctic Pollution and Territorial Sea Limits", reproduced as Appendix "A" in *Can. H. C. Deb.*, at 5923-4 (15 April 1970).

not imply that the status of ice floes and ice islands is not important. Since they are in fact capable of some occupation for scientific or even for military purposes, it is advisable that they be subjected to some legal regime. Their status will now be examined, along with that of ice shelves.

PART V

The Legal Status of Ice Shelves and Ice Islands in the Arctic

Ice islands, as well as ordinary ice floes, are being used by scientists and technicians as drifting stations to carry on research programs in the Arctic Ocean. The question may arise as to what state has jurisdiction over such islands. Indeed, such question did arise in 1970 when a homicide was committed on Ice Island T-3, and the question of jurisdiction has not yet been resolved. Numerous ice islands have been located in the Arctic, and they appear to originate from ice shelves off the north coast of Ellesmere Island bordering on the Arctic Ocean. Canada has not yet issued geographical coordinates to determine the baselines of its territorial waters in the Arctic but, when it does, it will have to decide what status should be given to the Ellesmere Island ice shelf. This brief study will inquire into the legal status of ice shelves and ice islands, and examine the question of state jurisdiction over Ice Island T-3 in relation to the *Escamilla Case*.

I. — ICE SHELVES

The legal status of ice shelves in international law has never been determined but there appears to be a consensus among interested states that they ought to be considered as land. Such would seem to be the intent of Article VI of the Antarctic Treaty of 1959, which specifies that the treaty applies "to the area south of 60 degrees South Latitude, including all ice shelves"; in other words, the treaty covers not only *terra firma* but *glacies firma*. These huge ice-tongues are partly afloat, but their thickness and quasi-permanency render them much more like land than water. As pointed out by Ivor Richardson with respect to the Ross Ice Shelf within the New Zealand sector, "for the purposes of navigation, it makes no difference if a permanent barrier is composed of frozen water or land"; [1] one is as effective a barrier to navigation

---

[1] Ivor RICHARDSON, "New Zealand's Claims in the Antarctic", 33 *New Zealand L.J.*, at 40 (Feb. 1957).

as the other. The permanency of the Ross Ice Shelf as a barrier to navigation is certainly quite evident when one considers that its thickness is said to vary from 500 to 1500 feet [2] and that it is land-locked in an immense bay between Victoria Land and Marie Byrd Land. The 1959 Treaty, however, did not limit its assimilation of the shelf ice to land to the case of the Ross Ice Shelf; it applies to all ice shelves in the Antarctic, and some of them in the other sectors are far from being as large, as thick and permanent as the Ross Shelf. Indeed, some of the ice shelves are only semi-permanent, in the sense that seaward sections break off and float away to form ice islands. A similar phenomenon occurs in the Arctic, although to a much more limited extent. A brief investigation into the physical characteristics of the Arctic ice shelves must be carried out before attempting to determine the legal consequences.

1. DESCRIPTION OF ICE SHELVES

On 14 August 1946, when the U.S. Air Force spotted by radar a huge ice mass, very much thicker than the surrounding ice floes and having an area of some 200 square miles, it had found a fragment of an ice shelf. [3] When two more were found in 1950, the search for their place of origin was intensified. As a result of a study of RCAF trimetrogon photographs, some "twenty-eight ice islands, varying in size from a mile to 7 or 8 miles across were found, as well as a considerable number of smaller fragments". [4] Historical research also showed that early explorers had described large ice floes, which were possibly fragments of ice shelves. Peary had probably found the place of origin of those islands when he

---

2   *Ibid.*

3   L. S. KOENIG, "Discovery of Ice Islands on U.S.A.F. Flights over the Arctic Ocean", in L. S. KOENIG et al., "Arctic Ice Islands", 5 *Arctic,* 68-75 (1952). This same ice island was seen again in October 1965 and it had maintained its original triangular shape, with an area of about 125 km[2]; see D. LINDSAY, "Ice Islands", 20 *Ice,* at 8 (April 1966).

4   K. R. GREENWAY, "Additional Information from Flights and Photographs in the Canadian Arctic", in L. S. KOENIG et al., *ibid.* 75, at 78.

spoke about a "peculiar ice-foot" and of a "glacial fringe" [5] located north of Ellesmere Island.

Dr. Hattersley-Smith was probably the first to trace scientifically the origin of the ice islands of the Arctic Ocean to the ice shelves of northern Ellesmere Island. The conclusion he arrived at in 1952, which has been confirmed since, was quite clear: "It is the periodic breaking-off of large areas of this shelf which has formed the ice islands at present drifting in the Arctic Ocean and channels of the Canadian Archipelago." [6] Ice shelves are known to have existed off the northeast coast of Greenland and between the islands of Severnaya Zemlya as well as those of Franz Josef Land. Two ice shelves still exist in the Svalbard archipelago, a large one off the southeast coast of Nordaustlandet and a small one on the east coast of Edgeöya. [7] However, it seems that the more important ice shelves left in the Arctic to-day are located off the coast of Ellesmere Island. The northern part of this large island resembles Greenland and the Antarctic continent in that it is partly covered with glaciers projecting ice lobes far deep into the fiords; these glaciers are partly responsible for the formation of the landward part of the ice shelves. As for the seaward projection, it is the result of an accumulation of snow on sea ice over a long period of years. Dr. Hattersley-Smith describes the formation of the shelf ice north of Ellesmere Island as follows:

> In the inner parts of the fiords, where the ice appears to be very thick, the main glaciers and their tributary glaciers seem to have been the chief sources of supply; in the outer parts of the fiords and along the coast between the fiords the shelf ice seems to have grown mainly through the accumulation of snow on sea ice. [8]

---

[5]   Moira DUNBAR, "Historical references to Ice Islands", in L. S. KOENIG et al., *ibid.*, 83, at 92.

[6]   G. HATTERSLEY-SMITH, "Comments on the Origin of the Ice Islands", in L. S. KOENIG et al., *ibid.*, 95, at 102.

[7]   See Map 514, entitled "Barentshavet", published by the Norsk Polarinstitutt, Oslo, 1960. The writer is grateful to Dr. Tore Gjeldsvik of the Norsk Polarinstitutt for pointing out that those two ice shelves are still in existence.

[8]   G. HATTERSLEY-SMITH, *supra* note 6, at 99.

Ice shelves are, therefore, the product of land as well as sea; each contributes a separate part which eventually forms such a perfect union that it is impossible, in most cases, to find the demarcation line between the sea ice and the glacier. Ice shelves front much of the fiords of Ellesmere Island. The landward part of the shelves is of considerable thickness, as indicated by some of the ice islands like T-3, which was described as being 190 feet thick; [9] the outer part of the ice shelves is about 100 to 150 feet thick. [10]

Until 1962, there were four major ice shelves north of Ellesmere Island (Figure 7). [11] The *Milne Ice Shelf* covers the entire fiord and projects about two miles beyond the mouth of Milne Fiord, which is approximately 10 miles wide. Although the other three ice shelves under review have suffered considerable breaking-up in recent years, the Milne Ice Shelf has remained intact. [12] Part of its resistance seems to come from the fact that it is the only one welded to a main glacier tongue which appears to be aground. The *Ayles Ice Shelf* covered two-thirds of Ayles Fiord until about 1966, and extended about two miles beyond the mouth of the fiord. In April 1966, it was noticed that "only scattered ice islands and slivers of ice shelf" remained, [13] and a 1967 report indicated that the ice shelf had completely disintegrated. [14] The *M'Clintock Ice Shelf* covered the full entrance of the fiord and extended three miles beyond until about 1966. An aerial survey of April 1966 showed that "only scattered disoriented fragments of ice shelf (or small islands)" were left; [15] by 1967, this ice shelf had also

---

[9]   Max C. BREWER, "Drifting Stations in the Arctic Ocean", in *Proceedings of the Arctic Basin Symposium,* at 305 (1963).
[10]   G. KONECNY et al., "Studies on Ice Movements on the Ward Hunt Ice Shelf by means of Triangulation-Trilateration", 19 *Arctic,* at 337 (1966).
[11]   Reproduced from G. HATTERSLEY-SMITH, "The Ward Hunt Ice Shelf: Recent Changes of the Ice Front", 4 *Journal of Glaciology,* at 416 (1963).
[12]   G. HATTERSLEY-SMITH, "Note on ice shelves off the north coast of Ellesmere Island", Vol. 22, No. 1, *The Arctic Circular,* at 13-14 (1965-1966).
[13]   *Ibid.,* at 13.
[14]   See G. HATTERSLEY-SMITH, "Report", in 23 *Ice,* at 9 (April 1967).
[15]   G. HATTERSLEY-SMITH, *supra* note 12, at 13.

completely disintegrated. [16] The *Ward Hunt Ice Shelf*, projecting north of Disraeli Fiord, is by far the largest of the four main ice shelves. Until 1962 it measured some 45 miles in length and extended an average of 10 miles seaward beyond the main coastline. Dr. Hattersley-Smith described the ice shelf in the following terms: "West of the Markham Bay re-entrant, the ice shelf has maintained, as far west as Cape Discovery, an unbroken band averaging about 16 km. in width from the outer coast and extending far up Disraeli Fiord." [17]

Between August 1961 and April 1962, extensive fragmentation of the Ward Hunt Ice Shelf occurred; it was estimated that about 596 km. [2] of ice shelf was calved during that period. [18] Five large ice islands were born during the calving, as well as a number of smaller ones (Figure 7); four of the islands proceeded together westward preserving their original position, and are following the general direction of the clockwise movement of the current around Beaufort Sea. [19] The fifth island proceeded east and eventually entered Robeson Channel between Greenland and Ellesmere Island. [20] Radar reflectors were placed on this fifth island (WH-5) so as to be able to follow its drift and thus provide further data on the currents involved. [21] The ice island was subsequently traced into Baffin Bay where it eventually broke up. [22] The Ward Hunt Ice Shelf has been under close observation since the fragmentation of 1961-1962, but there has been no further calving apparently, and the ice movement has been very slight; indeed, the special observations obtained between 1964 and

---

[16] See G. HATTERSLEY-SMITH, *supra* note 14.

[17] G. HATTERSLEY-SMITH, "Ice Conditions off the North Coast of Ellesmere Island", *Report No. Misc. G-8*, at 10, Defense Research Board, Canada (1962).

[18] G. HATTERSLEY-SMITH, "The Ward Hunt Ice Shelf: Recent Changes of the Ice Front", *supra* note 11, at 418.

[19] See D. LINDSAY, "Sea Ice Reconnaissance", in F. Müller, "Glacier Research", 20 *Canadian Geographic Bulletin*, at 188-189 (1967). See also D. LINDSAY et al., "Ice Islands, 1967", 21 *Arctic*, at 103-106 (1968).

[20] See D. C. NUTT and L. K. COACHMAN, "A note on ice island WH-5", 16 *Arctic*, at 204-206 (1963).

[21] See G. HATTERSLEY-SMITH, *supra* note 11, at 423.

[22] See D. C. NUTT, "The drift of the ice island WH-5", 19 *Arctic*, at 244-262 (1966).

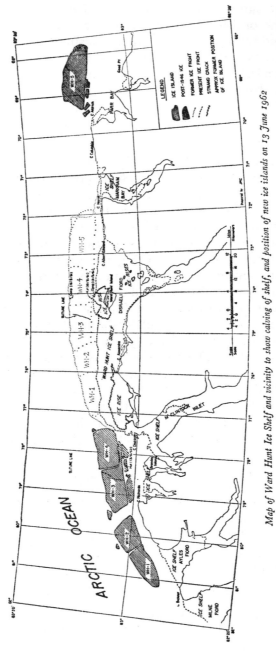

Map of Ward Hunt Ice Shelf and vicinity to show calving of shelf, and position of new ice islands on 13 June 1962

Reproduced from the *Journal of Glaciology*, Vol. 4, No. 34, at **416** (1963).

FIGURE 7.   MAJOR ICE SHELVES OFF ELLESMERE ISLAND.

1965 suggest that "the ice shelf is in a stagnant condition". [23] Its front now extends only slightly north of Ward Hunt Island, located at the entrance of Disraeli Fiord.

2. LEGAL ASPECT OF ICE SHELVES

It appears from the foregoing that the only places in the Arctic where ice shelves could cause a legal problem in the delimitation of territorial waters and, by definition, of the continental shelf are located on the north coast of Ellesmere Island and on the east side of the Svalbard archipelago. Two of the four major ice shelves known to have existed in recent times off the north coast of Ellesmere Island have disappeared. Ayles and M'Clintock ice shelves, which extended two or three miles beyond their respective fiords, have completely disintegrated since 1967 and no longer pose any legal problem. The two remaining ice shelves are Milne and Ward Hunt. The Milne Ice Shelf extends an average of about two miles beyond the entrance of the fiord, the closing line of which is about 10 miles; this means that, if the ice shelf is assimilated to land, the edge of it ought to serve as the baseline for the measurement of Canada's territorial waters. The Ward Hunt Ice Shelf still extends an average of about four miles beyond the entrance of Disraeli fiord; however, because of the presence of Ward Hunt Island at the outer edge of the shelf at the entrance of the fiord, the baseline for measuring territorial waters coincides roughly with the edge of the ice shelf, projecting only a mile or two beyond the baseline. It follows, therefore, that ice shelves in the Canadian Arctic cause little, if any, legal difficulty. In view of the considerable disintegration of the Ward Hunt Ice Shelf and the complete disintegration of neighbouring ones, it is suggested that it would be somewhat unrealistic for Canada to assimilate the remaining ice shelves to land in the measurement of its territorial waters north of Ellesmere Island. Unlike the Antarctic continent, there is no active inland ice sheet or glacier on Ellesmere Island pushing ice shelves forward; [24] thus there is little chance

---

23   C. KONECNY et al., *supra* note 10, at 342.
24   This is the phenomenon which has been observed at Halley

of the remaining ice shelves eventually regaining their former seaward position and affecting the location of baselines. Indeed, the remaining ice shelves might well disintegrate completely and become ice islands.

As for the ice shelves on the east side of the Svalbard archipelago, the one off the east coast of Edgeöya is rather small and would not greatly affect the drawing of territorial waters along the coast of that island. The ice shelf off the southeast coast of Nordanslandet, however, appears to extend a considerable distance — perhaps three or four miles — beyond actual land. The ice cliff or glacier, of which it is part, is indicated to be over 2,000 feet high and covers most of this large island. [25] It is not known to the writer if the glacier is an active one, which would affect the precise limit of the ice shelf, but it certainly appears to be a permanent phenomenon. Having regard therefore to the size and permanency of the ice shelf in question, it would seem only normal that Norway be allowed to assimilate it to land in the drawing of the territorial waters off that island.

II. — ICE ISLANDS

As stated by Professor Bishop, "the question may be asked whether large floating 'ice islands' in the Arctic may be subject to territorial sovereignty when expeditions remain in occupation of them for considerable periods". [26] In dealing with this problem, a distinction could be made between two types of ice islands: the "ice islands" properly so-called, which are huge fragments detached from ice shelves off Ellesmere Island, and the "ice floes" which are large pieces of sea ice constituting the pack ice. Although the first presents more sturdiness as an embarcation, both types can be occupied and

---

Bay, a British survey station operating in the Antarctic since 1956. See Sir Vivian FUCHS, "Life Cycle of a Polar Station", *The Geographical Magazine*, at 460-467 (1967).

[25] See Map 2282 entitled "The Greenland and Barents Seas", published by the British Admiralty in 1872, with additions and corrections to 1960.

[26] BISHOP, *International Law Cases and Materials*, at 409, note 17 (3rd ed., 1971).

used for essentially the same purposes, and may be treated together. Being capable of occupation, can these ice islands be considered floating pieces of territory ? Or are they perhaps more in the nature of ships ? Or do they possibly constitute a special phenomenon of nature not yet capable of legal qualification ? A closer look at their physical characteristics and at the kind of use and occupation to which they may be subjected may help in determining the legal status they should be given. What follows is a representative sampling of the ice islands which have been used thus far as floating research stations by the United States and the Soviet Union.

1. DESCRIPTION AND OCCUPATION OF ICE ISLANDS

(1) T-3 or Fletcher's Ice Island (U.S.)

This tabular iceberg is a fragment of one of the Ellesmere Island ice shelves and was originally about 150 feet in thickness. It is the sturdiest and largest ice island to have been occupied in the Arctic Ocean. It was originally described as measuring 31 miles in circumference and 5 miles across at the narrowest part. [27] Ten years later it was described as being four by nine miles [28] and, in 1972, it measured four by seven miles and its thickness had decreased to about 100 feet. [29] It was continuously occupied by the Americans until May 1954, and reoccupied periodically until October 1961, a year and a half after it had become grounded in about 130 feet of water, some 88 miles northwest of Barrow, Alaska. In 1962, heavy storms caused a major portion of T-3 to refloat and it was then re-occupied, this time by the U.S. Navy; research stations have been operating on the ice island since then, and will probably continue to do so for a long time to come. So long as T-3 remains in the Pacific Gyral north of Alaska and Canada, it serves as an excellent research platform for geophysicists, biologists, meteorologists and other scientists; highly

[27]   See A. P. CRARY et al., "Preliminary Report on Scientific Work on 'Fletcher's Ice Island', T-3", 5 *Arctic*, at 212-213 (1952).
[28]   See Max C. BREWER, *supra* note 9.
[29]   See *U.S.A.* v. *Escamilla* (No. 71-1575), *Brief for Appellee*, prepared by J. W. Williams, at p. 13 (1971).

classified research is also reportedly pursued on T-3 by the Electronics Defense Research Laboratory. [30] Life for the personnel on this ice island presents no great problem since it can be supplied by aircraft. The only major difficulty for the future of the island is the possibility of it being caught by the transpolar drift whenever it gets close to the North Pole; this was the fate of another ice island, Arlis II.

(2) ARLIS II (U.S.)

This 70-foot-thick ice island was unusual in that it presented certain characteristics of land; Leonard Le Shack of the Office of Naval Research gives the following description:

> This 3.5 by 1.5 ice island with its piles of rocks and boulders looks, even to the most discerning observer, remarkably like a snow-covered land mass. Its gently rolling topography, similar to a snow-covered meadow, differs markedly from the surrounding characteristic pack ice, whose perfectly flat surfaces alternate with their, jumbled, blocky, broken ice. From "dunes" of glacial debris, the ARLIS II ice slopes gently, like a seashore, until it reaches the pack ice "ocean". [31]

A sketch of the island prepared by the same author confirms the visual impression of land rather than ice (Figure 8); [32] he suggests, as did others, that this peculiar phenomenon might be the "land" which Cook and other explorers are said to have seen in the Beaufort and Lincoln Seas during the early part of the century.

The United States took possession of this ice island immediately upon locating it north of Alaska at 73°10′N. and 156°05′W., in May 1961, and occupied it continuously for four years. Unlike T-3, Arlis II failed to follow the Pacific Gyral around the Beaufort Sea; it was caught in the transpolar current after nearly reaching the Pole, and proceeded east in the Greenland Sea. It was evacuated in May 1965 at 66°43′N. and 27°01′W., in the Denmark Strait between Greenland and

---

[30]   Ibid., at 12.
[31]   Leonard A. LE SHACK, USNR, "Arlis II: New Arctic Drift Stations", Naval Research reviews, at 12 (Sept. 1961).
[32]   Ibid., at 16.

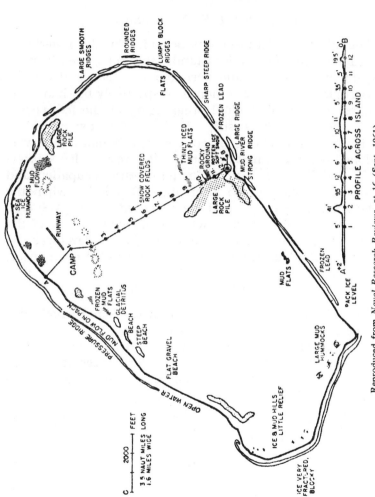

Reproduced from *Naval Research Reviews*, at 16 (Sept. 1961).

FIGURE 8.   SKETCH OF ICE ISLAND ARLIS II.

Iceland. In spite of its land-like appearance, it was definitely only a large piece of ice shelf; it disintegrated in the warm waters of the Atlantic and dumped its rocks onto the ocean floor.

(3) Other U.S. ice stations

The other five drift stations occupied by the Americans were ordinary ice floes (not ice islands) and, consequently, were considerably less secure and permanent. *Alpha* and *Charlie* were occupied for 17 and 9 months respectively but had to be evacuated because of gradual breaking-up of the ice, particularly at the end of the airstrips. [33] *Arlis I* was a small 8-foot-thick ice floe and was occupied for only 6 months; it was abandoned because it had drifted too far west. [34] Ice stations *Arlis III* and *IV* were planned for temporary occupation and were evacuated as planned after about 3 months, when the specific studies envisaged had been carried out. [35] Although only two of these five ice floes were abandoned because of the breaking-up of the ice, it seems that all of them developed the usual pressure ridges, tension cracks and leads of open water.

(4) North Pole 6 (USSR)

North Pole 6 was organized on an ice island which, like the American T-3, is believed to have originated from ice shelves off northern Ellesmere Island. [36] It measured 13.8 by 8.3 kilometers [37] and was thick enough [38] never to develop fractures during its three and a half years of continuous occu-

---

[33] See Max C. BREWER, *supra* note 9, at 306; also Louis O. QUAM, "Arctic Basin Research", *Naval Research reviews* 1, at 6-7 (1966).

[34] See Louis O. QUAM, *ibid.*, at 10.

[35] *Ibid.*, at 10-11.

[36] See V. F. BURKANOV, "Floating ice islands in the Central Arctic", noted in 12 *Arctic Bibliography*, at 136, note 70459 (1965) and V. D. DIBNER, "Floating ice islands and the glaciers which originated them", also in 12 *Arctic Bibliography*, at 211, No. 71014.

[37] See K. A. SYCHEV, "On a drifting ice island", noted in 12 *Arctic Bibliography*, at 875, No. 76053 (1965).

[38] Its thinest edge seemed to measure from about 5 up to 12 meters, since meltwater was combatted in summer by boring holes in the ice which varied from 4.8 to 12.1 meters in depth. See V. S. ANTONOV, "At the last stage", noted in 12 *Arctic Bibliography*, at 55-56, No. 69821 (1965).

pation. [39] The ice island was located north of the Chukchi Sea at 74°24′N. and 177°06′W. when first occupied in April 1956; it drifted right across the Arctic Ocean, following the transpolar current, and was abandoned as it entered the Greenland Sea. Life on the island posed no major problem, and its temporary inhabitants were once entertained by visiting artists from Moscow. [40]

(5) North Pole 7 (USSR)

North Pole 7 was established on an ice floe in April 1957 and was occupied for two years; the station was set up at 82°06′N., 164°11′W., north of the Chukchi Sea. It drifted north and eventually east into the transpolar current, where it was abandoned at 85°14′N., 33°03′W., in April 1959, heading toward Greenland. By this time the ice floe had become too short for aircraft landings. In April 1961, North Pole 7 was spotted by a plane of the Royal Canadian Air Force off the east coast of Baffin Island; it is believed that the floe drifted into Robeson Channel between Ellesmere Island and Greenland, and proceeded south into Baffin Bay. [41] Three weather buildings were still on the floe but the sun had melted about 14 feet of ice; one of the buildings had settled to the point where a diesel generator, left inside and insulating the ice beneath, had gone through the roof. [42] Obviously the surface melting of the ice does pose problems to personnel on ice floes.

(6) Other Soviet ice stations

It seems that Soviet scientists have occupied only two ice islands properly so-called, NP6 and NP19, all the others being ordinary ice floes. In the course of their various activities they have, therefore, experienced the numerous and various diffi-

---

[39] See P. A. GORDIENKO, "Scientific Observations from, and the Nature of Drift of the 'North Pole' Stations", in N. A. OSTENSO (ed.), *Problems of the Arctic and Antarctic No. 11*, at b-5 (1966).

[40] See V. M. DRIATSKII, "The International Geophysical Year in the Central Arctic", noted in 12 *Arctic Bibliography*, at 224-225, No. 71109 (1965).

[41] See Moira DUNBAR, "The drift of North Pole 7 after its abandonment", 6 *Canadian Geographer*, at 129-142 (1962).

[42] *The Polar Times*, at 13 (Dec. 1961).

culties which are associated with life on floating ice; the data collected by the Soviet stations established beyond any doubt that living on an ice floe can hardly be compared to living on land. In reviewing the accomplishments of the first ten ice stations, Gordienko points out that ice fracturing and hummocking constitute definite hazards to life; part of his description of the gradual breaking-up of the ice floes is reproduced below:

> Ice fracture, compression, and hummocking are hazards to life on the polar pack. Every polar explorer knows from personal accounts and log books the difficulties that members of the drift expeditions encounter. (Table 2 gives a full list of all fracturing and pressure ridging to which the "North Pole" stations were subjected.) The ice pack broke up and hummocked more than 450 times around "North Pole" stations; 95 of these cases occurred within the station camp. Not one station escaped the onslaught of the elements, no matter in what region they drifted. Fifty-seven times the break-up and pressuring of ice forced the occupants to shift their camps to new sites on more stable ice floes. [43] (The table referred to is reproduced here.)

It appears obvious that the main reason for the moving of camps by Soviet scientists has been the danger to life; the danger resulted mainly from ice conditions at the camp site or from the condition of the airstrip used for supplies. In so far as the evacuation of the ice stations themselves is concerned, the main reason seems to have been to avoid being caught by the outflow current leading to the Greenland Sea.

2. LEGAL APPRAISAL OF ICE ISLANDS

Keeping the above description in mind, the main question to examine is whether an ice island should be assimilated to land or to a ship. To consider ice islands as floating pieces

---

[43]   P. A. GORDIENKO, *supra* note 39, at b-5. The table referred to in the passage cited is reproduced herein. Note that, since the preparation of this table covering the first 9 stations only, the USSR has continued its operations on a number of other ice stations. In April 1972, it established North Pole 21, after abandoning North Pole 16 near the Canadian Arctic archipelago. — See P. FINN, "Veteran Arctic explorer claims first for Russia", *The Montreal Star*, Aug. 15, 1972, at A-20.

TABLE

LARGE ICE FRACTURES AND COMPRESSIONS OBSERVED DURING DRIFTS OF THE "NORTH POLE" STATIONS IN THE VICINITY OF THE CAMP AND AT THE SCIENTIFIC INSTALLATIONS

Station and Years of Drift	Phenomena Observed Outside the Camp		Fractures and Hummocking Within the Camp		Total Number of Phenomena During Drift Period	Comments
	Fractures, Channels, Ice Thinning	Compression, Hummocking	Fractures	Hummocking		
"North Pole-1" 1937/38	6	?	4	?	10?	Camp was re-established 4 times
"North Pole-2" 1950/51	1	2	2	10	15	Camp was re-established 5 times
"North Pole-3" 1954/55	2	20	2	15	39	Camp was re-established 4 times
"North Pole-4" 1954/55	13	16	—	—	23	Camp was re-established 1 time
"North Pole-4" 1955/56	10	11	—	—	21	Camp was re-established 1 time
"North Pole 4" 1956/57	34	29	—	—	63	Camp was re-established 2 times
"North Pole-5" 1955/56	total of 90 occurrences		total of 11 occurrences		101	Camp was re-established 4 times
"North Pole-5" 1956	5	7	2	2	16	Camp was re-established 4 times
"North Pole-6" 1956/59	up to 15/IX 1959 when the station was abandoned no fracturing occurred within the ice island				16	
"North Pole-7" 1957/58	8	8	4	2	16	
"North Pole-7" 1958/59	3	6	4	4	15	Camp was re-established 4 times
"North Pole-8" 1959/60	17	13	4	4	38	Camp was re-established 4 times
"North Pole-8" 1960/61	9	12	—	—	21	
"North Pole-8" 1961/62	6	8	12	11	37	Camp was re-established 14 times
"North Pole-9" 1960/61	19	4	8	2	33	Camp was re-established 10 times On 26 March camp was threatened with destruction and the party was evacuated.
Total of 14 annual drift cycles *	Outside the camp ice fracturing, hummocking and compressions were observed 353 times.		Within the camp ice fracturing, hummocking and compressions were observed 95 times.		448	The camp and its installations were re-established 57 times.

* Excluding the drift of station "North Pole-6".

Reproduced from Problems of the Arctic and Antarctic No. 11, ed. by N. A. Ostenso, at b-6 (1966)

of territory would present an element of logic, since they are but fragments of ice shelves which may be legally assimilated to land. If that is so, all ice islands in the Arctic might have to be considered as coming under Canadian sovereignty, since they all seem to have originated from Ellesmere Island which is part of Canadian territory. Or does an ice shelf fragment become a *res nullius* once detached and subject to territorial acquisition by the first occupant ? If so, does the new territorial sovereignty continue as long as the ice island is occupied, regardless of the drift path which it follows ? Extending this kind of logic soon reveals that it is somewhat unrealistic to continue considering ice shelf fragments as land, after they have become movable and have drifted away from their place of origin on to the high seas. The same reasoning applies, *a fortiori,* to ordinary ice floes which are not of territorial origin. Ice islands do not have the qualities of permanency and stability which are basic characteristics of any piece of territory. Even if an ice island could somehow be anchored in the Arctic Ocean or grounded in a shallow sea, [44] the consequences of considering it as territory of the occupying state would be inacceptable in international law; such action would be contrary to the Convention on the High Seas which provides that "[t]he high seas being open to all nations, no state may validly purport to subject any part of them to its sovereignty" (Art. 2). Two of the 1958 Conventions on the Law of the Sea make it quite clear that an island must be land before it can be legally considered an island, with its own territorial waters. Article 10 of the Convention on the Territorial Sea specifies that "an island is a naturally-formed area of land". [45] The

---

[44]   Ice island T-3 became grounded in May 1960 in about 130 feet of water northwest of Barrow. See Max C. BREWER, *supra* note 9. It has also been reported that "two huge 'ice islands' had grounded themselves in 90 feet of water just 20 to 30 miles north of the Prudhoe Bay area" (see Max B. SKELTON, "Ice Islands May Become Moorings", *The Ann Arbor News* (Feb. 20, 1969), at 33). Plans are now being made to increase their weight so much that they will remain grounded and serve as moorings and drilling platforms (see Clair BALFOUR, "Ice Islands studied as drilling platforms", *The Globe and Mail*, May 13, 1969, at B-14).

[45]   This article was adopted by a vote of 37 to 6, with 14 abstentions. See WHITEMAN, 4 *Digest of Int'l L.*, at 295 (1965).

qualification "naturally-formed", which was not in the draft of the International Law Commission, adds an important element to the legal definition of an island; it also indicates clearly that states consider as vital the basic principles of freedom of the seas and territorial integrity. The same concern is reflected in Article 5 of the Convention on the Continental Shelf, which provides that the various devices constructed by states to explore and exploit the continental shelf "do not possess the status of islands" (Para. 4). Under these treaty limitations, it is even impossible to consider as islands the artificial coral-type "islands" constructed in the Persian Gulf in order to drill for oil; *a fortiori*, such limitations eliminate the possibility of assimilating ice islands to land capable of territorial sovereignty.

But, if ice islands cannot be assimilated to land, can they perhaps be regarded as ships ? Ice islands are indeed used very much like research ships to study the ocean floor, the currents, the winds, etc. As far back as 1932, Gidel asked himself the question: "Les îles flottantes sont-elles des navires ?" [46] Having retained the ability to navigate as the essential criterion of a floating apparatus qualifying as a ship, he answers the question in the negative. However, he does go on to say that, if a floating island is equipped with propellers activated by motors, it may be assimilated to a ship since it is then able to navigate in the traditional sense. [47] Gidel was not discussing the ice-type of floating islands, but it is submitted that the same reasoning is substantially applicable. In other words, it is conceivable that modern technology might enable man to control the movements of an ice island in such a way that it is actually being navigated. Cmdr. Paul Frazier of the United States Navy, referring to ice islands, affirms without hesitation: "These are nothing more than floating 'ships of ice' which must be supplied by air support." [48] Up to now these ice stations have been devoted to peaceful uses and

---

[46] GIDEL, I *Le Droit international public de la Haute Mer*, at 66 (1932).

[47] *Ibid.*, at 68.

[48] *Proceedings of the Amer. Soc. of Int. Law,* at 165 (1958).

may be assimilated to merchant vessels, but, in time of war, they could become warships; quoting again from Cmdr. Frazier, "with additional slight modification these same scientific platforms could become effective 'aircraft carriers' or 'advance bases' for defense in the event of global war". [49] Gordon Smith, discussing Canada's claim in the Arctic in 1966, also prefers to compare ice islands to ships rather than to land, but he believes that the analogy "soon breaks down because the movements of an ice island, up till the present time at least, cannot be controlled as those of a ship can be". [50] Charles Hubert, of France, made a case recently for the necessity of defining the legal status of artificial islands, saying that it was a new mode of occupation of the sea, and traditional maritime law was no longer adequate to cope with this new situation. [51] The same may be said of natural ice islands; they constitute a new way of navigating and possibly occupying the sea. The suggestion is that ice islands ought to be considered as ships when occupied and appropriated. Such ice islands would be classified as public or private ships in the same way as ordinary ships are, depending mainly on whether or not they are engaged in the performance of public acts. They could be subject to the 1958 Convention on the High Seas, in so far as its provisions relating to ships may be made applicable. The same criterion of applicability could be followed for the relevant principles of customary law. Of course, if the use of ice islands should become extensive enough, it would be advisable for interested states to agree on a special convention governing such use. Having regard to the uses already being made and those contemplated, one can ask if such a convention should not be adopted in a near future. Otherwise, questions of state jurisdiction are bound to occur.

---

[49]   *Ibid.*

[50]   G. W. SMITH, "Sovereignty in the North: The Canadian Aspect of an International Problem", in R. St.J. MACDONALD (ed.), *The Arctic Frontier*, at 249 (1966).

[51]   Charles HUBERT, "Les îles artificielles", 71 *R.G.D.I.P.*, at 342-368 (avril-juin 1967).

III. — STATE JURISDICTION OVER ICE ISLAND T-3: THE ESCAMILLA CASE [52]

The facts. — On the evening of July 16, 1970, the shooting of the leader of a 19-man joint government-industry research team, one Bennie Lightsy of Louisville, Kentucky, took place in a hut on Ice Island T-3. The ice island was then floating in the Arctic Ocean at 84°45.8′ North latitude and 106°24.4′ West longitude, [53] within the so-called "Canadian" sector, at approximately 185 nautical miles from the Canadian Arctic islands. Lightsy was shot with a rifle held by one Mario Escamilla, a Mexican-born American citizen from California. Following a report about the incident, an American investigation team flew to the ice island and made an investigation on the spot. It took Escamilla into custody, flew him to Thule (a US Air Force Base in Greenland) for a change of plane and then to Dulles airport in Virginia. This having been the first touchdown on U.S. territory, he was brought before a magistrate in the District Court for the Eastern District of Virginia where the airport is located and charged with murder in the first degree. He was subsequently indicted by a grand jury for the lesser offence of second degree murder. After a trial before Judge Oren R. Lewis and a jury, Escamilla was convicted of involuntary manslaughter and sentenced to commit-

---

[52] For a previous discussion of the Escamilla Case, see the following: Andreas G. RONHOVDE, "The Escamilla Case in Court", 24 *Arctic* at 139 (1971); D. PHARAND, "State Jurisdiction over Ice Island T-3: The Escamilla Case", *id.*, at 83-89 (1971); Daniel WILKES, "Law for Special Environments: Ice Islands and Questions Raised by the T-3 Case", *The Polar Record*, Vol. 16, No. 100, 23-27 (1972); Rear Admiral C. O. HOLMQUIST, "The T-3 Incident", *U.S. Naval Institute Proceedings* 40-53 (1972); and Andreas G. RONHOVDE, *Jurisdiction over Ice Islands : the Escamilla Case in Retrospect*, published by The Arctic Institute of North America, 18 pp. (Nov. 1972). See also the following dealing with similar problems: Richard D. BILDER, "Control of Criminal Conduct in Antarctica", 52 *Virginia L. Rev.* 1-54 (1970); *Regina* v. *Tootalik* (1969) 71 *WWR* 435; F. M. AUBURN, "The White Desert", 19 *I.C.L.Q.* 229-256 (1970); and F. M. AUBURN, "International Law-Sea Ice — Jurisdiction", 48 *Can. Bar Rev.* 776-782 (1970).

[53] The geographic coordinates were given at the trial by Dr. Kenneth Hunkins, of the Lamont Geological Observatory of Columbia University. The Observatory has been tracking T-3's position since 1952, by taking 20 to 30 fixes a day. See *U.S.A.* v. *Escamilla* (No. 71-1575), Brief for Appellee, prepared by J. W. Williams, at 12 (1971).

ment in the custody of the Attorney General for a period of three years. The case was appealed and argued before a three-judge panel of the U.S. Court of Appeals for the Fourth Circuit in December 1971, and then re-argued before the Fourth Circuit sitting in full bench in June 1972. The Court of Appeals ordered a new trial because of an omission in the judge's charge to the jury, the accused was re-tried on the reduced charge of involuntary manslaughter and he was acquitted in November 1972.

The issue of jurisdiction. — The U.S. government exercised criminal jurisdiction under Title 18, United States Code, Section 7(1) which extends the special maritime and territorial jurisdiction of the United States to "the high seas". The prosecution argued that Ice Island T-3 must be deemed to be "high seas" and that there was no difference in terms of maritime jurisdiction whether an offence took place on board a vessel or in the sea itself. The defence contended that the "high seas" provision of section 7 did not confer any more than the traditional admiralty and maritime jurisdiction requiring a nexus to a vessel which Ice Island T-3 was not. In order to cover ice islands, specific legislation would be required in the same way as it was in 1856 to extend US jurisdiction to certain guano islands. In addition, the defence argued that T-3 was under the territorial sovereignty of Canada by virtue of the "sector theory". Having heard arguments of counsel and the testimony of a Department of State witness that the Canadian Government had waived jurisdiction, Judge Lewis decided to take jurisdiction. He did not deal specifically with the questions of international law which had been raised and seemed to have rested his finding of criminal jurisdiction primarily on the nationality of the accused and the national character of the research station operating on T-3. [54] As for the Court of Appeals, its panel of six judges was evenly divided

---

[54] See *U.S.A.* v. *Escamilla (No. 71-1575). Brief for Appellant*, prepared by W. E. McDaniels and F. X. Grossi, at 12-13 (1971), and Andreas G. RONHOVDE, *Jurisdiction over Ice Islands : The Escamilla Case in Retrospect*, published by the Arctic Institute of North America, at 3-6 (Nov. 1972).

on the question of jurisdiction and so the district court's exercise of jurisdiction was affirmed. [55]

Comment. — It is generally agreed that there are four possible bases for the exercise of state jurisdiction: territory, nationality, protection of special state interests such as security, and protection of certain universal interests permitting jurisdiction over crimes such as piracy. In the present context we are concerned with the first two bases and the two following points should be commented upon: territorial jurisdiction in relation to Canada and personal jurisdiction in relation to the United States.

Territorial jurisdiction is derived from sovereignty and gives a state exclusive jurisdiction — subject to agreements to the contrary and to diplomatic immunities recognized by international law — to all persons and things found on its territory. The exclusiveness of jurisdiction is such that a state's forcible removal of a person from another state's territory is a violation of the latter's territorial sovereignty and involves the international responsibility of the former. The question which arose here was whether Canada's territorial sovereignty could be considered as extending to the T-3 incident, since it took place within the Canadian Arctic sector. More specifically, is the sector theory, invoked by Senator Pascal Poirier in 1907 in support of Canada's claim to Arctic islands north of the mainland, to be relied upon now to claim sovereignty right up to the Pole ? On this point it might be recalled that Prime Minister Trudeau stated, in reply to a question in the House of Commons on March 10, 1969, that in his opinion, the sector theory did not apply to the waters or ice. [56] This opinion is quite sound, considering the physical realities of the Arctic Ocean. The sector theory has never been recognized in international law as a valid basis for the acquisition of sovereignty over territory and has never been invoked — not even by the U.S.S.R. — as a means of acquiring sovereignty over the pack ice of the Arctic Ocean. This does not mean that the sector theory could not be used eventually as a convenient device to delimit the Arctic regions for the purpose of pollution control by the coastal states or for some other specific purpose. It does mean, however, that the theory in question — and it remains only a theory — cannot be invoked to claim territorial jurisdiction. It is not surprising, therefore, that the Canadian Government decided to waive jurisdiction. What is somewhat surprising, however, is that the Note expressing the waiver also stated that "[t]he Canadian Government continues to reserve its position on the question of jurisdiction over the alleged offence..." [57] In other words, it is only the actual exercise of jurisdiction which is being waived and not jurisdiction itself. It is not clear then on what basis the reservation is made, unless it is on the sector theory or on the fact that Ice Island T-3 was originally detached from Ellesmere Island ice shelf and is still considered as a floating part of Canadian territory. [58] Both of these possibilities are unlikely and, it is suggested, of no legal validity. The trial judge in the *Escamilla Case* would have been quite right in discarding the argument of Canadian jurisdiction, even in the absence of an express waiver.

Personal jurisdiction is based on nationality and extends to all nationals, regardless whether they are inside or outside a state's territory. In practice, however, states usually refrain from exercising jurisdiction over their nationals in respect of acts done on the territory of another state and, in case of conflict, territorial jurisdiction is generally recognized as taking

---

[57]   For a quotation of the essential part of the Note, see Terrance WILLS, "Arctic rule and the ice island killing", in *The Globe and Mail*, May 19, 1971, at 8. This part of the Note was also read into the record by the trial judge: see *U.S.A. v. Escamilla (No. 71-1575), Brief for Appellee*, prepared by J. W. Williams, in Appendix at 18 (1971).

[58]   The wedding of a Canadian couple on T-3 in May 1973 would seem to indicate that the RCMP might consider the ice island as part of Canadian territory. It is reported that RCMP constable Ross Pollock and Diane Underwood were married by Inspector Vic Irving, commanding officer of the Eastern Arctic patrol, in the mess hall of T-3, after unfolding the Canadian flag in front of the 16 members of the American expedition. See *The Globe and Mail*, May 3, 1973, at W8, and *The Ottawa Citizen*, May 5, 1973, at 16.

precedence over personal jurisdiction. But, who has jurisdiction over offenses committed by nationals in places not under the sovereignty of any state, such as on a ship on the high seas ? In such a case, jurisdiction over criminal offenses generally belongs to the state of the flag. The rule that the state of the flag has jurisdiction over everything which takes place aboard ship is so well established that a coastal state cannot exercise its criminal jurisdiction on board a foreign ship passing through its territorial waters to arrest a person for a crime committed on board during passage, unless the consequences of the crime extend to the coastal state. Regardless of the exact basis for this rule — be it the fiction that a ship is considered as a floating portion of territory or not — the validity of the rule is not in question. If Ice Island T-3 had been assimilated to a ship, the Escamilla incident would have been deemed to have taken place aboard an American ship on the high seas and there would have been no problem of jurisdiction. [59] It is interesting to notice that Canada's Note said that it "would not object to having the drifting ice formation in question treated as a ship for the purposes of the particular legal proceedings concerned in order to facilitate the course of justice and, if it is considered necessary, for the purpose of the legal proceeding in question". [60] This could be construed as an admission that the ice island was on the high seas, a status which Canada rejects for the Arctic Ocean. In any event, the prosecution did not rely on the ship analogy and the judge did not deal with it. Instead of asking the Court to construe the term "vessel" in the U.S. legislation so as to include T-3, the prosecution asked that the term "high seas"

---

[59]   The ship analogy was very ably discussed by Dr. Ronhovde recently in relation to the Escamilla Case. (See RONHOVDE, *supra* note 54, at 11-14.) He expresses skepticism about the analogy because of the problems it raises. Without minimizing the importance of those problems, this writer believes that a special Arctic convention could usefully incorporate the analogy and formulate rules governing the use of ice islands and ice floes. The relevant provisions of the High Seas Convention could be made applicable, some could be modified and new ones could be introduced, so as to insure the establishment of a reasonably complete legal regime. Otherwise, similar incidents are bound to recur and a legal vacuum might be found to exist.

[60]   See *supra* note 57.

be interpreted to encompass ice islands. Interestingly enough, it found support in Canada's Arctic Waters Pollution Prevention Act in its interpretation of "high seas". The Canadian Act, which applies to "arctic waters", defines those waters in two ways. In the first place, they cover waters up to 100 nautical miles from land and, in the second place, they include all waters above the submarine areas which Canada has the right to exploit; this means, in Canadian terms, to the edge of the continental margin or over 150 miles into the Beaufort Sea. For the second type of arctic waters it is specified that the Act applies whether or not those waters are "in a frozen or a liquid state". [61] The ice is, therefore, clearly assimilated to water and not to land for purposes of pollution prevention. It is not clear if Judge Lewis accepted the argument that "high seas" include ice islands, as his finding of jurisdiction appeared to rest on personal jurisdiction. This basis seems to be quite sound when one considers that the accused, the victim and the rest of the station personnel were all American citizens. Furthermore, the whole research program was administered by the Naval Arctic Research Laboratory located at Point Barrow, Alaska. In these circumstances, it is suggested that the exercise of criminal jurisdiction by the United States was quite justifiable under the general principle of personal jurisdiction based on nationality.

---

[61] Sec. 3(2), *Arctic Waters Pollution Prevention Act*, chap. 47, 18-19 Eliz. II, 1969-70.

PART VI

Oil Pollution Control in the Arctic

The importance of the problem of oil pollution control and prevention in the Arctic was given clear recognition by the Canadian Government on April 8, 1970, when it introduced the Arctic Waters Pollution Prevention Bill in the House of Commons. [1] In spite of strong objections on the part of the United States against certain provisions considered to be contrary to existing international law, the Bill was endorsed without a dissent by the House of Commons. It was given royal assent on June 26, 1970 and came into force by proclamation on August 2, 1972, along with the Regulations

---

[1] *Arctic Waters Pollution Prevention Act*, Chap. 47, 18-19 Eliz. II, 1969-70. For readings which comment on the Canadian Arctic legislation, see the following: R. B. BILDER, "The Canadian Arctic Waters Pollution Prevention Act: New Stresses on the Law of the Sea", 69 *Mich. L. Rev.*, 1-54 (1970); J.-Y. MORIN, "Le progrès technique, la pollution et l'évolution récente du droit de la mer au Canada, particulièrement à l'égard de l'Arctique", 8 *C.Y.I.L.* 158-248 (1970); L. LEGAULT, "Canadian Arctic Waters Pollution Prevention Legislation", in L. M. ALEXANDER (ed.), *Proceedings of the Fifth Annual Conference on the Law of the Sea Institute*, Rhode Island, 294-300 (1970); D. M. JOHNSTON, "The Arctic Marine Environment: A Managerial Perspective", *ibid.*, 312-318; D. M. JOHNSTON, "Canada's Arctic Marine Environment: Problems of Legal Protection", 29 *Behind the Headlines*, 1-7 (July 1970); L. F. E. GOLDIE, "International Principles of Responsibility for Pollution", 9 *Col. J. Trans. L.* 283-330 (1970); M. COHEN, "The Arctic and the National Interest", 26 *Int'l J.* 52-81 (1970-71); B. K. CARNAHAN, "The Canadian Arctic Waters Pollution Prevention Act: an Analysis, 31 *Louisiana L. Rev.* 632-649 (1971); L. HENKIN, "Arctic Anti-Pollution: Does Canada Make — or Break — International Law ?". 65 *A.J.I.L.* 131-136 (1971); R. H. NEUMAN, "Oil on Troubled Waters: The International Control of Marine Pollution", 2 *J. Mar. L. & Com.* 349-361 (1971); G. SUTTON, "Pollution Prevention in the Arctic — National and Multinational Approaches Compared", 5 *Ottawa L. Rev.* 32-64 (1971); L. C. GREEN, "International Law and Canada's Anti-Pollution Legislation", 50 *Oregon L. Rev.* 462-503 (1971); D. WILKES, "International Administrative Due Process and Control of Pollution — The Canadian Arctic Waters Example", 2 *J. Mar. L. & Com.* 499-539 (1971); J. A. BEESLEY, "Rights and Responsibilities of Arctic Coastal States: The Canadian View", 3 *J. Mar. L. & Com.* 1-12 (1971); D. M. JOHNSTON, "Marine pollution control: law, science, and politics", 28 *Int'l J.* 69-102 (1972-73); A. E. UTTON, "The Arctic Waters Pollution Prevention Act, and the Right of Self-Protection", 7 *U.B.C. Law Rev.* 221-234 (1972).

envisaged by the Act. Canada considered existing international conventions inadequate for the protection of coastal states against the threat of oil pollution and, with the oil activities on the increase ever since the discovery at Prudhoe Bay in 1968, felt that the situation was sufficiently serious and urgent to adopt unilateral measures. The stated objective behind this novel legislation is to protect the delicate ecological balance of the Canadian Arctic. The Government was careful to underline that it would have preferred an international solution to the problem, but decided to act unilaterally after failing to obtain satisfactory results on the international plane, both at the Brussels Conference of 1969 and, afterwards, in its bilateral talks with the United States.

The purpose here is to: I — examine briefly the extent of the problem of oil pollution in the Arctic regions; II — survey existing conventions bearing on oil pollution generally; III — analyse the Canadian legislation and its legal basis in international law; and IV — assess the future of oil pollution control in the Arctic.

I. — THE PROBLEM OF OIL POLLUTION CONTROL IN THE ARCTIC

Three major oil spills immediately come to mind when mentioning oil pollution: the stranding of the Liberian tanker *Torrey Canyon* in 1967, the Santa Barbara blowout of 1969 and the grounding of the Liberian tanker *Arrow* in 1970. A brief study of these spills can give an idea — albeit a remote one — of the damage which would result if such spills were to occur in the Arctic.

The stranding of the *Torrey Canyon* on the Seven Stones' reef in the English Channel, on March 18, 1967, while laden with 119,328 tons of crude oil, was the cause of millions of dollars of damage to both the British and the French coasts. [2]

---

[2] The material facts of the *Torrey Canyon* incident are set out in full in a publication by the Secretary of State for Home Department, *Coastal Pollution : Observations on the Report of the Select Committee on Science and Technology*, 244 pp. (January 1969). For the international law aspects of the "Torrey Canyon", see the following: A. E. UTTON, "Protective Measures and the 'Torrey Canyon'", 9 *Boston Col-*

In order to reach the French coast, the oil had to travel a distance of over 200 miles. After long proceedings instituted in Singapore by the British Government and in Rotterdam by the French Government, the owners and charterers of the tanker agreed to pay a total of 3 million pounds in final settlement of the claims of the two governments. [3] This was half of the actual amount which the two governments had estimated their damage to be. And, of course, this cannot take into account the undetermined, but nevertheless very real, effects on marine life and its environment.

The Santa Barbara blowout occurred on January 8, 1969, while the Union Oil Company was drilling a well about 5 miles offshore in 188 feet of water. [4] The well had been drilled to its total planned depth of 3,479 feet when it began gushing mud. The engineers managed to stop the mud flow from the pipe, but the gas and oil apparently found passage outside the wall of the well and began discharging at various points along a distance of about 800 feet. It was estimated that the oil spill amounted to between 200 and 500 barrels a day. It took a month to bring the leak under control and, even after that, oil continued to leak intermittently from contaminated rocks. The slick of oil eventually spread on beaches along the channel shore for a distance of about 30 miles. Here, as in the case of the *Torrey Canyon*, it was impossible to measure

---

lege *Indus. and Com. Law R.* 613-632 (1968); E. D. BROWN, "The Lessons of the Torrey Canyon", *Current Legal Problems* 113-136 (1968); V. P. NANDA, "The 'Torrey Canyon' Disaster: Some Legal Aspects", 44 *Denver L. J.* 400-425 (1967); E. DU PONTAVICE, *La pollution des mers par les hydrocarbures (A propos de l'Affaire du "Torrey Canyon")*, 142 pp. (1968). See also an excellent review by L. F. E. GOLDIE of the following books: *In the Wake of the Torrey Canyon*, by Richard PETROW (1968); *Oil and Water : The Torrey Canyon Disaster*, by Edward COWAN (1968); *Torrey Canyon Pollution and Marine Life*, edited by J. E. Smith (1968); *The Wreck of the Torrey Canyon*, by C. GILL and F. BOOKER (1967).

    [3] See "Torrey Canyon" (Agreement on Claims), reproduced from the British Hansard, in 9 *Int'l Legal Materials*, at 633-635 (1970).

    [4] For a discussion of the technical aspects of the Santa Barbara blowout, see V. E. McKELVEY, "The Origin, Incidence, Effects and Means of Prevention and Control of Oil-Well Blowouts", *Subsea Mineral Resources and Problems Related to Their Development*, Geological Survey Circular 619, at 19-22 (1969).

the damage done to the ecological balance of the marine environment concerned.

The grounding of the Liberian Tanker *Arrow* on Cerberus Rock in Chedabucto Bay, Nova Scotia, on February 4, 1970, was carrying some 108,000 barrels of Bunker C fuel oil and spilled more than half the cargo. Dr. P. D. McTaggart-Cowan, who headed the task force operations for the Canadian Government, summed up the resulting damage and cleaning-up difficulties in his letter to the Minister of Transport:

> Of the 375 miles of beautiful shoreline in Chedabucto Bay, 190 miles was contaminated to a greater or lesser extent by the *Arrow's* cargo and our efforts on the beaches cleaned only 30 miles. The remaining shoreline is virtually uncleanable unless one resorts to chemical methods which themselves would place the marine fauna and flora of the Bay in jeopardy to an extent unacceptable to your Task Force.
>
> Oil from the tanker *Arrow* moved from Chedabucto Bay as a result of mechanisms not yet clearly understood and fouled the beaches of Sable Island from one end to the other, even though Sable Island is over 100 miles from Chedabucto Bay. In the process an additional 4,800 birds lost their lives. [5]

It should be noted that the cost of the clean-up operations to the Canadian Government was about 4 million dollars [6] and that those measures could not prevent the lethal effects on wildlife and the long term ecological effects on the marine environment.

Such oil spills directly affect the whole web of living creatures in the sea. The following passage explains the complex interaction which takes place between marine organisms.

> The history of life in the ocean is one of interaction between the living creatures and the oceanic environment —

---

[5] See *Report of the Task Force — Operation Oil (Clean-up of the Arrow oil spill in Chedabucto Bay)* to the Minister of Transport, Vol. I, at 2 (1970).

[6] See "Govt. out $4 million in Arrow cleanup job", the *Ottawa Citizen,* Jan. 25, 1971, at 12, where the Minister of Transport is reported as quoting that figure.

the water, the air, and the land. To a large extent the shapes and habits of each living creature in the sea have been molded by that environment. Each has adjusted to and has been shaped by the ocean, and over the millions of years a series of delicately adjusted, interlocking relationships have developed. The life of all parts of the ocean is linked — the plankton to herring and mackerel, to tuna and shark, to squid and whale. [7]

It must be emphasized that the complex ecosystem just described, and applicable to oceans in general, is infinitely more delicate and precarious in the cold waters of the Arctic seas. The Arctic ecosystem is young and unstable, [8] and biological damage caused by a major oil spill would affect the whole pattern of reproduction. [9] The adverse consequences on such a vulnerable environment would be all the greater that cleaning-up operations — which are always costly and only partially successful in limiting ecological damage — are far more difficult to carry out in cold waters. A foretaste of such difficulty was gained by Canada in the clean-up operations of the *Arrow* spill where attempts to ignite slicks of that oil were virtually unsuccessful because the temperature of the water was close to freezing point. [10] One can readily imagine the difficulties of cleaning-up operations in the freezing waters of the Arctic which, in addition, are generally covered with ice floes. David P. Hoult, of the Massachusetts Institute of Technology, states that "the oil will tend to spread *under the ice*, at the oil water interface, and collect in pockets at the inter-

---

[7] *Marine Science Affairs*, Annual Report of the President to the Congress on Marine Resources and Engineering Development, at 17 (April 1970).

[8] On the characteristics of ecosystems in polar regions, see M. J. DUNBAR, *Ecological Developments in Polar Regions. A Study in Evolution* (1968). For a good description of the marine ecosystem in the Arctic, see M. E. BRITTON, *Special Problems of the Arctic Environment*, at 38-41; manuscript distributed at Conference on Canada-US Law of the Sea Problems, Toronto (16-17 June 1971). Dr. Britton illustrates in particular the food chain or dependency of organisms on others in the Arctic Ocean.

[9] See Fu-Shiang CHIA, "Reproduction of Arctic Marine Invertebrates", in 1 (NS) *Marine Pollution Bulletin*, at 78-79 (1970).

[10] See H. BOYD, "Oil Poses Urgent Problems in Canada", in 1 (NS) *Marine Pollution Bulletin*, at 69 (1968).

face". [11] He also estimates that "(a) super tanker, breaking up in an ice field would create a pool of oil about a mile in radius with a mean thickness of 1 foot. Thus, in contrast to the problem in temperate climates, the oil spill on ice does not form thin films." [12] It would be very difficult, if not impossible, to retrieve such thick films of oil and they would take a long time to disappear in the below-zero temperatures of the Arctic waters. Dr. Richard Warner, of Memorial University of Newfoundland, speaks of the slow degradation process of oil in such waters as follows:

> ... decomposition (of oil) in the Arctic oceans, whose temperatures are at 0°C (32°F) or below throughout the year, would be very slow indeed. Where oil is exposed to still lower temperatures, for instance when carried onto shorelines and ice floes, biochemical decay would be virtually nonexistent, and the oil would persist for decades, perhaps centuries ... evaporation rates of the highly toxic "lighter fractions" of crude oil slicks are believed to be greatly slowed. The net effect is to significantly prolong the time during which the sensitive marine organisms are exposed to the toxic influences of the lighter hydrocarbons. [13]

As for the possible damage to wildlife which could result from a major oil spill in the Arctic, Dr. A. H. MacPherson of the Canadian Wildlife Service, gives the following opinion:

> Direct mortality of wildlife from a large oil gush or a tanker accident could be enormous. In spring heavy oil pollution in open water off the floe-edge in the Beaufort Sea or Hudson Bay would unquestionably trap very large proportions of the Arctic populations of swans, ducks, geese, gulls, guillemots, murres, fulmars, jaegers and phalaropes. Crude oil is toxic to many birds and would presumably be also to mammals attempting to remove it from their pelts with their tongues. Polar bears and Arctic foxes might suffer

---

[11]   D. P. HOULT, "Marine Pollution", *Concentrating on the Effects of Hydrocarbons in Sea Water*, at 5; manuscript distributed at Conference on Canada-US Law of the Sea Problems, Toronto (16-17 June 1971).

[12]   *Ibid.*

[13]   Brief prepared for the Canadian Wildlife Service, 14 Aug. 1969, quoted by James Woodford in *The Violated Vision*, at 62 (1972). For a similar point of view on the slow degradation of oil in Arctic waters, see M. J. DUNBAR, *Environment and Good Sense*, at 55 (1971).

on the sea-coasts; muskrats, beavers, mink, otter and lesser species would doubtless be affected by a major spill on the Yukon River or in the Delta of the Mackenzie. Seals also appear vulnerable to crude oil spills. . . . [14]

The problem of transporting oil from Prudhoe Bay is not yet resolved. True, for the moment, the debate is whether to build a pipeline across Alaska or the Mackenzie Valley in order to carry oil to the United States, but the eventual use of the Northwest Passage is far from being discounted. It could be used to carry oil to the East Coast and possibly to Europe. Some estimate that as much as $600,000 a day could be saved by using the Northwest Passage as compared to the cost of building and operating a transcontinental pipeline. [15] With the valuable data obtained by the *Manhattan* during her two voyages in 1969 and 1970, there is nothing to prevent the development of huge icebreaking tankers possessing the necessary shaft horsepower to make the Northwest Passage, including M'Clure Strait. This, however, only adds to the possibility of an oil spill occurring. The force of polar ice is a giant one to contend with, as the *Manhattan* found out on her return voyage in 1969, when the ice of Lancaster Sound knocked out a huge panel from her hull, spilling 15,000 barrels of ballast water. [16] Of course, it was pointed out that the accident happened in the unprotected section of the hull and that any tanker carrying oil would be fully reinforced. The fact remains that such a possibility had not been guarded against and that similar accidents are bound to occur in the eventuality of tanker traffic developing.

In addition to transporting oil through the Northwest Passage by supertanker icebreakers, one must not discount the possibility of doing so through the Arctic Ocean itself. If a surface ship can navigate through the polar ice of M'Clure Strait, there is an excellent chance that it can manage the same kind of polar ice in the Arctic Ocean. And plans are

---

[14]   Manuscript entitled "The Oil Rush and the Arctic Environment", quoted by James Woodford in *The Violated Vision,* at 61 (1972).
[15]   B. KEATING, "North for Oil. Manhattan Makes the Historic Northwest Passage", 137 *National Geographic,* 374 at 376 (1970).
[16]   *Ibid.,* at 391.

not limited to using large surface tankers, they envisage submarine tankers as well. General Dynamics Corporation announced some time ago that it had made proposals to five oil companies to build 170,000-ton nuclear-powered submarine tankers. These submarines would be 900 feet long, with a beam of 140 feet and a hull depth of 85 feet. [17] Such submarines could carry oil not only to the United States through the Northwest Passage, if they can manage the somewhat shallow waters of Barrow Strait, but also to Europe through the Arctic Ocean under the pack ice. These are exciting possibilities and very positive ones for the future of the oil industry and for economic development generally, but we must take precautions to insure that we are not destroying the environment and ourselves in the process. Let us see to what extent the precautions already taken on the international plane insure adequate protection of the Canadian Arctic waters against oil pollution.

II. — OIL POLLUTION CONTROL IN INTERNATIONAL CONVENTIONS UP TO 1970

The intention here is not to make a complete analysis of international conventions on the subject [18] but rather to

---

[17] "Transportation", *Canadian Petroleum*, at 14-15 (Feb. 1970).
[18] Such an analysis was done admirably by Prof. J. C. SWEENEY in his scholarly article "Oil Pollution of the Oceans", 37 *Fordham L. Rev.* 155-208, at 186-194 (1968), where he summarized the efforts done on the international plane up to 1968. For the sake of completeness, mention should be made of the North Sea Oil Pollution Convention of 1969 but it will not be reviewed since it has no application to the Arctic. The Convention provides for cooperation among the Contracting Parties (Belgium, Denmark, France, Germany, Netherlands, Norway, Sweeden and the United Kingdom) in dealing with pollution of the North Sea by oil, by reciprocal information on the presence of oil slicks and assistance in remedial measures. The text of the Convention may be found in 9 *Int'l Legal Materials,* at 359 (1969) and 74 *Revue générale de droit international public,* at 230 (1970). For further readings on the question of international control of oil pollution, in addition to some mentioned in Footnote 1 above, see the following: A. I. MENDELSOHN, "Maritime Liability for Oil Pollution — Domestic and International Law", 38 *Geo. Wash. L. R.* 1-31 (1969); a Comment: "Oil Pollution of the Sea", 10 *Har. Int'l L. J.* 316-359 (1969); A. HOVANESIAN, "Post Torrey Canyon: Toward a New Solution to the Problem of Traumatic Oil Spillage", 2 *Conn. L. Rev.* 632-647 (1970); N. D. SHUTLER, "Pollution of the Sea by Oil", 7 *Houston L. Rev.* 415-441 (1970); N. J.

concentrate on the 1969 Brussels conventions after making a very brief historical review of the main international provisions before then.

1. INTERNATIONAL PROVISIONS BEFORE THE 1969 BRUSSELS CONVENTIONS

In 1926, at the instance of the United States government, a Preliminary Conference on Oil Pollution of Navigable Waters was held in Washington. It was attended by 12 seafairing countries and produced a Convention which established prohibited zones, varying from 50 to 150 miles from the coast, within which commercial ships were not to discharge oil or oily mixtures with a certain oil content. The Convention, however, did not receive the necessary five ratifications and never entered into force.

The next Conference was not held until 1954, this time in London, at the initiative of the British Government. Thirty-two countries were represented and they adopted the *International Convention for the Prevention of Pollution of the Sea by Oil*. The Convention went into force on July 28, 1958, twelve months after ratification or accession by 10 countries including 5 having at least 500,000 gross tons of tanker tonnage (Art. XV). The Convention established prohibited zones, extending from 50 to 150 miles from the coast, within which

---

HEALY, "The International Convention on Civil Liability for Oil Pollution Damage, 1969", 1 *J. Mar. L. & Com.* 317-323 (1970); N. A. WULF, "International Control of Marine Pollution" 25 *J.A.G. Journal* 93-100 (1971); O. SCHACHTER & D. SERWER, "Marine Pollution Problems and Remedies", 65 *A.J.I.L.* 84-111 (1967); P. N. SWAN, "International and National Approaches to Oil Pollution Responsibility: An Emerging Regime for a Global Problem", 50 *Oregon L. Rev.* 506-586 (1971); W. W. MAYWHORT, "International Law — Oil Spills and Their Legal Ramifications", 49 *N.C.L. Rev.*, 996-1003 (1971); M. HARDY, "International Control of Marine Pollution", 2 *Nat. Res. J.* 296-348 (1971); G. KOJANEC, "Compétences des Etats et réglementation internationale récente en matière de pollution de la mer: un cas de dédoublement fonctionnel", 41 *Annuaire de l'A.A.A.* 35-40 (1971); Y. DINSTEIN, "Oil Pollution by Ships and Freedom of the High Seas", 3 *J. Mar. L. & Com.* 363-374 (1972); L. C. CAFLISCH, "International Law and Ocean Pollution: The Present and the Future", 8 *Belgian Rev. Int'l L.* 28-33 (1972); V. PETACCIO, "Water Pollution and the Future Law of the Sea", 21 *I.C.L.Q.* 15-21 (1972); N. A. WULF, "Contiguous Zones for Pollution Control", 3 *J. Mar. L. & Com.* 537-557 (1972).

commercial ships of over 500 tons gross tonnage were not to discharge oil or any oily mixture which would foul the surface of the sea (Art. III and Annex "A"). Provisions were made for the installation of oily-water separators on ships and of oily waste receiving facilities in the main ports. Because of the flag state principle, no agreement was reached on a surveillance procedure of the high seas, and it was left up to each country to take proceedings against the owners of its ships in case of breach of the Convention. Any contracting government, however, could provide any other contracting party with written evidence of contraventions, which put the latter under an obligation to investigate and institute proceedings if necessary (Art. X). In 1962, the Convention was amended to increase the number of prohibited zones and extend their breadth from a minimum of 50 to one of 100 miles. There is now a specific Canadian Western Zone which extends to 100 miles from the nearest land along the west coast of Canada, as well as a North-West Atlantic Zone of 100 miles along the east coast of Canada. [19] The 1962 amendments came into force in May 1967. The Convention was amended again in 1969 to further reduce permissible oil discharges at sea and to prohibit altogether any such discharge by tankers within 50 miles from the nearest land. Unfortunately, these amendments are not yet in force. It must be underlined that the Convention, even as amended in 1962 and 1969, does not cover cases of accidental pollution.

In 1958, the Geneva Conference on the Law of the Sea adopted four conventions, three of which contain provisions relating to pollution of the seas. The *Convention on the High Seas* provides that "every state shall draw up regulations to prevent pollution of the seas by the discharge of oil from ships or pipelines or resulting from the exploitation and exploration of the seabed and its subsoil, taking account of existing treaty provisions on the subject" (Art. 24). The intent was obviously to emphasize the obligations of states to prevent oil

---

[19]   See *ANNEX A*, 2 (a) and (b), "Amendments to the International Convention for the Prevention of Pollution of the Sea by Oil, 1954", reproduced in *Canada Treaty Series* No. 29, at 14 and 16 (1967).

pollution, whether as a result of navigation or through exploration and exploitation. The *Convention on the Continental Shelf* specifies that "exploration of the continental shelf and the exploitation of its natural resources must not result in any injustifiable interference with . . . the conservation of the living resources of the sea" (Art. 5(1)), and adds that "the coastal state is obliged to undertake, in the safety zones, all appropriate measures for the protection of the living resources of the sea from harmful agents" (Art. 5(7)). Here again the general intention is clear that states have a duty to explore or exploit their continental shelf in such a way as not to pollute waters of the high seas above and thereby affect its living resources. The *Convention on the Territorial Sea and the Contiguous Zone* contains a general provision on the contiguous zone which empowers a coastal state to "exercise the control necessary to: (a) prevent infringement of its . . . sanitary regulations within its territory or territorial sea; (b) punish infringement of the above regulations within its territory or territorial sea" (Art. 24). The coastal state is therefore given a protective and preventive jurisdiction in a zone of the high seas, in order to insure the respect of its sanitary regulations within its territorial waters. This provision is now generally interpreted as enabling the coastal state to enact oil pollution control regulations and to enforce them within the contiguous zone. Furthermore, it may be reasonably argued that the passage of a polluting ship in territorial waters is not innocent, since a passage is considered innocent only "so long as it is not prejudicial to the peace, good order or security of the coastal State" (Art. 14(4)). A ship which damages the marine environment and territorial interests of the coastal state, it is submitted, constitutes a threat to its living in peace and security.

No provision so far is made for accidental oil pollution damage but, after the 1967 *Torrey Canyon* disaster, the question took on more practical importance. It was clearly demonstrated what catastrophic consequences such a massive spill can have and how difficult it is to obtain compensation.

The *Institute of International Law* studied the question of accidental pollution of the seas and, at its Edinburg session in September 1969, agreed upon certain important provisions which are having a considerable influence on the development of international law. One provision, which enables the coastal state to take protective measures, in the event of an imminent danger of pollution following an accident on the high seas, was adopted with only slight modification at the Brussels Conference a few months later. The Institute suggested also that all states should take appropriate measures in relation to the design and equipment of ships to prevent pollution of the seas. It then went on to provide that the coastal state has the right to prohibit ships not conforming with those standards from crossing their territorial sea and contiguous zone. The article in question reads:

> States have the right to prohibit any ship that does not conform to the standards set up in accordance with the preceding articles for the design and equipment of the ships, for the navigation instruments, and for the qualifications of the officers and members of the crews, from crossing their territorial seas and contiguous zones and from reaching their ports. [20]

In other words, a ship which does not meet certain anti-pollution standards is considered a threat to the coastal state. The latter may protect itself by prohibiting the passage of such ship not only within its territorial waters but also on the high seas within its contiguous zone. Although this provision finds a legal basis in the Territorial Sea Convention of 1958 already referred to, the Brussels Conference was not quite prepared to adopt it.

2. THE TWO BRUSSELS CONVENTIONS OF 1969

The Brussels Conference of 1969 was called at the initiative of IMCO and was attended by delegates of close to 40 countries. The Conference was presented with two draft conventions: one, dealing with the rights of the coastal state

---

[20] INSTITUTE OF INTERNATIONAL LAW (Edinburg Session), *Resolutions adopted by the Institute . . .*, Art. VI, at 8, Geneva (December 1969). For a report of the study leading up to the adoption of the Resolutions, see 53 *Annuaire de l'Institut de Droit international*, Tome I, at 547 (1969).

to take certain measures on the high seas against pollution damage: the other covers the liability of the owner of the ship causing pollution. What follows is an analysis of the main provisions of those two conventions.

(1) International Convention Relating to Intervention on the High Seas in Cases of Oil Pollution Damage (1969) [21]

Scope of the Convention. — The Convention is limited to pollution damage caused by the spillage of oil and does not cover other pollutants. "Oil" is defined as meaning "crude oil, fuel oil, diesel oil and lubricating oil" (Art. II(4)). Some of the delegations were in favour of enlarging the scope of the Convention to include other pollutants, but it was generally felt that the inclusion of other polluting agents would create serious problems of interpretation in the absence of an agreed list. [22] There was also some discussion at the Conference on whether the Convention should cover interventions in the territorial sea as well as the high seas. However, it was decided that this would cause confusion, since the rights of the coastal state in its territorial waters were already wider than those conferred by the Convention.

The whole operation of the Convention is linked to the concept of "maritime casualty", since no measure against possible pollution damage may be taken until there has been a "maritime casualty" (Art. I). The restrictive definition of this expression will be seen later. As for the meaning of "ship", it includes any sea-going vessel, but it specifically excludes warships or government ships used only on non-commercial service (Art. I(2)). It also excludes a floating craft which would be used as a device for the exploration or exploitation of the resources of the sea-bed and subsoil of the ocean (Art. II(2b)).

Nature of the incident justifying measures. — The main provision on measures to be taken by the coastal state is Article I which provides as follows:

---

[21] Reproduced in 9 *Int'l Legal Materials,* at 25-35 (1970).
[22] See generally IMCO Brussels Conference 1969, LEG/CONF/ C.I./S.R., 1 & 2.

> Parties to the present Convention may take such measures on the high seas as may be necessary to prevent, mitigate or eliminate grave and imminent danger to their coastline or related interests from pollution or threat of pollution of the sea by oil, following upon a *maritime casualty*, which may reasonably be expected to result in major harmful consequence (emphasis added).

This article is basically the same as had been adopted by the Institute of International Law, but it makes an important change in substituting "maritime casualty" for "accident". The expression "maritime casualty" is defined as meaning "a collision of ships, stranding or other incident of navigation, or other occurrence on board a ship or external to it resulting in material damage or imminent threat of material damage to a ship or cargo" (Art. II(1)). In addition to a "maritime casualty", there must be an actual or threatened pollution damage directed at the coastline or "related interests". This expression is defined as including fisheries activities, tourist attractions, the health of the coastal population, conservation of living marine resources and of wildlife (Art. I(4)). It may conceivably include other related interests not specifically mentioned, since the definition is not exhaustive.

It follows from this analysis of Article I that two conditions must be met before the coastal state can take protective measures: (1) material damage (actual or imminent) to the ship or cargo, and (2) pollution damage (actual or imminent) to the coastline or related interests of the coastal state. The first condition becomes the key to the whole operation of the Convention and the existence of it is difficult, if not impossible, for the coastal state to determine.

Procedure for enforcing the measures. — Although the coastal state may decide when to take protective measures, it cannot exercise that right without following a prescribed procedure. Before taking any measure, the coastal state must, in principle, consult with other states affected and it must notify the proposed measures to persons or states having interests which can reasonably be expected to be affected (Art. III). This means that the coastal state must first determine the owners of the ship and cargo in order to notify them.

Since the ownership of the cargo is normally within the knowledge of the flag state, it would have been a more practical and efficient procedure to require the flag state to notify the cargo owners. It is only in cases of extreme situations that the coastal state is dispensed with the notification and consultation procedure. The article in question stipulates: "in cases of extreme urgency requiring measures to be taken immediately, the coastal state may take measures rendered necessary by the urgency of the situation, without prior notification or consultation or without continuing consultations already begun" (Art. III(d)). Naturally, if this course of action is followed, the coastal state must be in a position to show that the emergency situation did really exist and that the measures taken were justified.

Nature and proportionality of the measures. — It is up to the coastal state to decide what type of measures it will take but, whatever they are, they must be proportionate to the damage either actual or threatened. The Convention provides that any Party which has taken measures in contravention of the Convention "shall be obliged to pay compensation to the extent of the damage caused by measures which exceed those reasonably necessary to achieve the end mentioned in Article I" (Art. VI). In other words, if a coastal state takes measures going beyond what was "reasonably necessary" to protect its coastline or related interests, it must pay compensation to the owners of the ship or cargo, or both, for any loss resulting from the excessive measures.

A number of states, particularly Canada, felt that the obligation to pay such compensation ought to be limited to cases where the states of the ship or cargo were Parties to the Private Law Convention on Civil Liability for Oil Pollution Damage. The Canadian delegation presented a proposal to link up the two Conventions in that way. The purpose of the amendment was explained by Mr. Stanford who is reported as follows:

> A coastal State should not be required to undertake the potential financial obligations imposed by Article VI of the Public Law Convention in relation to States which

are not prepared to accept the corresponding financial obligations in the Private Law Convention. [23]

He specified that ". . . a coastal State should not be obliged to pay for excessive damages caused to a ship or its cargo while the flag State or the State that represented the shipowners' interest . . . remained free from any obligation towards the nationals of the coastal State which had suffered massive pollution damage". [24] Most of the 37 delegates present expressed considerable symphathy for the principle behind the Canadian proposal but, when the Canadian delegation insisted for a roll call vote, only 9 supported it. [25]

Settlement of disputes. — In case of controversy relating to the measures taken by the coastal state, it is submitted, upon request of any party concerned, to conciliation or, if conciliation fails, to arbitration. The non-exhaustion of local remedies is not a ground to refuse a request for conciliation or arbitration (Art. XIII).

General comment. — In spite of certain shortcomings, this Convention does represent a very important step toward the protection of the coastal state. For the first time, the coastal state is expressly recognized as having a right to take certain unilateral measures on the high seas in order to protect itself against a threat of pollution damage. By the same token, it represents a recognition of the necessity to impose certain limitations on the traditional principle of the freedom of the high seas and the corollary rule of the flag state jurisdiction. The Convention, however, is far from being in force yet. It has been signed by 21 states and it must be ratified or acceded to by 15 states before entering into force (Art. XI). Canada was rather dissatisfied with the lack of adequate protection afforded to the coastal state; it abstained from voting on the adoption of the Convention at the Conference and did not sign the Convention subsequently.

---

[23]   IMCO Document LEG/CONF/C.I./S.R., 12, at 4.

[24]   *Ibid.*

[25]   *Ibid.*, at 13. The nine states in question were Australia, Ghana, Guatemala, India, Indonesia, New Zealand, Philippines, Syria and Yugoslavia.

(2) *International Convention on Civil Liability for Oil Pollution Damage (1969)* [26]

Scope of the Convention. — The Convention is restricted to pollution damage due to one source only, namely oil. This limited scope is normal, since the sister convention relating to intervention on the high seas is also limited to pollution damage caused by oil. "Oil" is defined as meaning "any persistent oil such as crude oil, fuel oil, heavy diesel oil, lubricating oil and whale oil, whether carried on board a ship as cargo or in the brinkers of such a ship" (Art. I(5)). This definition is essentially the same as the one in the sister convention previously studied.

The area of application of the Convention is limited to liability for damage done to the "territory" of the contracting states (Art. II). This includes the territorial waters (Act. II) but does not include any contiguous zone. However, the liability envisaged by the Convention does cover "preventive measures" taken to prevent or minimize pollution damage, and such measures could well have been taken on the high seas. This Convention, like the Public Law Convention, does not apply to warships or government ships used only for non-commercial service (Art. XI).

Nature of the liability. — There was considerable discussion at the Brussels Conference on whether the liability for pollution damage should be a strict one or should be based on fault or negligence. There was even more debate on the question of who should bear the liability: the owner of the ship, the owner of the cargo or both. Finally, a form of strict liability of the owner [27] of the ship was adopted. It is a mitigated form of absolute liability, since the owner may avoid being liable, if the incident causing the damage results from any of the following: an act of war, an act or omission of a third party, the negligence of a government responsible for navigational aids, or the act or omission of the person or

---

[26]   Reproduced in 9 *Int'l Legal Materials,* at 45-64 (1970).

[27]   "Owner" is defined as including the operator of the ship, in order to cover the situation of socialist countries where the state owns the ships.

state suffering the damage (Art. III). Furthermore, the liability is a limited one, providing the owner is not found at fault. The liability of the ship owner is then limited to $125. per ton of the ship's tonnage, with a maximum of 14 million dollars (Art. V(1) & (2)). In order to ensure payment in the event of liability, the owner must constitute a fund by depositing the amount or a sufficient guarantee with a court or other competent authority in his country (Art. V(3)). Furthermore, if a ship carries more than 2,000 tons of oil, the owner must maintain insurance for the limits of liability prescribed (Art. VII). The major and obvious defect of the system just described is that an innocent victim of pollution damage is not fully protected. This was pointed out by some of the countries represented at the Conference, particularly by Canada which advocated a joint liability of the owners of the ship and cargo, with the setting-up of an international compensation fund. The Canadian position was explained by Mr. Wershof and is reported in part as follows:

> His delegation was glad to note that they included strict liability on the owner but could not agree with the exceptions. The basic position taken by his country was that innocent victims must be assured of compensation up to the limit of actual credible damage. They realized that shipowners alone could not assume the whole burden, and had therefore put forward a plan which involved joint liability between the ship and the cargo. [28]

The Conference was not ready to accept Canada's proposal and accepted instead the British compromise proposal which is the principle incorporated in the Convention.

Settlement of disputes. — The enforcement of the Convention is left to the courts of the contracting Parties. Action for compensation by a coastal state is brought in its own courts and the judgment will be recognized by the other contracting

---

[28]   See IMCO Document LEG/CONF/C.I./S.R. 17, at 11. During the subsequent debate on the Arctic Waters Pollution Prevention Bill, the Minister of Transport, the Hon. Donald C. Jamieson, stated that "the conventions produced by the conference fell far short of what Canada considers to be satisfactory, particularly as to liability for pollution damage". See *Can. H.C. Deb.* Vol. 114, No. 50, at 2698-9 (22 Jan. 1970).

states, except if the judgment was obtained by fraud or if the defendant was not given reasonable notice and fair opportunity to present his case (Articles IX and X).

General comment. — This Convention does represent a considerable progress in incorporating the principle of strict liability on the part of the shipowner in case of pollution damage. For instance, the proof of liability in the *Torrey Canyon* case would still have been necessary if it had gone to the end. The owners there continued to deny liability throughout, in spite of the fact that the Seven Stones were notorious navigational dangers, that an error in navigation was admitted and that the Liberian Board of Investigators recommended the revocation of the Master's licence because of negligence. [29] Looking at the negative side of the Convention — and this is its main shortcoming — it may very well leave a coastal state with partial compensation in case of a huge oil spill. This was recognized by the Conference and a resolution was adopted requesting IMCO "to elaborate as soon as possible, through its Legal Committee and other appropriate legal bodies, a draft for a compensation scheme based upon the existence of an International Fund". [30] The resolution specifies that such a scheme should take two principles into account: (1) victims should be fully compensated, and (2) the shipowner should, in principle, be relieved of the additional financial burden now imposed by the Convention.

As for the entry into force of the Convention, it necessitates ratification or accession by 8 states, including 5 with not less than 1,000,000 gross tons of tanker tonnage (Art. XV). It has been signed by 20 states but has not yet received the necessary number of ratifications or accessions. Canada was quite dissatisfied with the limited liability provisions of the

---

[29] *Secretary of State for Home Department* (U.K.), *Coastal Pollution : Observations on the Report of the Select Committee on Science and Technology*, at 5-6 (Jan. 1969).
[30] "Resolution on Establishment of an International Compensation Fund for Oil Pollution Damage", reproduced in 9 *Int'l Legal Materials*, at 66-67 (1970). The Fund was in fact established by special convention signed at Brussels on December 18, 1971. For the text of the International Compensation Fund Convention, see 66 *A.J.I.L.*, at 712-733 (1972).

Convention, voted against its adoption at the Conference and has not subsequently signed it.

It was in the light of the above conventions, the two more important ones not yet in force, that Canada decided to adopt unilateral measures to protect its Arctic regions against the pollution threat posed by the present exploitation of oil in permafrost and its eventual transportation through ice-infected waters.

III. — OIL POLLUTION CONTROL LEGISLATION FOR THE CANADIAN ARCTIC (1970)

The purpose here is to review the main features of the Canadian legislation and examine the international validity of some of its provisions in the light of the relevant principles of the law of the sea.

1. MAIN PROVISIONS OF THE ARCTIC WATERS POLLUTION PREVENTION ACT

Preamble. — The preamble of the Act gives a good indication of the basic reasons for this somewhat unprecedented legislation. It recites that Parliament has an obligation to see not only that the natural resources of the Canadian Arctic are developed and exploited, but also that the Arctic waters adjacent to Canada are navigated only "in a manner that takes cognizance of Canada's responsibility for the welfare of the Eskimo and other inhabitants of the Canadian Arctic and the preservation of the peculiar ecological balance that now exists in the water, ice and land areas of the Canadian Arctic". [31] The basic objective of the legislation is therefore to permit the economic development of the Canadian Arctic while, at the same time, preserve its unique marine environment.

Geographic application (Figure 9). — The Act applies to "arctic waters" which are defined as being those "adjacent to the mainland and islands of the Canadian Arctic within the

---

[31] *Supra* note 1.

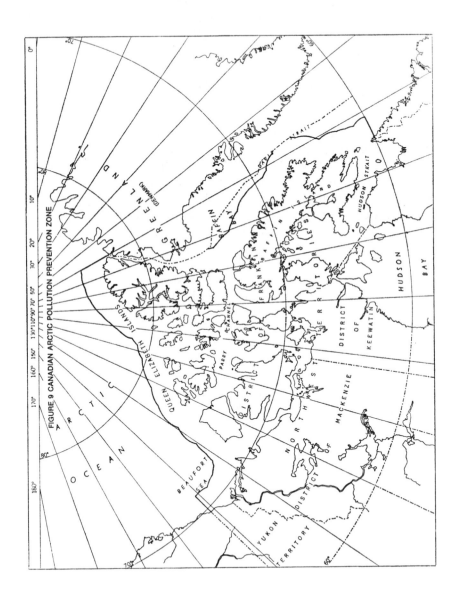

FIGURE 9 CANADIAN ARCTIC POLLUTION PREVENTION ZONE

area enclosed by the sixtieth parallel of the north latitude, the one hundred and forty-first meridian of longitude and a line measured seaward from the nearest Canadian land a distance of one hundred nautical miles . . . " (Sec. 3(1)). An exception is made to this distance on the east side of the archipelago where the limit is the median line between Greenland and the nearest Canadian land. In other words, the northerly limit of the Arctic waters as defined extends 100 miles from the mainland into the Beaufort Sea, beginning at the 141st meridian and running in a general northeasterly direction along the coastline of the Canadian Arctic Archipelago until it reaches the 60th meridian. The pollution prevention zone in question cannot be interpreted as extending to the North Pole as some commentators would have it. [32] The expression "arctic waters" is further defined as including waters adjacent to the areas above described where such adjacent waters overlies "submarine areas Her Majesty in right of Canada has the right to dispose of or exploit" (Sec. 3(2)), that is the waters above the continental shelf. More specifically, the pollution prevention zone extends only 100 miles in relation to navigation or shipping, but extends beyond that in relation to the exploitation of the continental shelf, Canada having already issued permits as far as 140 miles off the mainland coast in the Beaufort Sea. The Act also specifies that the waters envisaged include those "in a frozen or a liquid state". This was felt necessary to specify, since in most of the area covered by the legislation, waters are in a frozen state for the greater part of the year.

Type of pollution prohibited. — The Act prohibits and provides stiff penalties for the deposit of "waste" in the Arctic waters or on the mainland or islands where such waste may enter the Arctic waters. The definition of "waste" is a very comprehensive one and includes any substance that, if added to any waters, would degrade or alter the waters "to an extent

---

[32]   See R. H. NEUMAN, "Oil on Troubled Waters: The International Control of Marine Pollution", 2 *J. Mar. L. & Com.* 349, at 355, footnote 17 (1971), and G. SUTTON, "Pollution Prevention in the Arctic — National and Multinational Approaches Compared", 5 *Ottawa L. Rev.* 32, at 41 (1971).

that is detrimental to their use by man or by any animal, fish or plant that is useful to man . . . and . . . includes anything that, for the purposes of the Canada Water Act, is deemed to be waste" (Sec. 2(1)). Under the Canada Water Act, the Governor-in-Council may make regulations prescribing that certain substances, concentrations of substances and treatments of water are deemed to be waste. [33] This definition, of course, goes far beyond the usual persistent oils and includes all forms of pollutant agents. Fortunately, the Act goes on to provide that "the Governor-in-Council may make regulations . . . prescribing the type and quantity of waste, if any, that may be deposited . . . ." (Sec. 4(3)). The Regulations, which came into effect on August 2, 1972, contain two provisions relating to permissible waste resulting from non-shipping activities: one covering domestic waste and the other, industrial waste. Non-shipping activities envisage essentially those connected with the exploration and exploitation of the Arctic lands and submarine areas. The type and quantity of industrial waste permitted are determined by reference to three other statutes: the Oil and Gas Production and Conservation Act, the Territorial Lands Act and the Public Land Grants Act. The 1972 Regulations do not apply to the deposit of waste by a ship, so that the latter is fully subject to the comprehensive definition quoted above.

Nature of liability. — The Act imposes civil liability, for the deposit of waste, upon persons exploring or exploiting natural resources of Canadian Arctic lands or submarine areas, as well as upon "the owner of any ship that navigates within the Arctic waters and the owners of the cargo of any such ship" (Sec. 6(1)). Such liability is "absolute and does not depend upon proof of fault or negligence . . . ." (Sec. 7(1)). These provisions, which impose absolute liability on the ship and cargo owners, were the cause of the delay in bringing the Act into force. The Communiqué issued by the Canadian Government at the time the Act was proclaimed gives the following explanation:

---

[33] *Canada Water Act,* 18-19 Eliz. II, 1969-1970, Sections 2(2) and 16 (1)(a).

The chief stumbling block concerned the desire of shipowners and cargo owners to obtain insurance to cover pollution liability and the absence of such insurance due to the fact that before the Arctic Waters Pollution Prevention Act was drafted the need for this kind of coverage did not exist.

Following extensive consultations with marine underwriters and a more positive assessment of the situation by the international shipping community, a way has now been found whereby the absolute liability which the Act places on shipowners and cargo owners for any pollution resulting from the passage of their ship through Arctic waters can be insured. [34]

The way which was found to obtain insurance covering the absolute liability principle incorporated in the Act was to attach a number of exceptions in the Regulations. The latter provide that the underwriter will not be liable where:

(a)   the deposit of waste was caused by an act of war, hostilities, civil war or insurrection, or a natural phenomenon of an exceptional inevitable and irresistible character;

(b)   the deposit of waste was wholly caused by the act or omission of a person, other than the ship owner or a servant or an agent of the ship owner, done with intent to cause damage;

(c)   the deposit of waste was wholly caused by the negligence or wrongful act of a government or other authority responsible for the maintenance of navigation lights or other aids to navigation in the exercise of that responsibility; or

(d)   the deposit of waste was caused by wilful misconduct on the part of the ship owner. [35]

More succinctly expressed, although possibly not as accurately, the four exceptions are: *a*) force majeure, *b*) intentional act of a third party, *c*) act or omission of the government responsible for navigational aids and *d*) intentional act of the ship owner. With all these exceptions it is obvious that to continue

---

[34] See *Communiqué Arctic Waters Pollution Prevention Act to be Proclaimed*, at 2, published by the Department of Indian Affairs and Northern Development, No. 1-7239 (25 July 1972).
[35] *Arctic Waters Pollution Prevention Regulations*, secs 5 & 6 (1972).

qualifying this type of liability as "absolute" is a misnomer. It is basically the well known principle of strict liability, with some variations in the traditional exceptions. Exceptions (a), (b) and (c) are found verbatim in the 1969 Brussels Civil Liability Convention. Exception (d) incorporates the under-lying principle found in all insurance law that liability attaches only for the negligent and not for the intentional acts of the insured. With these four exceptions it is therefore more accurate to qualify the nature of the liability envisaged as being a limited kind of strict liability. The liability is also expressly limited in amount.

Limits of liability. — The limits of the joint and several liability of the ship and cargo owners are not spelled out in the Act [36] but they are in the 1972 Regulations. The Regulations provide that the maximum amount of the liability in question shall "be determined by multiplying 2,000 gold francs by the number of tons of the ship's tonnage, but the maximum amount of such liability shall not exceed 210 million gold francs". [37] This maximum amount, however, may be reduced to cover any expenses reasonably incurred by the ship owner or underwriter in the taking of remedial measures. [38]

Proof of financial responsibility. — The Act imposes an obligation on any ship owner who wants to navigate within any shipping safety control zone of the Arctic waters to provide evidence of financial responsibility in the form of insurance or an indemnity bond (Art. 8(1)(d)). The form specified in the Regulations consists of two documents: a declaration by an underwriter stating that he insures the ship in the required amount and a duplicate copy of a special policy endorsement covering the ship for Arctic waters. The documents must be filed with the Minister and must remain in force so long as the ship is in any zone of the Arctic waters. [39]

Shipping safety control zones. — The Act provides for the establishment of shipping safety control zones and for

---

[36] *Ibid.,* sec. 11(2).
[37] *Ibid.,* sec. 14(1).
[38] *Ibid.,* sec. 14(2).
[39] *Ibid.,* sec. 11(1).

regulations prescribing certain standards of hull and fuel tank construction, navigational aids, manning of the ship, pilotage, icebreaker assistance and maximum quantity of cargo (Article 12 (1)). These prescribed standards apply to all ships, but those belonging to or being operated by a foreign sovereign power may be exempt upon proof that they comply with "standards substantially equivalent" (Article 12(2)). This exemption will probably include all warships and other ships owned or operated by a state for non-commercial service, otherwise, the Act would be contrary to the well-established principle of sovereign immunity.

A provision of fundamental importance relating to action envisaged by the coastal state to protect itself against pollution is Section 13. It reads as follows:

> Where the Governor in Council has reasonable cause to believe that a ship that is within the arctic waters and is in distress, stranded, wrecked, sunk or abandoned, is depositing waste or is likely to deposit waste in the arctic waters, he may cause the ship or any cargo or other material on board the ship to be destroyed, if necessary, or to be removed if possible to such place and sold in such manner as he may direct.

This article calls for comment with respect to the very serious nature of the action envisaged, namely the destruction of the ship. There is no doubt that, in principle, the action taken by the coastal state must be proportioned to the actual or threatened damage. This was the rule incorporated in the Brussels Convention Relating to Intervention on the High Seas and, although the provision does not expressly mention the principle of proportionality, it is surely implied in the qualifying words "if necessary" immediately after the word "destroyed". In other words, the ship or cargo, or both, will be destroyed only if other lesser means cannot adequately contain the pollution damage, actual or impending. This was the situation in the *Torrey Canyon* incident where the British authorities had to finally destroy the ship by bombing, after failing to remove the oil by other means. And this would have had to be done in the *Arrow* incident in Chedabucto Bay off Nova Scotia, if the experts had not succeeded in installing flanges to remove the rest of the oil from the tanker.

As for the establishment of the zones, an Order has been issued, at the same time as the Regulations, establishing 16 areas of the Arctic waters as shipping safety control zones. This Order will come into force 60 days after its publication in the Canada Gazette (Sec. II). No regulations have yet been adopted, however, specifying the standards required for navigation in those zones. Those standards will probably vary, depending on the time of the year and the location of the zone, since the delimitation of those zones seem to be based mainly on the ice conditions. Until those standards are adopted, only traditional shipping will presumably be allowed. This seems to be the intent behind the Communiqué which reads in part as follows:

> The regulations are designed to apply to *shipping normally passing through Arctic waters.* They do not at this time specify limitations with respect to size of ship or the amount of potential pollutant that may be carried. An intensive study of cargoes, destinations, and any pollutants presently being carried is under way to determine whether such limitations should be imposed in the future.
>
> The Ministers emphasized that the promulgation of the Act and the regulations should not, therefore, be taken as an indication that the government is prepared at this time to approve the passage of large oil tankers throughout Arctic waters.
>
> With careful design, proper navigational aids and competent crews, movement of oil by tanker through Arctic waters may be possible in the future. The Ministers said a great deal more study is required, however, following which it would be possible to establish by regulation the *maximum cargo* of oil that could be reasonably carried by one ship. [40]

It is reasonably obvious from the above that the Act cannot yet be adequately implemented without the additional regulations. Furthermore, the pollution prevention officers named so far are those for non-shipping activities only. Conceivably the pending regulations might be adopted before the coming into force of the Order establishing the zones.

Pollution prevention officers. — The Act provides for the nomination of pollution prevention officers and arm them with

---

[40]   *Supra,* note 35, at 3-4; emphasis added.

very extensive powers to carry out the action envisaged in the previous provisions. Not only may a pollution officer board any ship within a shipping safety control zone, but he may order such ship out of the zone and even seize the ship and its cargo. Indeed, Section 23(1) provides that, whenever a pollution prevention officer suspects on reasonable grounds that any provision of the Act or regulations has been contravened, a pollution prevention officer "may with the consent of the Governor in Council, seize the ship and its cargo anywhere in the arctic waters . . . ." Such ship or cargo may then be forfeited by a Court, upon conviction of the offence charged (Sec. 24). Here again, of course, a reasonable exercise of such powers must be envisaged, and the seizure of the ship or cargo should not be made unless the situation really warrants it. But, since these decisions will involve a question of personal judgment to be made quickly and in trying circumstances, difficulties of implementation are bound to arise. Conceivably, such situations might occur on the high seas where, in principle, the flag state has exclusive jurisdiction over its ships, and the only exceptions provided for in the High Seas Convention relate to the repression of slave trade and piracy. However, other exceptions are permitted under customary law, as will be discussed later. Furthermore, nothing prevents states from agreeing to the mutual policing of ships in certain areas of the high seas for specific purposes, such as is already done to a certain extent for the enforcement of conservation measures. Canada and the United States have given each other such powers in 1953 for the preservation of the halibut fishery in the Northern Pacific Ocean and Bering Sea. [41] And nothing could have prevented Canada and the United States in this instance to conclude a similar type of agreement relating to pollution prevention in the Arctic. Let us see why Canada decided to act unilaterally, and then discuss the legal validity of her action in international law.

---

[41] See Art. II of "Northern Pacific Halibut Convention", reproduced as a Schedule to Chap. 43, 1-2 Eliz. II, 1952-1953.

2. THE RATIONALE BEHIND THE CANADIAN LEGISLATION

(1) *The inadequacy of existing international law*

On April 15, 1970, the Prime Minister of Canada delivered an address to the Canadian Press in Toronto which outlined the rationale behind the new Bill against pollution in the Arctic. Having emphasized the absolute necessity and urgency to protect the Arctic marine environment against the possibility of an oil spill, Prime Minister Trudeau then explained that existing international law was inadequate to protect the coastal state, that effective international controls were necessary and that the government legislation was intended as an interim measure only. Such huge areas cannot be protected by Canada alone, he said, and "[j]ust as the Arctic environment is of benefit to many nations, so only, in the long run, will international controls be able effectively to protect it". He added that "Canada will press for the rapid introduction of a system of international environmental law to protect all vulnerable areas". [42] However, he believed that such an adequate international regime could not be expected within the next few years and stated that, "[u]ntil such a *régime* exists, therefore, Canada must take steps to ensure that irreparable harm will not occur in the interim". [43] The Prime Minister went on to make a statement which indicates clearly that he regarded existing international law as being inadequate and that the proposed legislation came close to going beyond it.

> The biosphere is not divided into national compartments, to be policed and protected by national regulations. Yet neither is the current state of international law sufficiently developed to permit instant and effective protection for the Canadian Arctic against activities which are already under way. Our pollution legislation is without question at the outer limits of international law. We are pressing against the frontier in an effort to assist in the development of principles for the protection of every human being on this planet. [44]

---

[42]   P. E. TRUDEAU (Rt. Hon.), "Canada Leads Fight Against Pollution", *Statements and Speeches,* No. 70/3, at 2 (15 April 1970).
[43]   *Ibid.,* at 3.
[44]   *Ibid.*

There is no question that the new legislation went beyond what was generally considered as being permitted by the law of the sea, in so far as it allowed a coastal state to exercise jurisdiction over another ship on the high seas so as to protect itself against pollution. As already indicated, the Brussels Convention Relating to Intervention on the High Seas in Cases of Oil Pollution Damage does not come into operation until the ship itself is threatened with material damage, regardless of the imminence of danger to the coastal state. Furthermore, the requirements imposed upon the coastal state in the actual initiation of protective measures are too stringent to be capable of effective application.

On April 16, 1970, the Minister for External Affairs, Mitchell Sharp, further explained the rationale behind the new legislation. He emphasized that Canada had found itself compelled to proceed unilaterally since it had failed in its attempts to obtain an international regime. He referred specifically to the efforts made by Canada at the Brussels Conference of 1969 and stated that "[w]hile the main thrust of the bill under debate is preventive, that of the Brussels Conventions is remedial and liability oriented". [45] The Minister, however, explained that Canada hoped for an eventual international regime. "The bill we have introduced", he said, "should be regarded as a stepping-stone toward the elaboration of an international legal order which will protect and preserve this planet Earth for the better use and greater enjoyment of all mankind." [46] He further specified that Canadian Government officials had met with representatives of the American Government on two occasions, March 11 and March 20, 1970, to discuss the main features of the legislation about to be introduced, plus subsequent discussions in Washington between the Canadian Ambassador, Marcel Cadieux, and the U.S. Under-Secretary of State for Political Affairs, Alexis Johnson. "Unfortunately", said Mr. Sharp, "it did not prove possible for the two governments to reach agreement on all

---

[45]   M. SHARP (Hon.), "Preserving Canada's Arctic Environment", *Statements and Speeches,* No. 70/5, at 4 (16 April 1970).
[46]   *Ibid.,* at 2.

aspects of these questions, as has since been made known by the United States Government." [47] The Minister was referring here to a U.S. Press Release on April 15, [48] in which the United States Government had challenged the international validity of the Canadian legislation, in the light of the traditional principles of the law of the sea. The Press Release stated in particular that the United States intended "shortly to ask other interested states to join in an international conference designed to establish rules for the arctic beyond national jurisdiction by international agreement". [49]

On April 17, the Canadian Government handed a Note, in reply to the United States, in which it repeated its preference for an international regime and stated that it was "the earnest hope of the Canadian Government that it will be possible to achieve internationally accepted rules for Arctic navigation within the framework of Canada's proposed legislation". [50] The rest of the Canadian Note relates to the legal basis for the new legislation, which will now be discussed.

(2) *The legal basis for the legislation : self-defence or self-protection ?*

The State Department statement of April 15, 1970, concentrates its opposition to the proposed Canadian legislation on its legal validity in international law. It emphasizes throughout that the proposed legislation is contrary to the principle of the freedom of the high seas. More specifically, it contends: "International law provides no basis for these proposed unilateral extensions of jurisdictions on the high seas, and the U.S.A. can neither accept nor acquiesce in the assertion of such jurisdiction." [51] The statement ends by suggesting to the Canadian Government that it submit the matter to the International Court of Justice for adjudication.

---

[47]   *Ibid.*, at 7.
[48]   See text of the U.S. Press Release reproduced in *Can. H.C. Deb.*, as Appendix "A", at 5923 (15 April 1970).
[49]   *Ibid.*
[50]   See Summary of Note reproduced in *Can. H.C. Deb.*, as an Appendix, 6027, at 6029 (17 April 1970).
[51]   See *supra* note 48.

Canada refused to submit the question to the Court and modified its acceptance of jurisdiction [52] so as to exclude any dispute relating to the anti-pollution prevention legislation. [53] In this writer's opinion, the exclusion of the Court's jurisdiction was rather unfortunate. [54]

---

[52]   For an excellent study of the new acceptance of jurisdiction by Canada, see R. St. J. MACDONALD, " The New Canadian Declaration of Acceptance of the Compulsory Jurisdiction of the International Court of Justice", 8 *C.Y.I.L.* 3-38 (1970).

[53]   In his Toronto speech to the Annual Meeting of the Canadian Press, Prime Minister Trudeau dealt with the question of submitting the measure to the International Court. He stated that what was involved was not simply a matter of losing a case in the World Court:

> What is involved, rather, is the very grave risk that the World Court would find itself obliged to find that coastal states cannot take steps to prevent pollution. Such a legislative decision would set back immeasurably the development of law in this critical area. In short, where we have extended our sovereignty, we are prepared to go to court (this is a reference to Bill C-203, introduced at the same time, extending Canada's territorial waters from 3 to 12 miles). On the other hand, where we are only attempting to control pollution, we will not go to court until such time as the law catches up with technology. See *supra* note 42, at 3-4.

Indeed, on the same day that the Government introduced the Bill, the Canadian Ambassador at the United Nations, Yvon Beaulne, transmitted a letter to the U.N. Secretary-General withdrawing Canada's acceptance of the International Court's jurisdiction over "disputes arising out of or concerning jurisdiction or rights claimed or exercised by Canada . . . in respect of the prevention or control of pollution or contamination of the marine environment in marine areas adjacent to the coast of Canada." (See text of the letter to the Secretary-General reproduced in 22 *External Affairs,* at 130-131 (1970).)

[54]   First of all, if Canada was that unsure of the adequacy of international law, it could have invoked the reciprocity clause against the United States and, because of the latter's Connally reservation, would have been entitled to claim successfully that this was a domestic dispute over which the Court had no jurisdiction. This, it will be recalled, was successfully done by Norway against France in the *Norwegian Loans Case* in 1957, following which France withdrew her Connally-type reservation. Now, if the United States had used the subterfuge of having another state, let us say Japan, to challenge the Canadian legislation in the World Court, it is submitted the Canadian Government ought to have had sufficient confidence in the legal basis of its legislation and in the World Court to be ready to stand behind it. The Court has shown sufficient readiness in the past to develop international law in maritime cases, particularly in the *Anglo-Norwegian Fisheries Case,* to warrant that confidence. And Canada, it should be added, has found that decision most advantageous in the drawing of its straight baselines both on the east and on the west coasts. It is suggested that, by invoking existing legal concepts, Canada could have convinced the Court to enlarge their scope and extend their application to this new situation.

Now coming to the international validity of the legislation, the Canadian Government states that it is based on self-defence. Its Note to the United States very plainly specifies that "[t]he proposed anti-pollution legislation is based on the overriding right of self-defence of coastal states to protect themselves against grave threats to their environment". [55] In introducing the Bill in the House of Commons, the Honourable Mitchell Sharp also invoked the same principle as a legal basis. He stated in reference to the Bill: "It is based on the fundamental principle of self-defence and constitutes state practice, which has always been accepted as one of the ways of developing international law." [56]

Before commenting on the validity of self-defence as a legal basis, it is necessary to specify the exact nature of the jurisdiction being asserted. In the first place, the claim is not one of sovereignty over the waters in question. In this regard it is worth noting that, in spite of the recommendation of a Standing Committee of the House of Commons in December 1969 urging a declaration of complete sovereignty and control over all waters of the Canadian Arctic Archipelago, [57] the Government has limited itself to saying that "the position of Canada has always been that these waters are regarded as Canadian". [58] It has yet to specify whether this really means "internal" waters. In the second place, Canada is not claiming "jurisdiction and control" [59] over the natural resources of the high seas. Thirdly, it is not claiming the right to prohibit the innocent passage of foreign ships in its territorial waters

---

[55] See *supra* note 50, at 6028.

[56] See *supra* note 45, at 6. It is clear from these two official statements that self-defence is the only legal basis which was advanced by Canada. Since then the concepts of "custodianship" and "delegation of powers" have been mentioned occasionally in support of the legislation. They are said to have originated in a speech made by Prime Minister Trudeau in October 1969 where he stated that "Canada regards herself as responsible to all mankind for the peculiar ecological balance that now exists so precariously in the water, ice and land areas of the Arctic archipelago". See *Can. H.C. Deb.*, at 39 (24 Oct. 1969).

[57] See *Standing Committee on Indian Affairs and Northern Development*, Proceedings No. 1, at 6-7 (16 Dec. 1969).

[58] *Supra* note 50, at 6029.

[59] This is what was claimed by the United States in 1945 over the natural resources of the subsoil and seabed of the continental shelf.

generally or in the Northwest Passage in particular. What Canada is claiming is the right to exercise a limited jurisdiction over foreign ships in an area of the high seas [60] contiguous to its coasts for the special purpose of protecting certain territorial (including territorial sea) interests. Those interests involve the delicate ecological balance of the Canadian Arctic, affect the lives of its inhabitants and are considered vital to the preservation of its territorial integrity. In order to protect this territorial integrity, Canada will insure that ships, within certain shipping safety control zones, meet adequate anti-pollution standards; it might go so far as to destroy, within the Arctic waters in question, a ship which is in distress, stranded, wrecked, sunk or abandoned and is actually polluting the waters or likely to do so. [61]

To qualify such an exercise of jurisdiction as "self-defence" is somewhat inaccurate, since it might not always be possible for Canada to prove that the situations envisaged by the Act constitute an actual threat to its territorial interests. Such a threat has to be established before self-defence becomes applicable. Professor Bowett points out in his study of the nature of self-defence in international law:

> The essence of self-defence is a wrong done, a breach of a legal duty owed to the state acting in self-defence . . . . The breach of duty violates a substantive right, for example the right of territorial integrity, and gives rise to the right of self-defence. It is this pre-condition of delictual conduct which distinguishes self-defence from the "right" of self-preservation and the "right" of necessity. [62]

Having regard to the restrictive application of self-defence as a legal concept, it is suggested that a wider and more flexible, but as adequate, a basis for the present purposes, is the

---

[60] The area extends to 100 miles from the Canadian Arctic coast which is the same distance approved internationally in 1962 as a prohibited zone for oil pollution on the east and west coasts of Canada. See *supra* note 19.

[61] *Ibid.* Sec. 13(1). This power is essentially the same as was recently grafted to pending legislation before the Parliament of the United Kingdom, after a series of collisions in the English Channel threatened pollution of its coasts. See report "Britain enacts law to sink, seize ships liable to foul coasts", *Globe and Mail*, at 1 (9 April 1971).

[62] D. W. BOWETT, *Self-Defence in International Law*, at 9 (1958).

concept of *"self-protection"*. This concept is one of the four recognized bases of state jurisdiction in international law, those bases being: "(a) territory . . . (b) nationality . . . (c) protection of certain state interests not covered under (a) and (b) . . .; and (d) protection of certain universal interests . . . ." [63] The "protective principle", as it is often called, permits the exercise of state jurisdiction to protect certain state interests considered of vital importance, such as security, property and the integrity of governmental processes. This might even extend to violations committed outside of the territory by a foreign national. [64] This right of self-protection is at the basis of most of the cases where coastal states have extended their jurisdiction unilaterally over ships on the high seas within a zone contiguous to their coast. The right has been recognized by the United States ever since the classic judgment of Chief Justice Marshall in the *Church* v. *Hubbart Case*. One of the underlying issues involved in that case was the right of Portugal to seize a foreign vessel on the high seas allegedly engaged in trade with its colonies contrary to Portugese law. Referring to this right, Marshall made the following statement:

> Any attempt to violate the laws made to protect this right, is an injury to itself which it may prevent, and *it has a right to use the means necessary for its protection*. These means do not appear to be limited within any certain marked boundaries, which remain the same at all times and in all situations. If they are such as unnecessarily to vex and harass foreign lawful commerce, foreign nations will resist their exercise. If they are such as are reasonable and necessary to secure their laws from violation, they will be submitted to (emphasis added). [65]

This opinion of Chief Justice Marshall, even if *obiter dictum*, contains a sound rule of reasonableness in the exercise of

---

[63]   Restatement, Second, Foreign Relations Law of the United States (1965), Section 10, cited in FRIEDMANN et al., *International Law Cases and Materials*, at 441 (1969).
[64]   On this point, see R. B. BILDER, "Control of Criminal Conduct in Antarctica", 52 *Virginia L. Rev.* 231, at 272. See in particular footnote 124 where he cites American case law in support.
[65]   6 U.S. (2 Cranch) 187, at 234-35 (1804), quoted in L. H. HYDEMAN and W. H. BERMAN, *International Control of Nuclear Maritime Activities*, at 227 (1960).

such jurisdiction and has been relied upon consistently. [66] The U.S. Treasury Department, for instance, invoked this opinion of Marshall, when it presented its case before the Ways and Means Committee of the House on support of the Anti-Smuggling Act of 1935. [67] It will be recalled that the Act authorized the President to establish customs' enforcement zones extending 50 nautical miles beyond the normal 12-mile customs zone, in order to prevent violation of the Act. On the basis of Marshall's opinion, Professor Yntema of the University of Michigan and the Treasury Department argued that "the only test of the extent to which a nation may extend its jurisdiction in proximate areas of the high seas is the test of reasonableness". [68] Professor Jessup adds his own comment: "It is believed that this is a sound position under international law. We then have a mixed question of fact and law as to whether enforcement of this Act will meet the test of reasonableness." [69]

Self-protection has been invoked also in relation to the continental shelf and the air space above the high seas. The Truman Proclamation of 1945 cites self-protection as one of the reasons for wanting to exercise jurisdiction over the natural resources of the continental shelf. [70] As for the extension of jurisdiction of coastal states over foreign aircraft within a zone of the high seas contiguous to their coasts, the most striking examples are the air defense identification zones (ADIZ) established by the United States in 1950 and those established by Canada (CADIZ) the next year. The United States fixed a zone extending up to 300 miles from its coast, within which foreign aircraft heading toward the coast are required to identify themselves. Canada's zone extends only

---

[66]   See HYDEMAN et al., *ibid.*, at 227-28, footnote 357.
[67]   See JESSUP, "The Anti-Smuggling Act of 1935", 31 *A.J.I.L.* 101, at 104-05 (1937).
[68]   *Ibid.*, at 105.
[69]   *Ibid.*
[70]   The Proclamation stated in its preamble that "self-protection compels the coastal nation to keep close watch over activities off its shores which are of the nature necessary for utilization of these resources". See Presidential Proclamation 2667, 10 Federal Register 12303 (1945), reproduced in 4 WHITEMAN, *Digest Int'l L.*, at 756-7 (1965).

180 miles, but it applies to all aircraft crossing the zone in any direction. As pointed out by Ivan Head, "ADIZ regulations do not purport to operate only in the event that the United States or Canada is attacked by armed force. For this reason they cannot be regarded by even their most ardent advocates as a form of self-defence, but must rather instead fall into the much broader category of 'self-protection'." [71] It should be added that stiff penalties are provided for violation of those air defence regulations and that Canada provides for the possibility of interception by military aircraft. Those regulations do not appear to have met with resistance on the part of other states and constitute important precedents for the legislation under consideration. In addition to the precedents already cited, Hydeman and Berman have surveyed numerous other cases of unilateral assertions of jurisdiction by various countries over the last 300 years. Their conclusion that customary law permits reasonable assertions of jurisdictions by the coastal state is expressed as follows:

> A rule of international law seems to have emerged which permits a coastal State to make reasonable assertions of jurisdiction and control in areas of the high seas contiguous to its territorial sea in order to protect vital interests in its territory or territorial waters. [72]

The reasonableness of the claim of jurisdiction is, of course, of fundamental importance, although always difficult to assess. It would seem, in this regard, that the seaward extent of any contiguous zone must depend on the nature and importance of the coastal interests to be protected. In the case of oil pollution control in the Arctic, having regard to the possible catastrophic consequences and in the light of the well known precedents, a distance of 100 miles appears to be most reasonable.

------

[71] I. L. HEAD, "ADIZ, International Law, and Contiguous Airspace", 3 *Alta L. Rev.* 182 at 192 (1964). On the question of contiguous air space zone generally, see also: J. A. MARTIAL, "State Control of the Air Space Over the Territorial Sea and the Contiguous Zone", 30 *Can. Bar Rev.* at 245 (1952); J. T. MURCHISON, *The Contiguous Air Space Zone in International Law* (Rev. ed., 1955); J. R. BROCK, "Legality of Warning Areas as used by the United States", 21 *J.A.G. Journal*, at 69 (1966-67).

[72] *Supra,* note 65, at 236.

It should be mentioned finally that the various Law of the Sea Conventions have confirmed self-protection as a proper legal basis for coastal state jurisdiction over the high seas for a number of purposes. The very concept of contiguous zone, incorporated in Article 24 of the Territorial Sea and Contiguous Zone Convention, is obviously based on the right of self-protection. The major defect of the contiguous zone there created, however, is the spatial limitation of 12 miles from the coast; this is completely inadequate for protection against oil pollution. That spatial limitation has been questioned by such prominent jurists as Jessup [73] and Bishop, [74] and it should certainly be revised at the next Law of the Sea Conference. In any event, protection against major oil spills does not appear to have been contemplated — certainly not in relation to the Arctic — in 1958 and, consequently, one has to fall back on customary law to determine what constitutes a reasonable distance as a protective zone.

Another concept which is based on the right of self-protection is that of "special interest" incorporated in the High Seas Fisheries Convention. Article 6 of the Convention states: "A coastal State has a special interest in the maintenance of the productivity of the living resources in any area of the high seas adjacent to its territorial sea." [75] This entitles the coastal state, in certain circumstances and under certain conditions, to adopt unilateral measures of conservation in areas of the high seas contiguous to its coasts (Art. 7).

Considering this imposing array of precedents for the use of self-protection for the exercise of coastal state jurisdiction in adjacent areas of the high seas, it is not surprising that Professor Andrassy expressed his preference for self-protection, as against self-defence and necessity, in his "Rapport provisoire" to the Institute of International Law on the ques-

---

[73] JESSUP, "The United Nations Conference on the Law of the Sea", 59 *Col. L. Rev.* 234, at 244 (1959).

[74] BISHOP, "General Course of Public International Law", 115 *Recueil des Cours* 147, at 304 (1965-II).

[75] Convention on Fishing and Conservation of the Living Resources of the High Seas, A/CONF. 13/L.54 (1958).

tion of a legal basis for a coastal state to take anti-pollution measures. Having quoted from Article 2 of the Convention on the High Seas which provides that "the freedom of the high seas is exercised under the conditions laid down by these articles and by *the other rules of international law*", he stated that the members of his Commission had examined customary law for a legal basis to justify coastal state measures and summed up the result as follows:

> Plusieurs membres mentionnent dans leurs observations le droit de légitime défense, le droit de nécessité ou le droit d'autoprotection. Le rapporteur estime que le droit *d'autoprotection* (self-protection) est suffisamment reconnu et développé en droit international pour compléter les dispositions ci-dessus citées des Conventions de Genève en ce qui concerne notre matière. Ce droit ne peut être invoqué que pour la protection des intérêts importants, en cas de danger imminent et grave, et en l'absence d'autres moyens appropriés pour parer à ce danger. [76]

Having expressed his own personal preference for self-protection, the Rapporteur then asked in a written question to the members of the Commission: "Admettez-vous la conception d'autoprotection comme justifiant l'action de l'État menacé en haute mer ?" A study of the answers given reveals that the majority agreed with Professor Andrassy that self-protection was the best legal basis to advance as a justification for a state to exercise jurisdiction on the high seas adjacent to its coasts in order to protect itself against pollution. [77]

This writer's opinion is that the right of self-protection had gained sufficient recognition by 1970, in both conventional and customary law, to justify Canada's anti-pollution legislation as a unilateral measure pending adequate international

---

[76] J. ANDRASSY, "Etude des mesures internationales les plus aptes à prévenir la pollution des milieux marins", 53 *Annuaire de l'Institut de Droit international,* Tome I, 547, at 565; emphasis and "(self-protection)" added (1969).

[77] See the observations of the Commission members on the various questions contained in the "Rapport provisoire", *ibid.,* at 614-652 and in the "Rapport définitif", at 673-711. The memoers of the Twelfth Commission were: Bishop, Dupuy, Koretsky, McWhinney, Münch, Muûls, O'Connell, Rousseau, Vallat, Verzijl and Charles de Visscher; see *id.,* at 547.

conventions. Since 1970, important steps have been taken toward the adoption of such conventions.

IV. — THE FUTURE OF OIL POLLUTION CONTROL IN THE ARCTIC

As indicated by Canada when introducing its legislation, the ideal would be to have an adequate international convention to protect the marine environment and the special rights of coastal states in that environment. Considerable progress has been made toward this ideal since the enactment of the Canadian legislation in 1970, particularly through the efforts of the Intergovernmental Working Group on Marine Pollution (IWGMP) set up on the recommendation of the Preparatory Committee for the U.N. Conference on the Human Environment. The IWGMP held meetings in London, Ottawa and Reykjavik which resulted in the adoption of Draft Articles of a Convention on Ocean Dumping [78] and of General Marine Pollution Principles. [79] Both of those instruments were introduced and acted upon at the Stockholm Conference.

The Draft Articles on Ocean Dumping were referred to the UN Seabed Committee at its session of July/August 1972 and to a pending intergovernmental conference to be held in London from 30 October to 13 November 1972. [80] Representatives of some 80 countries met at the London Conference and adopted the text of a Convention on the Dumping of Wastes and other Matter at Sea. The Ocean Dumping Convention requires contracting Parties to take effective measures to prevent marine pollution by dumping. More specifically, it prohibits completely the dumping of certain substances such as hydrocarbons and allows the dumping of other substances under special permits. Both of those categories of substances are specifically listed in the Convention. A third category

---

[78] See *Report of the Intergovernmental Meeting on Ocean Dumping*, 1 MOD/4, Annex D (15 April 1972).
[79] See *Report of the Intergovernmental Working Group on Marine Pollution at its Second Session*, A/CONF. 48/1 I.W.G.N.P. II/5, at 2-7 (22 Nov. 1971).
[80] See *Report of the Third Committee*, UN Conference on the Human Environment, A/CONF. 48/CRP. 14, at 6.

covers all other substances and these may be dumped under general permits issued on the basis of certain technical criteria. The Convention, which will come into force after ratification or accession by 15 countries, represents a great step forward in the protection of the marine environment. Unfortunately, it does not provide for an international enforcement machinery or a dispute settlement procedure.

As for the General Marine Pollution Principles, they were endorsed "as guiding concepts for the Law of the Sea Conference and the Intergovernmental Maritime Consultative Organisation (IMCO) Marine Pollution Conference scheduled to be held in 1973. . . ."[81] Although these 23 principles have no legal force for the moment — except those which could be considered already part of customary law — they were given formal collective endorsement by the 113 governments represented at the Conference and they will constitute very strong "guidelines" at the 1973 treaty-making conferences. Those principles impose a duty on states to protect the marine environment and to adopt measures to prevent marine pollution. One principle recognizes the right of coastal states to take protective measures against damage to its coastline and related interests:

> Following an accident on the high seas which may be expected to result in major deleterious consequences from pollution or threat of pollution of the sea, a coastal state facing grave and imminent danger to its coastline and related interests may take appropriate measures as may be necessary to prevent, mitigate, or eliminate such danger, in accordance with internationally agreed rules and standards. [82]

This principle gives considerably more powers to the coastal state than did the one contained in the 1969 Brussels Public Law Convention, in the sense that any accident — not necessarily one amounting to a "maritime casualty" — is sufficient for the coastal state to take measures. The principle is essentially the same as was adopted by the Institute of International

---

[81] *Ibid.,* at 8.
[82] *Supra,* note 79, Principle No. 21, at 6.

Law at its Edinburg Session of 1969. The qualification that the measures must respect internationally agreed norms is quite appropriate, since otherwise too much would be left to the subjective judgment of the potential victim. Some of those norms are already generally recognized and relate to the reasonableness and the proportionality of the measures in relation to the pollution danger.

In addition to the adoption of those principles as guidelines, the Stockholm Conference also took note of three principles which had been submitted by Canada at the Ottawa meeting of the IWGMP in November 1971, and it decided to refer them "to the 1973 IMCO Conference for *information* and to the 1973 Law of the Sea Conference for such *action* as may be appropriate". [83] Those three principles relate solely to the special rights of coastal states and the legal basis for such rights. They read as follows:

1. A state may exercise special authority in areas of the sea adjacent to its territorial waters where functional controls of a continuing nature are necessary for the effective prevention of pollution which could cause damage or injury to the land or marine environment under its exclusive or sovereign authority.

2. A coastal state may prohibit any vessel which does not comply with internationally agreed rules and standards or, in their absence, with reasonable national rules and standards of the coastal state in question, from entering waters under its environmental protection authority.

3. The basis on which a state should exercise rights or powers, in addition to its sovereign rights or powers, pursuant to its special authority in areas adjacent to its territorial waters, is that such rights or powers should be deemed to be delegated to that state by the world community on behalf of humanity as a whole. The rights and powers exercised must be consistent with

---

[83] *Supra,* note 80, at 8. Canada has already submitted "Draft Articles for a Comprehensive Marine Pollution Convention" to the 1973 March session of the UN Seabed Committee, which provide for a right of intervention in favour of the coastal state in much the same terms as those incorporated in the first of the three principles reproduced and discussed here. See U.N. Doc. A/AC.138/SC.III/L.28 (9 March 1973).

the state's primary responsibility for marine environmental protection in the areas concerned: they should be subject to international rules and standards and to review before an appropriate international tribunal. [84]

Those three principles, as noted by the Stockholm Conference, were neither endorsed nor rejected at the Ottawa meeting. However, some 21 delegations supported the general concept contained in the principles, others disagreed and still others reserved their position. [85] In these circumstances it is difficult to foresee what will be their ultimate fate at the Law of the Sea Conference, but they undoubtedly will be considered and they should be commented upon here. The *first principle* empowers the coastal state to exercise special pollution prevention authority in adjacent areas of the sea where functional controls of a continuing nature are necessary. Of course, Canada was thinking primarily of its 100-mile Arctic pollution prevention zone, when putting forth this proposal. Because of the precarious and highly vulnerable nature of the Arctic ecosystem, it presumably does require a degree of supervision and control higher than would other regions, and Canada feels that this can only be provided adequately by the coastal state. The emphasis here is on "effective prevention", since the ecosystem might never be able to recover from a marine pollution catastrophy. In these circumstances, this writer agrees that certain coastal states ought to be given this special marine prevention authority, providing its exercise is subject to proper international control. This is envisaged in the third principle. It remains a question as to whether states outside the Arctic regions should be given such authority, and the answer depends on the degree of vulnerability of the environment. Perhaps certain states that border on sea lanes heavily travelled by oil tankers should also have such authority. In any event, it would be unwise to give such special authority to all states and leave it to their complete discretion as to whether to exercise it or not. Certain basic norms relating to the vulnerability of the environment should be met before a state could qualify to have such an authority. The *second principle*

---

[84]   *Supra*, note 79, at 7.
[85]   *Ibid.*

empowers the coastal state to prohibit ships not complying with certain standards from entering the pollution protective zone established under the first principle. The standards are to be governed by internationally agreed norms or, in their absence, reasonable standards imposed of the coastal state. This is a considerable power to accord to the coastal state and it does infringe upon the traditional laissez-faire regime of the high seas, where the flag state has, in principle, exclusive jurisdiction. However, it is now being recognized that the freedom to navigate the high seas does not include the freedom to pollute either the seas themselves or the coast of states. The high seas constitute a shared resource to be used in common by members of the international community and, consequently, it must be used with reasonable regard to the interests of others. Otherwise, the freedom of the high seas will continue to lead to abuse and result in irreparable damage to both international and coastal state resources. The only way to avoid such disastrous consequences is for states to agree upon adequate standards of pollution prevention and control, accompanied by an effective enforcement mechanism. There should be a general, or preferably a regional, international system of supervision in the implementation of those standards. However, in order for the system to be really effective, a delegation of powers to the coastal states would be necessary. This is the purpose of the third principle. The *third principle* specifies the legal rationale behind the special rights and powers of the coastal state. The notion of self-defence is not mentioned, but rather the more sophisticated concept of delegation of powers. This concept, along with that of custodianship, is being advanced by Canada in other areas of the law of the sea, in particular with respect to the question of conservation and management of fisheries resources. As applied to pollution, the Canadian representative at the Geneva session of the Seabed Committee in August 1971 made the following statement concerning general and regional solutions which could be adopted:

> With regard to both the general and regional rules, the coastal states could be delegated the powers and related duties required for the effective prevention of pollution of

their environment, and indeed would in a sense become custodians for part of the marine environment on behalf of the international community. [86]

The concept is therefore predicated on the theory that, for the protection of certain internationally shared resources, the coastal state becomes the custodian of the world community and part of the seas adjacent to its coasts fall under its "custodial protection". [87] If this concept is properly defined and delimited, there is no reason why it cannot be used. However, because of the apparent relationship between the concepts of delegation of powers and custodianship on the one hand and the well known domestic law concepts of agency (or mandate) and trusteeship on the other, a number of questions arise. Where will the scope of the delegation of powers be spelled out ? To whom exactly is the delegatee to be accountable ? Is the delegator to retain the usual powers to suspend or withdraw his powers ? Will the custodian be acting on his own behalf as well as that of the international community ? Those are some of the questions which are bound to be raised, unless there is a proper delimitation of the legal concept on which the delegation of powers would rest. It is not very clear, for instance, upon reading the third principle proposed by Canada, if it is only the *exercise* of the special rights and powers which will be subject to international control or whether such control will include the *scope* of the rights themselves. It would be preferable that both be subject to international control, while leaving to the coastal state a sufficient degree of discretion to protect its own interests as well as those of the international community. This could be spelled out in a general convention which could formulate certain basic norms of a universal character and provide for

---

[86]   See statement by Mr. J. A. Beesley, dated August 5, 1971, at page 8 of text circulated at the Conference.

[87]   The expression is borrowed from J. L. Hargrove who has commented on the concept of delegation of powers in J. L. HARGROVE (ed.), *Law, Institutions & the Global Environment*, at 100-101 (1972). For an extensive comment on the concept of custodianship, see R. Y. JENNINGS, "A Changing International Law of the Sea", 31 *Cambridge L. J.* 32, at 44-48 (1972).

the possibility of regional agreements containing supplementary norms coupled with an adequate enforcement mechanism.

Adequate protection of the marine environment will, in the end, depend on the close cooperation of states grouped into regions, enabling them to take both regional and national action. A good beginning has been made in this regard by the Parties to the Oslo Convention signed on February 15, 1972. Those twelve Parties (West Germany, Belgium, Denmark, Spain, Finland, France, United Kingdom, Iceland, Norway, Netherlands, Portugal and Sweden) have expressly recognized that "concerted action by Governments at national, regional and global levels is essential to prevent and combat marine pollution", [88] and believed that "the States bordering the North-East Atlantic have a particular responsibility to protect the waters of this region". [89] Surely the five states bordering on the Arctic basin ought to feel that they have a similar responsibility to protect the waters of that region. The stumbling block here appears to be the USSR which has rejected Canada's proposal for an Arctic basin Conference and did not attend the 1972 Stockholm Conference. At that Conference, Norway offered to convene an international conference on the protection of the Arctic environment, but it is not known if there has since been any reaction on the part of the USSR. The USSR seems to feel thus far that it is sufficient for Arctic states to take protective measures individually. It is said to have approved of the Canadian Arctic legislation in 1970 and it has adopted certain anti-pollution measures itself in 1971. A Decree of the Council of Ministers of the USSR, dated September 16, 1971, approved the Statute of the Administration of the Northern Sea Route which provides as follows:

> The Administration of the Northern Sea Route attached to the Ministry of the Maritime Fleet has been established for the purpose of ensuring the safety of arctic navigation, as well as of taking measures to prevent and

---

[88] See paragraph 3 of the Preamble in *Convention for the Prevention of Marine Pollution by Dumping from Ships and Aircraft,* A/AC.138/SC.III/L.9 (13 March 1972).
[89] *Ibid.,* paragraph 6 of the Preamble.

eliminate the consequences of pollution of the marine environment and the northern coast of the Union of Soviet Socialist Republics. [90]

The Statute more specifically provides, *inter alia,* for the following: regulation of ship movement, areas of compulsory icebreaker escort or pilotage, air reconnaissance and guidance, rules of navigation in the Sea Route, requirements of equipment and supply, and the determination of the conditions of vessels before they sail along the Sea Route. [91] In order to insure that the standards and conditions above mentioned are met, the Chief of the Administration of the Northern Sea Route, his deputies and inspectors have the right to visit vessels and to prohibit them from sailing the Route if they do not conform with the prescribed standards. They may suspend icebreaker escort and pilotage, as well as navigation itself, in portions of the Route if this is warranted by navigation conditions or a threat of pollution. The Statute also provides for criminal prosecution against the masters and officers for violation of the regulations, as well as for civil liability if damage is caused. [92] The precise nature of the criminal responsibility or of the civil liability which could ensue is not mentioned. No action against the ship or cargo owners is envisaged, since presumably only Soviet ships navigate the Northern Sea Route. Indeed, it has always been regarded as a strictly national sea route. It is suggested, however, that this is not a sufficient reason to render unnecessary a regional agreement on marine pollution. Surely an oil spill, just about anywhere in the peripheral seas surrounding the Arctic basin, would be of concern to the Arctic states bordering that basin. An "Arctic Oil Pollution Prevention Convention", providing for the close cooperation of the Arctic states, would seem to command itself, in order to insure that adequate and coordinated protective measures are taken both at the regional and national levels. Arctic states might find that stricter norms of preven-

---

[90]   Sec. 1, "Statute of the Administration of the Northern Sea Route Attached to the Ministry of the Maritime Fleet", in 9 *Int'l Legal Materials,* at 645 (1972).

[91]   *Ibid.,* sec. 3.

[92]   *Ibid.,* sec. 6.

tion and control are necessary in that region of the globe, and their experts could combine their knowledge of the Arctic environment to formulate those norms. The big complaint at the moment is that little is known about the exact nature of that environment; therefore, cooperation in scientific research should be intensified so as to gain the necessary knowledge to formulate the protective norms. The enforcement of norms through third party settlement might be premature, but surely Arctic states could agree on the establishment of a Marine Pollution Fact Finding Commission. This would be composed of representatives of all five Arctic states. It would make full inquiries and report on the facts, in the event of a pollution damage incident. This would only be a beginning toward an adequate third party settlement procedure, but it would be better to make a beginning now before it is too late.

PART VII

The Arctic Continental Shelf and Seabed

The discovery of huge oil deposits at Prudhoe Bay on the north slope of Alaska in 1968 has given a tremendous impetus to exploratory activities in the Arctic regions, particularly in the Beaufort Sea area. With the expansion of those activities, it is not difficult to foresee problems of delimitation of continental shelf boundaries such as have arisen in the North Sea. The Arctic Ocean is far from being as shallow as the North Sea, but it does cover a very extensive continental shelf, particularly off the coasts of the Soviet Union, Alaska and Canada. The purpose of this part is to examine the physiography involved, investigate briefly the potential mineral resources, analyse the relevant principles of law and suggest boundary delimitations. The subject will be treated under the following headings: I — Physiography of the Arctic Continental Shelf and Seabed; II — Potential Natural Resources of the Arctic Continental Shelf and Seabed; III — The Law Applicable to Seaward Delimitation; IV The Law Applicable to Lateral Delimitation; V — The Legislation and Practice of Arctic States in Continental Shelf Delimitation; and VI — Suggested Delimitation of the Arctic Continental Shelf and Seabed.

I. — PHYSIOGRAPHY OF THE ARCTIC CONTINENTAL SHELF AND SEABED

1. Definition of Terms

An accurate use of geological and geographical terms presents difficulties for geologists and geographers; a fortiori, for lawyers. The intention here is to present a brief explanation of the main terms used throughout this study. [1]

---

[1] The material for this explanation of terms is taken mainly from three sources: I FAIRBRIDGE, *Encyclopedia of Oceanography*, 200-207 (1966); *Report of the Economic and Technical Working Group of the Ad Hoc Committee to study the Peaceful Uses of the Sea-Bed*

Ocean Floor — This is a general term used to designate all of the seabed with its various topographical and geological features.

Continental Shelf — This refers to the gently sloping (from about 1/8 of one degree to more than 3 degrees) shallow-water platform that extends from the coast to the point where the shelf "breaks". At this point there begins a relatively steep descent toward the abyssal plain. The average width of the continental shelves of the world is about 65 km (Figure 10), but it varies from less than one km to some 1,500 km, which is the case in the Barents Sea. The average depth at which the shelf terminates is approximately 130 meters but conventionally the edge of the shelf is assumed to be at 200 meters. The legal definition incorporated in the Convention on the Continental Shelf of 1958 defines it as being constituted of the "submarine areas adjacent to the coast" and as extending to "200 meters or beyong that limit, to where the depth of superjacent waters admits of the exploitation of the natural resources" (Art. 1). More will be said later about the implications and consequences of this definition.

Continental Slope — The term refers to the relatively steep (from as little as 3 degrees to over 45 degrees) descent beyond the outer limit of the continental shelf marked by a "break" indicating the end of the gently sloping platform and the beginning of the relatively steep descent. The slope extends to a point usually marked by a rise before reaching the abyssal plain. The width of the slope is generally 15-80 km

---

and the Ocean Floor beyond the Limits of National Jurisdiction, U.N. Doc. A/7230 (1968); K. O. EMERY, "Geological aspects of Sea-Floor Sovereignty", in Lewis M. ALEXANDER (ed.), *The Law of the Sea, Off-shore Boundaries and Zones*, at 138-159 (1967); O. K. LEONT'YEV and O. G. UDINTSVA, "Areas of the Main Morphostructure Elements of the Ocean Bottom", 13 *Soviet Geography : Review and Translation*, at 40 (1972), translated from Vestnik Moskovskogo Universiteta, Geografiya, No. 2, 47-51 (1971). It should be stated, however, that the authors of the last mentioned article suggest that the commonly accepted divisions of the ocean floor, which will be used in the present study, are inaccurate because they are based on levels of elevation and depth regardless of landform origins. Instead, they propose four major morphostructural elements: (1) the submarine margin of continents; (2) an intermediate zone; (3) the deep seabed, and (4) the mid-ocean ridges.

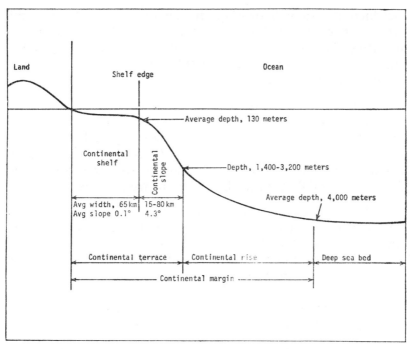

Reproduced from *Subsea Mineral Resources and Problems Related to Their Development*, Geological Survey Circular 619, at 2 (1969), published by the Department of the Interior, U.S.A.

FIGURE 10.   DIAGRAMMATIC PROFILE OF CONTINENTAL MARGIN.

and the depth of its lower edge is 1,400-3,200 meters. [2] The end of the slope marks "the general boundary between the light rocks of the continents and the denser rocks of the sea floor". [3]

Continental Terrace. — This is a general term referring to that submerged land mass composed of both the continental shelf and the continental slope.

Continental Rise. — This geomorphic feature is considered to be "an apron of detritus that has been carried down the continental slope". [4] Sometimes the sediments of the

---

[2]   I FAIRBRIDGE, *ibid.*, at 205.
[3]   K. O. EMERY, *supra* note 1, at 149.
[4]   K. HUNKINS, "Geomorphic Provinces of the Arctic Ocean", in J. E. SATER (coord. by), *Arctic Drifting Stations*, 365-376, at 367 (1968).

continental rise will overlap the continental slope and the latter will continue directly into the abyssal plain, thus eliminating the rise as a separate feature. When it is present, the rise may be as much as 1,000 km wide; its average depth is about 4,000 meters.

Continental Margin. — This is a general term used to indicate the undersea land mass extending from the emergent continent to the deep ocean floor; it is composed of the continental shelf, the slope and the rise. It also includes marginal plateaus such as the Chukchi Plateau and the Northwind Escarpment or Plateau in the Western Arctic Ocean.

Abyssal Plain. — This term refers to the deep ocean floor beyond the continental margin and is generally a "rolling plain from 3,000 to 5,500 meters below the surface of the sea". [5] Sea mounts, ridges and deep trenches are also found on the ocean floor.

2. PHYSIOGRAPHIC DESCRIPTION OF THE ARCTIC CONTINENTAL SHELF AND SEABED

The Arctic Ocean has an area of 14,000,000 km; it is the smallest and the shallowest of the earth's oceans, [6] its mean depth being only 1,205 meters. [7] The ocean is surrounded by large land masses whose extensive continental shelves constitute about one third of the seabed of the Arctic Ocean. What follows is a brief description of the continental margin of the Arctic states and of the deep seabed beyond.

(1) *The continental margin of the Arctic states*

Soviet Union. — The continental shelf along the coast of the USSR is the world's largest. All of the bordering seas (Barents, Kara, Laptev, East Siberian and Chukchi) are epicontinental seas. The table which follows, showing the

---

[5]   "Report of the Economic and Technical Working Group . . .", *supra* note 1, at 23.

[6]   I FAIRBRIDGE, *supra* note 1, at 49.

[7]   III FAIRBRIDGE, *The Encyclopedia of Geomorphology,* at 186 (1968).

area and mean depth of the seas in question, gives a fairly good idea of the extent of the continental shelf under those coastal seas. [8]

	Area ($10^9 m^2$)	Mean depth (m)
Barents Sea	1,405	229
Kara Sea	883	118
Laptev Sea	650	519
East Siberian Sea	901	58
Chukchi Sea	582	88

A good description of the continental shelf is given by the Committee on Polar Research in the following terms:

> The continental shelf north of Eurasia is the widest in the world, with widths of 850 km in the Barents Sea, while the part of the shelf north of Europe is cut by deep re-entrants. The best known of these cuts are the Svataya Anna and Voronin Troughs, which show depths of 500 m well into the Kara Sea. The shelf break north of Europe ranges between 350 and 500 m and is thus deeper than the world average. North of Asia, the shelf break is closer to the usual 200 m and appears to be unmarked by troughs, although canyons occur on the outer rim. North of Alaska and the Chukchi Sea, the continental shelf narrows from 25 to 40 km in width, with a shelf break at a depth of about 200 m. [9]

The whole continental margin (shelf, slope and rise) reaches far into the Arctic basin, particularly off the Chukchi and the Franz Josef Land shelves where the margins include plateaus and cones reaching into the deep basin.

United States (Alaska). — The Alaskan continental shelf extends fully into the Bering Sea and north of the Alaska coast, and it has a shelf break at about 200 meters in depth. It extends northward from the Bering Straits over 100 km and narrows down north of Alaska to less than 40 km.

---

[8] The table is taken from the *Handbook of Oceanographic Tables*, compiled by E. L. BIALEK of the U.S. Naval Oceanographic Office, at 51 (1966). Of course, the area mentioned for Chukchi Sea and Barents Sea can only be approximate until the lateral delimitations with Alaska and Svalbard are determined.

[9] COMMITTEE ON POLAR RESEARCH, *Polar Research, A Survey*, at 50 (1970).

Beyond the continental shelf of Alaska, there is a fairly wide slope and rise, particularly in the eastern section. The continental margin of the eastern section includes extensive plateaus advancing into the Canada Abyssal Plain. Senator Stevens of Alaska estimated that ". . . the continental margin off my home State of Alaska encompasses a greater area than the combined Continental Shelf of the remaining 49 States". [10]

Canada. — The Canadian Arctic continental shelf lies in deeper water than the Alaskan and Siberian shelves, due to the effect of weighting by continental ice mass. Pelletier describes the Canadian Arctic shelf as follows: "The sea floor of the outer continental shelf falls away gradually to the northwest, to a point 100-115 miles offshore where the water is 650 meters deep. Here, the true continental slope begins, marked by a major break in the bathymetric profile." [11] The continental shelf north of the Yukon and the Canadian Arctic Archipelago is relatively narrow and averages around 50 km. The Archipelago itself sits on a continental shelf landmass marked by a few depressions or channels some of which are more than 500 meters deep. The general limit of the continental slope is described as being "consistently 80-110 miles offshore". [12] The continental rise extends to 500 km. wide, and "[t]here is a smooth transition from the continental rise to the Canada Abyssal Plain". [13] It is stated by the Committee on Polar Research that: "In general, the stratigraphy and structure of arctic North America and the transition from the North American continental platform to the Arctic Ocean Basin typify the classic concept of an 'ideal' continental margin." [14]

De Leeuw gives the following description of the Canadian continental margin:

> The wide continental margin west of the Canadian Arctic Archipelago extends from the floor of the Abyssal

---

[10]   *Congressional Record*, No. 32, S2817 (10 March 1971).
[11]   B. R. PELLETIER, "Canadian Arctic Archipelago and Baffin Bay", in I FAIRBRIDGE, *supra* note 1, 157-167, at 161.
[12]   B. R. PELLETIER, *ibid.*, at 162.
[13]   K. HUNKINS, *supra* note 4, at 367.
[14]   See COMMITTEE ON POLAR RESEARCH, *supra* note 9, at 18-19.

Canada Plain where the gradient is less than 1:1000 (with an average depth of 3800m), crosses the broad continental rise, the continental slope and the continental shelf to the coast line, an average distance of 600 km. The margin's widest component is the rise, with its gradient gently increasing to the 2500 m isobath. Thence up to the 500 m isobath the continental slope is rather steady at 2°. Between Borden Island and Ellesmere Island however the constant slope only reaches the 1000 m isobath where it tends to flatten into a broad expanse with an average gradient 1:150 (less than 0.5°). [15]

It has been estimated that Canada's total continental margin comes to about 1.5 million square miles, which is nearly 40 per cent as large as the total land area of Canada, [16] and a good proportion of that margin lies in the Arctic.

Denmark (Greenland): The continental shelf north of Greenland breaks at a depth of about 300 meters instead of the usual 200 meters. The greater depth of the shelf is said to probably reflect "isostatic depression by the Greenland ice sheet". [17] The width of the shelf ranges from about 50 km under the Lincoln Sea to about 200 km under the Greenland Sea. The slope and rise, particularly the latter, are fairly extensive both toward the Pole Abyssal Plain and Spitzbergen. [18]

Norway (Svalbard). — The continental shelf around the Svalbard archipelago is very extensive; [19] indeed, most of it may be considered as a mere extension of Norway's mainland shelf. On the west side, the Svalbard shelf stretches as far as the Lena Trough which separates it from Greenland and,

---

[15]   M. M. DE LEEUW, "New Canadian Bathymetric Charts of the Western Arctic Ocean", 14 *Deep Sea Research*, at 496-497 (1967).

[16]   D. G. CROSBY, "A Brief Look at Canada's Offshore", 62 *Canadian Mining and Metallurgical Bulletin*, No. 685, 490-500, at 491 (May 1969).

[17]   K. HUNKINS, *supra* note 4, at 366.

[18]   See "Fig. 1. Physiographic provinces of the Norwegian-Greenland Sea" accompanying an article entitled "Morphology and evolution of the Norwegian-Greenland Sea", by G. L. JOHNSON and B. C. HEEZEN, in 14 *Deep-Sea Research* 755, at 756 (1967).

[19]   See Map 2281, *The Greenland and Barents Seas*, published by the Admiralty, London, 1872, corrected up to 1963.

on the east side, it extends to form part of the same continental shelf which surrounds Franz Josef Land, an archipelago belonging to the USSR. The continental slope and rise are also extensive, particularly to the north where they reach into the Barents Abyssal Plain.

(2) *The seabed beyond the continental margin* [20]

The seabed of the Arctic Ocean is not that of a single basin, as it was apparently still believed until 1948, but rather a complex of three major ridges and four large basins. In 1948, Soviet scientists discovered what is now known as the *Lomonosov Ridge* which is an undersea mountain extending some 1,800 kilometers. It runs from the continental margin off the New Siberian Islands to the one off Ellesmere Island and Greenland, passing at about 30 kilometers from the North Pole on the Atlantic side. It is the major feature dividing the Arctic Ocean basin, averaging about 3,000 meters in height, although it rises to 3,700 meters above the Amundsen Deep. Its width varies from 60 to 200 km and it has a smooth surface. The Arctic Ocean is thus divided into two main units: one on the Atlantic side and the other, on the Pacific side.

On the Pacific side of the Lomonosov Ridge, there is a second ridge, the Alpha Cordillera (or Mendleev Ridge). [21] It runs parallel to the Lomonosov Ridge from the continental

---

[20] The main sources used for the description of the major topographical features of the Arctic Basin are the following: I FAIRBRIDGE, *Encyclopedia of Oceanography,* 200-207 (1966); K. HUNKINS, "Geomorphic Provinces of the Arctic Ocean", in J. E. SATER (coord. by), *Arctic Drifting Stations,* 365-376 (1968); and A. F. TRESHNIKOV et al., "Geographic names of the main features of the floor of the Arctic Basin", *Problems of the Arctic and Antarctic* (in Russian), No. 27 (1967). This last article was translated for the writer by Professor Ann Kleimola, Ph.D., of the University of Nebraska.

[21] It is called "Alpha Cordillera" by the Americans because the ridge was recognized as the major feature of the Arctic basin by American scientists aboard the drifting ice station ALPHA in 1957. The Geographic Society of the U.S.S.R. called it "Mendeleev Ridge", after D. I. Mendeleev, an outstanding chemist who was one of the early investigators of the Arctic basin. Soviet scientists claim to have detected this ridge in 1949 during an air expedition.

margin of Ellesmere Island to that of East Siberia, veering toward Wrangel Island. It spreads to about 1,000 kilometers in width and ranges from 1,500 to 2,000 m. in height. It is broadly arch-shaped in profile and has a very rough surface. The two main basins on the Pacific side of the Lomonosov and formed by the Alpha Cordillera are the Makarov Deep (or Fletcher Abyssal Plain named after Col. J. O. Fletcher who installed the first scientific station on ice island T-3) whose depth reaches some 4,000 meters and the large Canada Deep or Abyssal Plain which covers an area of about 254,000 km. [2] The latter is described as being remarkably flat, with a uniform depth of 3,790 m. over a great portion of its surface.

On the Atlantic side of the Lomonosov Ridge, there is a third ridge made up of cone-shaped mountains of volcanic origin, which is a continuation of the Mid-Atlantic Ridge. It also runs parallel to the Lomonosov Ridge, extending from the abrupt depression (Lena Trough) north of Greenland to the deep area off the continental margin under the Laptev Sea. This ridge is referred to by American scientists simply as the Arctic Mid-Oceanic Ridge, whereas the Soviet scientists have named it the Gakkel Ridge, after Ya. Gakkel, who is said to have been the first to substantiate the hypothesis that the ridge in question was a continuation of the Mid-Atlantic Ridge. It is made up of subparallel ranges of cone-shaped mountains of volcanic origin, varying from 400 to over 4,000 meters in height. Its width appears to average about 500 kilometers for most of its length. The two main basins on the Atlantic side of the Lomonosov and formed by the Arctic Mid-Oceanic Ridge are the Amundsen Basin (also referred to as the Pole Abyssal Plain because of the location of the geographic North Pole) whose greatest depth goes to 4,500 meters and the Nansen Basin whose average depth is 3,450 meters, its greatest registered depth being 5,180 meters in the Fram part of the Basin (also referred to as the Barents Abyssal Plain). The continental margins off Spitzbergen and Franz Josef Land project partly across the Nansen Basin, so that it does not present as uniform a bottom as the Amundsen Basin.

II. — POTENTIAL NATURAL RESOURCES OF THE ARCTIC CONTINENTAL SHELF AND SEABED

The geological data on the Arctic submarine areas are still very inadequate but indications so far are quite promising. Those indications are derived from two main sources: (1) maps compiled from bottom samples and photographs and (2) actual discoveries on both the Eurasian and the North American sides of the Arctic basin.

1. MAPS, BOTTOM SAMPLES AND PHOTOGRAPHS

Both the Soviet and American scientists have been taking bottom samples and photographs of the Arctic Ocean floor in order to determine the nature of the sediments and have carried on seismic surveys to obtain information on the thickness of those bottom sediments. They have done so from ships [22] and from drifting ice stations. [23] As a result,

---

[22]   For a summary of surface and sub-surface navigation carried on by the U.S.S.R. and the U.S.A. in the Arctic Ocean see Part IV *supra*, "Freedom of the Seas in the Arctic Ocean". The primary purpose of those experimental voyages was to determine the possibility of navigation, but some research activities were performed. For instance, before the U.S.C.G. *Northwind* attempted to cross the Vilkitsky Straits of the Northeast Passage in August 1967, it had spent some time in the Barents and Kara Seas where American scientists studied the geological structure of the area. N. A. Ostenso is reported to have come back with a total of 14,400 miles of survey track, most of which was taken in those seas. — See R. PETROW, *Across the Top of Russia*, at 348 (1967). The U.S.S.R. is said to have sent a note to the United States, charging that the *Northwind* carried out a bottom-coring program in the continental shelf of the Kara Sea without permission and, therefore, in violation of the 1958 Continental Shelf Convention. — See PETROW, *id.*, at 351. It might be added that Mr. Petrow was aboard the *Northwind* throughout the trip.

[23]   Soviet scientists established their first drifting ice station in 1937 and resumed their research activities on ice stations in 1952. They have since operated some 21 such stations and have covered most of the Arctic Ocean, gathering data of various kinds. For a summary of their scientific observations, see P. A. GORDIENKO, "Scientific Observations from, and the nature of, the drift of 'North Pole Stations' ", in 11 *Problems of the Arctic and Antarctic,* Leningrad (1962), English translation edited by N. A. OSTENSO, b-1 to 19 (1966). American scientists have been carrying on research activities on drifting ice stations since 1952 when they first occupied Ice Island T-3. They began to take photographs of the Arctic Ocean bottom from Drifting Station Alpha in 1957 and they have been continuing a bottom-photograph program off Ice Island T-3 since 1963. From 1963 to 1970, they took 2,086 usable pictures while drifting some 13,000 km, passing over all

both the United States and the USSR have been able to publish maps which are helpful in trying to forecast in a tentative and preliminary way the seabed resource potential of the Arctic Ocean. In 1967, two Soviet scientists summarized "Soviet Research on Ocean Bottom Sediments"[24] and stated:

> The first composite map of the recent sediments of the marginal seas of the USSR has also been compiled for the Atlas of Lithological and Paleographical Atlas of the USSR as a result of the joint efforts of several institutes (Institute of Oceanography, Arctic Geological Research Institute, and the All-Union Geological Research Institute).[25]

They report also that they have produced geochemical maps of Arctic Ocean sediments.

Soviet scientists have also been active in taking bottom cores from their various drifting stations, in particular from drifting station North Pole 7. Six core-columns giving about 100 samples were taken from that station in the North Pole area on the eastern slope of the Lomonosov Ridge. Part of their report relates to the distribution of iron in the Arctic Basin sediments and the nature of the Lomonosov Ridge.[26]

As to the origin of the Lomonosov Ridge, Hunkin's suggestion is that the rifting or sea floor spreading which has taken place in the Arctic Ocean "apparently split off the outer edge of the continental shelf which now forms the Lomonosov Ridge". He adds that "[t]he smooth topography of this ridge and the match between the shelf and the Lomonosov Ridge outlines tend to support this idea".[27] In other words, if the Lomonosov is a continental shelf fragment, it would contain

---

major bottom features of the western part of the Arctic Ocean. — See K. HUNKINS et al., "The Floor of the Arctic Ocean in Photographs", 23 *Arctic* 175, at 176-177 (1970).

[24] See P. L. BEZRUKOV and A. P. LISITSYN, "Soviet Research on Ocean Bottom Sediments", 7 *Oceanology*, No. 5 (1967), translated by Scrypta Technica, Inc.

[25] *Ibid.*

[26] See T. I. LIN'KOVA, "Some Results of Paleomagnetic Study of Arctic Ocean Floor Sediments", translated from *The Present and Past of the Geomagnetic Field*, 279-281, Moscow, "Nauka" Press (1965).

[27] K. HUNKINS, "Arctic Geophysics", 22 *Arctic* 225, at 230 (1969).

the natural resources generally found in continental shelves, including petroleum.

As for the Alpha Cordillera and Mendeleev Ridge, American scientists summarize their findings from a bottom-photograph program started in 1957 in the following terms:

> In summary, photographs of arctic submarine ridges generally show soft sediments studded with erratic rocks. Outcrops of indigenous rocks were noted at only 2 sites. Animals such as fish, crinoids, shrimp and sponges were observed at over 80 per cent of the ridge stations. However, animal tracks and trails are rare. ... The arctic ridge system is similar to mid-oceanic ridges in having both soft sediment and rock outcrops, animal life and lack of trails. However, manganese nodules, so prevalent on the foothills and flanks of mid-oceanic ridges elsewhere are not observed in arctic photographs, nor are talus blocks. [28]

Two surprises are contained in this summary: a considerable presence of animal life and a complete absence of manganese nodules.

The petroleum potential in the Arctic Ocean floor, according to a Preliminary Map published by the United States Department of the Interior, would seem to be very considerable indeed. [29] The pink colour indicating offshore potential petroleum resources covers virtually all of the Arctic continental margins and part of the abyssal plains, such as the Canada Abyssal Plain starting under the Beaufort Sea. Of course, it must be emphasized that the map in question does not purport to give more than tentative indications of petroleum potential. The compilers of the map were careful to print the following note on the map itself:

> The delineation of sedimentary basins favorable for petroleum involves interpretations on which informed petroleum geologists often disagree. Because of the paucity of geologic data, the delineation of favorable areas offshore is highly speculative, and that shown here should be taken

---

[28]   K. HUNKINS et al., "The Floor of the Arctic Ocean in Photographs", 23 *Arctic* 175, at 184 (1970).
[29]   See "Preliminary Map, Potential Petroleum Resources", *Map 1-632* (Sheet 3 of 4) of *World Subsea Mineral Resources*, compiled by V. E. MCKELVEY et al. (1970).

> merely as a rough indication of the areas that seem most
> likely to contain petroleum accumulations. No commercial
> value should be attributed to any of these areas on the basis
> of these projections. [30]

As further explained by the authors in an article accompanying the map, the projections shown are not accurate enough to serve as a guide to exploration but "they may be useful to those concerned with the broad aspects of the character and distribution of seabed resources and the prospects for their development". [31] This describes accurately the present interest of the writer.

As for living resources, there is evidence of their presence in the Canada Abyssal Plain whose floor is apparently made up of fine-grained material which flowed down the continental slope and "is marked by a mosaic of interwoven tracks and trails together with small pits and mounts". [32] At one station, fresh trails were observed and were "composed of a central ridge of disturbed sediment bordered by V-shaped indentations. This type of trail is attributable to bottom-feeding fish which propel and support themselves on their pectoral fins, scooping up mud with their mouths as they move." [33] The authors point out, however, that in spite of the abundance of trails which appeared at all stations except one, animals themselves appeared at only 35 per cent of the stations.

Canada, for her part, has been active since at least 1960 in the study of her own continental shelf underlying the Arctic islands and extending into the Arctic Ocean. A capsule report of these activities, found in the 1970-71 Canada Year Book, gives an idea of their extent and nature.

> The continental shelf bordering the Arctic Ocean as
> well as the adjacent mainland, particularly near the delta
> of the Mackenzie River, and the islands of the Canadian
> Arctic Archipelago have been subjected to increasingly

---

[30]   *Ibid.*, at 29.
[31]   V. E. McKELVEY and F. F. H. WANG, *World Subsea Mineral Resources* — A Discussion to Accompany Miscellaneous Geologic Investigations Map 1-632 (1969).
[32]   *Supra* note 28, at 185.
[33]   *Ibid.*, at 187.

intensive scientific study and mineral resource exploration during the past 15 years. Coordinated and continuing programs of research and survey have studied the bedrock geology, the development of the terrain, the sediments on the sea floor and the nature and history of the icecaps. Gravity, seismic, aeromagnetic, geomagnetic and geothermal investigations have obtained information on the physical characteristics and structure of the rocks beneath the surface, and the nature and stability of the crust underlying the islands, the continental shelf and the continental slope. A complementary program of geodetic, topographic and hydrographic surveys has provided the necessary background maps and charts, and information about both terrestrial and marine physiography for these studies. [34]

2. ACTUAL DISCOVERIES

The actual discoveries of natural resources on the Arctic Ocean floor so far have been limited to oil and gas. On the North American side, oil has been found in considerable quantity in at least three places, and so has gas. In early 1968, Atlantic Richfield and Humble Oil companies made an unprecedented oil discovery on the northern slope of Alaska, near Prudhoe Bay, opening on the Beaufort Sea. The combined recoverable reserves were conservatively estimated at 5 to 10 billion barrels. On July 16, 1968, Atlantic Richfield published a report made by the consulting firm of De Golyer and MacNaughton which reads as follows:

> In our opinion this important discovery could develop into a field with recoverable reserves of some five billion to ten billion barrels of oil which would rate it as one of the largest petroleum accumulations known to the world today . . .

> The estimate of five billion to ten billion barrels is a reasonable expectation for a structure of the size indicated by seismic interpretation with the sand characteristics and saturation which have been shown by the productive intervals in the two wells. [35]

---

[34] CANADA (Dominion Bureau of Statistics), *Canada Year Book,* at 13 (1970-1971).

[35] Quoted by J. C. REED in "Oil Developments in Alaska", 15 *The Polar Research* 7-17, at 10 (1970).

The oil strike at Prudhoe Bay, less than 200 miles from the Yukon boundary, has spurred companies to intensify their exploration efforts in the nearby Canadian shelf advancing under Beaufort Sea and underlying the Canadian Arctic archipelago. It was reported in January 1970, that "[s]eismic sections from under the Beaufort Sea, shot last year for Operation Arctiquest, indicate giant structures up to 5,000 feet thick, which, if oil bearing, could yield oil accumulations as large as any in the world". [36] Operation Arctiquest, started in 1969, consists of geological and geophysical studies covering a 200,000 square-mile area, both on shore and off-shore into the Beaufort Sea, extending from Prudhoe Bay to Banks Island. Ernie Pallister, a consulting geologist, is reported as stating with respect to the Beaufort Sea structure: "There is no doubt in my mind that immense reserves are there to be found." [37] A few weeks later, on 14 January 1970, Imperial Oil Enterprises Ltd. made an important discovery of medium gravity crude oil at its Atkinson Point well. [38] This well is located some 500 miles east of Prudhoe Bay on the northwestern part of the Tuktoyaktuk Peninsula, part of Canada's mainland and which advances into the south east edge of the Beaufort Sea, close to the entrance of Amundsen Gulf. The well is reported to be only 13 feet above sea level and lies within the geological province of the Beaufort Sea continental shelf where sediments are believed to be thicker. [39] World Oil reported, in its March issue of 1972, Imperial Oil's recording that "Atkinson Point H-25 on the northwestern Tuktoyaktuk Peninsula flowed at a rate of 2000 bopd on a DST of the top of a Lower Cretaceous sandstone and conglomerate sequence at 5,700 feet". [40] These data, admitted Imperial, indicated "an encouraging and significant oil-bearing reservoir". [41]

---

[36] E. GRAY, "Challenger of North Oil Potential", *Oilweek* 20-23, at 21 (5 January 1970).

[37] *Ibid.*

[38] B. PAMENTER, "Arctic strike spurs scramble for data", *Oilweek*, at 16 (26 January 1970).

[39] *Ibid.*

[40] See "Imperial confirms 2,000 bopd flow from Arctic wildcat", 174 *World Oil*, No. 4, at 71 (March 1972).

[41] *Ibid.*

These important strikes at Prudhoe Bay in 1968 and at Atkinson Point in 1970 provided added impetus for the other companies to continue and increase their activities. Panarctic Oils Ltd., which is a joint venture between private enterprise and the Federal Government in which the latter holds 45% of the shares, has been particularly active. It has just completed its fourth year of activities, and the Vice-President in charge of operations wrote recently that the Company "shortly will satisfy its initial commitment to drill 20 wildcats to earn some 40,000,000 acres of land in the Canadian Arctic Islands, bringing its total land holdings to 55,000,000 acres". [42] He summarized the exploration activities of the company in the following terms:

> Activity accelerated considerably commencing in 1969 after discovery of the Prudhoe Bay (Alaska) oilfield. Prior to that only three wells had ever been drilled in the Arctic Islands. Since 1969, 16 additional exploratory wells have been drilled. *Two major gas fields have been discovered.* Nine drilling rigs operated by five separate companies are presently active. [43]

The two major gas fields in question are located at Drake Point on the Sabine Peninsula of Melville Island and the second one is on King Christian Island to the north east. The first discovery at a Drake Point well was followed by a second one 6 miles north announced on June 1, 1972. Panarctic is reported to have stated that the new well "tested 4.4 million cubic feet on dry gas from a depth of 3,574 to 3,781 feet". [44] The second major discovery mentioned by Vice-President of Panarctic, the one on Christian Island, is described as being located on a surface structure 5 x 10 miles, which is considered an average size structure in the area, some being more than 100 miles long, and about 25 of the 250 structures have been identified as "giants". [45] A third gas find

---

[42]   H. J. Strain, "Drilling in the High Arctic", 44 *Petroleum Engineer*, No. 1, at 34 (January 1972).
[43]   *Ibid.*, at 40: emphasis added.
[44]   See "Another Arctic gas find", *The Toronto Star*, at 15 (2 June 1972).
[45]   See J. R. Chilton et al., "Four discoveries highlight Arctic Islands exploration", 174 *World Oil*, No. 5, at 53 (April 1972).

was made just north of King Christian Island, on Ellef Rignes Island, but no details have been given as to its size. [46]

Late in February 1972, Panarctic made its first oil find in the Arctic Islands, on the Fosheim Peninsula of Ellesmere Island, at the bottom of Nansen Sound which leads to the Arctic Ocean. The oil discovered is said to be "sweet, medium gravity oil in a DST at 3,425 feet". [47] No other information was released but the discovery is considered significant.

The Canadian discoveries so far have been on shore but Panarctic has recently acquired an offshore area, and exploration activities are beginning to take place on the Canadian Arctic shelf. When one considers the geological similarities which apparently exist between the on-shore and off-shore areas, as well as the preliminary maps indicating the potential resources of the Arctic continental margins and beyond, there is reason to suggest that it is only a question of time for off-shore Arctic discoveries to be made, given sufficient development in deep water technology. In this regard, it is interesting to note that Humble Oil has recently devised "a system that will make possible the development and production of oil and gas in waters ranging from 700 to 1500 feet deep". [48] The important decision to be made at the moment is how best to transport the oil and gas from the North American Arctic to the south, having regard to local conditions, cost and the protection of the environment. Various methods are conceivable: surface tanker, submarine tanker, railway, highway, pipeline, even aircraft. Some of these methods are being seriously studied and it would seem that, in terms of present technology, pipelines will be chosen as the main medium of transportation.

On the Eurasian Union side of the Arctic, our information on natural resources potential is rather limited, except for the Preliminary Maps already referred to. However, there are also reports of oil discovery in the vast continental shelf off

---

[46]   *Ibid.*, at 55.
[47]   *Ibid.*
[48]   STANDARD OIL COMPANY, "The New Adventure", 141 *National Geography*, No. 6, at 6th unnumbered page (June 1972).

western Siberia. An article in the Komsomolskaya Pravda of August 16, 1967, reported that a huge oil deposit was found at only 20 to 25 meters deep and stated that "[t]he Tyeman region alone promises by 1980 — that is, in a dozen years — to yield as much oil as was produced in the entire Soviet Union last year". [49] A recent issue of Sovetskaya Rossiya is said to have reported to be estimated at 2 billion metric tons equivalent to 14 billion the recoverable reserves of that oil deposit to bbl". [50] It has been reported also that gas had actually been extracted from the seabed of the Kara Sea by 1970. The geological structure of the shelf was compared to that of the Gulf of Mexico by Soviet geologists. [51]

Having regard to the potential mineral resources just briefly outlined, it is wise to start thinking about the delimitation of the Arctic continental shelf and seabed in the light of the developments which are now taking place toward the formulation of an adequate legal regime.

III. — THE LAW APPLICABLE TO SEAWARD DELIMITATION

The present debate in the United Nations Seabed Committee relating to the seaward limit of the continental shelf acquires special importance in the Arctic where we find the largest continental shelves in the world. This section will review the meaning of the present definition of the continental shelf and examine the main proposals for a redefinition in the light of their application to the Arctic.

1. THE PRESENT DEFINITION OF THE CONTINENTAL SHELF

The question of the outer edge of the continental shelf is dealt with in the Convention on the Continental Shelf of 1958. It came into force on June 10, 1964 and some 50 states are

---

[49] Quoted by A. PARDO in "Sovereignty Under the Sea", *The Round Table*, No. 232, 341, at 343 (October 1968).

[50] See "Siberian Field Another North Slope", *Petroleum Engineer International* 96, at 97 (July 1970).

[51] Reported in *Soviet News* (3 February 1970), at 58, and quoted by Wm. E. BUTLER, in *The Soviet Union and the Law of the Sea*, at 138, Footnote 13 (1971).

now Parties to the Convention. All of the five Arctic states have now ratified the Convention: the USSR (22 November 1960), the United States (12 April 1961), Denmark (12 June 1963), Canada (8 February 1970) and Norway (9 September 1971). In any case, even if they were not all Parties to the Convention, their rights to the continental shelf could not be disputed. It is generally agreed that such rights in favour of coastal states have become part of the legal concept of the continental shelf, under international customary law, since the nineteen fifties. [52] Even before acceding to the Convention, Norway had adopted national legislation claiming jurisdiction over submarine areas "as far as the depth of the superjacent waters admits of exploitation of natural resources". [53] It therefore relied on the exploitability criterion contained in Article 1 of the Convention, the text of which is as follows:

> For the purposes of these articles, the term "continental shelf" is used as referring (a) to the seabed and subsoil of the submarine areas adjacent to the coast but outside the area of the territorial sea, to a depth of 200 meters or, beyond that limit, to where the depth of the superjacent waters admits of the exploitation of the natural resources of the said areas; (b) to the seabed and subsoil of similar areas adjacent to the coasts of islands.

With the developing technology permitting the exploitation of the seabed and subsoil at increasing depths, the interpretation of this provision has become the subject of considerable controversy. More specifically, the question arises as to whether

---

[52] In his extensive study of the question of sovereignty over submarine areas back in 1950, Lauterpacht concluded that the continental shelf doctrine had already become part of customary international law. — See H. LAUTERPACHT, "Sovereignty over Submarine Areas", 27 *B.Y.I.L.* 376, at 393-398 (1950). Lord Shawcross came to a similar conclusion when he said: "By 1953 the practice of so many states, generally acquiesced in by the rest, had I think resulted in the acceptance of the principle that a State has *ipso jure* and without proclamation sovereign rights over submarine areas in its continental shelf as part of custom in international law." — See Lord SHAWCROSS, "The Law of the Continental Shelf with special reference to the North Sea", *The World Land Use Survey Discourses to the Twentieth International Geographic Congress* 35, at 36 (1964).
[53] See Sec. 1 of "Act No. 12 of 21 June 1963 relating to the Exploration for and Exploitation of Submarine Natural Resources", in *Survey of National Legislation*, prepared by the U.N. Secretariat, U.N. Doc. A/AC.135/11, at 46 (4 June 1968).

the exploitability criterion may serve as an adequate way of defining the limit of the continental shelf beyond 200 meters. It is now agreed that, regardless of the technical possibilities of exploitation of natural ressources of the seabed, there must be a limit beyond which the coastal state has no jurisdiction. The question remains "where should that limit be ?" This question has been examined by many but is still unresolved. [54] This study does not pretend to find a solution to the controversy — only a new international agreement or an interpretative declaration by the Parties to the Convention could do this effectively — but it does attempt to throw some light on three basic aspects of the continental shelf as a legal concept: (1) the notion of "natural extension", (2) the factor of "adjacency", and (3) the criterion of "exploitability".

(1) *The notion of "natural extension"*

The idea that the continental shelf is the natural extension or appurtenance of the land territory or domain over which the coastal state has complete sovereignty was at the basis of the Truman Declaration of 1945 which, as stated by the International Court in the *North Sea Continental Shelf Cases,* "soon came to be regarded as the starting point of the positive law on the subject". [55] Indeed, the Proclamation of President Truman on September 28, 1945, specified in its Preamble as one of the reasons for claiming jurisdiction over the mineral resources of the continental shelf that "the continental shelf may be regarded as an *extension of the landmass of the coastal nation and thus naturally appurtenant to it".* [56]

---

[54]   See, for instance, the 1970 Report of I.L.A. Committee on "Deep-Sea Mining", reproduced as Appendix F to the *Report by the Special Committee on Outer Continental Shelf to the Committee on Interior and Insular Affairs,* U.S. Senate, 100, at 112 (21 Dec. 1970), where it is stated: "At this stage the Committee is unable to put forward an agreed recommendation on the problem of the outer limit of the continental shelf."

[55]   (1969) *I.C.J. Rep.* 3, at 33-34. It is interesting to note in passing that the same notion of natural prolongation was at the basis of the Russian Declaration of September 26, 1916, claiming sovereignty over a number of islands which it considered "une extension vers le nord de la plateforme continentale de la Sibérie". — See Appendix in V. L. LAKHTINE, *Rights over the Arctic Regions,* Moscow (1928).

[56]   Reproduced in 4 WHITEMAN, *Digest of International Law,* at 756 (1965); emphasis added.

The Proclamation further stated that "these resources frequently form a *seaward extension of a pool or deposit lying within the territory*". [57] It is important to note that these were stated in the form of reasons and justifications for the Proclamation. The idea of the seaward extension of the land-mass is therefore at the very basis of the coastal state's jurisdiction over the continental shelf, and it was so recognized by the International Law Commission. [58]

As for the 1958 Convention on the Continental Shelf, it did not expressly incorporate the notion of natural extension or appurtenance, but it certainly appears to underlie one of its provisions which stipulates that "the rights of the coastal State over the continental shelf do not depend on occupation, effective or notional, or on any express proclamation" (Art. 2(3)).

The fundamental importance of the concept of "natural extension" was also emphasized by the International Court in the *North Sea Continental Shelf Cases*. [59] In refuting Germany's argument that a coastal state was entitled to a just and equitable share of the available continental shelf, the Court made the following pronouncement:

> . . . the doctrine of the just and equitable share appears to be wholly at variance with what the Court entertains no doubt is the most fundamental of all the rules of law relating to the continental shelf, enshrined in Article 2 of the 1958 Geneva Convention, though quite independent of it, — namely that the rights of the coastal State in respect of the area of continental shelf that constitutes *a natural prolongation of its land territory* into and under the sea exist *ipso facto* and *ab initio,* by virtue of its sovereignty over the land, and as an extension of it in an exercise of sovereign rights for the purpose of exploring the seabed and exploiting its natural resources. [60]

---

[57]   *Ibid.,* emphasis added.
[58]   For a discussion of the legal basis of the coastal state's jurisdiction, see (1956) *I.L.C. Yearbook* II, at 298.
[59]   This is clearly demonstrated by Professor JENNINGS, in "The Limits of Continental Shelf Jurisdiction: Some Possible Implications of the North Sea Case Judgment", 18 *Int'l & Comp. L.Q.* 812, at 821-825 (1969); emphasis added.
[60]   (1969) *I.C.J. Rep.* 3, at 22; emphasis added.

The court underlined again at a later stage in its judgment that "it is this *idea of extension* which is, in the Court's opinion, determinant". [61] The submarine areas constituting the continental shelf, said the Court, "may be deemed to be actually part of the territory over which the coastal State already has dominion, — in the sense that, although covered with water, they are a prolongation or continuation of that territory, *an extension of it under the sea*". [62] *In short, the coastal state has jurisdiction over submarine areas which may be considered as the natural extension or prolongation of its land territory.* But the question remains: "What does this mean in practical terms?" Leaving aside the question of "adjacency" for the moment, the criterion of "natural extension", as pointed out by Professor Jennings, brings in not only the geomorphological continental shelf but the continental slope also, since they are made up of the same type of rock. [63] The only difference between the two features is in the degree of slope or gradient. The continental rise, however, poses a problem. As seen earlier, it will often cover rock belonging partly to the slope and partly to the abyssal plain. In these circumstances, the only sure way to determine the limit of the natural extension is to stop at the inward edge of the continental rise rather than at its outward edge. Another reason which makes this preferable is the fact that the rise might sometimes be so wide that its outer edge could no longer be considered as being "adjacent to the coast". [64]

(2) *The factor of "adjacency"*

The element of adjacency or proximity is expressly mentioned in the Convention, and it has the specific function of qualifying and limiting the exploitability criterion. The importance of this function grows with the time, since technology makes it possible to exploit at ever increasing depths. Not only is this factor of "adjacency" expressly incorporated

---

[61] *Ibid.*, at 31; emphasis added. None of the dissenting judges expressed disapproval of this opinion.
[62] (1969) *I.C.J. Rep.* 3, at 31; emphasis added.
[63] See *supra* note 59, at 829.
[64] *Supra* note 59, at 830.

in the Convention but, taken as being synonymous to contiguity, it has always been considered as part of the justification for the coastal state's jurisdiction over the continental shelf. The operative part of the Truman Proclamation of 1945 specifies that the natural resources regarded as being subject to the jurisdiction and control of the United States are those "of the continental shelf beneath the high seas *but contiguous to the coasts* of the United States". [65] The Press Release issued on the same day specified that "[g]enerally, submerged land which is *contiguous to the continent* and which is covered by no more than 100 fathoms (600 feet) of water is considered as the continental shelf". [66] The importance of contiguity as a possible legal basis of jurisdiction over submarine areas was very carefully examined by Professor Lauterpacht in 1950. [67] He considered that, although contiguity may have served in the past as a basis for making exaggerated territorial claims, "[t]his does not mean that in a case such as that of submarine areas it does not represent the only solution consonant with convenience, economic necessities, and requirements of international peace". [68] The International Commission has also emphasized the importance of contiguity as a basis for jurisdiction over the continental shelf. In its report of 1956, the Commission states that it is not possible "to disregard the geographical phenomenon whatever the term — propinquity, contiguity, geographical continuity, appurtenance or identity — used to define the relationship between the submarine areas in question and the adjacent non-submerged land". [69] And the Commission adds: "All of these considerations of general utility provide a sufficient basis for the principle of the sovereign rights of the coastal state as now formulated by the Commission." [70]

As already seen the Commission suggested, and the Geneva Conference adopted, the expression "adjacent to" to

[65] WHITEMAN, *supra* note 56, at 757; emphasis added.
[66] *Ibid.*, at 758; emphasis added.
[67] See LAUTERPACHT, "Sovereignty over Submarine Areas", 27 B.Y.I.L. 376, at 423 et seq. (1950).
[68] *Ibid.*, at 430.
[69] (1956) *I.L.C. Yearbook* II, at 298.
[70] *Ibid.*

characterize the submarine areas whose natural resources are subject to the jurisdiction of the coastal State. In proposing the expression "adjacent to the coastal State", Dr. Garcia-Amador explained to the International Law Commission that those words placed a definite limitation on the submarine areas envisaged. He stated that "[t]he adjacent areas ended at the point where the slope down to the ocean bed began, which was not more than 25 miles from the coast". [71]

As for the International Court, it did not consider the factor of "adjacency" as being as fundamental in importance as that of "natural extension" to justify the exercise of jurisdiction by a coastal state, but it certainly did not reject it as an important consideration to impose a limit on the distance which a state may claim in the exercise of that jurisdiction. True, the Court was discussing the meaning of "adjacency" in the context of Article 6 of the Convention relating to boundary lines between opposite or adjacent states and not in the context of Article 1 relating to the outer limit of the continental shelf; however, it is submitted that the Court's interpretation of the expression "adjacent to" in the context of Article 6 is substantially applicable to the same expression in the context of Article 1. Indeed, the Court did not specifically refer to Article 6 when discussing the meaning and importance of "adjacency". After stating that "the idea of absolute proximity is certainly not implied by the rather vague and general terminology employed in the literature on the subject", [72] the Court went on to make a rather important pronouncement, albeit an *obiter dictum,* on the meaning of the expression "adjacent to" used in the Convention. It said in particular:

> To take what is perhaps the most frequently employed of these terms, namely "adjacent to", it is evident that by no stretch of the imagination can a point on the continental shelf situated say a hundred miles, or even much less, from a given coast, be regarded as "adjacent" to it, or to any coast at all, in the normal sense of adjacency, even if the

---

[71]   (1956) *I.L.C. Yearbook* I, at 134.
[72]   (1969) *I.C.J. Rep.* 3, at 30.

point concerned is nearer to some one coast than to any other. [73]

Now the Court did not say that a continental shelf may never extend to 100 miles. Indeed, the whole seabed of the North Sea consists of a continental shelf of less than 200 meters, except for the Norwegian trough along part of the Norwegian coast, and the median line between the United Kingdom and Norway is over 300 km. in places. [74] The Court was careful to specify that it was then referring to "the normal sense of adjacency", which implies "proximity" or "nearness". But it must have a wider meaning than that in the Convention; otherwise, the expression "adjacent to" would make no sense in Article 1, which incorporates the exploitability criterion; nor would it make more sense in Article 6, which envisages cases "where the same continental shelf is adjacent to the territories of two or more states" or "where the same continental shelf is adjacent to the territories of two adjacent States".

What the Court explained, in effect, was that the expression "adjacent to" in the Convention did not necessarily mean "proximate to". For instance, said the Court, "a point inshore situated near the meeting place of the coasts of two States can properly be said to be adjacent to both coasts, even though it may be fractionally closer to the one than the other. Indeed, local geographical configuration may sometimes cause it to have a closer physical connection with the coast to which it is not in fact closest." [75] As a consequence, the Court concluded that "[t]here seems ... to be no necessary, and certainly no complete, identity between the notions of adjacency and proximity". [76]

The fact remains, however, that the notion of adjacency was inserted and retained in the Convention for a purpose. It is interesting to note on this point that, when France acceded to the Convention in June 1965, it attached the following

[73] Ibid.
[74] See large scale map of the North Sea in back cover pocket of I North Sea Continental Shelf Cases — I.C.J. Pleadings (1968).
[75] (1969) I.C.J. Rep. 3, at 30.
[76] Ibid.

Declaration relating to Article 1 which states: "In the view of the Government of the French Republic, the expression 'adjacent' areas implies a notion of geophysical, geological and geographical dependence which *ipso facto* rules out an unlimited extension of the continental shelf." [77] It might also be significant that, of the 46 other states that have ratified or acceded to the Convention, only 3 have taken note or reserved their position with respect to the French Declaration: the United Kingdom, on January 14, 1966, [78] the United States on September 9, 1965, [79] and Canada on February 6, 1970. [80] However, without attaching undue importance to this fact, surely the purpose of inserting the qualifying adjacency factor must have been to impose some seaward limit to the jurisdiction of the coastal state. Otherwise, the sole limit would be the farthest point at which technology can permit exploitation, and the qualifying expression becomes meaningless.

(3) *The criterion of "exploitability"*

Article 1 of the Convention on the Continental Shelf limits the outer edge of the continental shelf "to a depth of 200 meters or, beyond that limit, to where the depth of the superjacent waters admits of the exploitation of the natural resources".

This so-called exploitability criterion has given rise to difficulties of interpretation right from the beginning, when it was discussed in the International Law Commission. It was first adopted by the Commission in 1951, abandoned in 1953, and retained again in the 1956 draft on a majority vote. [81] The purpose here is not to retrace the whole history of

---

[77] *Multilateral Treaties in respect of which the Secretary General performs depository functions* (List as at 31 December 1970), ST/LEG/SER/ D/4, at 376.

[78] *Ibid.,* at 378.

[79] *Ibid.*

[80] *Ibid.,* at 377.

[81] For a brief history of this criterion, see Commentary in the Report to the General Assembly in *I.L.C. Yearbook* II, at 213-214 (1953) and *I.L.C. Yearbook* II, at 296-297 (1956).

Article 1 of the Convention [82] nor to review the controversy which has been going on ever since over the proper interpretation of the exploitability criterion. The object rather is to present a simple proposition, namely that the fixed limit criterion of 200 meters was intended to be the normal limit and that the supplementary criterion of exploitability beyond that limit was meant to cover exceptional cases.

The Commentary to draft Article 67 (which became Article 1 of the Convention) explains why certain members of the Commission wished to re-introduce the exploitability criterion. The Commentary states: "While maintaining the limit of 200 meters in this article as the *normal limit* corresponding to present needs, they wished to recognize forthwith the right to exceed that limit if exploitation of the seabed or subsoil at a depth greater than 200 meters proved technically possible." [83] The eventual technical possibility to exploit at a greater depth than the normal limit of 200 meters therefore constitutes the first reason for the exception. The second reason advanced was to cover the case where there is no continental shelf in the normal sense but "where the depth of the sea would nevertheless permit of exploitation of the subsoil in the same way as if there were a continental shelf". [84] A reading of the summary records of the discussions which took place in the Commission bears out the accuracy of the Commentary just quoted from. In other words, *the exploitability criterion was intended to serve a supplementary role to the fixed limit criterion of 200 meters but was never meant to supplant it.* [85] Now, with the extensive interpretation which

---

[82] This was already done by Lt. B. H. Oxman (U.S.N.R.) of the Office of the Judge Advocate General; see *The Preparation of Article 1 of the Convention on the Continental Shelf*, P.B. No. 182100 (1968). For a summary of the discussions on Article 1 at the Geneva Conference, see M. WHITEMAN, "Conference on the Law of the Sea: Convention on the Continental Shelf", 52 *A.J.I.L.* 629, at 633-634 (1958); see also J. A. C. GUTTERIDGE, "The 1958 Geneva Convention on the Continental Shelf", 35 *B.Y.I.L.* 102, at 106-110 (1959), and L. F. E. GOLDIE, "The Contents of Davy Jone's Locker — A Proposed Regime for the Seabed and Subsoil", 22 *Rutgers L. Rev.* 1-66, at 1-21 (1967).

[83] (1956) *I.L.C. Yearbook* II, at 296; emphasis added.

[84] *Ibid.*, at 297.

[85] A number of writers have expressed similar views and some of them are mentioned here. R. Young maintains that "there is no

is being given by some, the exception (exploitability criterion) is gradually replacing the rule (fixed criterion). A good
example of such extensive interpretation is that given by the
US Senate's Subcommittee on the Outer Continental Shelf,
chaired by Senator Metcalf, which interprets the definition of
the continental shelf as including "the entire continental
margin". [86]

The Report of the Special Subcommittee states in particular:

> The exploitability clause read together with the adja-
> cency clause clearly connotes an expanding boundary which
> at any given time extends to the limit of exploitability then
> existing within an ultimate limit of adjacency. Adjacency

---

evidence in the preparatory work for the Convention, either in the
International Law Commission or at the Conference, of any thought
that the shelf regime should apply to the great ocean depths". See "The
Limits of the Continental Shelf — And Beyond", *Proc. Amer. Soc. of
Int'l. L.* 229, at 330 (1968). Max Sorensen states: "The legal concept
of the continental shelf cannot reasonably be understood, even in its
widest connotation, as extending far beyond the geological concept."
See his dissenting opinion in the *North Sea Continental Shelf Cases*,
(1969), *I.C.J. Rep.* 3, at 249. J. Andrassy maintains: "The framers of
the Convention intended that the exploitability test only supplement
the 200-meter isobath test in exceptional circumstances; in normal
times they considered the isobath test controlling." See *International
Law and Resources of the Sea*, at 87 (1970). The Commission to Study
the Organization of Peace, presided by Professor Louis Sohn, came to
the conclusion that "whatever the reasons for its inclusion, the exploitability criterion was originally regarded as subordinate in importance
to the 200-meter depth line". — *The United Nations and the Bed of
the Sea*, at 23 (March 1969). As for the opinion of Soviet jurists,
Professor Butler states that, in their view, there is no basis for interpreting Article 1 of the Convention as permitting an extension of sovereign
rights to explore and exploit the deep seabed. — Wm. E. BUTLER, *The
Soviet Union and the Law of the Sea*, at 145 (1971). He adds: "These
jurists also find nothing in the proceedings of the International Law
Commission to justify such an interpretation; throughout its discussions, the commission is said to have assumed that there existed a
natural, geological limit to the shelf beyond which sovereign rights
to explore and exploit the seabed are not granted." This is essentially
the view of S. Nikolaev who concludes: "The criterion of the 200-meter
depth clearly defines the average outer limit of geological shelf and
therefore is of most vital importance." — S. NIKOLAEV, "Where is the
limit of national jurisdiction", *Soviet State and Law* 53-61, at 60 (1971);
this article published in Russian was translated for the writer by
Professor Ann Kleimola (Ph.D.), of the University of Nebraska.

[86] See *Report by the Special Subcommittee on the Outer Continental Shelf to the Committee on Interior and Insular Affairs*, Washington, at 29 (1971).

> as applied to the legal Continental Shelf means the seaward
> limit of the natural prolongation of the submerged land
> continent. The submerged land continent encompasses the
> geomorphic shelf, slope and rise. [87]

When it is recalled that the average depth of the seaward
edge of the rise is 4,000 meters, it becomes obvious that the
fixed limit criterion of 200 meters of the continental shelf has
been left behind 20 times over. Indeed, we are no longer
talking about the continental shelf; we are construing Article 1
of the Convention as if the draftsmen had defined the submerged areas without reference to any specific feature. However, the fact is that the International Law Commission was
quite familiar with the different features of submerged areas
and indeed, when it decided to retain the exploitability criterion, considered the idea of eliminating altogether the expression "continental shelf" and retaining simply the expression
"submarine areas" which already appeared in the definition.
As clearly stated in the Commentary, "[t]he majority of the
Commission decided to retain the term 'continental shelf'
because it is in current use and because the term 'submarine
areas' used without further explanation would not give a sufficient indication of the nature of the areas in question". [88]
In other words, the whole purpose of retaining the term "continental shelf" was to impose a definite limitation upon the
submarine areas envisaged. This intention was impliedly confirmed by the 1958 Conference when it defeated an amendment introduced by Panama which would have excluded from
the definition of the continental shelf any limitation in figures
and would have retained the geological criterion only. The
amendment proposed that the usual expression "continental
shelf" be used to designate the continental margin of the
seabed composed of the shelf and the slope, up to deep-sea
oceanic basins. [89] It was defeated by a vote of 38 to 4, with
26 abstentions. [90] In these circumstances, one must agree
with the conclusion of the Soviet jurist Nikolaev that "the

---

[87]   *Ibid.*, at 16.
[88]   (1956) *I.L.C. Yearbook* II, at 297.
[89]   *Conférence des Nations Unies sur le droit de la mer*, Vol. VI:
4ᵉ Com.; A/Conf. 13/42, at 147 (1958).
[90]   *Ibid.*, at 57.

participants in the Conference were not inclined to include the slope in the juridical concept of the continental shelf". [91]

However, in spite of the intention of the International Law Commission and the 1958 Conference to impose a limit in the light of foreseeable technological developments, the fact is that technology is developing to the point where the exploration and exploitation are becoming possible much beyond the continental shelf as contemplated in the Convention. It was reported recently that the *Glomer Challenger* had "bored 4,264 feet into the bottom of the Arabian Sea beneath 11,610 feet of water". [92] In addition, exploitation of manganese nodules will soon be possible at depths ranging up to 5,000 metres. Mr. McKelvey of the United States stated in the Seabed Committee of the U.N. on 14 March 1972 that "24 companies from various countries intended to finance in the summer of 1972 a programme to test the continuous line bucket dredging system, which had been invented in Japan and was designed to recover Pacific sea-floor nodules from depths ranging to 5,000 metres". [93] Considering these developments, the definition of 1958 has simply become obsolete. [94]

---

[91] S. NIKOLAEV, "Where is the limit to national jurisdiction", *Soviet State and Law* 53-61, at 60 (1971); this article published in Russian was translated for the writer by Professor Ann Kleimola (Ph.D.), of the University of Nebraska.

[92] See Walter SULLIVAN, "4 Years of Sea Drilling Yields Vast Lore", in *N.Y. Times*, at 1 (29 May 1972).

[93] See *A/AC.138/S.C.1/SR.37*, at 13 (17 March 1972). The representative of Japan described the "continuous line bucket" technique in the following terms: "It consisted of a continuous wire cable suspended from two winches at either end of a ship. The buckets, essentially scoops, were attached at intervals of the wire cable. They were lowered vertically from the ship to the seabed; then, turning horizontally, each bucket in turn took its scoop from the seabed. The buckets were then raised vertically and emptied into the ship." See *A/AC.138/S.C.1/SR.38*, at 8 (16 March 1972).

[94] It must be stated, of course, that some commentators do suggest to keep the definition as it is and exploit to the maximum the exploitability criterion. This is the opinion of the U.S. National Petroleum Council (which prepared a report for the Department of the Interior), of L. W. Finlay (former manager, Government Relations Department, Standard Oil Company, New Jersey), and O. L. Stone (General Counsel for Shell Oil, New York). See *N.P.C. Report on Petroleum Resources under the Ocean Floor* (1969); L. W. FINLAY, "The Outer Limit of the Continental Shelf", 64 *A.J.I.L.* 42-61 (1970), and O. L. STONE, "Some Aspects of Jurisdiction Over National Resources Under the Ocean Floor", 3 *Natural Resources Lawyer* 155-194

Either it must be changed to fit the facts or restrict the facts to the definition. The first solution is, of course, the more reasonable course to follow and is being proceeded with.

2. Redefinition of the Continental Shelf

The redefinition of the continental shelf has been the subject of considerable study and debate during the past several years. This debate has been particularly active since August 1967, when Ambassador Pardo of Malta made his proposal at the United Nations to consider the sea floor and subsoil beyond the limit of national jurisdiction as a common heritage of mankind. [95] He suggested to reserve the deep sea area exclusively for peaceful purposes and to have it administered by an international agency for the benefit of all peoples. [96] The implementation of such a proposal presumes, of course, that agreement must be reached as to the limit of national jurisdiction. The outer limit of the continental shelf must be fixed, and it is on the determination of that outer limit that disagreement begins. Some states advocate a narrow shelf, others suggest a wide one, [97] and various criteria are

(1970). It should be added that Professor Oda, of Japan, has also interpreted the exploitability criterion in such a way that "all the submarine areas of the world have been theoretically divided among the coastal states at the deepest trenches". He hastens to add, however, that he is in favour of a revision and that he "does not suggest that, as *lex ferenda*, the deep sea should be divided among the various coastal states". See S. ODA, "Proposals for Revising the Convention on the Continental Shelf", 7 *Colum. J. Transnat'l. L.* 1-31, at 9 (1968).

[95] See U.N. Doc. A/6695 (XXII), (18 August 1967).

[96] Ambassador Pardo has explained his proposal in a number of places outside the United Nations. See "Sovereignty under the Sea", *The Round Table* 341-355 (1968); "Panel: Whose is the Bed of the Sea", *Proc. Amer. Soc. Int'l. L.* at 216-229 (1968); "An International Règime for the Deep Seabed: Developing Law or Developing Anarchy", 5 *Texas Int'l. Law Forum* 204-217 (1969); and statement in front of the U.N. *ad hoc* Seabed Committee, U.N. Doc. A/AC135/WG.1/S.R.7, at 48-53 (27 June 1968).

[97] The same holds true for individuals and associations. Among those who suggest a *narrow shelf*, see the following: L. F. E. GOLDIE (200 m.) in "Deep-Sea Mining", *Report of Fifty-Third Conference of the I.L.A.*, at 206 (1968); L. HENKIN (200 m. plus a buffer zone) in *Law for the Sea's Mineral Resources*, at 105 (1968); R. YOUNG (300 m. or 100 miles) in "Panel: Whose Is the Bed of the Sea", *Proc. Amer. Soc. Int'l. L.*, at 233 (1968); Senator PELL (550 m. or 50 miles) in S. Res. 33, 115 *Congressional Record*, at 1330 (21 January 1969); J. ANDRASSY (200 m. or 30 miles plus a buffer zone), in his book *International Law*

proposed to indicate the extent of the shelf. The criteria are based on exploitability, geology, depth, distance, or a combination of depth and distance. [98] Due to the difficulties of reaching agreement on a redefinition of the shelf, the efforts at the United Nations have focused on the legal regime and machinery which will apply to the international area of the seabed beyond the continental shelf properly so-called or the limits of national jurisdiction, leaving such limits to be determined later. Of course, it is difficult, if not impossible, to discuss adequately the legal regime of the international area without reference to the limits of national jurisdiction. Consequently, the debates and proposals have touched upon the delimitation of the continental shelf and, to the extent that they do, they will be reviewed briefly. The most comprehensive proposal presented thus far is that of the United States and special attention will be devoted to it. The present section will be divided as follows: (1) — U.N. Seabed activities; (2) — U.S. draft convention and (3) — Urgency and perspectives of a redefinition.

(1) *U.N. seabed activities*

The Pardo proposal was well received by the General Assembly and, on December 18, 1967, the Assembly decided "to establish an *Ad Hoc* Committee to study the peaceful

---

and the Resources of the Sea, at 118-119 (1970); the Commission to Study the Organization of Peace, presided by Louis Sohn (200 m. or 50 miles) in *The United Nations and the Bed of the Sea*, at 24 (March 1969); and the World Peace Through Law Center (200 m.) in *Revised Draft Treaty Governing the Exploration and Exploitation of the Ocean Bed*, Pamphlet Series No. 14, Geneva (1971).

Among those in favour of a *wide shelf*, see the National Petroleum Council, L. W. Finlay and O. L. Stone, who all suggest that the coastal state has jurisdiction already as far as and including part of the continental rise: see *supra* note 94. See also Hollis D. Hedberg, "The National-International Jurisdictional Boundary on the Ocean Floor", in 1 *Ocean Management* 83-118 (1973).

[98] For an excellent discussion of the advantages and disadvantages of these criteria, see Lewis M. Alexander, *Alternative Regimes for the Continental Shelf*, a paper prepared for *Pacem in Maribus*, Preparatory Conference on the Legal Framework and Continental Shelf, University of Rhode Island, January 30 to February 1, 1970. See also "Statement of Lewis M. Alexander" in *Hearings before the Special Subcommittee on Outer Continental Shelf...*, Part 2, at 483-490, Washington (1970).

uses of the sea-bed and the ocean floor beyond the limits of national jurisdiction". [99] At its Rio de Janeiro meeting of 30 August 1968, the Committee reached an agreement on certain basic principles, two of which are relevant here: 1) there is an area of the seabed, ocean floor and subsoil beyond the limits of national jurisdiction and 2) there should be a precise boundary for the area. [100]

In November of the same year, a Standing Committee of 42 members was established to elaborate principles governing the eventual exploitation of natural resources beyond the limits of national jurisdiction. The Committee's membership has now reached 91 and its mandate covers not only the question of the seabed but all of the law of the sea issues, so that it has in fact become and is often referred to as the Preparatory Committee for the Third Law of the Sea Conference. This Conference is scheduled to be held in 1973, at which time a decision on the basic question of limits should be reached. In the meantime, the General Assembly has adopted a Declaration of Principles in December 1970 [101] and the Seabed Committee has gone ahead with its work.

The Declaration of Principles, adopted by the General Assembly on December 17, 1970, by a vote of 108 in favour, none against, with 14 abstentions, represents the most tangible accomplishment of the United Nations on the whole question of revising the Law of the Sea, in the light of technological developments and a proper balance between the interests of the members of the international community taken collectively and those of its members taken individually, particularly the developing countries. The principles themselves relate only to the area beyond the limits of national jurisdiction and do not cover the delimitation of that area,

---

[99]   Resolution 2172 (XXII), (18 Dcember 1967).

[100]   *Report of the Ad Hoc Committee to Study the Peaceful Uses of the Sea-Bed and the Ocean Floor Beyond the Limits of National Jurisdiction,* U.N. Doc. A/7230 (1968).

[101]   Resolution 2749 (XXV), U.N. Doc. A/C.1/544, reproduced in 9 *Int'l. Legal Materials,* at 220 (1971) and *Dep't. State Bull.,* at 155 (1971).

but they presume that there is such an area. Indeed, the Preamble of the Declaration affirms that "there is an area of the seabed and the ocean floor, and the subsoil thereof, beyond the limits of national jurisdiction, the precise limits of which are yet to be determined". [102]

Using these fifteen principles as guidelines, the Seabed Committee, divided into three subcommittees since 1971, proceeded with its 3-point mandate to prepare draft threaty articles on the following: 1) the legal regime and machinery governing the international area beyond the limits of national jurisdiction, 2) the subjects and issues to be discussed at the Third Law of the Sea Conference, the continental shelf being specifically mentioned and 3) the preservation of the marine environment. As for the question of limits, an understanding was reached in 1971 that "the matter of recommendations concerning the precise definition of the area (beyond the limits of national jurisdiction) is to be regarded as a controversial issue on which the Committee would pronounce". [103] It was further agreed that:

> While each Sub-Committee will have the right to discuss and record its conclusions on the question of limits so far as it is relevant to the subjects allocated to it, the main Committee will not reach a decision on the final recommendation with regard to limits until the recommendations of Sub-Committtee II on the precise definition of the area have been received ... [104]

It should be pointed out, however, that Subcommittee II took so long to agree on a list of issues that it had little time left for debate on substance and did not deal with the re-definition of the continental shelf. It was rather in Plenary or in Subcommittee I, when dealing with the legal regime and machinery of the international area, that states either presented specific proposals or touched upon the question

---

[102] *Ibid.*

[103] *Report of the Committee on the Peaceful Uses of the Sea-Bed and the Ocean Floor Beyond the Limits of National Jurisdiction.* — G.A. Official Records: 26th session, Sup. No. 21 (A/8421), at 5 (1971).

[104] *Ibid.*, at 8.

of limits in the course of debate. The main proposals and suggestions which have been made in U.N. debates concerning the delimitation of the seabed area of exclusive national jurisdiction may be classified as follows: continental margin, 200 miles, 200 miles or 2,500 metres, 200 miles or 550 meters, 200 miles or 200 meters, 200 meters, 200 meters or 40 miles, 200 meters plus a trusteeship zone over the continental slope and part of the rise. The latter proposal is that of the United States and is part of a comprehensive draft convention on the international seabed area. It is the most detailed proposal presented so far in the Committee and deserves to be examined separately. It becomes all the more important within a study of Arctic seabed delimitation that it is the only such proposal presented by an Arctic state.

(2) *The U.S. draft convention*

The U.S. draft convention, proposing a continental shelf limited to 200 meters plus a trusteeship zone over the slope and part of the rise, is based essentially upon a study made by the President's Commission on Marine Science (the Stratton Commission) completed in 1969. It disregards the recommendation made the previous year by the National Petroleum Council which had interpreted the 1958 Continental Shelf Convention as giving coastal states exclusive jurisdiction over the natural resources of the continental margin.

Stratton Commission. — The President's Commission made an extensive study of the new legal-political framework which should govern the exploration and exploitation of mineral resources underlying the high seas and recommended the adoption of a 200-meter isobath or 50-mile limit, whichever is the greater. The recommendation to the President reads as follows:

> The continental shelf of each coastal State, for purposes of the Convention on the Continental Shelf, shall be redefined so that its seaward limit is fixed at the 200 meter (656 feet) isobath or 50 nautical miles from the baselines used for measuring the breadth of its territorial sea, whichever alternative gives the coastal State the greater

area for permanent, exclusive mineral resources exploration and exploitation. [105]

A second recommendation made by the President's Commission is to create an intermediate zone beyond the continental
shelf as newly defined as far as the 2,500 meter (8,200 feet)
isobath or 100 nautical miles from the baselines of the territorial sea, whichever gives the greater area. Only the coastal
state or its licensees would be authorized to explore and
exploit the mineral resources within that zone. [106] Beyond
that, the Commission recommends the establishment of an
international regime the details of which are to be defined
later. The Commission's recommendations were followed by
a formal oceans policy statement by President Nixon.

Nixon proposal. — On May 23, 1970, President Nixon
made a formal announcement of the United States Oceans
policy. "At issue", he said, "is whether the oceans will be
used rationally and equitably and for the benefit of mankind
or whether they will become an area of unrestrained exploitation and conflicting jurisdictional claims in which event the
most advanced States will be losers." [107] The essential operative part of the declaration reads as follows:

> Therefore, I am today proposing that all nations adopt
> as soon as possible a treaty under which they would
> renounce all national claims over the natural resources
> of the seabed beyond the point where the high seas reach
> a depth of 200 metres (218.8 yards), and would agree to
> regard these resources as the common heritage of man-
> kind. [108]

The proposal then goes on to provide for an international
regime, with a trusteeship zone outside the continental shelf
as redefined. The President's announcement was transmitted
to the Chairman of the U.N. Seabed Committee and it specified

---

[105] Commission on Marine Science, Engineering and Resources,
Vol. 3, *Marine Resources and Legal-Political Arrangements for Their
Development*, at VIII-5 (1969).
[106] *Ibid.*
[107] "Statement by the U.S. President on Ocean Policy", U.N.
Doc. A/AC 138/22 (25 May 1970), reproduced in 9 *Int'l Legal Materials*
806, at 807 (1970).
[108] *Ibid.*

that the United States would introduce specific proposals at the next meeting of the Committee to implement the stated objectives.

At a hearing before the Special Subcommittee on outer continental shelf the following week, the Under Secretary of State explained why the United States had opted for a narrowshelf. He stated in particular: "For the United States to propose a concept of broad extension of national jurisdiction would have indirect, but serious, national security implications, and would impede the freedom of scientific research and other uses of the high seas." [109] He also underlined that a 200-meter limit is the only figure stated in the Convention and added that "[i]ts choice was also dictated by the difficulties involved in interpreting the adjacency and exploitability criteria of the Continental Shelf Convention". [110] The proposed Convention was then formally introduced in the Seabed Committee.

Draft U.S. convention. — On August 3, 1970, the United States delegation submitted a *Draft United Nations Convention on the International Seabed Area* [111] as a working paper for discussion purposes in the UN Seabed Committee. This draft convention incorporates the Nixon Proposal that the continental shelf would end at the 200-meter isobath with a maximum baseline of 60 nautical miles. The proposal provides also for an international trusteeship area composed of the continental slope and part of the rise. The part of the rise is defined for the moment as extending to "a line, beyond the continental slope . . . where the downward inclination of the surface of the seabed declines to a gradient of 1: —". [112] It is stated in a footnote that "the precise gradient should be

---

[109] "Clarifications of Presidential Proposal on Oceans", reproduced from U.S. Dept. of State Press Release No. 162, of May 27, 1970 in 9 *Int'l Legal Materials* 821, at 824-825 (1970).

[110]   *Ibid.*, at 826.

[111]   See U.N. Doc. A/AC.138/25 (3 August 1970), reproduced in 9 *Int'l Legal Materials*, at 1046-1080 (1970), and in *Report of the Committee on the Peaceful Uses of the Sea-Bed and the Ocean Floor Beyond the Limits of National Jurisdiction*, U.N. Doc. Sup. No. 21 (A/8021), at 130-176 (1970).

[112]   U.N. Doc. A/AC.138/25, at 7 (3 August 1970).

determined by technical experts, taking into account, among
other factors, ease of determination, the need to avoid dual
administration of single mineral deposits, and the avoidance
of including excessively large areas in the International
Trusteeship Area". [113] It is still not clear, therefore, what is
the exact portion of the rise which will be included in the
trusteeship zone.

Reaction to the U.S. proposal. — The U.S. proposal has
met with opposition both in the United States and in the
Seabed Committee.

In the United States, the Senate's Special Subcommittee
on Outer Continental Shelf objected that "[t]he offer to re-
nounce our sovereign rights beyond the 200 meter isobath
could cast a cloud on our present title to the resources of
our continental margin" [114] and stated that it would press for
the incorporation of its caveats in subsequent revisions of the
US proposal. [115]

In the Seabed Committee, the reaction to the U.S. draft
convention has been mixed. States, like Canada, that have a
large continental margin are very reluctant to accept the
200-meter isobath as representing the fixed limit of the continental shelf. It is pointed out that, under the U.S. proposal,
the United States itself would retain nearly all of its physical
shelf and so would the USSR, since their shelf break is generally at depths shallower than 200 meters. [116] On the other
hand, the other three Arctic states would lose considerably.
Canada, in particular, would lose about 18% of its physical
shelf, [117] mainly because the break of most of its Arctic shelf
occurs at a depth beyond 200 meters and reaching as far as
650 meters before the true slope begins. Norway and Den-

---

[113]   *Ibid.*
[114]   *Report by the Special Subcommittee on Outer Continental
Shelf to the Committee on Interior and Insular Affairs*, at 29 (21 December 1970).
[115]   *Ibid.*, at 33.
[116]   J. A. BEESLEY, *Exploration and Exploitation of the Seabed*,
World Peace Through Law Conference, Belgrade, at 10 (21 July 1971),
typewritten copy circulated at the time of delivery.
[117]   *Ibid.*, at 11.

mark would also lose a considerable portion of their Arctic shelf to the trusteeship zone, since the shelf break off Greenland and Spitzbergen occurs at greater depths than 200 meters. [118]

In order to help solve the problem of redefinition of the continental shelf and to expedite matters generally in seabed activities, Canada made a three-point proposal in March 1971. The three points may be summarized as follows: 1) that a *minimum non-contentious area* of the international seabed region be determined quickly by having all states define their continental shelf claims; 2) that a *transitional international machinery* be established to regulate exploration and exploitation in this minimum non-contentious international area, and 3) that coastal states agree to make voluntary contributions to an *international development fund* of a fixed percentage of their revenues from off-shore exploitation in the area within their national jurisdiction.

The proposal was repeated at the Belgrade Conference of World Peace Through Law in July 1971 by Canada's legal adviser for the Department of External Affairs who explained with respect to the interim redefinition of the shelf that

> If a state did not have a clear idea as to where its interests lie, then it could specify the maximum limit beyond which it would never claim in any event. The effect of this definition of national claims would be that, as of a given date, the international community would be provided with a definition of the minimum non-contentious area of the seabed beyond national jurisdiction. [119]

Mr. Beesley added that this would ensure that a very large percentage would definitely be used for the benefit of mankind and it would permit the simultaneous establishment of an international machinery to manage the development of the non-contentious area. [120]

The developing countries also have considerable difficulty in accepting the Nixon proposal mainly because of the fact

---

[118] *Ibid.*
[119] *Ibid.*, at 25.
[120] *Ibid.*, at 25-26.

that the 200-meter limit of the continental shelf is coupled with a trusteeship zone within which the coastal state exercises a considerable degree of jurisdiction. On this point, Kuwait's position is probably fairly representative and its statement of March 14th, 1972, reads as follows:

> The developing countries also had grave misgivings about the creation of a trusteeship zone in which coastal States would be entitled to exercise additional rights and privileges. The area lying beyond the limits of national jurisdiction should be as large as possible and should not be diminished by a trusteeship zone which would give preference to one group of States at the expense of the international community. Furthermore, the creation of such a zone would be contrary to the concept of the common heritage of mankind. [121]

(3) *Urgency and perspectives of a redefinition*

Urgency. — Progress toward a redefinition of the continental shelf has been slow thus far. Indeed, the solution to this most fundamental question seems to have been postponed until the Third Law of the Sea Conference. This does not mean, however, that there is no urgency for such a redefinition. On the contrary, there exist definite indications that the matter is a condition precedent for the normal and peaceful development of seabed activities. One such indication is the Moratorium Resolution adopted by the General Assembly on December 15, 1969. The resolution in question imposes a moratorium on all exploitation of the deep seabed until the question of a regime for its exploitation is settled. It declares:

> that, pending the establishment of the aforementioned international regime:
>
> (a) States, persons, physical or juridical, are bound to refrain from all activities of exploitation of the resources of the area of the sea-bed and ocean floor, and the subsoil thereof, beyond the limits of national jurisdiction;
>
> (b) No claim to any part of that area or its resources shall be recognized. [122]

---

[121] A/AC.138/SC.I/SR 38, at 4-5 (16 March 1972).
[122] Resolution D, A/RES/2574 (XXIV), (15 January 1970).

Commanding a majority in the General Assembly, the developing countries were able to force through this resolution by a vote of 62 to 28, with 28 abstentions and 9 being absent. Only three developed countries (Finland, Sweden, Yugoslavia) supported the resolution. Although any such resolution by the General Assembly can only have the force of recommendation, it cannot be disregarded and, indeed, caused some concern to the Chairman of the US Senate Subcommittee on the Outer Continental Shelf. One of the questions on which he asked the opinion of the Legal Adviser of the State Department was "what position does the State Department anticipate toward U.S. nationals who express an intention to exploit minerals from the deep seabed, such as manganese nodules ?" [123] The opinion given was that if that event materialized "prior to the establishment of an internationally agreed regime, we would seek to assure that their activities are conducted in accordance with relevant principles of international law, including the freedom of the seas and that the integrity of their investment receives due protection in any subsequent international agreement". [124]

Regardless of the fact that General Assembly resolutions on this subject are not legally binding decisions for the member states, the United States recognized that it "is required to give good faith consideration to the Resolution in determining its policies". [125] Indeed, it must have felt that there was considerable urgency in having agreement reached on the delimitation of the continental shelf and the legal regime beyond, since the Nixon Proposal was made less than six months after the adoption of the Moratorium Resolution. It should be noted further that the President's proposal also calls on other nations to join the United States in an interim policy under which all permits for exploration and exploitation beyond 200 meters would be issued "subject to the international regime to be agreed upon". [126] The proposal further

---

[123] See Letter from Lee Metcalf to John R. Stevenson, dated 23 December 1969, reproduced in 9 *Int'l Legal Materials*, at 831 (1970).
[124] *Ibid*, at 832.
[125] *Ibid*.
[126] *Ibid*.

provides that "a substantial portion of the revenues derived by a State from exploitation beyond 200 metres during this interim period should be turned over to an appropriate international development agency for assistance to developing countries". [127] It is obvious that the main purpose of the interim period proposal is to ensure that exploration and exploitation of the deep seabed continues, and to give entrepreneurs the necessary protection for their investments during that period.

Another indication of the urgency of reaching agreement on the limits of national jurisdiction is found in the speeches of some of the developing countries at the 1972 March session of the Seabed Committee in New York, alleging that a certain number of western countries, either directly or through their national corporations, had already begun the exploitation of the international seabed area. [128] Kuwait in particular made the following statement:

> A major problem yet to be solved was that of defining the limits of the area beyond national jurisdiction. The time had come to tackle that problem with courage, realism and in a manner that would do justice to the concept of common heritage.
>
> . . . . . .
>
> Many, if not all, of the developing countries were seriously concerned about the course events were taking. They would appreciate receiving formal assurances from all States connected with such activities that no commercial exploitation of the resources of the sea-bed and ocean floor beyond the limits of national jurisdiction would be undertaken before the establishment of the international regime. [129]

Not having received the assurances requested, Kuwait introduced a "draft decision" at the end of the March session,

---

[127]   *Ibid.*

[128]   See in particular Chile's statement of March 9, 1972, in A/AC.138/SC.I/SR.35, at 13-14 (13 March 1972); as well as Kuwait's intervention of March 16, 1972, in A/AC.138/SC.I/SR.38, at 4-5 (16 March 1972).

[129]   A/AC.138/SC.I/SR.38, at 5 (16 March 1972).

at a plenary meeting of the Seabed Committee, the operative part of which reads as follows:

> Decides also that all arrangements made or to be made for the commercial exploitation of the resources of the area prior to the establishment of the regime shall have no legal validity and shall not form the legal basis for any claims with respect to any part of the area or its resources. [130]

Since no notice of the draft resolution had been given, the Chairman ruled that there could be no discussion of the document but he did say that it could be discussed at the next session of the Committee to be held in Geneva in July-August 1972. This ruling, however, did not prevent the delegations of Algeria, Cameroons, Chile, China, India, Libyan Arab Republic, Mauritania, Nigeria, Pakistan, Peru and Yemen to express their solidarity with the delegation of Kuwait. In addition and on the very next day, a Note was sent by the Secretary-General to the members of the Seabed Committee asking them to provide relevant information, pertaining to deep-sea mining activities carried on by their nationals, before April 30, 1972. The purpose of this request by the Secretary-General was undoubtedly to enable the Secretariat to complete the Progress Report which the Chairman of Subcommittee I had mentioned previously when he asked states to provide the fullest information on their deep-sea activities. As it happened, very few states provided the U.N. Secretariat with the relevant information requested and the Kuwait proposal was not really discussed at the 1972 July-August meeting of the Sea-bed Committee. However, Kuwait requested that its proposal be included in the Committee's report to the General Assembly.

Regardless of the recommendatory nature of the 1969 Moratorium Resolution and of the eventual outcome of the Kuwait proposal, the urgency of reaching agreement on the basic issue of limits is clearly evident. The question which remains is: what are the perspectives for reaching such an agreement ?

---

[130]   See A/AC.138/L.II.

Perspectives. — The prospects of reaching an early agreement on a redefinition of the continental shelf do not appear good at the moment. The reason simply is that there are very real difficulties in trying to define limits of exclusive national jurisdiction in such a way as to protect adequately the interests of states with a wide shelf and those of states with a narrow one. The *200-meter isobath* is out of the question as an adequate solution: it is neither representative of the average nor of the maximum depth of the shelf break. The world average shelf depth is estimated to be about 132 meters and the shelf break occurs at depths up to 650 meters in the Arctic. Except for the United States, such a criterion would be unsuitable to all of the Arctic states since a considerable proportion of their shelf breaks at depths greater than 200 meters. This is the case for about 35% of Canada's Arctic shelf and about 25% for that of the U.S.S.R. The corresponding portion of the shelf off Spitzbergen and Greenland is of similar magnitude.

The *continental margin* would likewise seem unacceptable: it includes features (slope and rise) which are beyond the real shelf and, in addition, would give very little to states with a narrow shelf, the entire margins of such shelves being also usually narrow. As for the Arctic states, all of their continental margins are wide and such a criterion would be most favourable to them but it remains unsatisfactory for the great majority of the other states.

The 200-mile proposal, espoused by Pardo of Malta and incorporated in a draft ocean space treaty, appears so far to have gained the greatest number of adherents in the U.N. Sea-bed Committee. This would give a uniform breath of exclusive national jurisdiction to all coastal states, except those that are shelf-locked, and would generally benefit Latin American and African countries, as well as a few Asian ones. Consequently, if one can speak of a trend emerging from the debates in the Sea-bed Committee, it would seem to be toward accepting the 200-mile proposal. The concepts of economic zone and patrimonial sea advanced by certain African and Latin American countries are quite similar to Pardo's proposal, and those countries would probably be willing to accept it. The 200-mile proposal has the advantage of not only providing a limit which is easily determined but it goes a long way to accommodate the generality of states. In his speech of March 23, 1971, in the Sea-bed Committee, Ambassador Pardo reviewed the various criteria in the light of their general acceptability and the practical difficulties of application. He came to the conclusion that a fixed distance of 200 miles was the most feasible criterion to use. He summarized his conclusion in the following terms:

> Taking into account the general interest of the international community to keep the widest possible area of ocean space open to the non-discriminatory access of all, and taking into account the fact that some coastal States have already proclaimed that their jurisdiction extends to 200 miles from their coasts, my delegation has come to the reluctant conclusion that, to avoid prolonged debate and haggling, it has become necessary to establish a distance of 200 miles from the nearest coast as the outer limit of coastal State jurisdiction in ocean space. ... Three or four States may have legitimate claims to an ocean space jurisdiction exceeding 200 miles from their coasts which are founded on the depth criterion of the 1958 Geneva Convention on the Continental Shelf. I believe that, if moderation is shown, the interests of these States can be fully satisfied. [131]

The few states in question include Canada, the U.S.S.R. and the United States (Alaska); they would lose part of their shelf or margin. Canada, for instance, would lose the eastern portion of the Grand Bank and the Flemish Cap, all of which it presently claims as a natural extension of its land-mass. Theoretically, it is always possible that some proviso be attached to the 200-mile criterion so as to include the wider shelves claimed by those few states. Practically, it is doubtful that the other states would agree to such a solution, considering that those few states would already benefit to the maximum from the 200-mile strip. Consequently, it would seem

---

[131] See *Statement Delivered by Dr. Arvid Pardo, Permanent Representative of Malta to the United Nations in the Main Committee* (typewritten copy circulated at the time of delivery), at 65 (23 March 1971).

that the straight 200-mile criterion offers the best chance of agreement.

IV. — THE LAW APPLICABLE TO LATERAL DELIMITATION

Disputes have not yet arisen over the lateral boundaries of the Arctic continental shelves but, with the intensity of exploratory activities, problems of boundary delimitation are bound to arise. Will the states concerned agree on the equidistance principle to delimit their respective continental shelves or will they use some other method ? Are there special circumstances which ought to be taken into account ? To what extent may the decision of the International Court in the *North Sea Continental Shelf Cases* assist the Arctic states in their delimitation problem ? These are the kind of questions which will arise when delimitation negotiations begin, if they have not already begun.

The problem of delimitation of lateral boundaries received little attention in the early development of continental shelf doctrine. The Truman Proclamation of 1945 simply stated: "In cases where the continental shelf extends to the shores of another State, or is shared with an adjacent State, the boundary shall be determined by the United States and the State concerned in accordance with equitable principles." [132] It was in the International Law Commission that the problem was really examined for the first time. In its provisional draft of 1951, the Commission merely proposed that such boundary problems should be settled by agreement and, in the absence of agreement, by arbitration. [133] In 1953, after receiving guidance from a Committee of hydrological experts on the delimitation of territorial waters, "the Commission now felt in the position to formulate a general rule, based on the principle of equidistance . . .". [134] The draft article, agreed upon by the Commission in 1953, was retained in its 1956 report, with

---

[132]   4 WHITEMAN, *Digest of International Law*, at 757 (1965).
[133]   (1951) *I.L.C. Yearbook* II, at 143.
[134]   (1953) *I.L.C. Yearbook* II, at 216.

only a minor change, and was subsequently adopted as Article 6 of the Convention by the Geneva Conference in 1958. Para. 2 of Article 6 reads as follows:

> Where the same continental shelf is adjacent to the territories of two adjacent States, the boundary of the continental shelf shall be determined by agreement between them. In the absence of agreement, and unless another boundary line is justified by special circumstances, the boundary shall be determined by application of the principle of equidistance from the nearest points of the baselines from which the breadth of the territorial sea of each State is measured. [135]

It is not clear from the text itself what is meant to be the substantive rule, if any, envisaged by the provision, since it is silent as to what should be the basis of the agreement mentioned. However, it does appear quite clear from a study of the preparatory works of the Convention that the principle of equidistance was meant to be the general rule and serve at least as the starting point in negotiations. The relevant Commentary of the International Law Commission reads as follows:

> The rule (equidistance) thus proposed is subject to such modifications as may be agreed upon by the parties. Moreover, while in the case of both kinds of boundaries (median and lateral) the rule of equidistance is the general rule, it is subject to modification in cases in which another boundary line is justified by special circumstances. As in the case of the boundaries of coastal waters, provision must be made for departure necessitated by any exceptional configuration of the coast, as well as the presence of islands or of navigable channels. [136]

In other words, the Convention provides that the ordinary basis on which delimitation of continental shelf boundaries is to be made is the equidistance principle. This view finds consid-

---

[135]   For an extensive study of Article 6, which the present writer found very useful, see Etienne GRISEL, "The Lateral Boundaries of the Continental Shelf and the Judgment of the International Court of Justice in the North Sea Continental Shelf Cases", 64 *A.J.I.L.* 562-593 (1970); see also M. WHITEMAN, "Conference on the Law of the Sea: Convention on the Continental Shelf", 52 *A.J.I.L.* 629-659, at 648-654 (1958).
[136]   (1953) *I.L.C. Yearbook* II, at 216; words in brackets added.

erable support in the practice of states in general [137] and that of the Arctic states in particular. [138] The equidistance rule is subject, however, to two exceptions: an agreement on a different rule and the existence of special circumstances. The first exception simply means that states remain free to depart from the equidistance principle to any degree and on whatever basis they wish, in order to arrive at an acceptable delimitation. For instance, in the 1970 Agreement between Saudi Arabia and Iran in the upper Persian Gulf, the Parties modified the geographical equidistance rule in order to take into account the presence of certain islands and allot them the normal territorial waters around them. [139] As for the second exception, the presence of "special circumstances", it is impossible to be exhaustive in the determination of such circumstances, but three are specifically mentioned in the Commentary above quoted: an exceptional configuration of the coast, the existence of islands and the presence of navigable channels. A fourth type of special circumstance was also mentioned by the British hydrographer, R. H. Kennedy, at the 1958 Geneva Conference: "the possession by one of the two States concerned of special mineral exploitation rights or fishery rights . . .". [140] For instance, a state having made prior investment and exploitation might be able to invoke that as constituting a special circumstance. Another possible situation which might be equated to a special circumstance is the possession of a historic title. This is not mentioned in the Continental Shelf Convention, but it is provided for in the Territorial Sea Convention. Article 12 of that Convention specifies that the median line rule for the delimitation of territorial waters between opposite or adjacent states does not apply "where it is necessary by reason of historic title or other special cir-

---

[137] For a review of state practice relating to the equidistance rule, see M. LACHS in (1969) *I.C.J. Rep.* 3, at 228.

[138] See Section V *infra*, "The Legislation and Practice of Arctic States in Continental Shelf Delimitation."

[139] See Richard YOUNG, "Equitable Solutions for Offshore Boundaries: the 1968 Saudi Arabia-Iran Agreement", 64 *A.J.I.L.*, at 152-157 (1970).

[140] See "Summary Records of the Fourth Committee (Continental Shelf)", *U.N. Conference on the Law of the Sea*, A/CONF.13/42, at 93 (1958).

cumstances to delimit the territorial seas of the two States in a way which is at variance with this provision". By analogy, such historic title might also be considered a special circumstance in the delimitation of a continental shelf boundary.

Naturally enough, the determination of the existence of special circumstances and the extent to which they warrant a departure from the general rule will often cause difficulty in practice. If it is impossible for the Parties to arrive at an agreement, they should submit the matter to arbitration or to the International Court. In the *North Sea Continental Shelf Cases,* the Court held that the equidistant principle was not applicable because Germany was not a party to the Convention, but it nevertheless found that the equidistance rule should be departed from because it led to an inequitable result due to the markedly concave coast of Germany as opposed to the convexed coasts of its neighbours. [141] As was emphasized by the Court, what is important is to reach an equitable solution and not to find one method of delimitation.

To sum up the law on the question of delimitation of continental shelf boundary, it may be stated that the general rule applicable is the median line but there may be a number of possible special circumstances constituting exceptions: exceptional configuration of the coast, the existence of islands, the presence of navigable channels, the possession of special mineral exploitation rights and the possession of a historic title. These exceptions to the general rule are consonant with the assumption made by the International Law Commission since it did note that "special circumstances would probably necessitate frequent departures from the mathematical median line". [142]

V. — THE LEGISLATION AND PRACTICE OF ARCTIC STATES ON CONTINENTAL SHELF DELIMITATION.

What follows is a summary of the national legislation and practice of Arctic states with respect to their continental

---

[141] (1969) *I.C.J. Rep.* 3, at 50.
[142] (1956) *I.L.C. Yearbook* II, at 271.

shelf delimitation, both seaward and lateral: 1 — Norway, 2 — Denmark, 3 — The U.S.S.R., 4 — Canada, 5 — The United States.

1. NORWAY

Although Norway did not accede to the 1958 Convention on the Continental Shelf before 1971, it adopted national legislation in 1963 which borrowed from the relevant provisions of the Convention.

The Royal Decree of May 31, 1963 incorporates the exploitability criterion of Article 1 of the Convention and the median line principle of Article 6. The Decree reads as follows:

> The seabed and its sub-soil in the submarine areas outside the coast of the Kingdom of Norway are subject to Norwegian sovereignty in respect of the exploitation and exploration of natural deposits, to such extent as the depth of the sea permits the utilisation of natural deposits, irrespective of any other territorial limits at sea, but not beyond the median line in relation to other states. [143]

It should be noted that the term "utilisation" in this unofficial translation is replaced by the term "exploitation" in the enactment of the following month.

Act No. 12 of 21 June 1963, relating to Exploration and Exploitation of Submarine Natural Resources incorporates also the "exploitability" criterion and the median line principle of delimitation. Section 1 of the Act reads:

> This Act applies to exploration for and exploitation of natural resources in the seabed or in its subsoil, as far as the depth of the superjacent waters admits of exploitation of natural resources, within as well as outside the maritime boundaries otherwise applicable, but not beyond the median line in relation to other states. [144]

Having quoted the above provisions, the Memorandum submitted by Norway to the U.N. Ad Hoc Committee on the

---

[143] *Legislation concerning the Norwegian Continental Shelf, with unofficial English translation,* published by the Royal Ministry of Industry and Handicrafts, at 4 (1970). The writer is very grateful to the Norwegian Embassy in Ottawa for supplying him with this publication.
[144] *Ibid.,* at 6.

Seabed states: "It follows from these enactments that the Government of Norway has applied the exploitation criterion of Article 1 of the Geneva Convention on the Continental Shelf for the purpose of delimiting the continental shelf of Norway. No mention has been made of the alternative 200-metre criterion contained in the Geneva Convention." [145]

As explained at a later date by the representative of Norway, Mr. Evensen, "Their purpose was not, however, to enable his country to claim sovereignty over large areas of the Atlantic and Arctic Oceans but rather to apply a more elastic rule than the 200-metre criterion, which was obviously unsuited to the geographical peculiarities of Norway's continental shelf." [146]

It is interesting to note that both the Decree and the Act of 1963 use the term "sovereignty" and not "sovereign rights". As is well known, the latter expression was used in the Convention to indicate that the rights of the coastal state are definitely limited to the natural resources of the seabed and the subsoil and do not affect the superjacent waters and air space. It must be pointed out, however, that the Norwegian Act of 1963 does go on later to provide that "[t]he rights of navigation and fishing are not affected by this Act." [147]

Insofar as the adoption of the median line principle is concerned, Norway has not only incorporated it in its national legislation but it has subscribed to it in the delimitation of the North Sea continental shelf. Its Agreement with the United Kingdom dated 10 March 1965, as well as the one with Denmark of 8 December 1965, are based on the equidistance principle. [148]

2. DENMARK

Denmark ratified the Convention on the Continental Shelf on June 12, 1963. It has also adopted a decree which incor-

---

[145]   U.N. Doc. A/AC.135/1, at 39 (11 March 1968).
[146]   U.N. Doc. A/AC.135/WG.1/SR.6, at 38 (26 June 1968).
[147]   *Supra* note 152, sec. 5, at 5.
[148]   See Article 4 of the United Kingdom-Norway Agreement reproduced in (1968) *I.C.J. Pleadings* I, at 105-107, and Article 4 of the Denmark-Norway Agreement reproduced in (1968) *I.C.J. Pleadings* I, at 126-127.

porates the definition of the continental shelf contained in
Article 1 of the Convention. The *Royal Decree of June 7, 1963,
on the Exercise of Danish Sovereignty over the Continental
Shelf* provides as follows:

> 1. Denmark exercises, for the purposes of exploration
> and exploitation of natural resources, sovereign rights over
> that part of the Continental Shelf which according to the
> Convention on the Continental Shelf ... belongs to the
> Kingdom of Denmark, cf. Section 2 below.
>
> 2. (1) Pursuant to Article 1 of the Convention the
> term "continental shelf" is used as refer-
> ring ... (*text of Article 1 of the Convention*). [149]

The same decree goes on to provide that the boundary of the
continental shelf in relation to foreign states whose coasts are
opposite or adjacent to the coasts of Denmark shall be the
median line in the absence of any special agreement. In practice, Denmark has adhered to this principle in its relations
with other countries. It concluded three treaties all of which
embody the equidistance principle: one with the Federal Republic of Germany (9 June 1965), [150] a second one with Norway (8 December 1965), [151] a third with the United Kingdom
(3 March 1966), [152] and a fourth with the Netherlands (31
March 1966). [153] The Agreement with the United Kingdom
foresees the conclusion of a further agreement, should any
single geological structure make it necessary to cross the dividing line in order to exploit it. [154] The Agreement with the
Netherlands provides that, should a difference of opinion arise
as to the position of any installation in relation to the boundary
line, the matter should be settled by a further agreement. [155]

---

[149]   Taken from the unofficial translation provided to the writer
by the Royal Danish Embassy in Ottawa. However, the text of this
Decree reproduced in a survey prepared by the U.N. Secretariat for the
Ad Hoc Seabed Committee uses the expression "Danish Sovereignty
shall be exercised ..." See U.N. Doc. A/AC.135/11, at 28 (4 June 1968).

[150]   Reproduced in *I.C.J. Pleadings* I, at 111 (1968).

[151]   *Ibid.,* at 126.

[152]   *Ibid.,* at 128.

[153]   *Ibid.,* at 138.

[154]   *Ibid.,* at 129, Article 4.

[155]   *Ibid.,* at 138, Article 2.

3. SOVIET UNION

The Soviet Union has been a party to the Continental Shelf Convention since November 22, 1960. By an internal decree, in 1968, it defined its continental shelf and provided for its delimitation with other states in accordance with criteria found in the Convention.

The *Edict of the Presidium of the USSR Supreme Soviet Concerning the Continental Shelf of February 6, 1968,* defines the continental shelf in its Article 1, as follows:

> The U.S.S.R. exercises sovereign rights over the continental shelf adjacent to the outer limit of the territorial sea of the U.S.S.R., for the purpose of exploring it and exploiting its natural resources. The continental shelf of the U.S.S.R. consists of the sea-bed and the subsoil of the submarine areas adjacent to the coast or to islands of the U.S.S.R. but outside the area of the territorial sea, to a depth of 200 meters or, beyond that limit, to where the depth of the superjacent waters admits of the exploitation of the natural resources of the said areas.
>
> The sea-bed and subsoil of depressions entirely surrounded by the continental shelf of the U.S.S.R., irrespective of their depth, are part of the continental shelf of the U.S.S.R. [156]

The first two paragraphs are straight forward and are unquestionably in accordance with Article 1 of the Convention. The third paragraph, however, does call for comment since it includes "depressions entirely surrounded by the continental shelf". Depressions, channels or troughs were not expressly mentioned in the Convention, but those features were discussed in the International Law Commission. In its Commentary to the definition article, the Commission stated that "[i]n the special cases in which submerged areas of a depth less than 200 metres, situated fairly close to the coast, are separated from the part of the continental shelf adjacent to the coast by a narrow channel deeper than 200 metres, such shallow areas could be considered as adjacent to that

---

[156] See Survey of National Legislation relating to the continental shelf prepared by the U.N. Secretariat, A/AC.135/11, at 58 (4 June 1968); and 7 *Int'l Legal Materials,* at 392 (1968).

part of the shelf." [157] The Commission did not intend apparently to include the channel or depression itself as part of the shelf; perhaps the only reason was that it did not foresee the possibility of exploiting it. The Commentary went on to say that "[i]t would be for the State relying on this exception to the general rule to establish its claim to an equitable modification of the rule." [158] In examining the continental shelf north of the coast of the USSR, there seems to be only one place where the provision relating to depressions could apply: it is in the Kara Sea where there are some deep re-entrants. As explained by the American Committee on Polar Research, "[t]he best known of these cuts are the Svataya Anna and Voronin Troughs, which show depths of 500 m well into the Kara Sea." [159]

As for the delimitation in relation to other states, the Decree provides, as does the Convention on the Continental Shelf that, in the absence of agreement or special circumstances, such delimitation shall be made in accordance with the equidistant principle. [160] In practice, the U.S.S.R. has applied that principle with Finland in the Baltic Sea (5 May 1967) [161] and with Poland in the Gulf of Gdansk and the South-eastern Baltic Sea (29 August 1966). [162] As for the delimitation in the Gulf of Finland, however, the USSR agreed with Finland (20 May 1965) to have the boundaries of their continental shelf coincide with those of their territorial waters established in 1940. [163] A further indication of the Soviet practice is found in a joint Declaration on the Continental Shelf of the Baltic Sea signed by the Soviet Union, Poland and East Germany on October 23, 1968. It stipulates that the delimitation of the continental shelf in the Baltic Sea must

---

[157]   (1956) *I.L.C. Yearbook* II, at 297.

[158]   *Ibid.*

[159]   Committee on Polar Research — *POLAR RESEARCH, A Survey,* National Academy of Sciences, at 50 (1970).

[160]   See Article 2 of the Decree, *supra* note 165.

[161]   For a translation of the treaty, see 7 *Int'l Legal Materials,* at 560 (1968).

[162]   9 *Int'l Legal Materials,* at 697 (1970).

[163]   For a translation of the treaty, see 6 *Int'l Legal Materials,* at 727 (1967).

be made in accordance with the principles of the 1958 Convention on the Continental Shelf, in particular Article 6. [164]

4. CANADA

Canada has ratified the Continental Shelf Convention only on February 6, 1970, and it has not yet enacted special national legislation implementing the Convention. Strictly speaking, this means that the Convention as such has not yet become part of Canadian domestic law. Treaties being made by the Executive, the intervention of Parliament is necessary to translate them into national legislation. Nevertheless, Canada did enact two laws in 1970 which contain operational definitions of the continental shelf. One is an amendment to the *Oil and Gas Production and Conservation Act* which makes the Act applicable, *inter alia,* to the following areas:

> those submarine areas adjacent to the coast of Canada to a water depth of two hundred meters or beyond that limit to where the depth of the superjacent waters admits of the exploitation of the natural resources of the seabed and subsoil thereof; [165]

The provision just quoted is taken, of course, from Article 1 of the 1958 Continental Shelf Convention. The other law which contains a reference to the continental shelf is the *Arctic Waters Pollution Prevention Act* of 1970. [166] The definition of "arctic waters" to which the Act applies includes "all waters . . . lying north of the sixtieth parallel of north latitude, the natural resources of whose subjacent submarine areas Her Majesty in right of Canada has the right to dispose of or exploit . . ." [167] It is obvious from those operational definitions found in two separate statutes that Canada has meant to subscribe to and take advantage of the definition of the continental shelf in the 1958 Convention. It should be

---

[164] See Wm. E. BUTLER, in *The Soviet Union and the Law of the Sea,* at 147 (1971).

[165] Sec. 3(a) *Act to amend the Oil and Gas Production and Conservation,* Chap. 43, 18-19 Eliz. II (1970).

[166] 18-19 Eliz. II (1969-1970).

[167] *Ibid.,* Article 301.

pointed out further that, when ratifying the Convention, Canada has inserted the following declaration in its instrument of ratification with respect to Article 1:

> In the view of the Canadian Government the presence of an accidental feature such as a depression or a channel in a submerged area should not be regarded as constituting an interruption in the natural prolongation of the land territory of the coastal state into and under the sea. [168]

This Declaration is understandable since Canada takes a geomorphological view of the continental shelf off its coasts and there are certain depressions and channels in it. The more important ones are found off Nova Scotia in the Gulf of Maine where there is a delimitation problem with the United States, off the Grand Bank of Newfoundland and between some of the islands in the Canadian Arctic archipelago. Following the geomorphological approach, Government practice indicates that Canada relies considerably on the exploitability criterion in determining the seaward limit of its jurisdiction over the continental shelf.

Its statement addressed to the U.N. Ad Hoc Seabed Committee, on March 8, 1968, specifies:

> In the view of the Canadian authorities, the present legal position regarding the sovereign rights of the coastal States over the resources of submarine areas extending *at least to the abyssal depths* is not in dispute. It follows that the proposed study should be confined to the problems of exploration of the resources of the deep ocean floor. [169]

A similar view was presented subsequently by Canada's representative, George Ignatieff, to the same Committee when he stated that "[t]here was no doubt that the areas over whose resources coastal States possessed sovereign rights included the *continental shelf and slope.*" [170] In 1969, the Minister for

---

[168] See *Multilateral Treaties in respect of which the Secretary General Performs Depository Functions* (List as at 31 December 1970), ST./LEG/SFRD/4, at 376 (1971).

[169] U.N. Doc. A/AC.135/1, at 33 (8 March 1968): emphasis added.

[170] Summary Record of the Fourth Meeting, U.N. Doc. A/AC./135/SR.4, at 24 (21 March 1968); emphasis added.

External Affairs recognized the necessity of redefining the continental shelf and stated Canada's stand as follows: "We are taking the position that the redefinition of the continental shelf must recognize coastal-state rights over the 'submerged continental margin' which consists of the continental *shelf and slope and at least part of the rise*." [171] A claim to the continental margin would therefore appear to be well established government policy. In April 1971, Canada's legal adviser for the Department of External Affairs, Alan Beesley, gave the following interpretation of the Continental Shelf Convention:

> We differ of course with those who read the Convention selectively, stressing the 200-meter isobath while ignoring the overriding provision laying down the exploitability test. We accept, however, that the Convention is a Continental Shelf Convention, not an abyssal depth convention, and that there is a limit to national jurisdiction and that the area beyond the shelf is also beyond national jurisdiction. I refer here to the geological shelf; that is to say, the continental margin. [172]

Mr. Beesley then went on to say that an accommodation solution to the question of limits would have to permit those few states like Canada to "retain their present jurisdiction out to the edge of the continental margin". [173]

In practice, Canada has granted exploratory permits off its east and west coasts, as well as in the Beaufort sea at considerable distances and depths. The permits extend as far as 425 miles east of Newfoundland and, off the west coast, cover a stretch of 500 miles from the Strait of Juan de Fuca area to the Dixon Entrance region. [174] As for the Arctic regions, the Minister for Energy, Mines and Resources, stated in the House of Commons on March 9, 1970 that "approxi-

---

[171] Hon. Mitchell SHARP, "The Law and Arms Control on the Seabed", *Statements and Speeches,* No. 69/19, at 2 (1969); emphasis added.

[172] J. A. BEESLEY, "Some Unresolved Issues on the Law of the Sea", 4 *Natural Resources Law* 629, at 631 (1971).

[173] *Ibid.*

[174] See Statement by Hon. J. J. Greene (Minister of Energy, Mines and Resources), in *Can. H.C. Deb.,* at 4569 (9 March 1970).

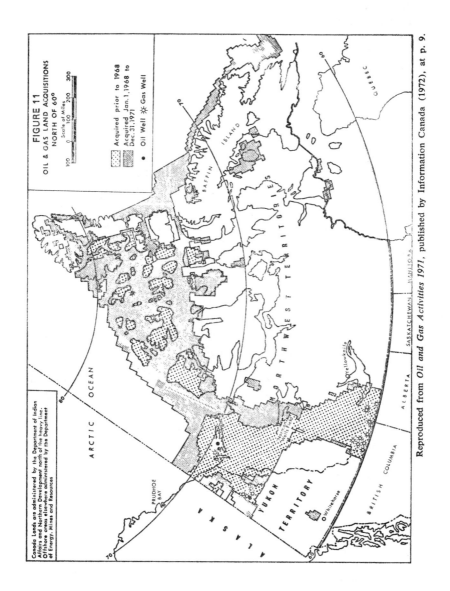

Reproduced from *Oil and Gas Activities 1971*, published by Information Canada (1972), at p. 9.

mately 150 million acres of oil and gas permits have been issued in the Arctic offshore". [175] He specified their location as follows: "These are situated in the Beaufort Sea region, where they extend as far seaward as 140 miles off the mainland coast, and in the Arctic islands regions where they cover most of the channels between the various islands." [176] (Figure 11). Having spoken of distances from shore, the responsible Minister went on to make the following statement about water depths.

> Here I would point out that the federal government has issued permits in water depths ranging to 2,200 meters — about 7,000 feet — in the Gulf of Maine region; to 3,700 meters — about 12,000 feet — in the Scotian shelf region; to 2,800 meters — about 9,000 feet — in the Grand Banks region; to 2,100 meters — about 6,800 feet — in the Labrador sea region; to 900 meters — about 3,000 feet — in the Arctic islands regions; and to 2,600 meters — about 8,500 feet — in the Beaufort Sea region. [177]

As for its continental shelf boundary delimitation with other states, Canada has no legislative enactment and it does not seem to have made any official pronouncement on the question. In the Arctic regions, Canada has two neighbours with which it must eventually conclude continental shelf boundary agreements: Denmark (Greenland) and the United States (Alaska). It is of interest that Canada and the United States have accepted the equidistant rule in a number of instances to delimit water boundaries, such as those of the Great Lakes and of Passamaquoddy Bay. More significantly, Canada relies on the equidistant rule in its negotiations with the United States over the continental shelf boundary in the Gulf of Maine. It has issued exploratory permits up to the median line, but this is not accepted as a proper demarcation by the United States. The latter invokes the "special circumstances" provision of the Continental Shelf Convention and it is reported to have sent a Note to Ottawa on February 21, 1970, refusing to "acquiesce in or recognize the validity of permits or other authorizations issued by the Government of

---

[175]   Ibid.
[176]   Ibid.
[177]   Ibid., at 4569-4570.

Canada to explore or exploit the natural resources of any part of the Georges Bank continental shelf". [178] So far as it is known to this writer, the matter has not yet been settled. Whether Canada will adopt the same attitude in the Beaufort Sea area remains a question. The geography there gives the United States a fairly convex coast whereas, in the same area, the Canadian coastline is markedly concave, thus being to the disadvantage of Canada. Without invoking the sector theory, which would be of very doubtful validity for a claim to sovereign rights over the continental shelf, [179] the United States and Canada could agree to use the 141st meridian. It is a convenient demarcation line and it has some historical significance. In the 1825 boundary treaty between Russia and Great Britain, the line of demarcation between the possessions of the Parties is specified to be the meridian line of the 141st degree "dans son prolongement jusqu'à la Mer Glaciale", [180] the latter phrase being translated "in its prolongation as far as the Frozen Ocean". [181] The same demarcation line is incorporated by reference in the 1867 cession treaty between Russia and the United States. [182] Should the United States and Canada agree to retain the 141st meridian line instead of the equidistance one as the demarcation line for their continental shelf, it would result in the gain of a small triangular piece for Canada. However, this gain disappears when reaching into the Canada Abyssal Plain where the median line becomes more favourable to Canada. A comparative study of the two lines must therefore be made in the light of the seaward or polar limit of the continental shelf.

5. United States of America

The United States has been a party to the Continental Shelf Convention since April 12, 1961, and was the first

---

[178] See *Time,* at 9 (9 March 1970). See also "U.S. questions validity of Canadian oil leases", *Globe and Mail,* at 1 (24 February 1970).

[179] On the applicability of the Sector theory in the Arctic, see this writer's dissertation: *La théorie des secteurs dans l'Arctique à l'égard du droit international,* 164 pp., Paris (1955).

[180] Recueil De Martens, N.S. II, at 428.

[181] Recueil De Martens, N.S. VI, at 686.

[182] Recueil De Martens, N.R., 2ᵉ Série, I, at 39.

country to assert jurisdiction over the continental shelf in the now famous Truman Proclamation of September 28, 1945. The Proclamation did not specify any outward limit to this assertion of jurisdiction and control, but the White House Press Release issued on the same day did. It stated that "[g]enerally, submerged land which is contiguous to the continent and which is covered by no more than 100 fathoms (600 feet) of water is considered as the continental shelf." [183] The Outer Continental Shelf Lands Act adopted in August 1953 [184] does not set any outward limit to the continental shelf of the United States. There is no national legislation implementing the 1958 Continental Shelf Convention but that is not necessary since, under the American Constitution, duly ratified treaties not only have force of law but take precedence over any internal law to the contrary. In practice, the United States has relied on the exploitability criterion. In 1961, the Department of the Interior granted a phosphate lease "in the Forty Mile Bank area some 40 miles off the California coast, where water depths range from 240 to 2,000 feet". [185] In 1968, oil and gas leases were issued in the Santa Barbara Channel in water depths up to 1,800 feet. [186] The Department is also reported to have published maps showing leases off the California coast up to a distance of 100 miles from the mainland and to a depth of 6,000 feet. [187] However, a change of government policy was formally announced by President Nixon on May 25, 1970, in which he advocated 200 meters as the limit of the continental shelf. [188]

---

[183] Quoted in 4 WHITEMAN, *Digest of International Law*, at 758 (1965).

[184] 67 *Stat.*, at 462 (1953).

[185] D. H. POPPER, Deputy Assistant Secretary for International Organization Affairs, "The Deep Ocean Environment: U.S. and International Policy", LIX *Dept. State Bull.*, at 172 (12 Aug. 1968).

[186] See "Coastal State Mineral Jurisdiction and the Continental Margin" as Appendix D to the *Report by the Special Committee on the Outer Continental Shelf* to the Committee on Interior and Insular Affairs, at 68, Washington (1971).

[187] *Ibid.*

[188] "Statement by the U.S. President on Oceans Policy", reproduced in IX *Int'l Legal Materials*, at 806 (1970). This statement was followed by a Draft Convention on the International Seabed Area submitted to the U.N. Seabed Committee on August 3, 1970.

Until the adoption of a 200-meter continental shelf limit in a general convention, the President proposed an interim policy and called on all states to join in its implementation. The President explained this interim policy as follows:

> I suggest that all permits for exploration and exploita-tion of the sea-beds beyond 200 metres be issued subject to the international regime to be agreed upon. The regime should accordingly include due protection for the integrity of investments made in the interim period. A substantial portion of the revenues derived by a State from exploitation beyond 200 metres during this interim period should be turned over to an appropriate international development agency for assistance to developing countries. [189]

This interim policy, as well as the 200-meter proposal, were severely criticized by the U.S. Special Subcommittee on Outer Continental Shelf. On the interim policy, the unanimous Report states: "We construe the President's policy proposal to mean that while pressing for international acceptance of the type of legal framework outlined in it, the United States should take no action which will in any way forfeit the present sovereign rights the United States enjoys in its continental margin." [190] More specifically, it added: ". . . we feel that during the interim period prior to the entry into force of a future seabed treaty, U.S. leases beyond the 200-meter isobath should not be issued subject to any future regime." [191]

What should be concluded in these circumstances as to the present continental shelf practice of the United States ? It would seem that the former practice of granting leases on the basis of the exploitability criterion would continue, but those leases would carry a proviso as to any future inter-national regime.

Insofar as its shelf boundary delimitation with other states is concerned, it must be taken to accept the equidistance rule incorporated in Article 6 of the Convention, since it has ratified

---

[189] "Statement by the U.S. President on Oceans Policy", *ibid.*, at 808.
[190] *Report of the Special Committee on Outer Continental Shelf . . . , supra* note 86, at 28.
[191] *Ibid.*, at 31.

that convention without reservation and, under its constitution, the convention has force of law. This rule is subject, of course, to "special circumstances" justifying a departure from it, and this is what the United States contends in the Gulf of Maine disagreement with Canada.

VI. — SUGGESTED DELIMITATION OF THE ARCTIC CONTINENTAL SHELF AND SEABED

When looking at a relief map of the Arctic Ocean floor [192] with a view to devising an equitable system of delimiting the continental shelf and seabed of the five Arctic states, one is impressed by the immense extension of the physical shelf into the Arctic basin. This shelf extension is so great that one would be tempted at first blush to suggest the partition of the whole seabed of this semi-enclosed sea among the bordering states. Such a division could be done either under the old sector theory, following boundary meridians to the North Pole, or under the equidistance principle incorporated in the Continental Shelf Convention of 1958. Since the resulting allocation would be of similar proportion under either method, it would be preferable to choose the equidistance principle, it being already accepted as a legal basis for continental shelf delimitation. However, presuming that such a system of apportionment would be acceptable to the Arctic states, it is not likely to be so for the other states of the international community. Indeed, it would be contrary to the fundamental concept that there *is* an area of the seabed which is beyond national jurisdiction and not subject to appropriation by individual states, as affirmed by the Declaration of Principles adopted by the General Assembly in 1970, without a dissenting vote. The fact that the Arctic Ocean is a semi-enclosed sea might justify the delegation of special powers to the bordering states for the exploitation of the international area on behalf of the international community, but would not justify doing away with an international area altogether. In

---

[192] Such a map was published by the National Geographic Society in October 1971, but permission to reproduce it was refused.

these circumstances, the simple solution just briefly considered, using only one criterion of delimitation, must be disregarded. In other words, the two usual types of boundary must be found: the seaward or polar boundary and the lateral boundary for each of the Arctic states.

The seaward or polar boundary should normally be determined on the basis of the same general criterion which will be used in the other oceans of the world. However, it could be that the general criterion might prove inequitable in the Arctic because of the immensity of the continental shelf. No general criterion has yet been agreed upon but, as indicated previously, the trend in the U.N. Seabed Committee is toward the acceptance of a fixed 200-mile limit from the coast. This trend has been more noticeable since the endorsement of the 200-mile proposal by Ambassador Pardo of Malta in March 1971. True, certain states refer to the submarine area in question as a patrimonial sea [193] and others advocate an economic zone, [194] but the nature of the claim is the same and the extent of the area envisaged appears to be substantially the same also. In these circumstances, the polar boundary of the Arctic continental shelf and seabed will be examined in the light of the 200-mile criterion, keeping in mind the maximum claim which Arctic states could make under the geomorphological criterion, that is the edge of the continental margin. More specifically, a comparison will be made between the application of the 200-mile sinuosity and that of the continental margin. Such a comparison indicates that the 200-mile contour line compares very favourably with that of the continental margin (Figure 12). Three states (Canada, Denmark and Norway) would keep all of their continental margin. The U.S.S.R. would lose only a small portion of her margin off the Chukchi and East Siberian Seas, but it would gain a considerable area beyond the continental margin off Severnaya Zemlya and Franz Josef

---

[193] For a summary of the Declaration of Santo Domingo adopted on June 9, 1972, where the concept of "patrimonial sea" is explained, see U.N. Doc. A/AC.138/SR.78 at 2-7 (20 July 1972).

[194] For the text of the conclusions of the General Report of the African States Regional Seminar on the Law of the Sea, where the nature of the "economic zone" is mentioned, see U.N. Doc. A/AC.138/79.

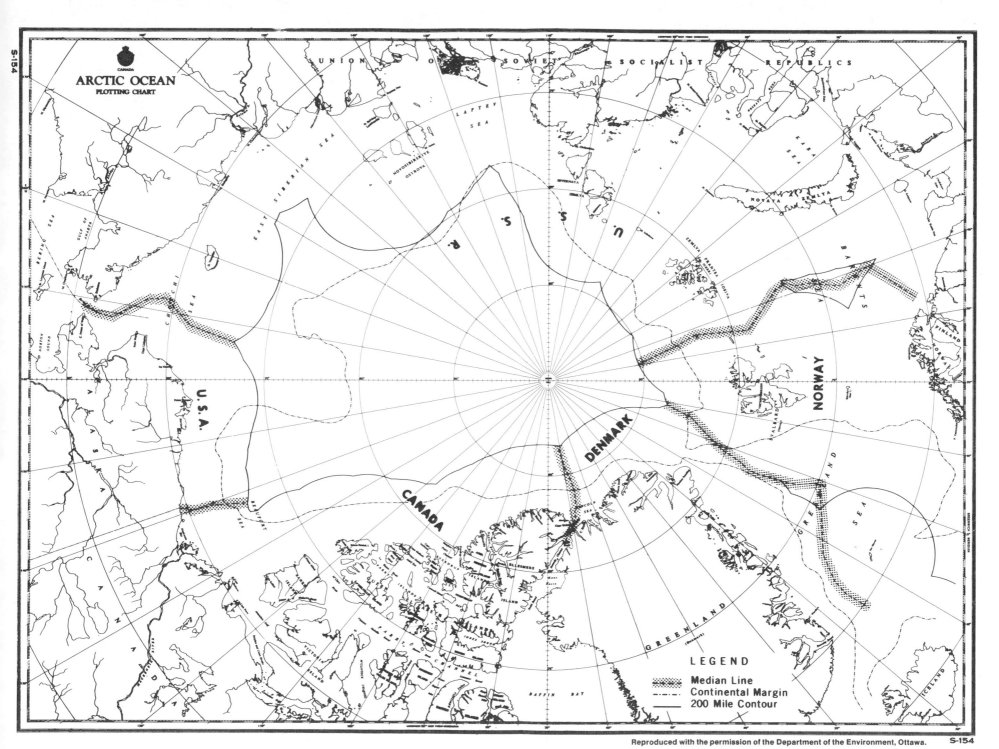

FIGURE 12   POSSIBLE DELIMITATIONS OF THE ARCTIC CONTINENTAL SHELF AND SEA-BED

Land. South of Franz Josef Land, the 200-mile criterion would leave a triangular piece in the center of Barents Sea which would normally constitute an international area. Considering that the area in question is undoubtedly part of the continental shelf, that it is relatively small and completely enclosed, the only practical solution appears to be to divide it between the two bordering states. By coincidence, the equidistance line divides the area in near equal parts and could be used for that purpose. The United States would lose substantial portions of two plateaus (Chukchi and Northwind) located at the western boundary of its margin, west of Point Barrow, Alaska, but would gain an area nearly as large extending along the coast, east of Point Barrow. The latter area offers the important advantages of being much more accessible from the coast and presenting a uniform surface. On the whole, it would thus appear that the 200-mile criterion for determining the polar boundary would give an equitable result and should be acceptable to the Arctic states.

The lateral boundaries, in the absence of agreement or special circumstances, should be determined by application of the equidistance principle provided for in the Continental Shelf Convention. So far, no continental shelf boundary agreement has been concluded among Arctic states, although negotiations may have already begun. Some of the states, in particular Canada and Norway, might be in a position to invoke the existence of special circumstances.

As for Canada, a boundary line based on the equidistance rule might not give an equitable result in the Beaufort Sea, because of the pronounced concave nature of Canada's coastline in that area. There would not seem to be a reasonable degree of proportionality between the extent of its continental shelf and the length of its coast measured in the general direction of its coastline. This, it will be recalled, was one of the guidelines suggested by the International Court in the *North Sea Continental Shelf Cases.* [195] Presuming that the seaward limit of the continental shelf is fixed at 200 miles from the coast, the equidistance line would adversely affect

---

[195]   (1969) *I.C.J. Rep.* 3 at 54.

Canada all the way to the seaward limit, since it is only beyond the 200-mile limit that the equidistance line starts turning away from the Canadian coastline. Canada might then wish to argue that this exceptional configuration of the coast constitutes a special circumstance and that the 141st meridian would be a more equitable boundary line to divide the continental shelf between itself and the United States. Actually, the 141st meridian itself might be deemed to constitute a special circumstance. Its historical significance goes back to the 1825 boundary treaty between Russia and Great Britain. It is not clear what was intended by the phrase "dans son prolongement jusqu'à la Mer Glaciale" [196] used in that treaty to qualify the boundary between Alaska and the Yukon, but it does lend support to the suggestion that the under-sea boundary ought to be the prolongation of the land boundary. In addition, Canada has used the 141st meridian in its *Arctic Waters Pollution Prevention Act* as the westerly boundary for its exercise of jurisdiction to a distance of 100 nautical miles from the coast. A third possible special circumstance upon which Canada could draw is that of "special exploitation rights". Indeed, the Canadian government has been issuing oil and gas permits in the Beaufort Sea for some time, using the 141st meridian as the westerly limit. [197] If this exercise of continental shelf jurisdiction is carried on without protest on the part of the United States, Canada might be deemed to have acquired a certain priority in exploitation rights. These three circumstances, either separately or collectively, might well qualify as "special" within the meaning of the Convention and warrant a departure from the equidistance rule, in order to arrive at an equitable boundary delimitation.

As for Norway, the application of that rule raises problems for both lateral boundaries on either side of the Svalbard archipelago. On the west side, the rule would be of doubtful application to determine the continental shelf boundary between Svalbard and Greenland.

---

[196]   See *supra* Note 189.
[197]   See Arctic Islands Index to Permit and Grid Area, Map No. 50, published by the Department of Indian Affairs and Northern Development, updated to 30 June 1972.

Indeed, Article 6 of the Continental Shelf Convention applies only "where the *same* continental shelf is adjacent to the territories of two adjacent states". In this case, the continental shelf of each state is already divided by a very deep trough known as the "Nansen Fracture Zone", so that there is definitely no continuity of shelf. The equidistance line would cut off the tip of the Yermak Plateau which clearly appertains to the Svalbard shelf; consequently, the equidistance line, if used at all, should be modified so as to allocate the triangular piece in question to Norway. On the east side of Svalbard, the use of the equidistance rule to establish the boundary with Franz Josef Land would not seem to produce a completely equitable result. The equidistant line runs between two islands: one being Victoria Island, a small island of 30,663 sq. st. miles resting on the edge of Franz Josef Land and the other, Kvitoya Island, being 96,963 sq. st. miles and belonging to the Svalbard group. Having regard to the fact that Kvitoya Island is over three times the size of Victoria Island, Norway could invoke the *North Sea Continental Shelf Cases* to obtain a more equitable boundary line. More specifically, it could argue that there should be a reasonable degree of proportionality between the extent of the continental shelf appertaining to its island and the length of the coast of the same island. It could also be that there are features of a geophysical and geological nature which should be taken into account in the determination of an equitable boundary between those two archipelagos, and it is up to the two countries concerned to do so in their negotiations.

As for the *international area* left in the centre of the Arctic basin, in principle it would be subject to the legal regime being presently devised in the U.N. Sea-bed Committee. However, due to the fact that the Arctic Ocean is a semi-enclosed sea and its international area would be completely surrounded by the continental shelf of the five bordering states, it might be found advisable for the international community to delegate its exploitation powers to those states. An agreement could be made with the International Sea-bed Authority whereby the Arctic states would exploit the international area on its behalf and be answerable to it. The terms of this agreement, of a semi-trusteeship nature, would have to ensure an equitable sharing of the benefits by the international community, considering in particular the needs of the developing countries, in accordance with the basic principles governing the exploitation of all international seabed areas.

To sum up the above discussion and suggestions relating to the delimitation of the Arctic continental shelf and seabed, the following propositions may be formulated.

1. Apportioning the whole of the Arctic seabed among the bordering states would be contrary to the United Nations Declaration of Principles of 1970; consequently, there must be an international area in the centre of the Arctic basin.

2. The seaward or polar boundary could be determined by application of the 200-mile criterion, which is gaining general acceptance for the determination of the limit of national jurisdiction; this would give Arctic states virtually all of their continental margin.

3. In principle, the lateral boundaries could be determined by the application of the equidistance rule provided for in the Continental Shelf Convention.

4. Canada could invoke the "special circumstances" provision in the delimitation of its boundary line with the United States in the Beaufort Sea.

5. Norway could invoke the "special circumstances" provision in the delimitation of its boundary with the U.S.S.R. between Svalbard and Franz Josef Land. The western boundary of Svalbard could not be determined by the equidistance rule, since there is no unity of shelf between Svalbard and Greenland; consequently, Norway should be entitled to the full limit of its shelf.

Conclusion

Each part having its own specific summary, the purpose here is simply to re-state in very general terms the answers given and the observations made in respect of each of the seven major questions examined.

Innocent Passage. — Canada having joined the USSR in adopting a 12-mile territorial sea in 1970, "gateways" of territorial waters now exist in both the Northwest and Northeast Passages. The right of innocent passage applies to both Passages but, since neither has ever been used for international navigation, those coastal states could suspend passage of foreign ships if it is essential to their security. It is suggested that, shoud those maritime routes be used by oil tankers. Canada and the USSR could suspend their passage in the event of their refusing to comply with reasonable pollution prevention measures, having regard to the special threat which such a passage would pose to the delicate marine environment of the Arctic.

Waters of the Canadian Arctic Archipelago. — The use of straight baselines to encircle the Canadian Arctic Archipelago has been under consideration by Canada for some time, particularly since the first voyage of the *Manhattan* in 1969. Since the adoption of a 12-mile territorial sea by Canada, it is no longer possible to suggest drawing two belts of territorial waters (one enclosing the islands south of Parry Channel and the other, around the Queen Elizabeth Islands north of the Channel), leaving a strip of high seas in the middle of the Northwest Passage. On the contrary, the presence of several small islands in the Passage create a link between the islands on either side and result in an overlap of territorial waters. The question therefore arises as to whether straight baselines could be drawn around the whole archipelago. This would mean closing Lancaster Sound, at the eastern end of the Passage, by a 54-mile line and the drawing of two straight baselines at the western end, one of 93 miles across Amundsen Gulf and the other of 108 miles across M'Clure Strait. Since no maximum length is provided for in the *Fisheries Case* of 1951 or the Territorial Sea Convention of 1958 and considering that the baselines would otherwise comply with the compulsory geographical criteria laid down by the Court and the Convention, it is suggested that such baselines would be permissible. The right of innocent passage, however, should continue to apply.

Historic waters. — Some writers have advanced the possibility of considering the waters of the Northwest and Northeast Passages as historic waters. If a historic title could be shown, the resulting status would be "internal waters" and innocent passage would not exist as of right. The burden of proving the existence of a historic title is a very heavy one: it presupposes the exercise of exclusive jurisdiction over those waters for a long period of time and the acquiescence in that jurisdiction by foreign states, particularly those primarily affected. A review of the maritime activities of the Soviet Union and Canada in the Arctic and their use of the sector theory in relation to the water areas indicate that it would be very difficult, if not impossible, for them to prove that the Passages in question meet the stringent requirements of historic waters.

Freedom of the seas. — In spite of the presence of the pack ice, it is submitted that the Arctic Ocean should be considered as "high seas". This opinion is based mainly on the fact that sub-surface navigation is possible there as in any other ocean and surface navigation is becoming increasingly possible also. With the exploitation of oil and gas on the North American side, it seems only a matter of time for the Arctic Ocean to be used for the transportation of those precious commodities.

Ice shelves and ice islands. — Since *ice shelves* are immoveable and are as much an obstacle to navigation as land, they should be assimilated in principle to the land-mass to which they are attached. In practice, however, the near-complete disintegration of the few remaining ice shelves in the Canadian Arctic renders this assimilation somewhat unnecessary in the delimitation of territorial waters. The ice shelf off one of the islands in the Svalbard archipelago, on the other hand, appears to be of sufficient dimension to warrant it being taken into account in the drawing of territorial waters off that island. As for *ice islands*, which are floating fragments of ice shelves, they still pose a problem. The main question is one of jurisdiction over an ice island, once it has been appropriated and occupied by a state. In 1970, the United States exercised criminal jurisdiction over Ice Island T-3, following an incident resulting in a homicide. It did so under its special maritime jurisdiction, maintaining that the ice island in queston should be considered as "high seas". The writer's suggestion is that an ice island, once occupied and under the control of a state, may be assimilated to a ship. Consequently, the Escamilla incident could have been deemed to have taken place aboard an American ship on the high seas.

Canadian pollution prevention legislation. — Because of what it considered as being inadequate protection afforded to coastal states by the Brussels Convention of 1969, Canada adopted the Arctic Waters Pollution Prevention Act in 1970. The Act, which came into force by proclamation on August 2, 1972, gives Canada control over foreign ships within a 100-mile zone from its Arctic coast, in order to protect the delicate ecological balance of the region against the possibility of a major oil spill. Canada justified its legislation on the principle of self-defence. The writer's opinion is that self-defence, which requires an actual threat of harm, can hardly justify the taking of certain preventive measures envisaged by the Act. It is suggested that a more adequate rationale could be based on the doctrine of "self-protection". This should enable a coastal state to take such measures on the high seas as are reasonably necessary for the protection of its legitimate territorial and related interests.

Continental shelf and seabed. — Technological progress has made the 1958 definition of the continental shelf somewhat obsolete and its redefinition has been the subject of considerable debate for a number of years. The 200-mile criterion seems to be gaining acceptance as a means of fixing the limit of national jurisdiction over the seabed, and this study considers its application to the Arctic. The conclusion is that this criterion would give Arctic states jurisdiction over virtually all the continental margin and ought to be acceptable as the seaward or polar limit. As for the lateral boundary between Arctic states, in principle it should be determined by the application of the equidistance rule. In the case of Canada and Norway, however, an exception might be warranted. Canada could perhaps invoke the "special circumstances" provision of the 1958 Continental Shelf Convention in the Beaufort Sea area and Norway could do the same for the delimitation of the boundary between Svalbard and Franz Josef Land.

Selected Bibliography

Bibliographical Sources

ARCTIC INSTITUTE OF NORTH AMERICA, *Arctic Bibliography*. Montreal and London: McGill-Queen's University Press. 16 volumes (1953-1972).

BUTLER, W. E., "Selected Bibliography", in *The Soviet Union and the Law of the Sea*. Baltimore and London: The Johns Hopkins Press 203-215 (1971).

CHRISTOL, C. Q., *Oil Pollution of the Marine Environment — A Legal Bibliography*. Washington: Government Printing Office (1971).

CORLEY, N. T., "Bibliography of Books Printed before 1800", 19 *Arctic* 77-98 (1966).

DARTMOUTH COLLEGE LIBRARY, *Dictionary Catalogue of the Stefansson Collection on Polar Regions*. Boston: G. K. Hall & Co. (1967).

DOUMA, J., *Bibliography on the International Court, including the Permanent Court 1918-1964; Corfu Channel Case* 190-195, *Anglo-Norwegian Fisheries Case* 201-207. Leyden: Sijthoff (1966).

DUPUY, R. J., "Bibliographie juridique et technique", in C. A. COLLIARD et al., *Le Fond des Mers* 181-205. Paris: Librairie Armand Collin (1971).

DUTILLY, A. A., *Bibliography of Bibliographies on the Arctic*. Washington: Catholic University of America Press (1945).

INNIS, H. A., "Recent Books on the Canadian Northland and the Arctic", 19 *Canadian Historical Review* 191-196 (1938).

KOERS, A. W., *The Debate on the Legal Regime for the Exploration and Exploitation of Ocean Resources : a Bibliography for the First Decade, 1960-1970*. Kingston: Law of the Sea Institute, University of Rhode Island, Special Publication No. 1 (1970).

OUDENDIJK, J. K., "Historical Sources and Literature", in *Status and Extent of Adjacent Waters* 153-157. Leyden: Sijthoff (1970).

ROBERTS, B., (Rapporteur), "Documentation", in *The Arctic Ocean*, Report of a Conference at Ditchley Park 14-17 May 1971, 42-46. Ditchley Park, Enstone, Oxfordshire (1971).

SATER, J. E., (Coordinated by), "Part IV — Bibliography", in *The Arctic Basin* 290-319. Washington: The Arctic Institute of North America (1963).

SCHMIDT, R. W., *Arctic and Subarctic Transportation : a Tentative Bibliography*. Maxwell Air Force Base, Air University (1949).

SMITH, G. W., "Bibliography", in *The Historical and Legal Background of Canada's Arctic Claims* 465-496. New York: Doctoral dissertation, Faculty of Political Science; Columbia University (1952).

UNITED STATES (Navy Hydrographic Office), "Bibliography" in *Oceanographic Atlas of the Polar Seas, Part II, Arctic* 133-139. Washington: U.S. Hydrographic Office (1958).

General
Arctic and Law of the Sea

ALEXANDER, L. M., (ed.), *The Law of the Sea : International Rules and Organisation for the Sea.* Proceedings of the Third Annual Conference of the Law of the Sea Institute June 24-27, 1968. Kingston: University of Rhode Island (1968).

ALEXANDER, L. M., (ed.), *The Law of the Sea : National Policy Recommendations.* Proceedings of the Fourth Annual Conference of the Law of the Sea Institute June 23-26, 1969. Kingston: University of Rhode Island (1969).

ALEXANDER, L. M., (ed.), *The Law of the Sea : The United Nations and Ocean Management.* Proceedings of the Fifth Annual Conference of the Law of the Sea Institute June 15-19, 1970. Kingston: University of Rhode Island (1970).

ALEXANDER, L. M., (ed.), *The Law of the Sea : A New Geneva Conference.* Proceedings of the Sixth Annual Conference of the Law of the Sea Institute 21-24 June 1971. Kingston: University of Rhode Island (1971).

ALEXANDER, L. M., and HAWKINS, G.R.S., (eds.), *Canadian-U.S. Maritime Problems, Law of the Sea Workshop, June 1971.* Kingston: Law of the Sea Institute, University of Rhode Island (1972).

ARMSTRONG, T., *Soviet Northern Development, with some Alaskan Parallels and Contrasts.* Alaska: Occasional Paper No. 2, Institute of Social, Economic and Government Research, University of Alaska (October 1970).

ARMSTRONG, T., "Northern Affairs in the Soviet Union", 19 *International Journal* 41-49 (1964).

BAIRD, P. D., and ROBINSON, J. L., "A Brief History of Exploration and Research in the Canadian Eastern Arctic", 30 *Canadian Geographical Journal* 136-157 (1945).

BALCH, T. W., "The Arctic and Antarctic Regions and the Law of Nations", 4 *American Journal of International Law* 265-275 (1910).

BAXTER, R. R., and TRISKA, J. F., *The Law of International Waterways, with particular regard to Inter oceanic Canals.* Cambridge: Harvard University Press.

BÉRIAULT, Y., *Les Problèmes politiques du Nord canadien.* Ottawa: Université d'Ottawa (1942).

BERNIER, J. E., *Master Mariner and Arctic Explorer.* Ottawa: Le Droit (1939).

BILDER, R. B., "Emerging Legal Problems of the Deep Seas and Polar Regions", 20 *Naval War College Review* 34-49 (1967).

BOWETT, D. W., *Law of the Sea*. Manchester: Manchester University Press (1967).

BROWN, E. D., *The Legal Regime of Hydrospace*. London: Stevens (1971).

BROWN, R. N., Rudmose. *The Polar Regions; a Physical and Economic Geography of the Arctic and Antarctic*. New York: E. P. Dutton and Co. London: Methuen (1927).

BURKE, W. T., "Ocean Sciences, Technology, and the Future of International Law of the Sea", in *The Future of the International Legal Order*, Volume 2, 183-264, Princeton: Princeton University Press (1970).

BUTLER, W. E., *The Soviet Union and the Law of the Sea*. Baltimore and London: The Johns Hopkins Press (1971).

BUTLER, W. E., "The Soviet Union and the Recent Development of the Law of the Sea", 3 *Chengchi Law Review* 153-165 (1970).

CANADA (Hydrographic Service), *Pilot of Arctic Canada*. Ottawa: Queen's Printer, Volume 1 (2nd ed., 1970), Volumes 2 and 3 (2nd ed., 1968).

COHEN, M., "The Arctic and the National Interest", 26 *International Journal* 52-81 (1970-71).

COLOMBOS, C. J., *The International Law of the Sea*. London and Harlow: Longmans Green & Co. Ltd. (6th ed., 1967).

COMMITTEE ON POLAR RESEARCH, *Polar Research, A Survey*. Washington: National Academy of Sciences (1970).

DE PAW, F., *Grotius and the Law of the Sea*. Bruxelles: Université de Bruxelles, Institut de Sociologie (1965).

DOLLOT, R., "Le droit international des espaces polaires", 75 *Recueil des Cours* 121-195 (1949).

DUNBAR, M., and GREENAWAY, K. R., *Arctic Canada from the Air*. Ottawa: Queen's Printer (1956).

ELDER, R. E., "Decision on Polar Sovereignty by Student Moot Court", 41 *American Journal of International Law* 656-659 (1947).

FAIRBRIDGE, R. W., (ed.), *Encyclopedia of Oceanography*, Volume 1. New York: Runhold Publishing Corp. (1966).

FERRON, O. de, *Le droit international de la mer*, 2 volumes. Paris: Droz & Minard (1958 et 1960).

FINNIE, R., *Canada Moves North*. New York: Macmillan Co. (1942).

FRIEDMANN, W., *The Future of the Oceans*. New York: George Braziller (1970).

FULTON, T. W., *The Sovereignty of the Sea*. Edinburgh: W. Blaskwood & Sons (1911).

GEORGE, P., *Les régions polaires*. Paris: A. Collin (2nd ed., 1950).

GIDEL, G., *Le Droit de la mer*, 3 volumes. Paris: Recueil Sirey (1932-1934).

GIDEL, G., *Les Pôles et le Droit des Gens*. Paris: Institut des Hautes Études Internationales (1950).

GREELY, A. W., *The Polar Regions in the Twentieth Century*. Boston: Little, Brown and Co. (1928).

GRZYBOWSKI, K., *Soviet Public International Law*. Leyden: Sijthoff (1970).

GULLION, E. A., (ed.), *Uses of the Seas*. New Jersey: Prentice-Hall Inc. (1968).

HARTINGH, F. de, *Les Conceptions soviétiques du Droit de la mer*. Paris: Pichon (1960).

HAYDON, R. D., "Polar Problems and International Law", 52 *American Journal of International Law* 746-765 (1958).

HEAD, I., *Canadian Claims to Territorial Sovereignty in the Arctic Regions*. Cambridge: Dissertation for LL.M., Harvard Law School (1960).

HYDE, C. C., "Acquisition of Sovereignty over Polar Areas", 19 *Iowa Law Review* 286-294 (1934).

INCH, D. R., "Examination of Canada's Claim to Sovereignty in the Arctic", 1 *Manitoba Law School Journal* 31-53 (1962).

"International Conference on the Deep Seas and Continental Shelf", 3 *Cornell International Law Journal* 105-204 (1970).

JOHNSTON, V. K., "Canada's Title to the Arctic Islands", 14 *Canadian Historical Review* 24-41 (1933).

JONES, S. B., *The Arctic : Problems and Possibilities*. New Haven: Institute of International Studies, Yale University (1948).

KIMBLE, G. H. T., and GOOD, D., (eds.), *Geography of the Northlands*. New York: John Wiley and Sons; London: Chapman and Hall (1955).

KING, W. F., *Report upon the Title of Canada to the Islands North of Mainland of Canada*. Ottawa: Department of the Interior (1905).

KONECNY, G., et al., "Studies on Ice Movements on the Ward Hunt Ice Shelf by means of Triangulation — Trilateration", 19 *Arctic* 337-342 (1966).

LAFUMA, J., *La place des régions arctiques dans l'économie et dans les problèmes politiques du monde actuel*. Paris: thèse, Faculté de droit (1949).

LAKHTINE, W. L., "Rights over the Arctic", 24 *American Journal of International Law* 703-717 (1930).

LAPENNA, I., *Conceptions soviétiques de Droit international public*. Paris: Pédone (1954).

LA PRADELLE, M. A. de G. de, *La Mer*, Doctoral Course. Paris: Les éditions internationales (1934).

LLOYD, T., "Some International Aspects of Arctic Canada", 24 *International Journal* 717-725 (1971).

LOW, A. P., *Cruise of the Neptune* 1903-1904. Ottawa: Queen's Printer (1906).

MACDONALD, R. St. J., (ed.), *The Arctic Frontier*. Toronto: University of Toronto Press (1966).

MASTERSON, W. E., *Jurisdiction in Marginal Seas with Special Reference to Smuggling*. New York: MacMillan Co. (1929).

McDougal, M. S., and Burke, W. T., "Crisis in the Law of the Sea; Community Perspectives versus National Egoism", 67 *Yale Law Journal* 539-589 (1958).

McDougal, M. S., and Burke, W. T., *The Public Order of the Oceans : A Contemporary International Law of the Sea.* New Haven: Yale University Press (1962).

Meyer, C. B. V., *The Extent of Jurisdiction in Coastal Waters.* Leyden: Sijthoff (1937).

Miller, D. H., "Political Rights in the Arctic", 4 *Foreign Affairs* 47-60 (1925).

Mitchell, M., *The Maritime History of Russia 848-1948.* London: Sidgwick & Jackson (1949).

Mouton, M. W., "The International Regime of the Polar Regions", 107 *Recueil des Cours* 175-285 (1962).

Naval War College, *Jurisdiction and Polar Areas, International Law Situations with Solutions and Notes, 1937.* Washington: Government Printing Office (1939).

Oudendijk, J. K., *Status and Extent of Adjacent Waters, a historical orientation.* Leyden: Sijthoff (1970).

Peary, R. E., *The North Pole.* New York: Stokes Co. (1910).

Petrow, R., *Across the Top of Russia.* New York: David McKay Co. (1967).

Plischke, E., *Jurisdiction in the Polar Regions.* Worcester, Massachusetts: Ph.D. dissertation, Department of History and International Relations, Clark University (1943).

Queneudec, J. P., *Droit maritime international.* Paris: Pédone (1971).

Reed, J. C., and Ronhovde, A. G., *Arctic Laboratory.* Washington: Arctic Institute of North America (1971).

Roberts, B., (Rapporteur), *The Arctic Ocean.* Report of a Conference at Ditchley Park 14-17 May 1971. Ditchley Park, Enstone, Oxfordshire (1971).

Robinson, J. L., "Conquest of the Northwest Passage by R.C.M.P. Schooner St. Roch", 30 *Canadian Geographical Journal* 54-72 (1945).

Sater, J. E., (coordinated by), *The Arctic Basin.* Washington: Arctic Institute of North America (1969).

Sater, J. E., et al, *Arctic Environment and Resources.* Washington: Arctic Institute of North America (1971).

Scott, J. B., "Arctic Exploration and International Law", 3 *American Journal of International Law* 928-941 (1909).

Sigrist, S. V., "Le Droit soviétique dans les régions polaires", 13 *Arbeitergericht* 982-987 (1928).

Smedal, G., *Acquisition of Sovereignty over Polar Areas.* Oslo: Norges Svalbard of Ishavs Undersokelser (1931). Olso: Gyldendal (1930).

Smedal, G., *De l'acquisition de souveraineté sur les territoires polaires,* traduit du norvégien par Pierre Rokseth. Paris: A. Rousseau (1932).

SMITH, G. W., "Sovereignty in the North: The Canadian Aspect of an International Problem", in R. St. J. MACDONALD (ed.), *The Arctic Frontier* 194-255 (1966).

SMITH, G. W., "The Transfer of Arctic Territories from Great Britain to Canada in 1880, and some Related Matters, as seen in Official Correspondence", 14 *Arctic* 54-73 (1961).

SMITH, H. A., *The Law and Custom of the Sea.* London: Stevens & Sons Ltd. (3rd ed., 1959).

SMITH, O. M., *Le statut juridique des terres polaires.* Paris : thèse, Faculté de droit (1934).

SOLLIE, F., "Arctic and Antarctic — Current Problems in the Polar Regions", 4 *Cooperation and Conflict, Nordic Studies in International Politics* 124-144 (1969).

SORENSON, M., "Law of the Sea", *International Conciliation* 195-256 (1958).

STANKA, V., *Institutions of the URSS active in Arctic Research and Development.* Washington: Government Printing Office (1963).

STEFANSSON, V., *Here is the Far North.* New York: Scribner (1957).

STEFANSSON, V., *Great Adventures and Explorations.* New York: Dial Press (1947).

STEFANSSON, V., *The Friendly Arctic.* New York: MacMillan Co. (1944).

STEFANSSON, V., *Arctic Manual* prepared under the direction of the Chief of the Air Corps. Washington: Government Printing Office (1953).

SVARLIEN, O., "The Sector Principle in Law and Practice, 10 *Polar Record,* No. 66, 248-263 (1963).

SVARLIEN, O., "The Legal Status of the Arctic", 52 *Proceedings of the American Society of International Law* 136-144 (1958).

TARACOUZIO, T. A., *The Soviet Union and International Law.* New York: MacMillan Co. (1935).

TARACOUZIO, T. A., *Soviets in the Arctic.* New York: MacMillan Co. (1938).

THOREN, R., *Picture Atlas of the Arctic.* New York: American Elsevier Publishing Co. (1969).

UNITED NATIONS, *First United Nations Conference on the Law of the Sea.* Official Records, 7 volumes. A/Conf. 13 (1958).

UNITED NATIONS, *Second United Nations Conference on the Law of the Sea.* Official Records, 2 volumes. A/Conf. 19/8 (1960).

UNITED NATIONS, *National Legislation and Treaties Relating to the Territorial Sea, the Contiguous Zone, the Continental Shelf, the High Seas and to Fishing and Conservation of the Living Resources of the Sea.* ST/LEG/SER.B/15 (1970).

VALLAUX, G., "Droits et prétentions politiques sur les régions polaires", *Affaires étrangères* 14-33 (1932).

VERZIJL, J. H. W., *International Law in Historical Perspective,* Volume IV (Stateless Domain). Leyden: Sijthoff (1971).

VYSHNEPOLSKII, S. A., "The Problem of a System of Law for the Arctic Regions", 7 *Soviet Press Translations* 371-376 (1952).

WALL, E. H., "Polar Regions and International Law", 1 *International Law Quarterly* 54-58 (1947).

WAULTRIN, R., "La question de la souveraineté des terres arctiques", 15 *Revue générale de Droit international public* 78-125, 185-209, 401-423 (1908).

WAULTRIN, R., "Le problème de la souveraineté des pôles", 16 *Revue générale de Droit international public* 649-660 (1909).

WHITEMAN, M. M., *Digest of International Law*, Volume 4. Washington: Government Printing Office (1965).

Part I

Innocent Passage in the Arctic

AMUNDSEN, R., *The Northwest Passage*, 2 volumes. New York: Dutton & Co. (1908).

ANDERSON, W. R., *Nautilus — 90° north*. Cleveland: The World Publishing Company (1959).

ARMSTRONG, T. E., *The Northern Sea Route*. London: Cambridge University Press (1952).

ARMSTRONG, T. E., "Northern Sea Route", 39 *Geographical Magazine* 23-25 (May 1966).

BERNIER, J. E., *Cruise of the "Arctic" 1906-1907*. Ottawa: Queen's Printer (1910).

BERNIER, J. E., *Cruise of the "Arctic" 1908-1909*. Ottawa: Queen's Printer (1910).

BLOOMFIELD, L. M., *Egypt, Israel and the Gulf of Aquaba on International Law*. Toronto: University of Toronto Press (1957).

BRUEL, E., *International Straits*, 2 volumes. London: Sweet & Maxwell Ltd. (1945).

BRUEL, E., "Les détroits danois au point de vue du Droit international", 55 *Recueil des Cours* 595-696 (1936).

BUTLER, W. E., "Soviet Concepts of Innocent Passage", 7 *Harvard International Journal* 113-130 (1965).

BUTLER, W. E., "Soviet Territorial Waters", 130 *World Affairs* 17-25 (1967).

BUTLER, W. E., "The Legal Regime of Russian Territorial Waters", 62 *American Journal of International Law* 51-77 (1968).

BUTLER, W. E., *The Law of Soviet Territorial Waters : A Case Study of Maritime Legislation and Practice*. New York: Frederick A. Praeger (1967).

BYRNE, J., "Canada and the Legal Status of Ocean Space in the Canadian Arctic Archipelago", 28 *University of Toronto Faculty of Law Review* 1-16 (1970).

CANADA, *Defense in the 70's*. Ottawa: Information Canada (1971).

CANADA (Hydrographic Service, Department of Energy, Mines and Resources), "Exploration of the Canadian Arctic, and the Search for the Northwest Passage", *Pilot of Arctic Canada*. Ottawa: Queen's Printer, Volume 1 (2nd ed. 1970).

CANADA, "Summary of Canadian Note Handed to the United States Government on April 16, 1970", *House of Commons Debates*, Appendix. Ottawa: Queen's Printer (17 April 1970).

CANADA (Standing Committee on External Affairs and National Defence), *Minutes of Proceedings and Evidence*, No. 25 (29 April 1970).

CARVER, J. E., "Northwest Passage: Commercial Seaway ?" 193 *Nautical Magazine* 37-39 (1965).

DAWSON, C. A., *The New Northwest*. Toronto: University of Toronto Press (1947).

DEAN, A. H., "The Second Geneva Conference on the Law of the Sea: The Fight for Freedom of the Seas", 54 *American Journal of International Law* 751-789 (1960).

DEAN, A. H., "The Geneva Conference on the Law of the Sea: What was Accomplished", 52 *American Journal of International Law* 607-659 (1958).

DEAN, A. H., "Freedom of the Seas", 37 *Foreign Affairs* 83-94 (1958-59).

DEDDISH, M. R., "The Right of Passage by Warships Through International Straits", 24 *Judge Advocate General Journal* 79-86 (1969-70).

DJALAL, H., *Statement before Sub-Committee II of the United Nations Seabed Committee*, 9-page text distributed by the Permanent Mission of the Republic of Indonesia (29 March 1972).

DODGE, E. S., *Northwest by Sea*. New York: Oxford University Press (1961).

DULBERGER, L., "Sonar Guides Submarines under Polar Ice", 34 *Electronics*, Nos. 12, 18, 19 (1961).

FITZMAURICE, G. Sir, "Some Results of the Geneva Conference on the Law of the Sea", 8 *International and Comparative Law Quarterly* 72-121 (1959).

FRANÇOIS, J. P. A., "Report on the Regime of the Territorial Sea", *Yearbook of the International Law Commission*, Volume II, 25-43 (1952).

GIDEL, G., "La mer territoriale et la zone contiguë", 48 *Recueil des Cours* 133-278 (1934).

GORDIENKO, P. A., "Scientific Observations from, and the Nature of, Drift of 'North Pole' Stations", in N. A. OSTENSO (ed.), *Problems of the Arctic and the Antarctic*, Collection of Articles No. 11, b1-b19. Washington: Arctic Institute of North America (1966).

GROSS, L., Passage Through the Strait of Tiran and the Gulf of Aquaba", 33 *Law and Contemporary Problems* 125-146 (1968).

GROSS, L., "The Geneva Conference on the Law of the Sea and the Right of Innocent Passage Through the Gulf of Aquaba", 53 *American Journal of International Law* 564-594 (1959).

HAMMAD, B. W., "The Right of Passage in the Gulf of Aquaba", 15 *Revue égyptienne de droit international* 118-151 (1959).

HARLOW, B. A., "Freedom of Navigation" in L. M. ALEXANDER (ed.), *The Law of the Sea : offshore boundaries and zones* 188-194. Columbus: Ohio State University Press (1967).

HILL, C. E., "Le régime des détroits maritimes", 45 *Recueil des Cours* 475-556 (1934).

INSTITUTE OF INTERNATIONAL LAW, *Resolutions Adopted by the Institute at the Session at Edinburgh (4-13 September 1969)*. Geneva: Imprimerie de "La Tribune de Genève" (1969).

JESSUP, P. C., *The Law of Territorial Waters and Maritime Jurisdiction.* New York: G. A. Jennings & Co. (1927).

JESSUP, P. C., "The U.N. Conference on the Law of the Sea", 59 *Columbia Law Review* 234-268 (1959).

JONES, J., "The Corfu Channel Case: Merits", 26 *British Year Book of International Law* 447-453 (1949).

KEATING, B., "North for Oil", 137 *National Geographic* 374-391 (1970).

KHOSBISH, A., *The Right of Innocent Passage.* Geneva: thesis, Geneva University (1954).

KRYPTON, C., *The Northern Sea Route and the Economy of the Soviet North.* New York: Frederick A. Praeger (1956).

LAPIDOTH, R., "Le passage par le détroit de Tiran", 73 *Revue générale de droit international public* 30-51 (1969).

LAPIDOTH, R., *Les Détroits en droit international.* Paris: Pédone (1972).

LARSEN, H. A., *The North West Passage,* 1940-1942 and 1944: the famous voyages of the Royal Canadian Mounted Police schooner "St. Roch". Ottawa: Queen's Printer (1958).

LAWRENCE, K. D., "Military-Legal Considerations in the Extension of Territorial Seas", 29 *Military Law Review* 47-95 (1965).

LEE, L. T., "Jurisdiction over Foreign Merchant Ships in the Territorial Sea: An Analysis of the Geneva Convention on the Law of the Sea", 55 *American Journal of International Law* 77-96 (1961).

MAC BRAYNE, S. F., "Right of Innocent Passage, 1 *McGill Law Journal* 271-276 (1954-55).

MAC CHESNEY, B., "The Altmark Incident and Modern Warfare; 'innocent passage' in Wartime and the Right of Belligerents to use Force to Redress Neutrality Violations", 52 *Northwestern University Law Review* 320-343 (1957).

MARSDEN, M., "Resources and Communications in the Arctic", in R. St. J. MACDONALD (ed.), *The Arctic Frontier* 26-56 (1966).

Mc DOUGAL, M., and BURKE, W. T., "Claims to Authority over the Territorial Sea", 1 *Philippine International Law Journal* 29-138 (1962).

NEATBY, L. H., *In Quest of the Northwest Passage.* London: Constable and Co. (1958).

PETROW, R., *Across the Top of Russia.* New York: David McKay Co. (1967).

"Peacetime Passage by Warships through Territorial Straits", 50 *Columbia Law Review* 220-225 (1950).

PHARAND, D., "Soviet Union Warns United States Against Use of Northeast Passage", 62 *American Journal of International Law* 927-935 (1968).

PHARAND, D., 'Innocent Passage in the Arctic", 6 *Canadian Yearbook of International Law* 3-60 (1968).

U.S. NAVAL OCEANOGRAPHIC OFFICE, *Sailing Directions for Northern USSR, Volume III*. Washington (amended up to 1967).

SELAK, C. B., "A Consideration of the Legal Status of the Gulf of Aquaba", 52 *American Journal of International Law* 660-698 (1958).

SELAK, C. B., "Fishing Vessels and the Principle of Innocent Passage", 48 *American Journal of International Law* 627-635 (1954).

SHAW, K. E., "Juridical Status of the Malacca Straits in International Law", 14 *Japanese Annual International Law* 34-47 (1970).

SLONIM, S., "Right of Innocent Passage and the 1958 Geneva Conference on the Law of the Sea", 5 *Columbia Journal of Transnational Law* 96-127 (1966).

SOKOLOV, A. L., "Drift of Ice in the Arctic Basin and Changes in Ice Conditions over the Northern Sea Route", in N. A. OSTENSO (ed.), *Problems of the Arctic and Antarctic*. Collection of Articles No. 11, J 1 - J 20. Washington: Arctic Institute of North America (1966).

STANKA, V., Institutions of the USSR Active in Arctic Research and Development. Washington: Government Printing Office (2nd ed., 1963).

"Statute on the Protection of the State Border of the USSR (1960)", in *Soviet Statutes and Decisions*, Volume 3, No. 4, 10-24. New York: International Arts and Sciences Press (1967).

"Statute of the Administration of the Northern Sea Route Attached to the Ministry of the Maritime Fleet", 9 *International Legal Materials* 645-646 (1972).

STEAD, G. W., "Current Canadian Coast Guard Operations in Ice", *The Polar Record*, Volume 12, No. 77, 147-155 (1964).

STEELE, G. P., *Seadragon under the Ice*. Toronto: Clarke, Irwin and Co. Ltd. (1962).

STEELE, G. P., *Seadragon, Northwest under the Ice*. New York: E. P. Dutton (1962).

STEVENSON, J. R., "Statement on U.S. Draft Articles on Territorial Sea, Straits and Fisheries Submitted to U.N. Seabed Committee", 65 *Department of State Bulletin* 261-268 (1971).

STRONG, J. T., "The Opening of the Arctic Ocean", *U.S. Naval Institute Proceedings*, Volume 87, No. 10, 58-65 (October 1961).

TRUDEAU-BÉDARD, N., "Souveraineté et passage du Nord-Ouest", 5 *Revue Juridique Thémis* 47-83 (1970).

TUNKIN, G., "The Geneva Conference on the Law of the Sea", 7 *International Affairs* 47-52 (1958).

UNITED NATIONS, *Laws and Regulations on the Regime of the Territorial Sea*. ST/LEG/SER. B/6 (1957).

UNITED NATIONS, *Convention on the Territorial Sea and the Contiguous Zone*. A/CONF. 13/L. 52 (1958).

UNITED NATIONS, *Supplement to the Laws and Regulations on the Regime of the Territorial Sea*. A/CONF. 19/5 and add. 1-3 (1960).

VERZIJL, J. N. W., The United Nations Conference on the Law of the Sea, Geneva, 1958", 6 *Netherlands International Law Review* 1-42 (1959).

VYSHNEPOLSKII, S. A., "The Problem of a System of Law for the Arctic Regions", translated in Soviet Press Translations, Volume 7, No. 10, 371-376 (1952).

WALDOCK, C. H. M., "The Release of the Altmark's Prisoners", 24 *British Year Book of International Law* 216-238 (1947).

WAULTRIN, R., "La question de la liberté de passage du Nord-Est", in "La question de la souveraineté des terres arctiques", 15 *Revue générale de droit international public* 401-423 (1908).

WRIGHT, Q., "Peacetime Passage by Warships through Territorial Straits", 50 *Columbia Law Review* 220-225 (1950).

Part II

Straight Baselines For the Canadian Arctic Archipelago

BAIRD, P. H., "Canadian Arctic Archipelago", in G. KIMBLE and D. GOOD (eds.), *Geography of the Northlands*. London: Chapman and Hall, 353 et seq. (1955).

BEAZLEY, B. P., "Territorial Sea Baselines", 48 *International Hydrographic Review* 143-154 (1971).

BROCK, J. R., "Archipelago Concepts of Limits to Territorial Seas", 19 *Naval War College Review* 34-97 (1966).

BUTLER, W. E., "The Legal Regime of Russian Territorial Waters", 62 *American Journal of International Law* 51-77 (1968).

COLLIN, E. A., "The Waters of the Canadian Arctic Archipelago", in *Proceedings of Arctic Basin Symposium* 128-137. Washington: Arctic Institute of North America (1963).

COQUIA, J. R., "The Territorial Waters of Archipelagoes", 30 *Annuaire de l'Association des Anciens Auditeurs de l'Académie de Droit International de La Haye* 35-53 (1960), and 1 *Philippine International Law Journal* 139-156 (1962).

DEAN, A., "The Second Geneva Conference on the Law of the Sea: The Fight for Freedom of the Seas", 54 *American Journal of International Law* 751-789 (1960).

DELLAPENNA, J. W., "Canadian Claims in Arctic Waters", 7 *Land and Water Law Review* 383-419 (1972).

EVENSEN, J., "The Anglo-Norwegian Fisheries Case and its Legal Consequences", 46 *American Journal of International Law* 609-630 (1952).

EVENSEN, J., "Certain Legal Aspects Concerning the Delimitation of the Territorial Waters of Archipelagos", *U.N. Doc. A/Conf. 13/18 (Preparatory Document No. 15)* 289-302 (1958).

FELICIANO, F. P., "Comments on Territorial Waters of Archipelagos", *Philippine International Law Journal* 157-177 (1962).

GOTLIEB, A. E., "The Canadian Contribution to the Concept of a Fishing Zone in International Law", 2 *Canadian Yearbook of International Law* 55-76 (1964).

HEAD, I. L., "Canadian Claims to Territorial Sovereignty in the Arctic Regions", 9 *McGill Law Journal* 200-226 (1962-63).

HODGSON, R. D., and ALEXANDER, L. M., *Towards an Objective Analysis of Special Circumstances*, Occasional Paper No. 13. Kingston: Law of the Sea Institute, University of Rhode Island (April 1972).

KENNEDY, R. H., "A Brief Geographical and Hydrographical Study of Straits which Constitute Routes for International Traffic", *Doc. A/Conf. 13/6 and Add. 1, Conference on the Law of the Sea, Official Records, Preparatory Documents*, Volume 1, 114-164 (1958).

KLEIN, C. B., "The Territorial Waters of Archipelagos", 26 *Federal Bar Association Journal* 317-323 (1966).

McCONNELL, W. H., "The Legal Regime of Archipelagos", 35 *Saskatchewan Law Review* 121-145 (1970-71).

MORIN, J. Y., "La zone de pêche exclusive du Canada", 2 *Canadian Yearbook of International Law* 77-106 (1964).

PHARAND, D., "The Waters of the Canadian Arctic Islands", 3 *Ottawa Law Review* 414-432 (1969).

REINHARD, W. G., "International Law: Implications of the Opening of the Northwest Passage", 74 *Dickenson Law Review* 678-690 (1970).

SHALOWITZ, A. L., *Shore and Sea Boundaries*. Washington: Government Printing Office, Volume 1 (1962).

SORENSEN, M., "The Territorial Sea of Archipelagos", 6 *Netherlands International Law Review* 315-331 (1959).

UNITED NATIONS, *Convention on the Territorial Sea and the Contiguous Zone*. A/Conf. 13/L. 52 (1958).

UNITED NATIONS, *Archipelagos Principles as proposed by the Delegations of Fiji, Indonesia, Mauritius and the Philippines*. A/AC. 138/SC. II/L. 15 (14 March 1973).

UNITED STATES (Department of State, Bureau of Intelligence and Research), *Limits in the Seas*, International Boundary Study, Series A, No. 46 (12 August 1972).

UNITED STATES (Department of State), "Sovereignty of the Sea", *Geographic Bulletin*, No. 3, Publication Number 7849 (April 1965).

WALDOCK, C. H. M., "The Anglo-Norwegian Fisheries Case", 28 *British Year Book of International Law* 114-171 (1951).

YOUNG, R., "The Anglo-Norwegian Fisheries Case", 38 *American Bar Association Journal* 243-245 (1952).

Part III

Historic Waters in the Arctic

BALCH, T. W., "Is Hudson Bay a Closed or an Open Sea ?", 6 *American Journal of International Law* 409-459 (1912).

BALCH, T. W., "The Hudsonian Sea is a Great Open Sea", 7 *American Journal of International Law* 546-565 (1913).

BLUM, Y. Z., *Historic Titles in International Law*. The Hague: Nijhoff (1965).

BOGGS, S. W., "National Claims in Adjacent Seas", 41 *Geographical Review* 185-209 (1951).

BOUCHEZ, L. J., *The Regime of Bays in International Law*. Leyden: Sijthoff (1964).

BOURQUIN, M., "Les baies historiques", in *Mélanges Sauser Hall*. Paris: Neuchatel, 37-51 (1952).

BREITFUSS, L., "Territorial Division of the Arctic", 8 *Dalhousie Review* 456-470 (1929).

CANADA (Department of Indian Affairs and Northern Development), *Documents Concerning Canadian Sovereignty in the Arctic*, list of 5 pages. Ottawa: Library of Department of Indian Affairs and Northern Development (1947).

CANADA, *Report of Advisory Technical Board on the Question of Canadian Sovereignty in the Arctic*. Ottawa: Public Archives (1920).

CANADA, "Exchange of Notes between Canada and Norway", *Canada Treaty Series*, No. 17 (1930).

DINWOODIE, D. H., "Arctic Controversy: The 1925 Byrd-MacMillan Expedition Example", 53 *Canadian Historical Review* 51-65 (1972).

DRAGO, L. M., "Dissenting Opinion in the North Atlantic Coast Fisheries Case", *Scott's Hague Court Reports* 195-207 (1916).

FRANKLIN, C. M., and McCLINTOCK, V. C., "Territorial Claims of Nations in the Arctic: An Appraisal", 5 *Oklahoma Law Review* 37-48 (1952).

GREEN, L. C., "Canada and Arctic Sovereignty", 48 *Canadian Bar Review* 740-775 (1970).

HARBEN, W. N., "Soviet Attitudes and Practices Concerning Maritime Waters — A Recent Historical Survey", 15 *Judge Advocate General Journal* 149-154 (1961).

HASHEM, Z., "Rationale of the Theory of Historic Bays with Special Reference to the International Status of the Gulf of Aquaba", 25 *Revue égyptienne de droit international* 1-65 (1969).

HEAD, I. L., "Canadian Claims to Territorial Sovereignty in the Arctic Regions", 9 *McGill Law Journal* 200-226 (1962-63).

HURST, Sir C., "The Territoriality of Bays", 3 *British Year Book of International Law* 42-54 (1922-23).

JOHNSON, D. H. N., "Acquisitive Prescription in International Law", 27 *British Year Book of International Law* 332-354 (1950).

JOHNSON, K., "Canada's Title to Hudson Bay and Hudson Strait", 15 *British Year Book of International Law* 1-20 (1934).

KONAN, R. W., "The *Manhattan's* Arctic Conquest and Canada's Response in Legal Diplomacy", 3 *Cornell International Law Journal* 188-204 (1970).

LAKHTINE, W. L., *Rights over the Arctic* (in Russian, with diplomatic notes of 1916 and 1924 in French, in appendix). Moscow (1928).

LAKHTINE, W. L., "Rights over the Arctic", 24 *American Journal of International Law* 703-717 (1930).

LORIOT, F., *La théorie des eaux historiques et le régime juridique du Golfe St-Laurent en droit interne et international* (typewritten copy). Québec: (1972).

MACGIBBON, I. C., "Customary International Law and Acquiescence", 33 *British Year Book of International Law* 114-145 (1957).

MALEK, C., "La théorie dite des "Baies historiques"", 6 *Revue de Droit international pour le Moyen-Orient* 100-173 (1957).

MCGRATH, P. T., "The Hudson Bay Dispute", *The Forthnightly Review* 125-136 (1 January 1908).

NICHOLSON, N. L., *The Boundaries of Canada, Its Provinces and Territories*. Ottawa: Queen's Printer (1964).

PEARSON, L. B., Canada Looks "Down North", 24 *Foreign Affairs* 638-647 (1946).

PHARAND, D., *La théorie des secteurs dans l'Arctique à l'égard du droit international*. Paris: thesis, Faculty of Law (1955).

PLISCHKE, E., *Jurisdiction in the Polar Regions*. Worcester: Ph.D. dissertation, Department of History and International Relations, Clark University, Massachusetts (1943).

ROUSSEAU, C., "Extension des eaux territoriales soviétiques dans la Baie de Vladivostock", 62 *Revue générale de droit international public* 63-72 (1958).

SMEDAL, G., *Acquisition of Sovereignty over Polar Areas*. Oslo: Gyldendal (1930). Oslo: Norges Svalbard of Ishavs Undersokelser (1931).

SMEDAL, G., *De l'acquisition de souveraineté sur les territoires polaires*. Traduit du norvégien par Pierre Rokseth. Paris: A. Rousseau (1932).

SMITH, G. W., *The Historical and Legal Background of Canada's Arctic Claims*. New York: Ph.D. dissertation, Faculty of Political Science, Columbia University (1952).

SMITH, G. W., "A Historical Summary of Maritime Exploration in the Canadian Arctic and Its Relevance in Connection with Subsequent and Recent Sovereignty Issues", in *Proceedings of the International Commission of Maritime History* (August 1970).

SMITH, G. W., *Territorial Sovereignty in the Canadian North : A Historical Outline of the Problem* NCRC — 63-7 (1963).

STROHL, M. P., *The International Law of Bays.* The Hague: Nijhoff (1963).

SVARLIEN, O., "The Legal Status of the Arctic", *Proceedings of the American Society of International Law* 136-143 (1958).

SVARLIEN, O., "The Sector Principle in Law and Practice", 10 *Polar Record,* No. 66, 248-263 (1960-61).

TARACOUZIO, T. A., *Soviets in the Arctic.* New York: MacMillan Co. (1938).

TAYLOR, A., *Geographical Discovery and Exploration in the Queen Elizabeth Islands.* Ottawa: Queen's Printer (1964).

UNITED NATIONS (Secretariat), *First United Nations Conference on the Law of the Sea, 1958, Preparatory Document No. 1, "Historic Bays".* A/Conf. 13/1 (1957).

UNITED NATIONS, "Juridical Regime of Historic Waters, including Historic Bays", *Yearbook of the International Law Commission,* Volume II, 1-26 (1962).

UNITED NATIONS, "Report on the Legal Regime of Historical Waters, 1962", *Yearbook of the International Law Commission,* Volume II, 1-30 (1962).

WALL, E. H., "The Polar Regions and International Law", *International Law Quarterly* 54-57 (1947).

Part IV

Freedom of the Seas in the Arctic Ocean

BULGAKOV, N. P., *The Extreme Boundary of Ice in Far Eastern Seas.* Washington: U.S. Naval Oceanographic Office (1967).

BURKHANOV, V. F., "Soviet Arctic Research", translated from 5 *Priroda* 21-30 (1957) by E. R. Hope. Ottawa: Defence Research Board (1957).

CLUTE, A. R., "The Ownership of the North Pole", 5 *Canadian Bar Review* 19-26 (1927).

DOLLOT, R., "Le Droit international des espaces polaires", 75 *Recueil des Cours* 118-200 (1949).

DONN, W. L., and SHAW, D. M., "The Heat Budgets on Ice Free and on Ice-Covered Arctic Ocean", 71 *Journal of Geographical Research* 1087-1093 (1966).

GORMLEY, W. P., "The Development and Subsequent Influence of the Roman Legal Norm of "Freedom of the Seas"", 40 *University of Detroit Law Journal* 561-595 (1963).

GORMLEY, W. P., "The Unilateral Extension of Territorial Waters: The Failure of the United Nations to Protect the Freedom of the Seas", 43 *University of Detroit Law Journal* 595-730 (1966).

HEAD, I. L., "Canadian Claims to Territorial Sovereignty in the Arctic Regions", 9 *McGill Law Journal* 200-226 (1962-63).

LAKHTINE, W. L., "Rights over the Arctic", 24 *American Journal of International Law* 703-717 (1930).

LYON, W., "The Submarine and the Arctic Ocean", *The Polar Record*, No. 75, 699-705 (1962-63).

MAYBOURN, R., (Capt.), "Problems of Operating Large Ships in the Arctic", 24 *The Journal*, The Institute of Navigation, 135-146 (1971).

MOUTON, M. W., "The International Regime of the Polar Regions", 107 *Recueil des Cours* 175-284 (1962).

McKITTERICK, T. E. M., "The Validity of Territorial and Other Claims in Polar Regions", 21 *Journal of the Society of Comparative Legislation* 89-97 (1939).

"Panel: Legal Problems and the Political Situation in the Polar Areas", *American Society of International Law Proceedings* 136-174 (1958).

PARTRIDGE, B., "The White Shelf: A Study of Arctic Ice Jurisdiction", 87 *U.S. Naval Institute Proceedings* 51-57 (1961).

PHARAND, D., "Freedom of the Seas in the Arctic Ocean", 19 *University of Toronto Law Journal* 210-233 (1969).

ROUSSEAU, C., "URSS: Essais de projectiles téléguidés dans le Pacifique — Manœuvres aéro-navales et essais atomiques dans les mers de Barents et de Kara", 67 *Revue générale de droit international public* 401-404 (1963).

SMITH, G. W., "Sovereignty in the North: The Canadian Aspect of an International Problem", in R. St. J. MACDONALD (ed.), *The Arctic Frontier*, University of Toronto Press (1966).

SCOTT, J. B., "Arctic Exploration and International Law", 3 *American Journal of International Law* 928-941 (1909).

STRONG, J. T., "The Openings of the Arctic Ocean", 87 *U.S. Naval Institute Proceedings* 58-65 (October 1961).

UNITED NATIONS, *Memorandum on the Soviet Doctrine and Practice with Respect to the Regime of the High Seas.* A/CN 4/38 (1950).

UNITED NATIONS, *Convention on the High Seas.* A/Conf. 13/L 53 (1958).

UNITED STATES (Department of State, Bureau of Intelligence and Research), *U.S.-Russia Convention Line of 1867*, International Boundary Study, No. 14 (Revised) (October 1965).

VALLAUX, C., "Droits et prétentions politiques sur les régions polaires", *Affaires étrangères* 14-33 (1932).

Part V

The Legal Status of Ice Shelves and Ice Islands in the Arctic

ARMSTRONG, T. E., *Illustrated Glossary of Snow and Ice.* London: University Press (1966).

AUBURN, F. M., "International Law — Sea Ice — Jurisdiction", 48 *Canadian Bar Review* 776-782 (1970).

AUBURN, F. M., "The White Desert", 19 *International and Comparative Law Quarterly* 229-256 (1970).

BILDER, R. B., "Control of Criminal Conduct in Antarctica", 52 *Virginia Law Review* 1-54 (1970).

BREWER, M. C., "Drifting Stations in the Arctic Ocean", in *Proceedings of the Arctic Basin Symposium* 305-307. Washington: Arctic Institute of North America (1963).

BULGAKOV, N. P., *The Extreme Winter Boundary of Ice in Far Eastern Seas*. Washington: U.S. Naval Oceanographic Office, Translation (1967).

CRARY, A. P., "Arctic Ice Island and Ice Shelf Studies", 11 *Arctic* 3-42 (1958) and 13 *Arctic* 32-50 (1960).

DUNBAR, M., "The Drift of North Pole 7 after its Abandonment", 6 *Canadian Geographer* 129-142 (1962).

FLETCHER, J. O., "Three months on an Arctic Ice Island", 103 *National Geographic Magazine* 489-504 (1953).

GORDIENKO, P. A., "Scientific Observations from, and the Nature, of Drift of the 'North Pole' Stations", in N. A. OSTENSO (ed.), *Problems of the Arctic and Antarctic*, Collection of Articles No. 11, b 1 - b 19. Washington: Arctic Institute of North America (1966).

HATTERSLEY-SMITH, G., "The Ward Hunt Ice Shelf. Recent Changes of the Ice Front", 4 *Journal of Glaciology* 415-424 (1963).

HATTERSLEY-SMITH, G., *Ice Condition off the North Coast of Ellesmere Island*. Ottawa: Defence Research Board, Report No. Misc. G-8 (1962).

HATTERSLEY-SMITH, G., "The Rolls on the Ellesmere Ice Shelf", 10 *Arctic* 32-44 (1957).

HATTERSLEY-SMITH, G., "The Ellesmere Ice Shelf and the Ice Islands", *The Canadian Geographer* 65-70 (1957).

HATTERSLEY-SMITH, G., "Note on Ice Shelves off the North Coast of Ellesmere Island", 22 *Arctic Circular* 13-14 (1965-66).

HATTERSLEY-SMITH, G., "Northern Ellesmere Island 1953-1954", 8 *Arctic* 3-36 (1955).

HOLMQUIST, C. O., "The T-3 Incident", *U.S. Naval Institute Proceedings* 40-53 (1972).

JOHNSON, D. H. N., "Artificial Islands", 4 *International Law Quarterly* 203-215 (1951).

KONECNY, G., and FAIG, W., "Studies of Ice Movements on Ward Hunt Ice Shelf by Means of Triangulation-Trilateration", 19 *Arctic* 337-342 (1966).

KOENIG, L. S., et al., "Arctic Ice Islands", 5 *Arctic* 67-103 (1952).

LINDSAY, D., et al., "Ice Islands, 1967", 21 *Arctic* 103-106 (1968).

MARSHALL, E. W., "Structural and Strategraphic Studies of the Northern Ellesmere Ice Shelf, 8 *Arctic* 109-114 (1955).

McDaniels, W. E., and Grossi, F. X., Brief of Appellant in *U.S.A.* v. *Escamilla*, No. 71-1575 (1971).

Nutt, D. C., "The Drift of the Ice Island WH-5", 19 *Arctic* 244-262 (1966).

Pharand, D., "State Jurisdiction over Ice Island T-3: The Escamilla Case", 24 *Arctic* 83-89 (1971).

Quam, L. O., "Arctic Basin Research", *Naval Research Reviews* 1-15 (October 1966).

Regina v. *Tootalik E4-321 (1969) 71 Western Weekly Reports 435.*

Rodahl, K., *L'archipel flottant* (Translation). Paris: Arthaud (1954).

Rolland, L., "Alaska, maison de jeu établie sur les glaces au-delà de la limite des eaux territoriales", 11 *Revue générale de droit international public* 340-345 (1904).

Ronhovde, A. G., *Jurisdiction over the Ice Islands : The Escamilla Case in Retrospect.* Washington: Arctic Institute of North America (November 1972).

Ronhovde, A. G., "The Escamilla Case in Court", 24 *Arctic* 139 (1971).

Sater, J. E., (Coordinated by). *Arctic Drifting Stations.* Washington: Arctic Institute of North America (1968).

Sokolov, A. L., "Drift on Ice in the Arctic Basin and Changes on Ice Conditions over the Northern Sea Route", in N. A. Ostenso (ed.), Problems of the Arctic and the Antarctic, Collection of Articles No. 11, j1 - j20. Washington: Arctic Institute of North America (1966).

Swithinbank, C. W. M., "Ice Shelves", 121 *Geographical Journal* 64-76 (1955).

U.S.A. v. *Escamilla* (No. 71-1575). Judgment of United States Court of Appeals for the Fourth Circuit, 25 typewritten pages (17 August 1972).

Williams, J. W., Brief for Appellee in *U.S.A.* v. *Escamilla*, No. 71-1575 (1971).

Wilkes, D., "Law for Special Environments: Ice Islands and Questions Raised by the T-3 Case", 16 *The Polar Record*, No. 100, 23-27 (1972).

Yakovlev, G. N., "Ice Research in Central Arctic", in N. A. Ostenso (ed.), *Problems of the Arctic and the Antarctic*, Collection of Articles No. 11, j1 - j23. Washington: Arctic Institute of North America (1966).

Part VI

Pollution Control in the Arctic

"Agreement Concerning Pollution of the North Sea by Oil, 1969", reproduced in 9 *International Legal Materials* 359-364 (1970).

ANDRASSY, J., "Etudes des mesures internationales les plus aptes à prévenir la pollution des milieux marins", 53 *Annuaire de l'Institut de Droit international*, Tome 1, 547-711 (1969).

BEESLEY, J. A., "Rights and Responsibilities of Arctic Coastal States: The Canadian View", 3 *Journal of Maritime Law and Commerce* 1-12 (1971).

BILDER, R. B., "The Canadian Arctic Waters Pollution Prevention Act: New Stresses on the Law of the Sea", 69 *Michigan Law Review* 1-54 (1970).

BISHOP, W. W., "Exercise of Jurisdiction for Special Purposes in High Seas Areas beyond Outer Limit of Territorial Waters", a paper for the Sixth Conference of the Inter-American Bar Association, May 1949, reprinted in 99 *Congressional Record* 2586 (30 March 1953).

BOWETT, D. W., "The English Channel, Collisions and Coastal State's Jurisdiction: A Tentative Proposal", 3 *International Relations* 953-965 (1971).

BRITTON, M. E., "Special Problems of the Arctic Environment", in L. M. ALEXANDER and G. R. S. HAWKINS (eds.), *Canadian-U.S. Maritime Problems, Law of the Sea Workshop, June 1971*, 9-28. Kingston: Law of the Sea Institute, University of Rhode Island (1972).

BROWN, E. D., "International Law and Marine Pollution: Radioactive Waste and other Hazardous Substances", 11 *Natural Resources Journal* 221-255 (1971).

BROWN, E. D., "The Lessons of the Torrey Canyon", *Current Legal Problems* 113-136 (1968).

BUTLER, W. E., "Pollution Control and the Soviet Arctic", 21 *International and Comparative Law Quarterly* 557-560 (1972).

CAFLISH, L. C., "International Law and Ocean Pollution: The Present and the Future", 8 *Belgian Review of International Law* 7-33 (1972).

CARNAHAN, B. K., "The Canadian Arctic Waters Pollution Act: an Analysis", 31 *Louisiana Law Review* 632-649 (1971).

CAVARE, L., "Les problèmes juridiques posés par la pollution des eaux maritimes au point de vue interne et international", 68, *Revue générale de droit international public* 617-640 (1964).

CHARLIER, R. E., "Résultats et enseignements des conférences du droit de la mer", *Annuaire français de Droit international* 63-110 (1960).

CHIA, FU-SHIANG, "Reproduction of Arctic Marine Invertebrates", 1 *Marine Pollution Bulletin* (new series), No. 5, 78-79 (1970).

CLINGAN, Jr., T. A., "Third-Party Imitations of Canadian Legislation and the Implications for International Law Development", in L. M. ALEXANDER and G. R. S. HAWKINS (eds.), *Canadian-U.S. Maritime Problems, Law of the Sea Workshop, June 1971*, 68-74. Kingston: Law of the Sea Institute, University of Rhode Island (1972).

COHEN, M., "The Arctic and the National Interest", 26 *International Journal* 52-81 (1970-71).

"Convention on the Prevention of Marine Pollution by Dumping of Wastes and other Matter", 1972, reproduced in 11 *International Legal Materials* 1294-1314 (1972).

DELAPENNA, J. W., "Canadian Claims in Arctic Waters", 7 *Land and Water Law Review* 383-419 (1972).

DESPAX, M., *La pollution des eaux et ses problèmes juridiques*. Paris: Librairies Techniques (1968).

DINSTEIN, Y., "Oil Pollution by Ships and Freedom of the High Seas", 3 *Journal of Maritime Law and Commerce* 363-374 (1972).

DINWOODIE, D. H., "The Politics of International Pollution Control: The Trail Smelter Case", 27 *International Journal* 219-236 (1972).

DUNBAR, M. J., *Environment and Good Sense*. Montreal and London: McGill-Queen's University Press (1971).

DUNBAR, M. J., *Ecological Development in Polar Regions*. Englewood Clipp. New Jersey: Prentice-Hall (1968).

DU PONTAVICE, E., *La pollution des mers par les hydrocarbures* (A propos de l'Affaire du "Torrey Canyon"). Paris: Pichon et Durand-Auzias (1968).

GOLDIE, L. F. E., "International Principles of Responsibility for Pollution", 9 *Columbia Journal of Transnational Law* 283-330 (1970).

GREEN, L. C., "International Law and Canada's Anti-Pollution Legislation", 50 *Oregon Law Review* 462-503 (1971).

HARDY, M., "International Control of Marine Pollution", 2 *National Resources Journal* 296-348 (1971).

HARGROVE, J. L., (ed.), *Law, Institutions and the Global Environment*. New York: Oceana Publications Inc. (1972).

HEALY, N. J., "The International Convention on Civil Liability on Oil Pollution Damage, 1969", 1 *Journal of Maritime Law and Commerce* 317-323 (1970).

HENKIN, L., "Arctic Anti-Pollution: Does Canada Make — or Break — International Law ?", 65 *American Journal of International Law* 131-136 (1971).

HOULT, D. P., "Marine Pollution Concentrating on the Effects of Hydrocarbons in Seawater", in L. M. ALEXANDER and G. R. S. HAWKINS (eds.), *Canadian-U.S. Maritime Problems, Law of the Sea Workshop, June 1971*. Kingston: Law of the Sea Institute, University of Rhode Island (1972).

HOVANESIAN, A., "Post Torrey Canyon: Toward a New Solution to the Problem of Traumatic Oil Spillage", 2 *Connecticut Law Review* 632-647 (1970).

HYDEMAN, L. M., and BERMAN, W. H., *International Control of Nuclear Maritime Activities*. Ann Arbor: Braun-Brumfield Inc. (1960).

INTERGOVERNMENTAL MARITIME CONSULTATIVE ORGANIZATION, *Amendments to the International Convention for the Prevention of Pollution of the Sea by Oil, 1954, Resolution A. 175 (VI) adopted 21 October 1969*. A/VI/Res. 175 (16 January 1970).

International Convention for the Prevention of Pollution of the Sea by Oil, 1954, *Canada Treaty Series*, No. 31 (1958); amended on 11 April 1962, *Canada Treaty Series*, No. 29 (1967).

"International Convention on Civil Liability for Oil Pollution Damage, 1969", reproduced in 9 *International Legal Materials* 45-64 (1970).

"International Convention Relating to Intervention on the High Seas 1969", reproduced in 9 *International Legal Materials* 25-35 (1970).

"International Legal Aspects of Pollution", Proceedings of a Symposium Held in Vancouver in September 1970, 21 *University of Toronto Law Journal* 1-79 (1971).

JENNINGS, R. Y., "A Changing International Law of the Sea", 31 *Cambridge Law Journal* 32-49 (1972).

JOHNSTON, D. M., "Recent Canadian Marine Legislation: An Historical Perspective", in L. M. ALEXANDER (ed.), *Canadian-U.S. Maritime Problems, Law of the Sea Workshop, June 1971*, 63-67. Kingston: Law of the Sea Institute, University of Rhode Island (1972).

JOHNSTON, D. M., "Canada's Arctic Marine Environment: Problems of Legal Protection", 29 *Behind the Headlines* 1-7 (July 1970).

JOHNSTON, D. M., "The Arctic Marine Environment: a Managerial Perspective", in L. M. ALEXANDER (ed.), *The Law of the Sea : The United Nations and Ocean Management*. Proceedings of the Fifth Annual Conference of the Law of the Sea Institute June 15-19, 1970, 312-318. Kingston: University of Rhode Island (1970).

JOHNSTON, D. M., "Marine pollution control: law, science and politics", 28 *International Journal* 69-102 (1972-73).

JORDAN, F. E. J., "Recent Development in International Environmental Pollution Control", 15 *McGill Law Journal* 279-301 (1969).

KLOTZ, J. C., "Are Ocean Polluters Subject to Universal Jurisdiction — Canada Breaks the Ice", 6 *The International Lawyer* 706-717 (1972).

KOJANEC, G., "Compétence des États et réglementation internationale en matière de pollution de la mer: un cas de dédoublement fonctionnel", 41 *Annuaire de l'Association des Auditeurs et Anciens Auditeurs de l'Académie de Droit International de La Haye* 35-40 (1971).

KONAN, R. W., "The *Manhattan's* Arctic Conquest and Canada's Response in Legal Diplomacy", 3 *Cornell International Law Journal* 189-204 (1970).

LEGAULT, L. H. J., "The Freedom of the Seas: A License to Pollute ?", 21 *University of Toronto Law Journal* 39-49 (1971).

LEGAULT, L. H. J., "Canadian Arctic Waters Pollution Prevention Legislation", in L. M. ALEXANDER (ed.), *The Law of the Sea : The United Nations and Ocean Management*. Proceedings of the Fifth Annual Conference of the Law of the Sea Institute June 15-19, 1970, 294-300. Kingston: University of Rhode Island (1970).

LLOYD, T., "Canada's Arctic in the Age of Ecology", 48 *Foreign Affairs* 726-740 (1970).

Lucchini, L., "Pollution des mers par les hydrocarbures: les conventions de Bruxelles de novembre 1969 ou les fissures du droit international classique", 97 *Journal de droit international* 795-843 (1970).

Maywhort, W. W., "International Law — Oil Spills and their Legal Ramifications", 49 *North Carolina Law Review* 996-1003 (1971).

McKelvey, V. E., "The Origin, Incidence, Effects and Means of Prevention and Control of Oil-Well Blowouts", *Subsea Mineral Resources and Problems Related to their Development* (Geological Survey Circular No. 619), 19-22 (1969).

Mendelsohn, A. I., "Maritime Liability for Oil Pollution — Domestic and International Law", 38 *George Washington Law Review* 1-31 (1969).

Morin, J. Y., "Le progrès technique, la pollution et l'évolution récente du droit de la mer au Canada, particulièrement à l'égard de l'Arctique", 8 *Canadian Yearbook of International Law* 158-248 (1970).

Murphy, R. S., and Nyquist, D. (eds.), *International Symposium on Water Pollution Control in Cold Climates*. Washington: Government Printing Office (1971).

Nanda, V. P., "The "Torrey Canyon" Disaster: Some Legal Aspects", 44 *Denver Law Journal* 400-425 (1967).

National Petroleum Council, *Environmental Conservation*. Washington: The Oil and Gas Industries. Volume 1 (1971), Volume 2 (1972).

National Petroleum Council, *Law of the Sea — Particular Aspects Affecting the Petroleum Industry*. Washington (1973).

Neuman, R. H., "Oil on Troubled Waters: The International Control of Marine Pollution", 2 *Journal of Maritime Law and Commerce* 349-361 (1971).

"Ocean Pollution: An Examination of the Problem and an Appeal for International Cooperation", 7 *San Diego Law Review* 574-604 (1970).

O'Connell, D. M., "Continental Shelf Oil Disasters: Challenge to International Pollution Control", 55 *Cornell Law Review* 113-128 (1969).

"Oil Pollution of the Sea", 10 *Harvard International Law Review* 316-359 (1969); reprinted in *Environment Law Review* 349-389 (1970).

Petaccio, V., "Water Pollution and the Future Law of the Sea", 21 *International and Comparative Law Quarterly* 15-21 (1972).

Petrow, R., *In the Wake of the Torrey Canyon*. New York: David McKay Co. (1968).

Pharand, D., "The Implications of Canadian Marine and Arctic Legislation for the Development of International Law", in L. M. Alexander (ed.), *Canadian-U.S. Maritime Problems, Law of the Sea Workshop, June 1971*, 75-81. Kingston: Law of the Sea Institute, University of Rhode Island (1972).

Remond, M., *L'exploration pétrolière en mer et le droit*. Paris: Éditions Technip (1970).

SCHACHTER, O., and SERWER, D., "Marine Pollution Problems and Remedies", 65 *American Journal of International Law* 84-111 (1967).

SHARP, M., "Preserving Canada's Arctic Environment", *Statements and Speeches,* No. 70/5. Ottawa: Department of External Affairs (16 April 1970).

SHUTLER, N. D., "Pollution of the Sea by Oil", 7 *Houston Law Review* 415-441 (1970).

SIBTHORP, M. M., *Oceanic Pollution : A Survey and Some Suggestions for Control.* London: David Davies Memorial Institute of International Studies (1969).

SINGLETON, J. F., "Pollution of the Marine Environment from Outer Continental Shelf Oil Operations", 22 *South Carolina Law Review* 228-240 (1970).

SMITH, J. E., (ed.), *Torrey Canyon, Pollution and Marine Life.* London: Cambridge University Press (1970).

SUTTON, G., "Pollution Prevention in the Arctic — National and Multinational Approaches Compared", 5 *Ottawa Law Review* 32-64 (1971).

SWAN, P. N., "International and National Approaches to Oil Pollution Responsibility: An Emerging Regime for a Global Problem", 50 *Oregon Law Review* 506-586 (1971).

SWEENEY, J. C., "Oil Pollution of the Oceans", 37 *Fordham Law Review* 155-208 (1968).

TEDCLAFF, L. A., "International Law and the Protection of the Oceans from Pollution", 40 *Fordham Law Review* 529-564 (1972).

TRUDEAU, P. E., "Canada Leads Fight Against Pollution", *Statements and Speeches,* No. 70/3. Ottawa: Department of External Affairs (16 April 1970).

UNITED NATIONS, *First United Nations Conference on the Law of the Sea, 1958, Preparatory Document No. 8 "Pollution of the Sea by Oil".* A/Conf. 13/8 (1958).

UNITED NATIONS, *First United Nations Conference on the Law of the Sea, 1958, Secretariat Memorandum "Pollution of the Sea by Oil".* A/Conf. 13/37/169 (1958).

UNITED NATIONS (Secretariat), *Study on Marine Pollution which Might Arise from the Exploration and Exploitation of the Seabed and the Ocean Floor and the Subsoil thereof beyond the Limits of National Jurisdiction.* A/7924 (1970).

UNITED NATIONS (General Assembly), *Resolution Promoting Effective Measures for the Prevention and Control of Marine Pollution of 13 December 1969.* Doc. A/RES/2566 (XXIV) (12 January 1970).

UNITED NATIONS (Secretary General), *Study on Marine Pollution which Might Arise from the Exploration and Exploitation of the Seabed and the Ocean Floor and the Subsoil Thereof Beyond the Limits of National Jurisdiction.* A/AC. 138/13 (28 July 1969) and A/7924 (11 June 1970).

UNITED NATIONS, *Report of the Intergovernmental Working Group on Marine Pollution at its Second Session.* A/Conf. 48/1 WGMP. II/5 (22 november 1971).

UNITED NATIONS (General Assembly), *Convention for the Prevention of Marine Pollution by Dumping from Ships and Aircraft.* A/AC. 138/SC. III/L. 9 (15 March 1972).

UNITED NATIONS (Economic and Social Council), *Uses of the Sea. Study prepared by the Secretary-General.* E/5120 (28 April 1972), as amended by E/5120/Corr. 1 (23 June 1972).

UNITED NATIONS (General Assembly), *Report of the UN Conference on the Human Environment held at Stockholm, 5-16 June 1972.* A/Conf. 48/14 (3 July 1972).

UNITED NATIONS, *Report of the Intergovernmental Meeting on Ocean Dumping,* 1 MOD/4, Annex D (15 April 1972).

UNITED NATIONS (General Assembly), "Draft Articles for a Comprehensive Marine Pollution Convention, submitted by the delegation of Canada". A/AC. 138/SC. III L. 28 (9 March 1973), reproduced in 12 *International Legal Materials* 564-569 (1973).

UTTON, A. E., "The Arctic Waters Pollution Prevention Act, and the Right of Self-Protection", 7 *University of British Columbia Law Review* 221-234 (1972).

UTTON, A. E., "Protective Measures and the "Torrey Canyon", 9 *Boston College Industrial and Commercial Law Review* 613-632 (1968).

WILKES, D., "Effects of Key Provisions of the Canadian Arctic Waters Anti-Pollution Package", 15 *Polar Record,* 479-494 (1971).

WILKES, D., "International Administrative Due Process and Control of Pollution — The Canadian Arctic Waters Example", 2 *Journal of Maritime Law and Commerce* 499-539 (1971).

WULF, N. A., "Contiguous Zones for Pollution Control", 3 *Journal of Maritime Law and Commerce* 537-557 (1972).

WULF, N. A., "International Control of Marine Pollution", 25 *Judge Advocate General Journal* 93-100 (1971).

YATES, J. B., "Unilateral and Multilateral Approaches to Environmental Problems", 21 *University of Toronto Law Journal* 10-20 (1971).

Part VII

The Arctic Continental Shelf and Seabed

Note: This bibliography focuses primarily on the question of "limits" of the continental shelf.

ALEXANDER, L. M., (ed.), *The Law of the Sea : Offshore Boundaries and Zones.* Proceedings of the First Annual Conference of the Law of the Sea Institute June 27-30, 1966. Columbus: Ohio State University Press (1966).

ALEXANDER, L. M., *Alternative Methods for Delimiting the Outer Boundary of the Continental Shelf*. Washington: Office of External Research, Department of State (1970).

ALEXANDER, L. M., "Alternative Regimes for the Continental Shelf", a paper prepared for *Pacem in Maribus, Preparatory Conference on the Legal Framework and Continental Shelf*, January 30 to February 1, 1970. Kingston: University of Rhode Island (1970).

ALEXANDER, L. M., "Statement", in *Hearings before the Special Subcommittee on Outer Continental Shelf*, Part 2, 483-490 (1970).

ANDRASSY, J., "Application of the Geneva Convention, 1958, in Delimiting the Continental Shelf of the North Sea Area", 23 *Revue Égyptienne de droit international* 1-19 (1967).

ANDRASSY, J., *International Law and the Resources of the Sea*. New York: Columbia University Press (1970).

BEESLEY, J. A., *Exploration and Exploitation of the Seabed*. World Peace Through Law Conference, Belgrade: typewritten text (21 July 1971).

BEESLEY, J. A., "Some Unresolved Issues on the Law of the Sea", 4 *Natural Resources Law* 629-638 (1971).

BEZRUKOV, P. L., and LISITSYN, A. P., "Soviet Research on Ocean Bottom Sediments", 7 *Oceanology*, No. 5, translated by Scrypta Technica Inc. (1967).

BINGHAM, J. W., "Juridical Status of the Continental Shelf", 26 *Southern California Law Review* 4-20 (1952).

BOGGS, S. W., "Delimitation of Seaward Areas under National Jurisdiction", 46 *American Journal of International Law* 240-266 (1951).

BOUCHEZ, L. J., "The Exploration and Exploitation of Minerals on the Ocean Bed and its Subsoil", *Report of the Fifty-Second Conference of the International Law Association* 793-798 (1966).

BOUCHEZ, L. J., *The Outer Boundary of the Coastal State's Jurisdiction over the Seabed and its Subsoil*, paper presented at Preparatory Conference of *Pacem in Maribus*, Preparatory Conference on the Legal Framework and Continental Shelf, January 30 to February 1, 1970. Kingston: University of Rhode Island (1970).

BOWETT, D. W., "Deep-Seabed Resources: A Major Challenge", 31 *Cambridge Law Journal* 50-66 (1672).

BRIGGS, H. W., "Jurisdiction over the Seabed and Subsoil Beyond Territorial Waters", 45 *American Journal of International Law* 338-342 (1951).

BROWN, E. D., "The Outer Limit of the Continental Shelf", *Juridical Review* (No. 2) 111-146 (1968).

BROWNLIE, I., "Recommendations on the Limits of the Continental Shelf and Related Matters", in L. M. ALEXANDER (ed.), *The Law of the Sea : National Policy Recommendations* 133-158. Proceedings of the Fourth Annual Conference of the Law of the Sea Institute June 23-26. Kingston: University of Rhode Island (1969).

BURKE, W. T., "Ocean Sciences, Technology and the Future International Law of the Sea", in *The Future of the International Legal Order*, Volume 2, 183-264. Princeton: Princeton University Press (1970).

BUTLER, W. E., *The Soviet Union and the Law of the Sea*. Baltimore and London: The Johns Hopkins Press (1971).

CANADA (Department of Indian and Northern Affairs), *Oil and Gas Activities 1971*. Ottawa: Information Canada (1972).

CECCATTO, G. N., *L'évolution juridique de la doctrine du plateau continental*. Paris: Pédone (1955).

CHRISTY, F. T., "A Social Scientist Writes in Economic Criteria for Rules Governing Exploitation of Deep Sea Minerals", 2 *International Lawyer* 224-242 (1968).

COLLIARD, C. A., et al., *Le fond des mers*. Paris: Librairie Armand Colin (1971).

COMMISSION ON MARINE SCIENCE, ENGINEERING AND RESOURCES, *Marine Resources and Legal-Political Arrangements for their Developments*, Volume 3. Washington: Government Printing Office (1969).

COMMITTEE ON POLAR RESEARCH, *Polar Research, A Survey*. Washington: National Academy of Sciences (1970).

CROSBY, D. G., "A Brief Look at Canada's Offshore", 62 *Canadian Mining and Metallurgical Bulletin*, No. 685, 490-500 (1969).

DE LEEUW, M. M., "New Canadian Bathymetric Charts of the Western Arctic Ocean", 14 *Deep Sea Research* 449-504 (1967).

DE MESTRAL, A., "Le régime juridique du fond des mers: inventaire et solutions possibles", 74 *Revue générale de droit international public* 640-667 (1970).

DENORME, R., "The Seaward Limit of the Continental Shelf", in L. M. ALEXANDER (ed.), *The Law of the Sea : National Policy Recommendations*, Proceedings of the Fourth Annual Conference of the Law of the Sea Institute June 23-26, 263-274. Kingston: University of Rhode Island (1969).

DREYFUS, S., "Considérations sur le statut juridique du plateau continental et la conférence de Genève de 1958", 30 *Annuaire de l'Association des Auditeurs et Anciens Auditeurs de l'Académie de droit international de La Haye* 23-25 (1960).

ELY, N., "Seabed Boundaries Between Coastal States: the Effect to be Given Islets as Special Circumstances", 6 *International Lawyer* 219-236 (1972).

ELY, N., "The Limits and Conflicting Uses of the Continental Shelf", in L. M. ALEXANDER (ed.), *The Law of the Sea : Offshore Boundaries and Zones*. Proceedings of the First Annual Conference of the Law of the Sea Institute June 27-30, 1966, 174-179. Columbus: Ohio State University Press (1966).

EMERY, K. O., "Geological Aspects of Seafloor Sovereignty", in L. M. ALEXANDER (ed.), *The Law of the Sea : Offshore Boundaries and Zones*. Proceedings of the First Annual Conference of the Law of the Sea Institute June 27-30, 1966, 139-159. Columbus: Ohio State University Press (1966).

EUSTACHE, F., "Le fond des mers et le droit des gens", 97 *Journal du droit international* 844-897 (1970).

FINLAY, L. W., "Rights of Coastal Nations to the Continental Margins", 4 *Natural Resources Lawyer* 668-675 (1971).

FINLAY, L. W., "The Outer Limit of the Continental Shelf. A Rejoinder to Professor Louis Henkin", 64 *American Journal of International Law* 42-61 (1970).

FREEMAN, H. A., "Law of the Continental Shelf and Ocean Resources", 3 *Cornell International Law Journal* 105-120 (1970).

GIDEL, G., *Le plateau continental.* Fourth International Conference of the Legal Profession, International Bar Association, Madrid (July 1952). The Hague: Nijhoff (1952).

GOLDIE, L. F. E., "Where is the Continental Shelf's Outer Boundary ?", 1 *Journal of Maritime Law and Commerce* 461-472 (1970).

GOLDIE, L. F. E., "A Lexicographical Controversy — the Word 'Adjacent' in Article 1 of the Continental Shelf Convention", 66 *American Journal of International Law* 829-835 (1972).

GOLDIE, L. F. E., "The Exploitability Test: Interpretation and Potentialities", 8 *Natural Resources Lawyer* 434-477 (1968).

GOLDIE, L. F. E., "The Contents of Davy Jone's Locker — A Proposed Regime for the Seabed and Subsoil", 22 *Rutgers Law Review* 1-66 (1967).

GRISEL, E., "The Lateral Boundaries of the Continental Shelf and the Judgment of the International Court of Justice in the North Sea Continental Shelf Cases", 64 *American Journal of International Law* 562-593 (1970).

GRUNAVALT, R. J., "The Acquisition of the Resources of the Bottom of the Sea — A New Frontier of International Law", 34 *Military Law Review* 101-133 (1966).

GUTTERIDGE, J. A. C., "The 1958 Geneva Convention on the Continental Shelf", 35 *British Year Book of International Law* 102-123 (1959).

HEDBERG, H. D., "The National-International Jurisdictional Boundary on the Ocean Floor", 1 *Ocean Management* 83-118 (1973).

HEDBERG, H. D., "Limits of National Jurisdiction over National Resources of the Ocean Bottom", in L. M. ALEXANDER (ed.), *The Law of the Sea : National Policy Recommendations.* Proceedings of the Fourth Annual Conference of the Law of the Sea Institute June 23-26, 1969, 159-170. Kingston: University of Rhode Island (1969).

HENKIN, L., "A Reply to Mr. Finlay", 64 *American Journal of International Law* 62-72 (1970).

HENKIN, L., "The Extent of the Continental Shelf", paper at *Pacem in Maribus, Preparatory Conference on the Legal Framework and the Continental Shelf,* January 30 to February 1, 1970. Kingston: University of Rhode Island (1970).

HENKIN, L., *Law of the Sea's Mineral Resources*. New York: Institute for the Study of Science in Human Affairs of Columbia University (1968).

HOLLAND, H. F., "The Juridical Status of the Continental Shelf", 30 *Texas Law Review* 586-598 (1952).

HUNKINS, K., "Arctic Geophysics", 22 *Arctic* 225-232 (1969).

HUNKINS, K., et al., "The Floor of the Arctic Ocean in Photographs", 23 *Arctic* 175-189 (1970).

HUNKINS, K., "Geomorphic Provinces of the Arctic Ocean", in J. E. SATER (coordinated by), *Arctic Drifting Stations*, 365-376 (1968).

HURST, C. J. B. Sir, "The Continental Shelf", 34 *Transactions of the Grotius Society* 153-169 (1949).

HURST, C. J. B. Sir, "Whose is the Bed of the Sea ?", 4 *British Year Book of International Law* 34-43 (1923-24).

"International Conference on the Deep Seas and Continental Shelf", 3 *Cornell International Law Journal* 105-204 (1970).

JENNINGS, R. Y., "Jurisdictional Adventures at Sea: Who has Jurisdiction over the Natural Resources of the Seabed ?", 4 *Natural Resources Lawyer* 829-840 (1971).

JENNINGS, R. Y., "The Limits of Continental Shelf Jurisdiction: Some Possible Implications of the North Sea Case Judgment", 18 *International and Comparative Law Quarterly* 812-832 (1969).

JOHNSTON, D. M., "Law, Technology and the Sea", 55 *California Law Review* 449-472 (1967).

KAUFMAN, S., "Seabed Technology", 5 *Texas International Law Forum* 195-203 (1969).

KOULOURIS, M., "Les droits souverains sur le plateau continental", *Revue hellénique de Droit international* 292-308 (1971).

LABASTIDA, F., "The Continental Shelf and the Freedom of the High Seas", 3 *Cornell International Law Journal* 133-140 (1970).

LAUTERPACHT, H., "Sovereignty over Submarine Areas", 27 *British Year Book of International Law* 376-433 (1950).

"Legal Aspects of Seabed Petroleum and Mineral Resources Development", Offshore Technology Conference, 4 *Natural Resources Lawyer* 681-881 (1971).

LIN'KOVA, T. I., "Some Results of Paleomagnetic Study of Arctic Ocean Floor Sediments", translated from *The Present and the Past of Geomagnetic Field*. Moscow: "Nauka Press", 279-281 (1965).

LONGAVANT, E., "L'étendue du plateau continental", 22 *Droit maritime français* 131-143 (1970).

McKELVEY, V. E., and WANG, E. F. H., *Preliminary Maps of World Subsea Mineral Resources*. Washington: U.S. Geological Survey, Department of Interior (1970).

MOUTON, M. W., *The Continental Shelf*. The Hague: Nijhoff (1952).

MOUTON, M. W., "The Continental Shelf", 85 *Recueil des Cours* 347-463 (1954).

NIKOLAEV, S., "Where is the Limit of National Jurisdiction ?" (in Russian), *Soviet State and Law* 53-61 (1971).

ODA, S., "The Boundary of the Continental Shelf", 12 *Japanese Annual of International Law* 264-284 (1968).

ODA, S., "Proposals for Revising the Convention on the Continental Shelf", 7 *Columbia Journal of Transnational Law* 1-31 (1968).

OXMAN, B. H., "The Preparation of Article 1 of the Convention on the Continental Shelf", 3 *Journal of Maritime Law and Commerce* 245-305, 445-472 (1972).

PAGET, D., "Towards a Regime for the Seabed: An Examination of Official Proposals", 1 *Queen's Law Journal* 484-512 (1972).

PARDO, A., "An International Regime for the Deep Seabed: Developing Law or Developing Anarchy", 5 *Texas International Law Forum*, 204-217 (1969).

PARDO, A., "Sovereignty under the Sea", *The Round Table* 341-355 (1968).

PELLETIER, B. R., "Canadian Arctic Archipelago and Baffin Bay", in FAIRBRIDGE, *Encyclopedia of Oceanography*, Volume 1, 157-167 (1966).

"Post Torrey Canyon: Towards a New Solution to the Problem of Traumatic Oil Spillage", 2 *Connecticut Law Review* 632-647 (1970).

SCELLE, G., "Plateau continental et droit international", 59 *Revue générale de droit international public* 5-62 (1955).

SHAWCROSS, Lord, "The Law of the Continental Shelf with Special Reference to the North Sea", *The World Land Use Survey Discourses to the Twentieth International Geographic Congress* 35-42 (1964).

SHALOWITZ, A. L., *Shore and Sea Boundaries.* Washington: Government Printing Office, Volume 1 (1962), Volume 2 (1964).

SPECIAL SUBCOMMITTEE ON OUTER CONTINENTAL SHELF, *Report to the Committee on Interior and Insular Affairs*, Washington: Government Printing Office (1970).

STONE, O. L., "Some Aspects of Jurisdiction over National Resources under the Ocean Floor", 3 *Natural Resources Lawyer* 155-194 (1970).

TECLAFF, L. A., "Jurisdiction over Offshore Fisheries — How Far into the High Seas", 35 *Fordham Law Review* 409-424 (1967).

TRESHNIKOV, F., et al., "Geographic names of the main features of the floor of the Arctic Basin", *Problems of the Arctic and Antarctic* (in Russian) No. 27, 5-15 (1967).

UDINTSVA, O. G., and LEONT'YEV, O. K., "Areas of the Main Morphostructure Elements of the Ocean Bottom", 13 *Soviet Geography : Review and Translation* (1972), translated from Vestnik Moskovskogo Universiteta, Geografiya, No. 2, 47-51 (1971).

UNITED NATIONS, *Convention on the Continental Shelf.* A/CONF. 13/L.55 (1958).

UNITED NATIONS (Secretary General), *Definition of the Seabed and the Ocean Floor and the Subsoil thereof underlying the High Seas*

Beyond the Limits of Present National Jurisdiction. A/AC.135/19 (21 June 1968).

UNITED NATIONS (General Assembly), *Report of the Ad Hoc Committee to Study the Peaceful Uses of the Seabed and the Ocean Floor Beyond the Limits of National Jurisdiction.* A/7230 (1968).

UNITED NATIONS (Secretariat), *Survey of National Legislation Concerning the Seabed and the Ocean Floor, and the Subsoil thereof, underlying the High Seas Beyond the Limits of National Jurisdiction.* A/AC.135/11 and Corr. 1 and Add. 1 (4 June 1968, 13 August 1968 and 22 August 1968).

UNITED NATIONS (Secretariat), *Survey of Existing International Agreements Concerning the Seabed and the Ocean Floor and the Subsoil thereof underlying the High Seas Beyond the Limits of National Jurisdiction.* A/AC.135/10 (4 June 1968) and A/AC.135/10/Rev. 1 (12 August 1968).

UNITED NATIONS (Secretary General), *List of National Laws, Orders and Regulations Governing Exploration and Exploitation Procedures and Safety Practices Relating to the Seabed and Ocean Floor.* A/AC.135/11 (4 June and 13 August 1968).

UNITED NATIONS (Secretariat), *Supplement to the Survey of National Legislation Concerning the Seabed and the Ocean Floor and the Subsoil thereof Underlying the High Seas Beyond the Limits of Present National Jurisdiction.* A/AC.138/9 (11 March 1969).

UNITED NATIONS (General Assembly), *Report of the Economic and Technical Sub-Committee.* A/AC.138/17 (27 August 1969).

UNITED NATIONS (General Assembly), *Report of the Legal Sub-Committee covering its March and August, 1969, Sessions.* A/AC.138/18 (28 August 1969); A/AC.138/18Add. 1 (29 August 1969).

UNITED NATIONS (General Assembly), *Report of the Committee on the Peaceful Uses of the Seabed and the Ocean Floor Beyond the Limits of National Jurisdiction.* A/7622 and Add. 1 (1969).

UNITED NATIONS (General Assembly), *Draft United Nations Convention on the International Seabed Area.* A/AC.138/25 (3 August 1970).

UNITED NATIONS (General Assembly), *Report of the Committee on the Peaceful Uses of the Seabed and the Ocean Floor Beyond the Limits of National Jurisdiction, Supplement No. 21.* A/8021 (1970).

UNITED NATIONS (General Assembly), *Draft Ocean Space Treaty, working paper submitted by Malta.* A/AC.138/53 (23 August 1971) and A/AC.138/53/Corr. 1 (27 October 1971).

UNITED NATIONS (General Assembly), *Report of the Committee on the Peaceful Uses of the Seabed and the Ocean Floor Beyond the Limits of National Jurisdiction, Supplement No. 21.* A/8421 (1971).

UNITED NATIONS (Secretariat), *Comparative Table of Draft Treaties, Working Papers and Draft Articles.* A/AC.138/L.10 (28 January 1972).

UNITED NATIONS (General Assembly), *Kuwait : draft decision*. A/AC. 138/L.11 (30 March 1972) and A/AC.138/L.11/Rev. 1 (14 August 1972).

UNITED NATIONS (General Assembly), *Report of the Committee on the Peaceful Uses of the Seabed and the Ocean Floor Beyond the Limits of National Jurisdiction, Supplement No. 21.* A/8721 and Corr. 1 (27 November 1972).

UNITED NATIONS (Secretary-General), *Economic Significance, in Terms of Seabed Mineral Resources, of the Various Limits Proposed for National Jurisdiction.* A/AC.138/87 (4 June 1973).

VALLAT, F. A., "The Continental Shelf", 23 *British Year Book of International Law* 333-338 (1946).

VALLÉE, C., *Le plateau continental dans le droit positif actuel.* Paris: Pédone (1971).

WALDOCK, C. H. M., "The Legal Basis of Claims to the Continental Shelf", 36 *Transactions of the Grotius Society* 115-148 (1951).

WHITEMAN, M. M., "Conference on the Law of the Sea: Convention on the Continental Shelf", 52 *American Journal of International Law* 629-659 (1958).

YOUNG, R., "The Legal Status of Submarine Areas beneath the High Seas", 46 *American Journal of International Law* 225-239 (1951).

YOUNG, R., "Equitable Solutions for Offshore Boundaries: The 1968 Saudi Arabia-Iran Agreement", 64 *American Journal of International Law* 152-157 (1970).

YOUNG, R., "The Limits of the Continental Shelf — And Beyond", *Proceedings of the American Society of International Law* 229-236 (1968).

Indexes

I. — SUBJECT INDEX

II. — NAME INDEX

III. — GEOGRAPHICAL INDEX

IV. — SHIP INDEX